65.00

Law at the End of Life

Law at the End of Life

The Supreme Court
and Assisted Suicide

**Edited by
Carl E. Schneider**

Ann Arbor
THE UNIVERSITY OF MICHIGAN PRESS

2003   2002   4   3   2

Library of Congress Cataloging-in-Publication Data

Law at the end of life: the Supreme Court and assisted suicide / edited by Carl E.
   Schneider.
      p.   cm.
   Includes index.
   ISBN 0-472-11157-4 (cloth : alk. paper)
      1. Right to die—Law and legislation—United States.   2. Assisted suicide—
   Law and legislation—United States.   3. Political questions and judicial
   power—United States.   4. United States. Supreme Court.   I. Schneider, Carl,
   1948–

   KF3827.E87 L39   2000
   344.73′04197—dc21   00-034388

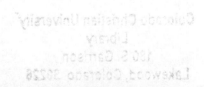

Contents

Political Questions, Judicial Questions, and the Problem of *Washington v Glucksberg*

Carl E. Schneider

Over a century and a half ago, Alexis de Tocqueville famously said, "Scarcely any political question arises in the United States that is not resolved, sooner or later, into a judicial question." Physician-assisted suicide superbly illustrates Tocqueville's acute observation. For a number of years, assisted suicide was the prototype of a (nonpartisan) political question. Interest groups brought it to public attention. Public discussion of it flourished. Legislatures debated it. Citizens in several states decided in referenda whether to make it legal. Almost suddenly, however, this classic political process was transformed into a judicial one by the startling and strongly stated opinions of the Second and Ninth Circuit Courts of Appeals. These opinions bid fair to take the power of decision away from political institutions by finding in the constitutional right of privacy an entitlement to the help of a physician in committing suicide. Now, in a case called *Washington v Glucksberg* (and, of course, its companion case, *Vacco v Quill*), the Supreme Court has reversed the decisions of the Second and Ninth Circuits.

When the political becomes judicial, the nature of the debate changes in crucial ways. In particular, the debate falls into the hands of lawyers, and discourse is limited to the arguments that are cognizable by the law. What is more, judicial opinions evoke considerably different—and considerably more difficult—kinds of responses from states, the other classic form of legal expression. For example, in evaluating a statute, we principally ask whether it produces a socially desirable result. In evaluating a judicial opinion, we principally ask whether the court reached the result required by law. The task of legislatures and referenda has generally been to decide whether assisted suicide is good public policy; the Supreme Court had only to decide whether the Constitution requires states to permit it. Almost everyone may reasonably have an opinion about what constitutes good public policy in matters of ordinary experience; it is hard to know what the Constitution requires unless you are familiar with a gruesomely large body of precedent.

There are other differences. For instance, a statute frequently attempts to address a problem completely and—the legislature usually hopes—with something like finality. A court is ordinarily obliged to decide only the case in front of it, and it is commonly thought that a narrow basis of decision is to be preferred to a broad one. Thus state statutes have either prohibited assisted suicide or, in Oregon, established a regime permitting and regulating it. In contrast, the Ninth Circuit opinion establishing a right to assisted suicide would have left many questions about the scope of the right and of governmental regulation to be decided through a combination of legislation and adjudication comparable to the quarter-century-long process in which the nature of the right to abortion has been worked out. Even the Supreme Court's opinion in *Glucksberg,* which declined to find a right to assisted suicide, is avowedly not final. Various Justices intimated in various ways that their views might change if litigants formulated their claim differently or if new evidence about how assisted suicide might work arose.

When a political issue becomes a judicial one, public interest in it does not end, of course. What is more, political activity surrounding it rarely ends either. Interested people may hope to change the judicial result. Sometimes they proceed judicially by trying to persuade the court either to overrule itself expressly or to erode its precedent by reinterpreting it. Sometimes they try to find room in the judicial decision for legislative and social countermeasures. This often means that the political and the judicial become so much intertwined that any person interested in a social policy must understand the judicial approach to it.

Unhappily, that understanding is too often hard to come by. As I have just explained, the judicial approach to political problems and the language courts employ in discussing them will often seem arcane, abstruse, and artificial to the laity. Even though America is an exceptionally judicialized country, the constraints, purposes, and discourse characteristic of courts are widely misunderstood. For example, even journalists who specialize in covering courts tend to see judicial holdings as simple, unabashed expressions of opinions about the relative merits of contending social policies. To be sure, there is a good deal of expert writing about judicial decisions, but it is ordinarily hidden away in law reviews and judicial opinions where the laity cannot easily find it, and too often it is also hidden away in language the laity cannot easily penetrate.

In short, a world in which the political and the judicial interact needs a discourse that makes sophisticated explanation and criticism of judicial opinions available to the public that is concerned with the political questions that have become confided to courts. It was to help provide this explanation and criticism that the University of Michigan Law School and the University of Michigan Program in Society and Medicine sponsored a conference on *Glucksberg* on November 14–15, 1997, only a few months after the case was decided. One goal of the conference was to solicit views from people of varied backgrounds, and the participants thus included a physician, a medical historian, and a medical sociologist. Even the lawyers had diverse experiences. Two were conventional lawyer-bioethicists, one had been a genetic counselor, one was an expert in criminal procedure and constitutional law, one was a Ph.D. in economics who specializes in antitrust law, and one was an English scholar of comparative law.

The papers given at this conference—which this volume publishes—undertook several tasks. They (1) asked what the Supreme Court's opinion in *Glucksberg* means as a judicial decision that is part of a continuing political process; (2) criticized the opinion as a piece of legal analysis, as a social document, and as a set of principles for the practice of medicine; (3) reflected on the principles that should animate legal thinking about assisted suicide; and (4) discussed the way institutional authority to decide questions of public policy should be allocated among and wielded by governmental institutions.

This volume begins its work in part I by setting *Glucksberg* in the context in which it arose. Part I, that is, contains a chapter that offers a brief description of how social practices surrounding the end of life and the law regulating decisions at the end of life have developed. In particular, chapter 1 tells the story of *Cruzan v Director, Missouri Department of Health,* a pivotal decision in which the Supreme Court first opened the door to the possibility that the Constitution speaks to the way law may attempt to govern medical decisions. In addition, chapter 1 outlines some of the basic legal issues *Glucksberg* raises.

Part II undertakes the difficult work of explaining the opinions in *Glucksberg*. First, what do the opinions actually say? One might expect this question to be completely straightforward. One would be pitiably mistaken. In this case, the Court was necessarily working on complex and controversial legal ground, and the Justices thus had some difficulty in deciding what they thought and in saying what they meant. Second, part II asks what *Glucksberg* means as a precedent. Might the Court later change its mind? Does *Glucksberg* entirely remove courts from supervising decisions at the end of life? Third, was *Glucksberg* correct as a matter of constitutional law? These decisions fall within one of the most mysterious areas of constitutional jurisprudence—the Fourteenth Amendment's protection of "liberty"—and thus raise momentous questions about whether the Court interpreted the Constitution and its own doctrine correctly and even about the legitimacy of the Court's power to act.

Two chapters engage these questions. Chapter 2 is by Sonia Suter—a promising young legal scholar whose writing on the intersection between law and medicine is given depth by her experience as a genetic counselor. She undertook to provide the volume's basic exposition and analysis of the opinions in *Glucksberg*. Her article vividly reveals a problem that almost invariably characterizes judicial treatments of political problems—that judicial opinions are tentative, tenebrous, partial, and ambiguous. The Justices in *Glucksberg* unanimously agreed that the lower court should be reversed. But Ms. Suter probes beyond the apparent unanimity of the Justices and sees ambivalence about assisted suicide, the state's interests in regulating it, and even the legitimacy of the Court's authority to supervene the state's regulations.

Judicial ambivalence and disagreement and the ambiguous opinions to which they give rise lead to controversies over what the opinions say about the law today and bode for the law tomorrow. There is an element of the artificial in these exercises in *explication de texte*. After all, the Justices generally do not draft their own opinions and are often unfamiliar with the problems under adjudication. Thus reading their opinions for hints about what is on their minds is quite futile. On the other hand, the opinions have both judicial meaning and political meaning. They have judicial meaning because the language in the opinions becomes law at least formally; they have political meaning exactly because of the political power the Court's moral authority generates (and because of the popular misunderstanding that the Court pronounces on the merits of public policy).

For these reasons, the antagonists in the assisted-suicide debate started spinning the opinions even before they were announced to turn judicial pronouncement into political benediction. Chapter 3 both criticizes this process at its worst and exemplifies it at its best. That chapter is by Yale Kamisar, who is the foremost student of the law of euthanasia. Since 1958, when he published his first article on the subject, Professor Kamisar has energetically attacked proposals to make euthanasia easier, and today he is one of the most vociferous critics of assisted suicide. He shows in shrewd detail how proponents of assisted suicide have tried to transform what looked like the setback of *Glucksberg* into a step forward. He then lustily argues point by point that—however ambivalent the Justices may be—*Glucksberg* was a crucial victory for opponents of assisted suicide. However, while Professor Kamisar is parti pris, he is a fair-minded lawyer, and he subtly examines the possibility that *Glucksberg* may contain the seeds of future judicial intervention in the law at the end of life—as by creating some kind of constitutional right to palliative care.

Professor Kamisar's discussion implicitly deals with another problem— that the judicialization of politics politicizes the judicial process. A century ago Mr. Dooley memorably averred that the Supreme Court follows the election returns, and half a century ago during the fight over Roosevelt's proposal to "pack" the Court someone wittily remarked of the Court's sudden acquiescence in New Deal legislation, "A switch in time saves nine." More recently and relevantly, the Court's travails with race and abortion have given it reasons to think carefully about its political power and position. Professor Kamisar's discussion shows how questions about the Court's response to the political situation in which it works may have affected its choices in *Glucksberg*.

Part II, then, investigates *Glucksberg's* meaning for the law and politics. Part III expands that investigation to look more directly at how *Glucksberg* seems to have been understood and now is likely to influence medical practice at the end of life. Rebecca Dresser, the author of chapter 4, is a leading lawyer-bioethicist. A professor of both law and medicine, she examines the opinions in *Glucksberg* to decipher its meaning for the way doctors may treat patients and patients may refuse treatment. Her chapter suggests how complex policy-making has become in an age of judicialized politics. The Court in *Glucksberg* declined to make assisted suicide a constitutional right, and it expressly commended the political process as a means of writing rules for assisted suicide. But Professor Dresser suggests that *Glucksberg* in fact stirs doubt about the constitutional status of several practices at the border between life and death. Like Professor Kamisar, for example, she speculates that the Court may have announced some kind of right to palliative care. More, she shows how ambiguous apparently clear principles become when they meet the realities of clinical practice.

But Professor Dresser's argument goes yet further. She announces a theme that several other chapters will pursue. She suggests that decisions at the end of life are ultimately most affected not by the law but by the attitudes of doctors and their patients. In other words, she raises the question whether law itself—whether born of political deliberation or judicial decision—can effectively regulate behavior about which people feel deeply and which takes place far from the observation of the state. In short, one reading of Professor Dresser's chapter sees *Glucksberg* as a case in which the judiciary nominally declines to intervene in the political process but in which it can hardly help making policy even while it cannot truly affect practice.

Howard Brody, the author of chapter 5, is a physician who has been one of the principal advocates of assisted suicide. In his chapter, Brody asks how well the courts have understood clinical practices at the end of life and modern bioethical views of them. He suggests that two ethical ideas have been central to clinical practice at the end of life in the United States: the principle that there is a moral difference between refusing treatment and committing suicide, and the principle that a physician may legitimately treat a patient's pain even when that treatment seems likely to cause the patient's death. He argues that the Second and Ninth Circuits seemed not to have achieved an adequate comprehension either of the clinical status of these ideas nor the ideas themselves. While he is relieved that the Supreme Court "at least wiped the slate clean," he concludes that it failed to announce "any superior view" and that the Justices generally seemed to have only a poor sense of the bioethical arguments at issue in the case. Like Professor Dresser (indeed, like virtually all the participants on both sides of the debate), Dr. Brody is centrally concerned that dying patients receive capable and kind medical treatment. He believes such care is likeliest when doctors accept the two principles he discusses, and he is troubled that courts have had so much difficulty appreciating them.

Part IV takes us from discussions of what *Glucksberg* means for courts, for legislatures, and for clinical practice to questions about how institutional authority should be distributed and wielded in a democracy in which the political so regularly becomes judicial. Christopher McCrudden, the author of chapter 6, is a distinguished English authority on comparative and international law. He meticulously examines the way courts throughout the world have assessed claims of a right to assisted suicide. He finds that it is becoming common practice for courts to rely on the authority of foreign courts and a developing international understanding of human rights. He demonstrates that the United States Supreme Court has been a conspicuous exception to these trends. His discussion thus raises some provocative questions about the judicialization of political issues. Is that process a desirable, even a necessary, way of giving effect to some transcendent vision of human rights? What happens to the principle of democratic government when courts interpret their country's statutes and constitutions in light of supranational standards?

In chapter 7, I use the example of assisted suicide to examine directly the desirability and even the legitimacy of resolving political issues judicially. I argue that judges are poorly suited by training for such tasks, that little in the working of courts or in the doctrines at their disposal properly equips them to make informed and wise decisions, and that there is no reason to think that the democratic organs of government will not reach decisions that are at least as sound. In addition, I use the chapter to offer readers a detailed survey of what otherwise might be missing from the volume—the arguments about states' interests in regulating assisted suicide that have been so central in both the political and judicial debates over assisted suicide.

In asserting authority to resolve the kind of political issue at stake in *Glucksberg*, courts have more or less directly consulted views about both the morality of assisted suicide and the legitimate scope of governmental power over intimate decisions. Part V, then, examines these issues from several perspectives. In chapter 8, Martin Pernick, a prominent medical historian, takes us back to the beginning of this century and the fascinating story of a physician and filmmaker who advocated euthanasia of the "unfit." Professor Pernick delicately explores the light this story sheds on our present concerns about slippery slopes, the claims of medical authority, and the cultural debates over issues like assisted suicide.

No small part of the criticism of the transformation of the political into the judicial has arisen from unhappiness about the courts' ability to formulate satisfactory principles for resolving cases. In chapter 9, Peter Hammer, a young legal scholar who is also an economist, undertakes an ambitious project—reconsidering the conventional judicial understanding of the way courts should conceptualize conflicts between the individual and the community. This project is an important attempt to stretch beyond the limits and exhaustion of the conventional understanding. Professor Hammer proposes a new analytic framework based on the ways individuals think about their own interests and social interests and on the way society may think about its own interests and those of its members. The challenge he raises is whether courts may be able to use this framework for reaching some wise resolution of the problems assisted suicide presents.

Chapter 10 is by Arthur Frank, a sociologist who had cancer and who has since then devoted himself to talking with patients and studying their narratives of illness. His essay takes us past the generalities and abstractions that so often characterize the discourse of both political and judicial institutions to the patients, families, friends, and doctors whose lives and deaths are the real stuff of the assisted-suicide debate. For Frank, questions about whether that debate should be resolved politically or judicially fade into insignificance. He doubts that satisfactory answers to the human realities can come from law at all (although he also presents an imaginative proposal of his own for the law at the end of life).

In chapter 11, I try to explain why Frank and the other contributors who wonder about the law's ability to regulate medical decisions at the end of life wisely may be right and to return us to Tocqueville's reflection on American life and law. Tocqueville said that when every political issue becomes judicial, political discussion must adopt the language of the law. In my essay, I suggest that that language is often inapt for issues like assisted suicide. Such issues ask us to think about what is right for one individual at one moment. But law is a system of social regulation that must make general rules for many people over long periods and that must be concerned for the regularity of its own procedures and the coherence of its own doctrines. This is law's strength and virtue. Nevertheless, it means that what law must say and what people should do may often be unhappily different. Thus, this essay suggests that the judicialization of politics raises questions not just about judicial competence and authority, but also about the way we discuss political and moral issues.

The volume closes with two judicial opinions—that of the Ninth Circuit in *Compassion in Dying v Washington* and that of the Supreme Court in *Washington v Glucksberg*. They are here to give the reader the texts on which the essays in this volume comment (for however judicialized our politics, basic judicial texts are usually not adequately available even to interested lay readers). I reprint these opinions for another reason as well. This is not a book about whether it is right or wrong for doctors to help patients commit suicide or even about whether it is good policy to make assisted suicide a crime. It is a book about the efforts of our federal courts to decide what role they should play in decisions about assisted suicide. One of the contributors is an eminent opponent of assisted suicide, another an eminent proponent. (The rest of the contributors had not written about the topic and were invited partly for that reason.) The reader, however, may want a clearer statement of the underlying arguments for and against assisted suicide. The Ninth Circuit's opinion is the most aggressive—one might even say combative—defense of a right to assisted suicide imaginable. The Supreme Court's opinion is a less adamant but still plain rebuttal of that argument.

Part I

Glucksberg in Context

CHAPTER 1

The Road to *Glucksberg*

Carl E. Schneider

This volume contains a series of essays on the United States Supreme Court's opinion in *Washington v Glucksberg,*[1] the case that presented the question whether laws making it criminal to help a person commit suicide are unconstitutional. These essays are written by scholars in several disciplines for a broad audience that may include doctors, lawyers, ethicists, and the general public. In this opening chapter, therefore, I want to provide some background that might make these essays and the difficult legal issues they raise more accessible to such an audience.

Before *Glucksberg: Cruzan* and *Quinlan*

I begin, as a student of the common law must, with a case. In the earliest minutes of January 11, 1983, a twenty-five-year-old woman named Nancy Beth Cruzan was driving down Elm Road in Jasper County, Missouri. Her car went off the road. When a policeman arrived, he found her lying face-down in a ditch ten meters from her car. She was not breathing. Her heart had stopped. An ambulance quickly arrived. Minutes later, its medical team got Nancy's heart and breathing started again. But Nancy remained in a coma.

As the days turned to weeks, it became clear that Nancy was in a "persistent vegetative state."[2] Her brain had been deeply and permanently damaged from being without oxygen for so long. She was unconscious, able only to respond reflexively to sounds and perhaps to pain. She lay curled up, her arms and legs contracted. She could not swallow. To make feeding her easier, her husband allowed surgeons to place a tube in her stomach through which she could be given food and water.

Eventually, Nancy's husband seems to have left the picture, and it was her parents who heard the doctors predict her future. They were told that Nancy was not legally dead, since some parts of her brain still worked. Nor was she terminally ill. Indeed, she might live another thirty years. But she would never regain consciousness.

On learning this, the Cruzans told the hospital to stop feeding Nancy through the tube so that she would die. The hospital refused to obey without a court order. A Missouri trial court issued that order, saying that Nancy would have wanted to die. However, the Missouri Supreme Court reversed the trial court. It found there was not enough evidence of what Nancy would have wanted to override the state's strong policy in favor of preserving life. In

December of 1989—almost seven years after the accident—the case reached the United States Supreme Court. What should that court have done?

This is really a remarkable question. The Supreme Court can generally decide for itself what cases to hear. It does not take most cases. This case might have seemed too easy a winner for Missouri to be worth reviewing. Nancy Cruzan did not fit many of the categories that are commonly invoked to justify stopping medical treatment. She wasn't dead; she was just kept alive by machines. She was not near death; on the contrary, she had many years to live. She was apparently not in pain, much less unbearable and unending pain. She had never used any of the formal means by which she could have announced in advance a wish to have medical treatment ended. She did not need "heroic measures" or "extraordinary means" to keep her alive. Indeed, she did not need medical care. She simply needed food and water.

To understand how remarkable a question the Supreme Court presented itself with, we need one more fact about its jurisdiction. The Supreme Court is, of course, the highest federal court. As such, its task is to resolve questions of federal law about which the lower federal courts disagree. But federal law is not responsible for defining homicide or regulating medical care. That is the prerogative of the states. The Supreme Court could only reach the *Cruzan* case by considering an argument that Nancy Cruzan had rights under the federal Constitution that Missouri had somehow violated. Thus, the claim in *Cruzan* was not that good social policy justified withdrawing food and water from Nancy, but that she had a constitutional right to compel the hospital to stop feeding her. The claim, in short, was that she had a "right to die."

How had America come this far? A few decades ago, things were quite different. Legally, of course, causing someone's death is punishable as homicide, even if the victim consented. And helping someone commit suicide is a crime in about two-thirds of the states. It was generally understood that both principles applied to failures to provide or continue medical care a patient needed to stay alive. Socially, most people believed (without having thought much about it) that doctors were above all committed to keeping their patients alive.

Nevertheless, in the real world of medical practice, things were more complicated. It was probably always true that, faced with particularly desperate cases, doctors deliberately let patients die. Indeed, hints would occasionally slip out that a doctor had actively hastened a death. As medical technology developed, doctors increasingly faced genuinely confounding choices about whether to use medicine's whole armory. Eventually, it became accepted, although not invariable, practice to issue orders against trying to revive an "irreversible, terminal, pain-ridden patient" when he stopped breathing or suffered heart failure.[3]

In short, the "law on the books" and the "law in action" were quite different. The law on the books said, "You must always treat a patient." But that law was often disobeyed. Prosecutors surely knew what was going on, but they rarely brought charges. Even when they did, the defendants were often sympathetic, and juries were reluctant to convict and judges to punish them.[4] Nevertheless, the very conflict between what the law said and what it did was widely criticized. Nor were doctors comfortable with either the moral or the legal risks they ran when they walked the line between the law on the books and the law in action.

In sum, there was real uncertainty and ambivalence about the role of both law and medicine at the end of life. This ambivalence was captured in a case from 1947—*Repouille v United States*.[5] Louis Repouille wanted to become a naturalized citizen. To do so, he had to show that he had been a person of "good moral character" for five years. However, he had had a thirteen-year-old boy who was mentally retarded, mute, and blind; who had malformed arms and legs; who could do nothing for himself; and who lived out his life in a crib. Repouille found it hard to care for the boy and his four other children, and one day he chloroformed the child. Repouille was convicted of manslaughter, but he was given a suspended sentence. (That is, he was put on probation but did not have to go to jail.) Was he a person of "good moral character"?

The court, in an opinion by Learned Hand, one of America's most admired judges, saw many moral perplexities but held "that only a minority of virtuous persons would deem the practise [of killing such a child] morally justifiable, while it remains in private hands, even when the provocation is as overwhelming as it was in this instance."[6] However, Judge Jerome Frank, another eminent jurist, dissented. Notably, he did not argue that Mr. Repouille *was* a man of good moral character. Rather, he argued that the issue was so uncertain that the court should have sought information about the general public view of such conduct.[7]

Despite this ambivalence, or perhaps because of it, the law governing the end of life came under growing pressure. Medical advances multiplied questions about when to stop or withhold treatment. Doctors had ever more reason to fear both criminal and civil liability for decisions not to treat. Furthermore, a small but convinced movement sought to liberalize the law. That movement was earnestly confident that the law was backward and barbaric, and it labored to reform it. Still, these issues were not broadly discussed, and the public remained uninformed, uncertain, and uneasy about the law at the end of life.

The first major change in both public and legal attitudes came, of course, with a case. In 1976, the New Jersey Supreme Court encountered Karen Ann Quinlan.[8] She was a twenty-two-year-old woman who had fallen into a persistent vegetative state. In other words, she lay in a coma from which doctors said she could not recover. She could not breathe on her own and was kept alive by a machine (called a respirator) that helped her breathe. She could not eat on her own and was fed by means of a tube. She was expected to die within a year, and possibly much sooner.

After prayer and consultation with priests, Karen's father asked a court to appoint him his daughter's guardian and to let him have the respirator removed so that she might die. The trial court said no, but the state supreme court said yes. Citing *Roe v Wade,* the American abortion decision, the court held that patients have a constitutional right to refuse medical treatment. That right, the court continued, "should not be discarded solely on the basis that her condition prevents her conscious exercise of the choice."[9] It said that "[t]he only practical way to prevent destruction of the right is to permit the guardian and family of Karen" to decide what she would have done had she been able to decide for herself.[10] Since the court had "no doubt . . . that if Karen were herself miraculously lucid for an interval" she would not want the respirator, the court authorized her father to order its removal.[11]

Why was the *Quinlan* case crucial? As I suggested, it arose when the time was ripe, when the issue was becoming more common and more problematic. Karen Quinlan unforgettably embodied the reformers' claims. She was by all accounts a lively and engaging person harshly struck down. Her father was by all accounts a decent, thoughtful, and devastated man struggling to do his best under the worst circumstances. Day after day, the Quinlans won the public's deepest attention and profoundest sympathy. Further, the case was importantly different from earlier causes célèbres. They had typically involved prosecutions of people who had already taken the law into their own hands in a "mercy killing." But in *Quinlan* the family was respectfully asking for governmental authority to end their daughter's life.

Ultimately, then, *Quinlan* legitimated discussion about the issues it raised. More, it confirmed the respectability of the Quinlans' position. And, in legal terms, it held not just that patients could refuse even lifesaving treatment, but that they had a constitutional right to do so, a right that survived even their ability to exercise it. By phrasing the issue in constitutional terms at this early stage in public discussion, the court gave the reformer's position special moral and legal authority.

Nevertheless, *Quinlan* did not liberalize the law as much as another case might have. First, its issue was whether to withhold medical care, not to withhold food and water or actively to kill the patient. Second, the medical care being withheld could have been called "extraordinary" or "heroic." Third, the court assumed that Karen Quinlan was dying anyway, so that the question could be not whether to cause her to die, but whether her death should be prolonged.[12] Finally, *Quinlan*'s dramatic message was dulled by an ironic fact. When her father ordered the respirator removed, Karen Quinlan confounded the doctors by not dying. Indeed, she lived on for nine more years.

Whatever *Quinlan*'s direct effects, it initiated a period of vigorous legal activity and public discussion. A series of judicial decisions stated a "right to refuse treatment," even where that treatment had kept the patient alive. This right was both constitutional and based on the common law principle that a doctor could not treat a patient unless the patient gave "informed consent." In 1976, the date of *Quinlan,* California enacted a law authorizing what came to be called "living wills." Living wills are documents in which a person states that, should he become irrevocably incompetent while fatally ill, his doctors should (under specified circumstances) withdraw any treatment designed to keep him alive. Some states have also created the "durable power of attorney." This document allows its signer to appoint someone to make medical decisions—including withdrawal of treatment—for him if he becomes incompetent. By 1990, forty states had enacted living will statutes, and thirteen permitted durable powers of attorney.[13]

These statutory developments dissatisfied many reformers because most people never use them. But where were the reformers to turn next? In the American federal system, the easiest way of getting national action is through a ruling by the U.S. Supreme Court. Further, when Americans think about a social issue, they think in terms of rights. These facts brought the reform movement to the case with which I began, the case of Nancy Cruzan. Although Missouri provided for living wills, Nancy had not written one. Did she nevertheless have and exercise a constitutional "right to die"?

A majority of the Supreme Court appears to have held in *Cruzan* that a competent person has a constitutional right to refuse "unwanted medical treatment."[14] But, by a vote of five to four, the Court held that Missouri could prevent Nancy's parents from withdrawing treatment. The Court said that the constitutional right was a right to choose, and Nancy had never chosen to refuse treatment and now was physically incapable of making any kind of choice at all: "[A]n incompetent person," the Court said, "is not able to make an informed and voluntary choice to exercise a hypothetical right to refuse treatment or any other right."[15]

The Court did seem to say that Nancy need not have expressed her choice formally, in a living will. But Missouri could insist that evidence of any informal choice be "clear and convincing." The evidence of Nancy's choice lay in a "'somewhat serious [1/2 hr.] conversation with a housemate friend that if sick or injured she would not wish to continue her life unless she could live at least halfway normally. . . .'" The United States Supreme Court agreed with the Missouri Supreme Court that this testimony was not clear and convincing evidence that Nancy would truly have wanted to be denied food and water in her present circumstances.

The majority's opinion provoked two angry dissents. Justice Brennan wrote for himself and two other Justices. He insisted that Nancy had a "fundamental right" to "be free from unwanted medical attention." This meant "a right to evaluate the potential benefit of treatment and its possible consequences according to one's own values and to make a personal decision whether to subject oneself to the intrusion."[16] The fact "that Nancy Cruzan is now incompetent," Justice Brennan thought, could not "deprive her of her fundamental rights."[17] True, she could not personally exercise her right to "choose to die with dignity."[18] But the Court was constitutionally obliged to try to decipher what she would have done had she been conscious. And in doing so, it was obliged to look to all the available evidence, even if it was not "clear and convincing."

Justice Stevens wrote a lone dissent. He agreed with Justice Brennan that Nancy had a fundamental right. But it was not, as the majority and Justice Brennan believed, a right to choose. It was a right to a decision in her best interests. Since there was "no reasonable ground for believing that Nancy Beth Cruzan ha[d] any *personal* interest in the perpetuation of what the State has decided is her life,"[19] her parents should have been allowed to order the hospital to stop feeding her.

On its face, *Cruzan* appeared to be a setback for the reformers. After all, the Court decided against Nancy's parents. Nevertheless, on balance *Cruzan* has been a trumpet call in a crescendoing reform effort. Even though the Cruzans lost, the Court apparently announced some kind of constitutional "right to die." The Court thus opened the door to the prospect of a series of cases limiting the ability of the states to regulate law at the end of life.

Further, like *Quinlan, Cruzan* has transformed public debate. Both cases received wide publicity. Both cases confronted the country with sympathetic parents arguing in the most earnest and appealing terms to be allowed to end their daughter's life. Of course, it is hard to measure the public's feelings about these questions. But some indication may be found in the fact that a book on how to commit suicide was for months a best-seller. More systematically, Justice Brennan quoted a poll purporting to find "that 80% of those surveyed favored withdrawal of life support systems from hopelessly ill or irreversibly comatose patients if they or their families requested it."[20] However, much depends on how pollsters phrase their questions. One regional poll found that 50 percent of those asked felt that "the Supreme Court should . . . approve removal of the feeding tube" in *Cruzan*. But when asked whether "the Supreme Court should . . . allow Ms. Cruzan to starve to death?" only 25 percent said yes.[21]

The evolving public mood has had practical manifestations. Publicity about *Cruzan* "helped assure passage by Congress of the Patient Self-Determination Act. . . ."[22] That law requires all health care institutions that receive federal aid to tell patients they have a right to refuse medical treatment and to employ advance medical directives like living wills and durable powers of attorney. But perhaps the most remarkable aftermath of *Cruzan* was the efflorescence of a movement to make it legal for doctors to help patients commit suicide. The remarkably rapid development in support for that movement is suggested by developments in the state of Washington. There, citizens can propose statutes and vote them directly into law. Initiative 119 would have been the first statute in the industrialized world directly authorizing doctors to kill patients who had less than six months to live and who had asked the doctor in writing to do so.

Initiative 119 would arguably have passed except for one man in Michigan. A week before the election, Dr. Jack Kevorkian met with two middle-aged women in a cabin in a park outside of Detroit. He provided one of them with a machine he called a "mercytron." This machine allowed her to inject herself with a fatal drug. Kevorkian furnished the other woman with a way to breathe carbon monoxide and thus suffocate. As Kevorkian watched, both women killed themselves.

Kevorkian publicized this event with great avidity. But many people found him and his crusade frightening. He acted alone, without formally established procedures for ensuring that the women had received adequate medical care, that they were competent, or that they truly and firmly wanted to die. Neither woman was fatally ill. One of them complained of incessant and unbearable pain, but at least one doctor later said that her disease was short-term, treatable, and should have caused only manageable pain. In short, Kevorkian was so much every patient's nightmare that he apparently shifted public opinion from its original 60 to 30 percent support of the proposal to a 54 to 46 percent rejection of it at the election.[23]

Nevertheless, the fact that so substantial a portion of the population was willing to vote for so substantial a change in the law was striking. And this was only the beginning. In 1992, precisely the same percentage of the voters in a California referendum expressed a similar willingness. In 1994, the voters of Oregon approved a referendum by a vote of 51 to 49 percent that authorized doctors to prescribe drugs that competent, terminally ill patients could use to commit suicide. And in 1997, after the Oregon legislature had exercised its power to revoke the statute the voters had passed, the voters of Oregon voted once again for the proposal, this time by a vote of 60 to 40 percent.

Particularly significant from our point of view is the number of courts that have announced some kind of constitutional defect in assisted-suicide statutes. In 1993, a Michigan trial court judge made such a ruling in a case involving Kevorkian,[24] although the Michigan Supreme Court reversed that ruling in 1994.[25] In that same year a federal trial court in Washington found the Washington assisted-suicide statute unconstitutional.[26] More significantly, that decision was upheld by the Ninth Circuit Court of Appeals in an en banc decision,[27] and the Second Circuit found the New York assisted-suicide statute unconstitutional.[28] The two circuit court opinions used importantly different reasoning. The Ninth Circuit found in the Due Process Clause of the Fourteenth Amendment a "liberty interest in determining the time and manner of one's own death"[29] and concluded none of the state's interests was sufficiently strong to overcome that liberty interest. The Second Circuit held that the New York statute violated the Equal Protection Clause of the Fourteenth Amendment. That clause requires that similarly situated people be treated similarly. The court reasoned that all terminally ill people are similarly situated but that, under New York law, they were treated differently: terminally ill people who were kept alive with medical help could die by refusing that help while terminally ill people who did not need such help could not die by refusing it.

The United States Supreme Court has now, in the two opinions that are the subject of the essays collected in this book, reversed the holdings of both the Ninth and the Second Circuits. Those opinions—*Washington v Glucksberg*[30] and *Vacco v Quill*[31]—are described in these essays,[32] so I will not review them here. These questions bring us up to the present and conclude our brief investigation of the historical and legal background to the Court's decision in *Glucksberg*. There is, however, one more story to tell about Nancy Cruzan. After the Supreme Court ruled against her parents, they went back to the same judge in the same courtroom in Missouri. They said they had found "new evidence," the testimony of three of Nancy's friends who said she had told them she wouldn't want to "'live like a vegetable' on medical machines."[33] Once again, the judge authorized the Cruzans to have the hospital remove the feeding tube. This time, no one appealed the court order. In December of 1990, the hospital obeyed the Cruzans' instructions, and on December 26, Nancy Beth Cruzan died.

Glucksberg

It may be helpful to supplement this brief summary of the background of *Glucksberg* with a brief introduction to some of the principal issues that case raises. It has become truly hard to know what the law at the end of life ought to do in particular cases or where it ought to draw its lines in general. In some of these cases, the real question may be what constitutes death. In them, the issue is not whether to keep the patient alive, but whether the patient is already dead. In other cases, there are real and perplexing questions about the best medical course to follow even if the only goal is to prolong the patient's life. In yet other cases, there are strong reasons for deferring to the patient's preference even if that preference is for death. If a truly competent patient who is genuinely about to die and who is in unrelievable pain irrevocably wishes to refuse "heroic" medical care, who are we to say he is wrong? Cases in all these categories, then, make it hard to say that life-sustaining treatment should never be withdrawn. The Ninth Circuit's description of one of the plaintiffs in *Compassion in Dying* makes this point painfully clear:

> Jane Roe is a 69-year-old retired pediatrician who has suffered since 1988 from cancer which has now metastasized throughout her skeleton. Although she tried and benefitted temporarily from various treatments including chemotherapy and radiation, she is now in the terminal phase of her disease. In November 1993, her doctor referred her to hospice care. Only patients with a life expectancy of less than six months are eligible for such care.
> Jane Roe has been almost completely bedridden since June of 1993 and experiences constant pain, which becomes especially sharp and severe when she moves. The only medical treatment available to her at this time is medication, which cannot fully alleviate her pain. In addition, she suffers from swollen legs, bed sores, poor appetite, nausea and vomiting, impaired vision, incontinence of bowel, and general weakness.[34]

But here we meet the slippery-slope problem. "Slippery slope" is the phrase lawyers use to describe the following kind of argument: "There is nothing wrong with doing A. A in itself is unobjectionable. But if you do A, you will soon wind up doing B, and B *is* objectionable. Therefore, you should not do A." The idea, of course, is that once you start off doing the desirable A, you find yourself helplessly sliding down a slope toward the undesirable B.

But as I must often tell my students, slippery-slope arguments are, logically, unconvincing. If the first step is right, it is right even though the second step is wrong. If the second step is wrong, then it simply should not be taken. But that should not prevent taking the first step, since there is no logical reason the second step must be taken just because the first one was. Indeed, there is a logical reason to stop before reaching the bottom, since the whole slippery-slope argument assumes that the top of the slope is very different from the bottom.[35]

Logically, this refutation of the slippery-slope argument seems convincing. But as Justice Holmes memorably said, "The life of the law has not been logic; it has been experience." And the American experience of law at the end of life confirms, I think, the hazards of the slippery slope. For several reasons, this should not be surprising. First, slippery slopes work even if they logically shouldn't, partly because of the common law's method. The common law reasons from precedents. It asks whether each new case is essentially the same as some precedent. If so, it is decided in the same way. But if you decide a series of cases in the same way because each case was *almost* the same as its predecessor, the end of the series may wind up quite far from the beginning. You may start at the top of the slope and, without realizing it, inch your way down to the bottom.

Second, slippery slopes operate psychologically, not logically: "[T]hey work partly by domesticating one idea and thus making its nearest neighbor down the slope seem less extreme and unthinkable."[36] Yet a third reason we slide down slippery slopes is that there are people pushing us. Several organized groups ardently want to reform the law at the end of life. They are well aware that the public is afraid of the bottom of the slope; they have consciously calculated how to move us by small steps down the slope.

I have been suggesting that while slippery-slope arguments are not logically convincing, they are practically persuasive. A quick review of the American experience shows just how far along the slope we have moved.[37] Up through at least the 1950s, and perhaps through the 1960s, the reformers themselves framed the debate primarily in the very limited terms of (1) withholding or withdrawing (2) medical treatment from (3) competent adults who (4) suffered from a fatal illness, who (5) were in pain, and who (6) expressly refused treatment.

Observe how far we have come. Neither Karen Ann Quinlan nor Nancy Beth Cruzan was, so far as anyone can know, in pain. Quinlan might have appeared to suffer from a fatal illness.[38] Cruzan not only did not, but her life expectancy of thirty years was one of the arguments for causing her death. The issue in *Quinlan* was whether to withdraw medical care—a machine that helped her breathe. When Quinlan's father was asked about withdrawing food and water, he was shocked, as doctors and laymen alike would have been. But the Court in *Cruzan* barely noticed that the family wanted to withdraw food and water, not medical care as it is usually understood. Most significantly, neither Cruzan nor Quinlan refused treatment, and neither was competent to do so. Now voters in Oregon have twice adopted a referendum permitting physician-assisted suicide. And this describes only the movement of the law on the books. The law in action has also gone impressively far. It is hard to find out what goes on in the privacy of medical practice, but an impressive hint is given by the American Hospital Association. It believes "that 70 percent of the estimated 6,000 deaths that occur daily in the United States are somehow timed or negotiated with patients, family and doctors quietly agreeing on not using death-delaying technology."[39] And doctors like Timothy Quill acknowledge that some physician-assisted suicide is already occurring.[40]

Of course, a slippery slope is not a problem unless the bottom of the slope is bad. What is it that opponents of assisted suicide fear? First, as *Quinlan* reminds us, doctors can make mistakes.[41] We cannot want patients to die who think they are mortally ill but who in fact would recover. Second, there is the danger that patients who would rather live will be led by social pressure—by the emotional and economic distress of their families, by the impatience of their doctors, by the social symbolism embodied in a "right to die"—to ask for death. Third is the risk that the slide down the slippery slope will continue to encompass the only two remaining steps—active voluntary euthanasia and involuntary euthanasia.

Finally, we risk the lives of people who on some higher principle ought to live. Many of these will be ordinary people. But particularly jeopardized in this category will be people who are less than normal but not less than human. The American experience provides its share of disquieting impulses to end lives that observers think not worth living, or not worth supporting. Consider the words of the now-much-admired social reformer Charlotte Perkins Gilman, who in 1935 advocated "mercy killing" for "'incurable invalids', 'hopeless idiots', 'helpless paretics', and certain grades of criminals.'" She "asserted that 'the dragging weight of the grossly unfit and dangerous could be lightened'" in this way "'with great advantage to the normal and progressive.'"[42]

How can we summarize the lessons of the American experience with law at the end of life? Ultimately, I believe, it teaches us that we are condemned to uncertainty and sorrow. However deeply we think, we cannot know how to resolve every case. The strength of reason is too weak. However hard we try, we cannot write rules that will cause all cases to be decided as we would wish. The power of language is too poor. We are trapped in our own ambivalence about what is good and our own inability to attain even what we know is right.

Medical progress and the temper of our times have made the old rules unworkable. And surely rules that sentence the dying and the destroyed to prolonged and helpless agony can make the top of the slippery slope seem as cruel as the bottom. But the new rules to which we are moving seem fraught with peril. In part, I believe we must accept that the law need not and cannot by itself assume the whole social burden of these decisions. Some responsibility should and will be borne by patients themselves, by their doctors, and by their families. But I believe our best hope in this uncertainty lies in candid, open, and civil public discussion of an issue about which we will disagree entirely, passionately, and irreconcilably. How else can we make wise policy about law at the end of life in the democratic society to which we are committed?

I must close as I began, with a story. This is the true story of Carrie Coons, of Rensselaer, New York. This elderly lady fell into a persistent vegetative state. The doctors said her condition was hopeless and that she had no chance of recovery. Her eighty-eight-year-old sister asked a court to approve the removal of a feeding tube. The court agreed. Before the order could be carried out, however, her nurses asked her doctor to visit her. He found her awake and even alert. He described her legal problem to her. He asked what should be done. She replied, "These are difficult decisions." And she lapsed back into sleep.[43]

NOTES

1. 117 S Ct 2258 (1997).
2. Patients in this condition are unconscious and have lost higher cerebral functions. However, the brain stem, which controls "vegetative" functions, continues to work. See Ronald E. Cranford, *The Persistent Vegetative State: The Medical Reality (Getting the Facts Straight)*, Hastings Center Report 27 (Feb/Mar 1988).
3. In the Matter of Quinlan, 355 A2d 647, 667 (1976).
4. Yale Kamisar, *Some Non-Religious Views Against Proposed "Mercy-Killing" Legislation*, 42 Minnesota Law Review 969, 971 (1958).
5. 165 F2d 152 (1947).
6. Ibid. at 153.
7. Ibid. at 154–55.
8. In the Matter of Quinlan, 355 A2d 647 (1976). For a discussion of the historical importance of this case, see ch 9 of David J. Rothman, *Strangers at the Bedside: A History of How Law and Bioethics Trans-* *formed Medical Decision Making* (Basic Books, 1991).
9. 355 A2d at 664.
10. Ibid. at 664.
11. Ibid. at 663.
12. "[O]ne would have to think that the use of the same respirator or like support could be considered 'ordinary' in the context of the possibly curable patient but 'extraordinary' in the context of the forced sustaining by cardio-respiratory processes of an irreversibly doomed patient." Ibid. at 668.
13. *Cruzan v Director, Missouri Department of Health,* 497 U.S. 261, 290 n2 (1990) (O'Connor, J., concurring).
14. *Cruzan v Director, Missouri Department of Health,* 497 U.S. 261, 262 (1990).
15. Ibid. at 352.
16. Ibid. at 309.
17. Ibid. at 308.
18. Ibid. at 302.
19. Ibid. at 350.

20. Ibid. at 312 n11.
21. Gale P. Largey & Richard N. Feil, *Knowing the Public Mind,* 20 Hastings Center Report 3, 3 (July/Aug 1990).
22. Andrew H. Malcolm, "Judge Allows Feeding-Tube Removal," *New York Times,* Dec 15, 1990, § 1, at 10, col. 1.
23. Richard A. Knox, "Igniting a Deadly Debate," *Boston Globe,* Oct 27, 1991, 1.
24. *People v Kevorkian,* No. 93–11482 (Mich Cir Ct Wayne Cty Dec 13, 1993).
25. *People v Kevorkian,* 527 NW2d 714 (Mich 1994).
26. *Compassion in Dying v Washington,* 850 F Supp 1454 (WD Wash 1994).
27. *Compassion in Dying,* 79 F3d 790 (1996).
28. *Quill v Vacco,* 80 F3d 716 (1996).
29. 79 F3d at 793.
30. 117 S Ct 2302 (1997).
31. 117 S Ct 2293 (1997).
32. See particularly Sonia M. Suter, *Ambivalent Unanimity: An Analysis of the Supreme Court's Holding,* in this volume.
33. Andrew H. Malcolm, "Missouri Family Renews Battle Over Right to Die," *New York Times,* Nov 2, 1990, A14, col. 3.
34. 79 F3d at 794.
35. For a careful analysis of the slippery-slope argument, see Frederick Schauer, *Slippery Slopes,* 99 Harvard Law Review 361 (1985).
36. Carl E. Schneider, *Rights Discourse and Neonatal Euthanasia,* 76 California Law Review 151, 168 (1988).
37. For masterful treatments of the slippery-slope problem, see Yale Kamisar, *Some Non-Religious Views Against Proposed "Mercy-Killing" Legislation,* 42 Minnesota Law Review 969 (1958), and Yale Kamisar, *When Is There a Constitutional "Right to Die"? When Is There No Constitutional "Right to Live"?,* 25 Georgia Law Review 1203 (1991).
38. The *Quinlan* court seemed to believe that Quinlan was terminally ill, but that was in the face of the evidence available at the time, and, of course, it was wrong in fact.
39. Andrew H. Malcolm, "Right-to-Die Case Nearing Finale," *New York Times,* Dec 7, 1990, A24, col. 1.
40. See, e.g., Timothy E. Quill, *Death and Dignity: Making Choices and Taking Charge* (W. W. Norton, 1993).
41. As to error in diagnoses of the persistent vegetative state, Cranford notes that "even the generally accepted criteria, when properly applied, are not infallible. There have been a few unexpected, but unequivocal and well documented, recoveries of cognitive functions in situations where it was believed that the criteria were correctly applied by several neurologists experienced in the diagnosis of this condition." Cranford, *The Persistent Vegetative State* 29–30 (cited in note 2).
42. *The Right to Die,* 94 The Forum 297–300 (1935), quoted in Kamisar, *Some Non-Religious Views Against Proposed "Mercy-Killing" Legislation,* 42 Minnesota Law Review 969, 1019 (1958).
43. Sam Howe Verhovek, "Right-to-Die Order Revoked As Patient in Coma Wakes," *New York Times,* Apr 13, 1989, B3.

Part II

Reading *Glucksberg*

CHAPTER 2   **Ambivalent Unanimity:**
An Analysis of the Supreme
Court's Holding

Sonia M. Suter

The Problem

The Supreme Court's decisions in *Washington v Glucksberg*[1] and *Vacco v Quill*[2] upholding the Washington and New York bans on assisted suicide surprised few people who had been following that debate. Yet while the result was expected, the Court's unanimity was not. This is after all a Court that regularly decides hard cases by close votes.[3] Moreover, the Justices had already disagreed about questions related to assisted suicide. Finally, the significant public support for a right to assisted suicide at least for terminally ill, competent patients[4] made the unanimous decision even more surprising, at least if Mr. Dooley was right that "th' supreme coort follows th' iliction returns."

The Court was unanimous not only in finding the statutes constitutional, but in other respects as well. The Justices appeared to agree that there is no generalized right to assisted suicide, that the dying need adequate palliative care, that the distinction between withdrawing life support and physician-assisted suicide is rational, and that there is great value in leaving the "vigorous debate"[5] about the "morality, legality and practicality of physician-assisted suicide" to be continued and resolved by the American people through their state legislatures or referendums.[6]

But the issue before the Court concerned a complex political and bioethical problem. Not surprisingly, and in spite of these areas of broad agreement, the Court's apparent unanimity is crucially ambivalent. Indeed, only five Justices signed the Chief Justice's opinion, and one of them, Justice O'Connor, wrote a separate opinion. Moreover, Justices Stevens, Souter, and Breyer each wrote separately. While these different voices give richness to our understanding of the Court's holding and its future implications, they also reveal that beneath the united front upholding the constitutionality of the statutes lies a Court that is deeply divided and ambivalent about many aspects of the assisted-suicide debate. The Court is divided and ambivalent about the best approach to substantive due process; about the proper interpretation of cases central to this debate, such as *Cruzan v Director, Missouri Department of Health*[7] and *Planned Parenthood of South Eastern Pennsyl-*

vania v Casey;[8] about the role of doctors; and about the strength and proper characterization of the competing interests. But underlying and shaping this ambivalence are perhaps the most prevalent, though subtly expressed, sentiments: a deep sympathy for the plight of the terminally ill, a recognition of the enormity and irreversibility of ending life, and the sense that these are deeply personal and intimate issues best left to the body politic rather than the judiciary.

I want to focus primarily on three areas of judicial ambivalence: (1) the Court's ambivalence about the procedural posture of the case—that is, about whether it faced an "as-applied" or facial challenge to the statutes, (2) its ambivalence about the nature of the liberty interest that it rejected, and (3) its ambivalence about whether there might ever be a liberty interest in assisted suicide. Having described these ambivalences, I will conclude with some reflections on their meaning and implications, on the Court's historical experience with and conflicts over substantive due process, and on the politics of the Court.

The Opinions

Each of the cases before the Court concerned the Fourteenth Amendment. The *Glucksberg* respondents based their claims on the Due Process Clause; the *Quill* respondents invoked the Equal Protection Clause. While these provisions and the analytic methods the Court has developed to interpret them are more than familiar to lawyers, they are not to the laity. Therefore, before outlining Chief Justice Rehnquist's opinions for the Court, I begin by sketching the structure of Fourteenth Amendment law.

The Due Process Clause declares that the state may not "deprive any person of life, liberty or property, without due process of law." This clause not only guarantees fair procedure,[9] but also provides substantive rights by "barring certain government actions regardless of the fairness of the procedures used to implement them."[10] Although the Court has not defined the full scope of those substantive liberties, it has established that they include protection from some kinds of government interference in such areas as marriage, procreation, contraception, family relationships, child rearing, education, and refusal of unwanted medical treatment.[11]

Determining whether someone has a liberty interest is a tricky, obscure process. Indeed, as I shall show in the following discussion, the Justices in *Glucksberg* disagree as to the appropriate approach. However, even if a plaintiff has a liberty interest, government interference with the interest is not necessarily unconstitutional. Whether and when government action violates substantive due process depends on the nature of both the individual's and the state's interests.[12] The weightier the individual interest, the more rigorous the review. At one extreme—when "certain 'fundamental' liberty interests" are at stake—the court must apply "strict scrutiny" analysis. That is, state action is constitutional only if the "infringement is narrowly tailored to serve a compelling state interest."[13] At the other extreme—when no constitutionally protected liberty interest exists—courts use the "rational-basis" test. Government action will be upheld if it is "rationally related to legitimate government interests."[14] Thus substantive due process analysis involves two steps: (1) establishing whether the asserted right is a fundamental liberty interest and (2) analyzing the state interests under the appropriate standard.

Like the Due Process Clause, the Equal Protection Clause prohibits certain state actions. Specifically, it declares that the State shall not "deny to any person within its jurisdiction the equal protection of the laws." However, merely treating cases differently does not violate the Equal Protection Clause. The constitutionality of state-imposed distinctions or inequalities depends on their nature and thus on the standard of review. If state action "neither burdens a fundamental right nor targets a suspect class," the action is constitutional "so long as it bears a rational relation to some legitimate end."[15] However, when governmental actions "interfere with fundamental constitutional rights or . . . involve suspect classifications," courts will use more demanding standards of review.[16]

Having laid this groundwork, I can turn to the Chief Justice's opinions. In *Glucksberg,* the Court reviewed the Ninth Circuit's decision that the Washington statute prohibiting assisted suicide violated the Due Process Clause of the Fourteenth Amendment. Specifically, the Ninth Circuit found a "constitutionally-protected liberty interest in determining the time and manner of one's own death" and held that "insofar as the Washington statute prohibits physicians from prescribing life-ending medication for use by terminally ill, competent adults who wish to hasten their own deaths, it violates the Due Process Clause of the Fourteenth Amendment."[17]

In writing the opinion of the Court, the Chief Justice began by describing what he called the Court's "established method of substantive-due-process analysis."[18] He stressed that only interests that are "'deeply rooted in this Nation's history and tradition'"[19] and "'implicit in the concept of ordered liberty'"[20] deserve constitutional protection under the Due Process Clause.[21] In articulating his notion of substantive due process, the Chief Justice strenuously sought to restrict expansive autonomy-based justifications for fundamental liberty interests. Although he conceded that the liberty interests at stake in *Cruzan* and *Casey* were deduced in part "from abstract concepts of personal autonomy,"[22] he insisted that the fact that "many of the rights and liberties protected by the Due Process Clause sound in personal autonomy does not warrant the sweeping conclusion that any and all important, intimate and personal decisions are so protected."[23]

Having established his view of the proper approach to substantive due process review, Chief Justice Rehnquist surveyed our "Nation's history, legal traditions, and practices"[24] and readily concluded that suicide and assisted suicide are neither deeply rooted in our history and traditions nor implicit in the concept of ordered liberty. Consequently, he found no fundamental liberty interest in either suicide or assisted suicide. This conclusion virtually decided the case, because at that point, all Washington needed to show was that its statute was "rationally related to legitimate government interests."[25] Chief Justice Rehnquist identified a number of state interests—preserving human life, preventing suicide, protecting the integrity and ethics of the medical profession, protecting vulnerable groups, and avoiding the slippery slope toward euthanasia.[26] All these "unquestionably" met the rational-basis test, and consequently the Court upheld the statute.[27]

At issue in *Vacco* was the Second Circuit's holding that the New York law criminalizing assisted suicide violated the Equal Protection Clause. The Second Circuit had concluded that New York did not treat all terminally ill, competent individuals who wished to hasten their deaths equally. Those on life support could hasten their deaths by being removed from life support, whereas those who sought to hasten their deaths through assisted suicide could not do so legally.[28] At the root of this holding is the long-standing debate about whether a principled distinction exists between withdrawing life support and physician-assisted suicide.

Although the Second Circuit was not persuaded that such a principled distinction could be drawn, Chief Justice Rehnquist was. Instead, he concluded that causation and intent differ in the two cases. When life-sustaining treatment is removed or refused, he reasoned, the patient "dies from the underlying fatal disease or pathology; but if a patient ingests lethal medication prescribed by a physician he is killed by that medication."[29] Similarly, when a physician withdraws life-sustaining treatment he "intends, or may . . . intend, only to respect his patient's wishes,"[30] whereas when he assists a suicide, the physician "'must, necessarily and indubitably, intend primarily that the patient be made dead.'"[31] The Chief Justice was further moved by the fact that these distinctions are "widely recognized and endorsed in the medical profession and in our legal traditions." Therefore he found the distinction between withdrawing life support and assisting a suicide wholly rational.[32]

Chief Justice Rehnquist further concluded that the statute does not target a suspect class or rely on suspect classifications. Indeed, he reasoned, the combination of statutes prohibiting assisted suicide and allowing refusal of medical treatment does not "treat anyone differently than anyone else or draw any distinctions between persons," since "[e]veryone, regardless of physical condition, is entitled, if competent, to refuse unwanted lifesaving medical treatment" and everyone is prohibited from assisted suicide.[33] Moreover, since the distinction between killing and letting die is rational, any "uneven effect upon particular groups" is not of "constitutional concern."[34]

Finally, Chief Justice Rehnquist found that the same state interests described in *Glucksberg* justified New York's decision to allow refusal of life-sustaining treatment but to prohibit assisted suicide. Because preserving human life, preventing suicide, protecting the integrity of the medical profession, protecting the vulnerable, and avoiding the slippery slope to euthanasia are "valid and important public interests," he concluded that the legislation is rationally related to a legitimate end and therefore is constitutional.[35]

Was the Washington Statute Challenged on Its Face or as Applied?

Although every Justice joined the Court's holding in both cases, the Court was deeply divided on several important issues. One key area of division and ambiguity concerns the procedural nature of the challenge in *Glucksberg*— was the Court evaluating the Washington statute on its face or as applied? As I shall discuss in the next two sections, whether the Court found either statute constitutional "as applied" or "on its face" is related to two other areas about which the Court appeared ambivalent: (1) the proper formulation of the liberty interest that the *Glucksberg* Court rejected and (2) whether, after *Glucksberg,* anyone could assert some other kind of liberty interest in assisted suicide.

The difference between as-applied and facial review is important. "If a court holds a statute unconstitutional on its face, the state may not enforce it under any circumstances, unless an appropriate court narrows its application; in contrast, when a court holds a statute unconstitutional as applied to particular facts, the state may enforce the statute in different circumstances."[36] Upholding the statute against a facial challenge simply indicates that prohibitions of assisted suicide are constitutional in at least some instances.[37] Such circumstances are easy to imagine; few would argue for a constitutional right to assisted suicide in all cases. The Court's denial of a facial challenge would therefore only establish the lack of a generalized liberty interest in assisted suicide, that is, an interest that applies to everyone. It would not reveal whether terminally ill, mentally competent patients (or any other particularized group) have such a liberty interest. That issue would only be resolved through an as-applied challenge, for then the Court would have to examine whether those particular individuals in those particular circumstances have such a liberty interest. One of the strongest cases for the unconstitutionality of the challenged statutes is that they infringe the rights of terminally ill competent adults—the very plaintiffs in this case. If their as-applied challenge failed, little would be left in the arsenal of most other potential plaintiffs seeking to challenge the statutes.[38]

Despite the importance of the issue and despite the fact that several Justices disagreed about it, Chief Justice Rehnquist devoted little attention to clarifying whether the challenge was facial or as applied. Instead, he seemed ambivalent on this point. In many places he spoke as if the challenge were facial, in spite of evidence that he recognized that the respondents raised an as-applied challenge. He noted, for instance, that the respondents asserted a liberty interest that "protects the decision of a mentally competent, terminally ill adult to bring about impending death in a certain, humane and dignified manner."[39] Although he did not specifically say their claim was as applied, it clearly was intended to be. Without explanation, however, his framing of the question suggested he might instead interpret the challenge as facial: Because the Washington statute prohibits "'aiding another person to attempt suicide,'" the question he addressed was "whether the 'liberty' specially protected by the Due Process Clause includes a right to commit suicide which itself includes a right of assistance in doing so."[40] His failure to discuss the statute in terms of a specific class of individuals—mentally competent, terminally ill adults—implied the challenge was facial. More notably, after examining whether the interests in suicide and assisted suicide are deeply rooted in our nation's history and tradition, the Chief Justice concluded that the "asserted right to assistance in committing suicide is not a fundamental liberty interest protected by the Due Process Clause."[41] Such a statement strongly suggests he was addressing only a facial challenge.

The opinions of other Justices underscore this interpretation. Justice O'Connor, for example, explicitly characterized the challenges to both statutes as facial. She did not, however, dwell on this point. She merely noted that "in the context of these facial challenges" the Court need not resolve the "narrower question" posed by the respondents: "whether a mentally competent person who is experiencing great suffering has a constitutionally cognizable interest in controlling the circumstances of his or her imminent death."[42]

Justice Stevens shared Justice O'Connor's view that the challenge was facial. Unlike Justice O'Connor, however, he explained his interpretation. Although he acknowledged that the Ninth Circuit evaluated the Washington statute as it applied to "'the prescription of life-ending medication for use by terminally ill, competent, adult patients who wish to hasten their deaths,'"[43] he concluded that the Ninth Circuit did not have before it "any individual plaintiff seeking to hasten her death or any doctor who was threatened with prosecution for assisting in the suicide of a particular patient."[44] Because the challenge was only facial, the plaintiffs had to (and here he quoted Chief Justice Rehnquist) "show that the interest in liberty protected by the Fourteenth Amendment 'includes a right to commit suicide which itself includes a right to assistance in doing so.'"[45] Since the plaintiffs did not make such a showing, he concluded that the Court decided that the Washington statute was "not 'invalid on its face.'"[46]

Justices Stevens and O'Connor were not alone in their views. Justice Breyer also seemed to think the Court held only that the statutes were facially constitutional. Although he did not address the facial/applied issue specifically, he alluded to it in stating that the Court formulated the liberty interest broadly as "'a right to commit suicide with another's assistance,'" in contrast to his characterization of the interest as applied to a specific class of terminally ill, physically suffering, mentally competent individuals.[47] These statements, coupled with the fact that he joined Justice O'Connor's separate opinion "except insofar as it joins the majority,"[48] therefore suggest that he believed the Court held only that the statute was constitutional on its face.

Justice Souter's analysis is ambiguous. In a footnote, he declared that he saw "the challenge to the statute not as facial but as-applied" and that he understood "it to be in narrower terms than those accepted by the Court."[49] He did not clarify what he meant by "narrower." If he used the adjective as Justice O'Connor did, to distinguish as-applied challenges from facial challenges, this statement might suggest he believed the Court addressed only a facial challenge, even if he himself viewed it as as-applied. On the other hand, he also stated that "the statute's application to the doctors has not been shown to be unconstitutional,"[50] which might indicate that he believed the Court's holding was, after all, based on an as-applied challenge. It is hard to reconcile these two statements.

The procedural posture Justices Stevens and O'Connor (and possibly Breyer and Souter) attributed to the case seems consistent with much of the Chief Justice's language. Yet, as I suggested earlier, the Chief Justice's position was ultimately ambiguous. In fact, he specifically addressed and seemed to reject Justice Stevens's argument that the Court confronted only a facial challenge. The Chief Justice pointed out more than once that the Ninth Circuit had held that the statute was unconstitutional "*as applied* to terminally ill competent adults who wish to hasten their deaths with medication prescribed by their physicians."[51] In addition, he stressed that the Ninth Circuit specifically "emphasized that it was '*not deciding the facial validity* of [the Washington statute]'" and that it was exactly this holding that was before the Supreme Court.[52] Most important, though, his express statement of the Court's holding at the end of the opinion undermines Justices Stevens's and O'Connor's position that the Court only addressed a facial challenge. As the Chief Justice flatly wrote, the Washington statute "does not violate the Fourteenth Amendment, either on its face or *as applied* to competent, terminally ill adults who wish to hasten their deaths by obtaining medication prescribed by their doctors."[53]

While the Chief Justice seemed ultimately to reject the view that the challenge was only facial, he did not fully address Justice Stevens's rationale for that view. Justice Souter, however, briefly did so in his concurrence.[54] As he pointed out, the plaintiffs included not only the terminally ill patients who died while the case was pending, but also four physicians who sought declaratory and injunctive relief so that they would be able to help other dying patients commit suicide. Thus in Justice Souter's view the claim before the Court was that the Washington statute was unconstitutional "*as applied* to physicians treating terminally ill patients."[55] Moreover, he concluded that the "statute's *application* to the doctors ha[d] not been shown to be unconstitutional. . . ."[56]

Justice Souter's reasoning makes sense. Under Justice Stevens's view, it is hard to imagine a case brought on behalf of terminally ill patients and their doctors that would ever qualify as more than a facial challenge, since, by definition, terminally ill patients would probably not survive the lengthy period of the judicial process. Moreover, as Professor Kamisar notes, the statute applies to physicians, for it is their actions the law prohibits. As he suggests, this is much like the situation created when physicians "assert their patients' rights in challenging abortion restrictions" on behalf of their patients.[57]

Professor Kamisar also argues that there is no reason to assume that Justices Kennedy, Thomas, and Scalia did not share Chief Justice Rehnquist's view regarding the nature of the challenge.[58] If in fact they did, together with Justice Souter they comprised a majority of the Court that thought the statutes were constitutional facially and as applied.

In sum, even if, despite the Court's ambiguous language, one concludes that a majority rejected a constitutional right *for* terminally ill, mentally competent patients, the Court was anything but unanimous with respect to that holding, let alone the underlying reasoning. The vote was probably five to four. Justices O'Connor and Stevens were clear dissenters, for they thought the holding was based on only a facial challenge. Justices Breyer and Ginsburg presumably are the third and fourth dissenting votes.

What Is the Proper Formulation of the Liberty Interest That the Court Rejected?

Largely because of the ambiguity regarding whether the challenge was facial or as applied, the Court also appeared ambivalent about the nature of the liberty interest it rejected. In many ways, these issues are flip sides of the same coin.[59] If the Court held only that the Washington statute was constitutional on its face, then all that the Court established was the lack of a generalized liberty interest in assisted suicide, that is, an interest that applies to everyone. If, however, the Court held that the statute was constitutional as applied to terminally ill, mentally competent individuals, then the rejected liberty interest would look much narrower. But, as we shall see, the ambiguity concerns not only which individuals have been denied the asserted interest, but also what the breadth and nature of that interest is.

Chief Justice Rehnquist seemed to characterize the rejected liberty interest much like a generalized liberty interest in assisted suicide. Focusing on the statutory language, he defined it as "a right to commit suicide which itself includes a right of assistance in doing so,"[60] and he specifically rejected the "asserted right to assistance in committing suicide."[61] The Chief Justice's framing of the interest seems to be a deliberate recharacterization of the respondents' and the Ninth Circuit's formulation of it. He began by quoting the respondents' depiction of the interest as the "Fourteenth Amendment's guarantee of liberty protect[ing] the decision of a mentally competent, terminally ill adult to bring about impending death in a certain, humane and dignified manner."[62] In addition, he sprinkled his opinion with descriptions the Ninth Circuit and respondents used, including statements that citizens have a right to die and have interests in choosing "how to die," in controlling "one's final days," in "choosing a humane, dignified death," and in shaping their deaths.[63] Then, without explanation, he framed the interest quite differently—in terms of the statute's language.[64]

In one sense, the Chief Justice's characterization of the liberty interest is broader than the respondents' and the Ninth Circuit's, since he described an interest that applies to all classes of individuals. In fact, this broad characterization helps explain the Justices' confusion as to whether the Court ruled that the statutes were constitutional on their face or as applied, since it suggests he viewed the challenge as facial in spite of some comments to the contrary. In another sense, however, Chief Justice Rehnquist's description of the interest is more limited. While the Ninth Circuit and the respondents depicted an interest that applies to a narrow class of individuals, it arguably includes more than receiving assistance in committing suicide. A right to "bring about impending death," a right to die, and a right to control one's final days may include not only a right to commit suicide, but also a right to euthanasia.

That the Chief Justice reformulated the interest at issue is not in and of itself problematic. After all, a court is not bound to adopt the exact characterization that litigants use to describe their claims. However, Chief Justice Rehnquist's reformulation is confusing in light of his concluding statements that the Washington statute is not only constitutional on its face, but also "'as applied to competent terminally ill adults who wish to hasten their deaths by obtaining medication prescribed by their doctors.'"[65] This statement suggests that he *was* addressing the narrower (as-applied) version of the asserted liberty interest. That he would conclude the opinion by describing the interest narrowly after having deliberately reformulated the interest more broadly is curious. Moreover, it muddies the waters as to the nature of the liberty interest that the Court rejected.

The opinions of some of the Justices exacerbate this confusion. Justice O'Connor explained that she joined "the Court's opinions because [she agreed] that there is no *generalized right* to 'commit suicide.'"[66] This statement suggests Justice O'Connor thought the Court had not rejected an interest limited to a specific class of individuals. Indeed, she specifically stated that the Court need not address "the narrower question" the respondents presented: "whether a mentally competent person who is experiencing great suffering has a constitutionally cognizable interest in controlling the circumstances of his or her imminent death."[67] Her use of the term "narrower," however, fails to distinguish between a terminally ill, mentally competent individual's interest *in assisted suicide* and such a person's broader interest *in controlling the circumstances of his or her imminent death*. This ambiguity theoretically leaves open the possibility that the Court rejected the former interest in assisted suicide and did not analyze the second, broader interest in controlling death. Yet that interpretation is unlikely given Justice O'Connor's statement that there is no "generalized right" and given her belief that the Court dealt with only a facial challenge. In other words, Justice O'Connor's opinion suggests she believed the Court merely rejected a generalized right to assistance in committing suicide, which was not limited to a narrow class.

Justice Stevens also seemed to think that the Court only decided whether everyone has a constitutional right to suicide and assistance in committing suicide. Because he believed the Court only dealt with a facial challenge, he thought the only interest at issue was "'a right to commit suicide which itself includes a right to assistance in doing so.'"[68]

In spite of the Chief Justice's concluding statements, Justice Breyer also appeared to interpret the Court's characterization of the rejected liberty interest as Justices O'Connor and Stevens did. He, however, believed the Court erred in describing the interest as a "'right to commit suicide with another's assistance.'"[69] Indeed, he wrote separately largely because he took issue with the Court's formulation of the liberty interest.[70] He would have characterized it as a "right to die with dignity," at the "core of which would lie personal control over the manner of death, professional medical assistance, and the avoidance of unnecessary, and severe physical suffering."[71] In one sense, this description is broader than Chief Justice Rehnquist's because dying with dignity and controlling the manner of one's death stretch beyond assisted suicide to encompass euthanasia. In another sense, however, the interest is narrower because it is limited to individuals seeking to avoid "severe physical pain (connected with death)."[72]

Finally, perhaps more than any other Justice, Justice Souter emphasized how important a court's characterization of the asserted liberty interest is.[73] Moreover, he explicitly separated the two questions that the other Justices had conflated—who has the right and what the right is. Because he believed the challenge to the Washington statute was as applied, he thought the Court was "faced with an individual claim not to a right on the part of just anyone to help anyone else commit suicide under any circumstances, but to the right of a narrow class to help others also in a narrow class under a set of limited circumstances."[74] But Justice Souter was also concerned with the breadth and quality of the interest itself, irrespective of the number and kind of individuals to whom it applied. Thus, he described the interest as "a right to a physician's assistance in providing counsel and drugs to be administered by the patient to end life promptly." The right would apply to "a patient [who is] suffering imminent death, who anticipates physical suffering and indignity, and is capable of responsible and voluntary choices."[75] This characterization of the interest differs from Justice Breyer's in that the interest is only in counsel and assistance from a physician in taking one's own life, as opposed to a more sweeping interest in controlling the end of one's life.

Taken together, these opinions are ambivalent and ambiguous in two respects. First, the Court seemed divided as to whose liberty interest was rejected by the Court. Chief Justice Rehnquist's opinion is confusing because throughout he focused on a generalized right to assisted suicide, and then, without explanation, ultimately declared that the statute was constitutional both on its face and as applied to mentally competent, terminally ill individuals. Justices O'Connor, Stevens, Breyer, and, one would presume, Ginsburg (since she silently joined Justice O'Connor's opinion) were not persuaded by the Chief Justice's later statement and therefore believed the Court merely rejected a generalized interest in assistance in committing suicide. In contrast, Justice Souter suggested that the Court rejected a right to assisted suicide that applied to a limited class of individuals. Once again, we find that the vote was in reality probably five to four.

The Court was also ambivalent about the breadth and nature of the interest asserted, regardless of the class of individuals to whom it applied. Chief Justice Rehnquist and Justice Souter examined a right to receive assistance in committing suicide (or in the cases of physicians, a right to provide such assistance). In contrast, Justices Breyer and O'Connor envisioned a broader liberty interest in controlling the manner of one's death and avoiding unnecessary and severe pain and suffering. Thus, in several respects the Court was ambivalent in its unanimous holding.

Can There Ever Be a Constitutional Right to Physician-Assisted Suicide?

The Court was ambivalent about more than its holding. On various levels and to differing degrees, each of the Justices was ambivalent about whether the Court could ever find statutes like the ones at issue unconstitutional. Many of the Justices expressed ambivalence about the existence of a constitutionally cognizable liberty interest in assisted suicide, the nature of such an interest, and whether it would outweigh the competing state interests.

Let me return to the majority's position and its confusing language. The Chief Justice's reframing of the question before the Court leaves open the question whether a person might be able to assert some kind of liberty interest to assistance in committing suicide. Because the Chief Justice never explained why he concluded that the statutes were constitutional as applied specifically to terminally ill, mentally competent patients; because his discussion of the liberty interest focused on suicide generally; and because of the confusion as to whether the challenge was facial or as applied, it is not clear whether he actually determined that some narrower liberty interest exists.[76] It is possible—even likely—that, like Justice O'Connor, he believed the Court did not need to address that question because the state's interests outweighed any such liberty interest. Unfortunately, the Chief Justice's analysis of the state's interests does not resolve this problem. Since he concluded that the asserted "right" to commit suicide is not fundamental, he examined the state's interests only casually.[77] Thus, his analysis does not tell us whether the state's interests are strong enough to limit some new and fundamental liberty interest.

The Chief Justice fueled the fires of confusion when, in footnote 24, he stated that the Court's "opinion does not absolutely foreclose" Justice Stevens's intimation that "'an individual plaintiff seeking to hasten her death, or a doctor whose assistance was sought, could prevail in a more particularized challenge.'"[78] This statement has been dismissed as merely a political maneuver to persuade Justice Stevens, and perhaps other Justices, to sign the opinion.[79] Such a reading is quite plausible, especially since the Chief Justice offered this observation almost as an aside, in a delphic footnote. Yet, although his opinion is not written with as much sympathy to the respondents' claims as some of the other opinions, one could read his ambiguous language together with this footnote as permitting a "more particularized claim." True, it is hard to imagine a more particularized case than being at the end of one's life, in great pain, while still mentally competent. Nevertheless, one exists—the case of such a person who is also unable to obtain relief from pain without lapsing into a coma.[80] The language of the opinion, at least formally, leaves open the possibility that the Court would consider such a claim. On the other hand, the patient-respondents argued that they fell within the "small group" of individuals with "no choice between agony and unconsciousness, even with the best palliative care."[81] Since none of the Justices discussed whether they accepted that description, however, the question remains unresolved.

My guess is that the Chief Justice would not be sympathetic to claims brought by such plaintiffs because of his unambiguous commitment to cabining substantive due process. His historicist approach to substantive due process, which draws primarily from the past, and his highly restrained characterization of the nation's traditions and practices strongly suggest that he would not find *any* new formulation of the liberty interest to be "fundamental." Indeed, his opinion almost seems intended to warn away attempts to assert such new formulations. Thus, he would probably find it simple to uphold the constitutionality of the challenged statute. Given the number of valid state interests he described, it is virtually certain he would find a rational basis for statutes prohibiting assisted suicide.

In the end, the confusion regarding the Chief Justice's willingness to consider some new class of liberty interests may be primarily the result of his efforts to achieve a unanimous holding. But it may also reflect some ambivalence on his part and the part of one or more of the three Justices who silently joined his opinion—ambivalence because of a tension between sympathy for the needs and desires of patients like the plaintiffs and a decided reluctance to expand substantive due process and embroil the Court in new and unforeseeable perplexities. One cannot say for sure.

Justice O'Connor's ambivalence is even more striking. Not only was she expressly sympathetic to the respondents' plight,[82] but she also seemed open to, though uncertain about, the possibility that patients like them might have some sort of liberty interest, at least in principle. She was also unsure of the exact nature of such a liberty interest.

This uncertainty is suggested by the fact that, after noting that the majority recharacterized the issue presented by the respondents, Justice O'Connor herself ultimately reframed the issue. She began by noting that the respondents raised the question of "whether a mentally competent person who is experiencing great suffering has a constitutionally cognizable interest in *controlling the circumstances of his or her imminent death.*"[83] Both because she treated the challenge as facial and because of the weightiness of the state's interest in ensuring that decisions to hasten death are voluntary, Justice O'Connor concluded that the Court need not address the possibility that some more persuasive formulation of the right could be devised. Nevertheless, she then shifted gears and ended her opinion with a fresh characterization of the issue: "whether suffering patients have a constitutionally cognizable interest in *obtaining relief from the suffering* they may experience in the last days of their lives."[84] This issue, she decided, did not need to be resolved both because patients can obtain palliative care in Washington and New York and because it is so difficult to define terminal illness and to ensure that decisions are voluntary. Thus, she concluded that the prohibitions on physician-assisted suicide were justified, and she happily left the matter to be worked out in the laboratory of the states.[85]

It is hard to know how to interpret this shift in focus—a shift from interests in controlling the circumstances of one's death to interests in relief from suffering. Some suggest that it reveals Justice O'Connor's belief in a constitutionally protected right to palliative care.[86] At the very least, Justice O'Connor would seriously consider the constitutionality of such an interest if a state prohibited the use of palliative care that might hasten death. But in refusing to address whether terminally ill, mentally competent patients have a liberty interest in controlling the circumstances of their death, she left open the question whether these patients have a liberty interest in physician-assisted suicide, even if compelling state interests ultimately outweigh it. Perhaps Justice O'Connor was ambivalent about the nature of any liberty interest in physician-assisted suicide—whether the issue is controlling the circumstances of one's death or ultimately relief from pain. Alternatively, she might have simply intended to suggest that two different possible liberty interests might exist—an interest in controlling the circumstances of one's death and an interest in obtaining relief from pain. Either way, her opinion is consistent with the possibility that she might recognize some form of liberty interest related to physician-assisted suicide.

Justice Stevens, who may be the Court's foremost champion of the right claimed by the respondents, expressed his own, surprising, ambivalence. As I noted, he agreed with the Court's result purely for procedural reasons, that is, he believed the Court had before it only a facial challenge to the Washington and New York statutes. But he wrote separately to keep alive the constitutional question raised by the respondents[87] because he believed that at times an "interest in hastening death" is not only legitimate, but "entitled to constitutional protection."[88] Justice Stevens based this view on a much broader reading of *Cruzan* than Chief Justice Rehnquist's. He reasoned that *Cruzan* dealt with more than just a "liberty interest in refusing unwanted medical treatment."[89] It also protected an "interest in dignity, and in determining the character of [one's] memories that will survive long after [one's] death."[90] In Justice Stevens's view, *Cruzan* made "it clear that some individuals who no longer have the option of deciding whether to live or die because they are already on the threshold of death have a constitutionally protected interest . . . in deciding how, rather than whether, a critical threshold shall be crossed."[91]

Not only did Justice Stevens practically declare the existence of a constitutionally cognizable liberty interest in determining the circumstances of one's death in some cases, but he also argued passionately that this interest may, at times, outweigh the state's interests in prohibiting assisted suicide, the weightiness of which, he believed, varies with the circumstances.[92] In fact, he argued that all the relevant state interests lose their force when considered in the context of terminally ill, competent individuals who decide, rationally and voluntarily, to seek assistance in ending their lives. The normally weighty state interest in preserving life is substantially reduced when an individual is left only with the choice of *when,* rather than *whether,* to die.[93] In addition, the state's interest in protecting the vulnerable and preventing euthanasia is not applicable to terminally ill individuals who are competent and rational and who voluntarily decide to seek assistance in ending their lives.[94] Justice Stevens was similarly unpersuaded that the state's interest in preserving the integrity of the medical profession is sufficiently weighty when it comes to competent, rational, and terminally ill patients, especially those who have long-standing relationships with physicians who are "attentive to their patients' individualized needs."[95]

Having made the case for the flimsiness of the state's interests with respect to mentally competent, terminally ill patients, however, Justice Stevens was strangely reluctant to assert that the state's interests are "invalid with respect to the entire class of terminally ill, mentally competent patients."[96] His arguments fizzled as he resisted making the bold assertion that the liberty interest in controlling the time and manner of one's death should prevail with respect to all terminally ill, mentally competent patients. Indeed, having distinguished the mentally competent, terminally ill from the vulnerable, the depressed, and the mentally incompetent, Justice Stevens curiously failed to explain why he would not uphold a constitutional right to assisted suicide for the former against competing state interests. Ultimately, he said only that he did not "foreclose the possibility that an individual plaintiff seeking to hasten her death, or a doctor whose assistance was sought could prevail in a more particularized challenge."[97] Given his strongly worded arguments not only asserting a liberty interest in assisted suicide for the terminally ill and mentally competent, but also depreciating the state's interests in prohibiting assisted suicide for this limited category of individuals, it is astonishing that Stevens would ultimately conclude so little.[98]

Like Justice Stevens, Justice Souter seemed persuaded that the respondents had a liberty interest in assisted suicide but nevertheless concluded that the statutes were constitutional. It is hard to glean from his opinion how Justice Souter himself would weigh the competing interests. His opinion, however, suggests he might favor the claims of the respondents.

It is difficult to assess Justice Souter's views in part because of the nature of his preferred approach to substantive due process.[99] His approach to judicial review, like Chief Justice Rehnquist's, requires an examination of our nation's traditions. But unlike the Chief Justice's, it asks the Court not only to identify old principles but also "to understand [them] afresh by new examples and counterexamples."[100] This requires "reasoned judgment" and close and careful analysis of the opposing interests.[101] Rather than try to establish absolute principles,[102] the Court must "assess the relative 'weights' or dignities of the contending interests."[103] The goal is not to determine which is the stronger interest, but whether the legislature's balancing of the interests is reasonable and not arbitrary.

In analyzing the case, Justice Souter spent considerable time and attention rather generously characterizing the strength of the respondent's interests.[104] He placed the alleged right in the context of the long tradition of judicial protection of autonomy in controlling the treatment of one's mind or body. The decriminalization of suicide, Justice Souter reasoned, "opens the door to the assertion of a cognizable liberty interest in bodily integrity and associated medical care that would otherwise have been inapposite, so long as suicide, as well as assisting a suicide, was a criminal offense."[105]

But Justice Souter also situated the interest in physician-assisted suicide in the context of positive rights to medical intervention— for example, the right to medical assistance in securing an abortion.[106] In his view, both interests are intimately associated with the relationship between doctor and patient. The importance of this relationship bears on the state's interest in regulating it. Justice Souter noted that a physician's assistance and counsel in ending one's life can be as crucial as a physician's assistance in having an abortion. Without that assistance, patients might be driven to "crude[,] ... shocking and painful" methods of effectuating their right to end their lives.[107] Not only does the interest in a doctor's help in committing suicide resemble the right to an abortion, it also resembles interests in other kinds of decisions in which people are now understood to have the right to the help of a doctor—like the decision to withdraw life-sustaining treatment, nutrition, or hydration and to receive terminal sedation. Moreover, Justice Souter believed that, like abortion and these other decisions, physician-assisted suicide may fall within our traditions of medical care, traditions that envision a physician not as a mere "mechanic of the human body . . . but [as] one who does more than treat symptoms, one who ministers to the patient."[108]

Having warmly characterized the respondent's interests, Justice Souter concluded that they fall within the class of "'certain interests' demanding careful scrutiny of the state's contrary claim."[109] As weighty as these interests are, however, he was ultimately persuaded that the state's interests are "sufficiently serious" to make the statute constitutional.[110] In particular, he concluded that great factual uncertainty over the state's ability to protect "terminally ill patients from involuntary suicide and euthanasia, both voluntary and involuntary," was reason enough to conclude that the statutory prohibition was neither arbitrary nor "purposeless."[111] This uncertainty, he reasoned, is best resolved through legislative inquiry and experimentation rather than through the judicial process.[112] Thus, like Justice O'Connor, Justice Souter found no reason to decide whether the interest at stake "might in some circumstances, or at some time, be seen as 'fundamental' to the degree entitled to prevail."[113] He warned however, that he did not "decide for all time that the respondent's claim should not be recognized."[114]

Justice Souter's decision to uphold the statutes leaves uncertain how the scales tip in his personal balancing of the competing interests. His opinion suggests that he found the respondent's interests particularly important. Yet all we can confidently say is that he did not think the respondent's interests greatly outweighed the state's.[115] Like Justice Stevens, Justice Souter hesitated to push his arguments as far as they might go. He was reluctant to claim that the respondents had a constitutionally cognizable liberty interest, even though he hinted that they do. Nevertheless, he did suggest that if the data from legislative experimentation demonstrated that state regulation had real teeth, he would be willing not only to revisit the issue, but perhaps to find a right to assisted suicide for the mentally competent terminally ill.[116]

Finally, Justice Breyer too expressed ambivalence as to whether there is some form of a constitutionally cognizable liberty interest in assisted suicide. As I mentioned earlier, Justice Breyer believed that the Court had incorrectly formulated the liberty interest. He noted that if that interest were characterized as a "right to die" or "control . . . the manner of death, professional medical assistance, and the avoidance of unnecessary and severe physical suffering," our legal tradition might provide support for it.[117] In sum, Justice Breyer suggested, but did not decide, that the interest in such control over one's death may be similar to the rights, liberties, or interests the Court has deemed fundamental.[118]

Like Justices O'Connor and Souter, however, Justice Breyer found no need to resolve that issue. In his view, the respondents' liberty interests were not infringed by either statute because "the avoidance of severe physical pain (connected with death) would have to comprise an essential part of any successful claim" and there are no legal barriers to the provision of palliative care, even care that hastens death.[119] Were the state to inhibit the provision of palliative care, however, this liberty interest would be "more directly at issue," and the "Court might have to revisit its conclusions in these cases."[120]

As in Justice O'Connor's opinion, this shift in focus from the right to die to the interest in palliative care blurs the nature of the liberty interest. Was Justice Breyer merely concerned with the right to palliative care, or was he also largely sympathetic to a larger right to control the manner of one's death and to avoid unnecessary and severe physical suffering? Like Justice O'Connor, Justice Breyer seemed impressed with the former, since it is that right that he would consider revisiting if state laws impeded the provision of palliative care. But his initial formulation and discussion of the liberty interest at issue suggest he might also give serious attention to the constitutionality of an interest in controlling the manner of one's death. Thus, Justice Breyer might consider the constitutionality of a right to assisted suicide for the "very few individuals for whom the ineffectiveness of pain control can mean, not pain, but the need for sedation in a coma."[121] These individuals, his opinion suggests, may have potent liberty interests in controlling the manner of their death.

The differences between the two liberty interests Justices Breyer and O'Connor described—in controlling one's death and in palliative care—may have constitutional implications. The former interest is vaguer and broader, encompassing all manner of ways one might end one's life, including euthanasia. This Court surely would be extremely uncomfortable giving constitutional status to an interest so broadly defined as to include euthanasia. Moreover, while controlling the manner of one's death, as several of the Justices pointed out, is clearly not deeply rooted in our nation's traditions, obtaining palliative care may be more in keeping with the traditional rhetoric and goals of medicine. Thus, one might imagine that several, possibly even a majority, of the Justices would be far more amenable to recognizing a fundamental constitutional liberty interest in receiving palliative care than in controlling one's death.

Justice Breyer's and O'Connor's discussions of palliative care are, however, dicta. The plaintiffs never suggested they were denied such care, and neither Washington nor New York bans the use of pain relief, even when it may hasten death.[122] Therefore, the question whether palliative care is protected under the Due Process Clause was not before the Court. One could, however, imagine circumstances in which a doctor might be prosecuted for being too aggressive in providing pain relief. Justices Breyer's and O'Connor's dicta hint that such a prosecution would be constitutionally troublesome.

What makes these dicta particularly interesting is that they suggest that some of the Justices believe certain end-of-life rights might exist that do not require the state to let individuals control their *death,* whether through assisted suicide or otherwise. Instead, such rights might only require the state to ensure that people are not prevented from receiving adequate palliative care. The implications of finding such an interest are vast and extend beyond the scope of this chapter. They would raise, for example, all sorts of questions about access, adequacy of care, and what to do when existing palliative care cannot dull pain without putting an individual into a coma. At the very least, however, as I shall discuss later, these dicta coupled with the language of some of the other opinions reveal a certain deference to the medical profession and its existing end-of-life practices.[123]

Why Are the Justices Ambivalent?

We have seen that the Court was ambivalent in its unanimity. Moreover, virtually every opinion expressed ambivalence about whether there may sometimes be a liberty interest in controlling the manner of one's death and about the nature of that interest. So what does all of this mean?

Practically, I think it means that the bell has not yet tolled for all possible claims of a constitutional right to assisted suicide.[124] While the Court is surely reluctant to recognize such a right too easily, the door remains slightly ajar to some very narrowly framed claims—particularly, claims brought by "the very few individuals for whom pain cannot be controlled through palliative care without slipping into a coma."[125] The Court hardly issued a welcome to such claims. But the ambivalence expressed in virtually every opinion suggests that most if not all of the Justices might consider them.

The Court's ambivalence is revealing in other ways. First, the fact that the Justices agreed on a result despite their ambivalence demonstrates how seriously committed the Court is to formal unanimity. Indeed, this commitment might explain much of the strained reasoning and confusing language in many of the opinions. For example, the Chief Justice's broad framing of the issue, coupled with his narrow statement of the holding, probably reflects his desire to capture votes from all of the Justices. Those who wanted to reject the claim for the narrow class of terminally ill, mentally competent patients could do so. Those who were only prepared to decide that there is no generalized constitutional right to assisted suicide could find something on which to hang their hats.

Second, the ambivalence within and among the Court's opinions suggests a deeper ambivalence about many important issues. Underlying each opinion, either implicitly or explicitly, is the Court's thorny experience with the aftermath of *Roe v Wade*.[126] In deciding a quarter of a century earlier that the Due Process Clause protected a privacy right to abortion, the Justices were unprepared for the travails that would follow. Case after case arose in which they struggled to develop convincing principles to guide them in evaluating the stream of state efforts to regulate abortion. The Court agreed to revisit and ultimately upheld *Roe's* essential holding in *Planned Parenthood of South Eastern Pennsylvania v Casey*.[127] Yet, *Casey* revealed the many areas in which the abortion issue had divided the Court, including the validity of substantive due process, the basis for establishing liberty interests, and the standard of review. Although the *Glucksberg* and *Quill* Justices undoubtedly differ in their assessment of whether and how *Roe* and its progeny were problematic, surely all have found the Court's experiences following *Roe* unnerving.

It is easy to imagine how this nervousness fueled the Justices' ambivalence in *Glucksberg* and *Quill*. Surely each Justice feared that recognizing a constitutional liberty interest in assisted suicide, however narrowly or broadly defined, would lead to enormous difficulties, not least in establishing principles for assessing the constitutionality of legislative attempts to regulate assisted suicide. Thus, even though the Court was not unanimous about the procedural posture of the case, the nature of the liberty interest it rejected, or the liberty interests it might acknowledge in the future, the Court seemed united in its reluctance to embark upon another *Roe*-like experience and in its desire to tread warily across the shifting sands of substantive due process.

A related undercurrent shaping the Court's ambivalence in *Glucksberg* and *Quill* is its conflict over the proper approach to substantive due process. On one hand, Chief Justice Rehnquist attempted to rein in substantive due process methodology and put back in the bottle the autonomy genie that escaped in *Casey*. One senses a deep visceral discomfort with much of *Casey's* language, especially those statements that are often recruited in arguments for expanded substantive due process rights, such as: "at the heart of liberty is the right to define one's own concept of existence, of meaning, of the universe, and of the mystery of human life."[128] Thus, even though two important substantive due process cases—*Casey* and *Cruzan*—concerned interests that "sound in personal autonomy," the Chief Justice stressed that the true basis for a liberty interest is its rootedness in the nation's history and traditions,[129] not in autonomy.

Justice Stevens described a very different and more expansive substantive due process world where autonomy reigns supreme. Following *Casey,* it protects matters "'central to personal dignity and autonomy.'"[130] Finally, Justice Souter formulated yet another approach, one that requires careful framing, balancing, and analysis of the competing interests in conjunction with consideration of our nation's traditions. This approach, he suggested, offers the flexibility the Chief Justice's lacked, while avoiding the errors of substantive due process gone awry.[131]

The Justices not only differed in their understanding of substantive due process, but in their interpretation of two important substantive due process cases—*Cruzan* and *Casey*. Chief Justice Rehnquist strongly emphasized that the interest at stake in *Cruzan* was in refusing unwanted medical treatment, *not* in hastening death.[132] Moreover, he stressed, it was only an *inferred* liberty interest. Justice Stevens interpreted *Cruzan* differently, finding more than just a right to refuse medical treatment. In his eyes, *Cruzan* recognized an "interest in dignity, and in determining the character of the memories that will survive long after [one's] death."[133]

Not surprisingly, these different methods of analyzing substantive due process and different interpretations of *Casey* and *Cruzan* informed the Justices' characterizations of the liberty interests at stake. Chief Justice Rehnquist rejected the language of the respondents and the Ninth Circuit, which was reminiscent of *Casey's* language. Reluctant to perpetuate such language, he spoke only of an interest in suicide and assisted suicide (even as he alternated between describing it as a generalized interest and as one limited to a narrow class of individuals). Justice Stevens, who embraced a more expansive substantive due process, described a liberty interest in "hastening death,"[134] in "deciding how, rather than whether" one's life will end[135] and "in determining the character of [one's] memories that will survive long after [one's] death."[136] Similarly, although they did not discuss *Casey* or *Cruzan,* Justices O'Connor and Breyer seemed to share Justice Stevens's sense of those cases. Thus, they spoke of a "right to die," a right to "control . . . the manner of death,"[137] or a "constitutionally cognizable interest in the circumstances of [one's] imminent death."[138] Finally, probably because his approach to substantive due process requires careful articulation of the interest at stake, Justice Souter's description was exceedingly circumspect. He depicted an interest in "a physician's assistance in providing counsel and drugs to be administered by [a] patient to end life promptly," an interest that is limited to patients that suffer "imminent death [and] anticipate[] physical suffering and indignity, and [are] capable of responsible and voluntary choices."[139]

Finally, the ambivalence within and among the opinions probably reveals the Justices' sympathy for the plight of those who request help committing suicide. One senses in virtually all the opinions, especially the concurring opinions, a deep turmoil as they confronted this imponderable philosophical, ethical, and medical debate. Indeed, the ambivalence is so intense that each Justice almost seemed relieved to find a reason to postpone resolving the issue. Whatever contradictions the opinions demonstrated and whatever holding each of the Justices attributed to the Court's opinion, they were truly unanimous on that point.

Several other factors may explain the general reluctance to find a constitutional right at this time. First, many of the Justices seemed concerned about the difficulties of distinguishing among categories of individuals who might have a liberty interest.[140] They worried that no matter how narrowly one draws the lines, distinctions among these categories will ultimately prove unprincipled, and the descent down the slippery slope will accelerate.[141] As Justice Scalia asked in oral arguments, why limit the right to the terminally ill? Why not include those who will suffer in pain for several years?[142] Rather than attempt to distinguish among individuals whose interest in assisted suicide is constitutionally protected, it is conceptually easier to find no such right at all.

Moreover, even if those lines could be drawn conceptually, there is raging medical and legal uncertainty about how to define key terms, such as "terminal illness," "mental competence," "voluntariness," and "intent."[143] And even if medicine and law could agree on definitions, it would still be difficult to determine whether an individual is terminally ill, mentally competent, or voluntarily choosing to die.[144] By returning the matter to the states, the Court avoided these quandaries. Instead, Oregon and possibly other states[145] will face the day-to-day issues associated with legalizing assisted suicide for a narrow class of individuals.[146]

The Court's reluctance to announce a new right was also motivated by its deference to the medical community. As is typical in health-care cases, the Court relied on medical standards of care. Dicta in *Glucksberg* and *Quill* suggest that virtually all Justices support accepted medical practices in treating end-of-life patients, or, at least, believe these practices are not unconstitutional. In *Quill*, the Court unanimously found the medically accepted distinction between withdrawing life-sustaining treatment and physician-assisted suicide to be rational. As noted earlier,[147] Chief Justice Rehnquist found this distinction rational based on differences in causation and intent. When a physician withdraws life-sustaining treatment, the Chief Justice reasoned, the physician intends only to relieve pain; he neither intends to, nor does he, cause death. Rather, the underlying pathology causes death. In contrast, he continued, the physician who assists a suicide not only intends to, but actually does, cause death.

Even more noteworthy, however, was the Court's implicit blessing of the doctrine of "the double effect."[148] The Court accepted the medical view that the double effect is different from assisted suicide because the primary intent is to alleviate pain. In distinguishing assisted suicide from withdrawal of life support, Chief Justice Rehnquist placed "aggressive palliative care" that may sometimes hasten a patient's death—that is, the double effect—in the same category as withdrawal of life-sustaining treatment.[149] In both cases, he reasoned, the physician's "purpose and intent is, or may be, only to ease his patient's pain."[150] He even seemed to defend "terminal sedation," albeit in a footnote, when he rejected the respondents' claims that terminal sedation is fundamentally no different from assisted suicide because it results in a barbiturate-induced coma followed by death through starvation.[151] Just as states may permit withdrawal of life-sustaining treatment, he reasoned, so they may permit "palliative care related to [the] refusal [of medical treatment], which may have the foreseen but unintended 'double effect' of hastening the patient's death."[152]

In their discussions of the need for adequate palliative care, Justices O'Connor and Breyer even more overtly endorsed the medically accepted double-effect principle. By noting that state law does not prohibit physicians from "providing patients with drugs sufficient to control pain despite the risk that those drugs themselves will kill,"[153] they were a mere step away from asserting that suffering, terminal ill patients have a constitutional right to palliative care,[154] even if such a right relies on the double effect. At the very least, as Professor Kamisar points out, they imply that the "double effect principle is not only plausible but *necessary*."[155]

While Justice Stevens also implicitly defended medically accepted end-of-life practices, he rightly pointed out the difficulties in using intent or cau-

sation to distinguish between withdrawing life support and assisted suicide.[156] Physicians (and patients or their families) who participate in either,
he pointed out, may actually share the same intent: to hasten death, to end
suffering, or to honor the patient's wishes. Moreover, a physician's intent to
alleviate suffering may motivate actions that do more than ease pain; they
may actually *cause* death, as in the case of terminal sedation, when sedatives
intended to relieve pain are the actual cause of death. Indeed, "[t]he illusory
character of any differences between intent or causation" in these end-of-
life practices, he pointed out, is highlighted by the practice of terminal sedation.[157] In his view, terminal sedation is very much like assisted suicide in
terms of intent and causation. In both cases, the goal may be to ease suffering, and in both cases, the administration of medication is the "actual cause"
of death.[158] In the end, Justice Stevens reasoned, distinguishing among various end-of-life practices is a messy, case-by-case job, that cannot be tidied
by relying on causation or intent.

Although Justice Stevens was alone in his concerns about the Court's
reliance on intent and causation to distinguish between withdrawal of life
support and physician-assisted suicide,[159] even he ultimately shrank from
the implacable difficulties of drawing lines in individual cases. In part, all the
Justices simply exercised judicial restraint by failing to reach constitutional
issues unnecessarily. But the Court also was relieved to be free of the messy
task of determining when an act is really assisted suicide or merely the administration of palliative care. Ultimately, the Court left the day-to-day resolution of these murky problems to individual doctors, patients, and their
families, presumably under the belief that these individuals are far better
suited than the courts to sort out such intimate and personal matters.[160] If
the Court sought to influence medicine at all, it was by validating the double
effect and encouraging doctors to offer more and greater palliative care,
even if it should sometimes hasten death.[161] But ultimately, the Court deferred to the medical profession in placing faith in its ability to make appropriate distinctions in a world of blurry lines.

Finally, many of the Justices might have been concerned about the sociological and psychological effects of finding a constitutional right to assisted suicide. Abortion provides a pertinent analogy here. Arguably the constitutionality of abortion has made it far more socially acceptable today than
when it was illegal. One might even argue that abortion is now seen as appropriate for certain categories of pregnant women: for example, young
teens, women on welfare, and pregnant women carrying a fetus identified
with a birth defect. Indeed some people (arguably even some women in
these categories) might argue that there is a moral responsibility to abort in
these cases. What was once just a right has for some become a duty.

Some of the Justices might have worried that constitutionalizing the
right to assisted suicide would have similar effects. They might have feared
that, in time, the moral and social ethos would change so that suicide would
be seen not only as appropriate but as a moral responsibility. I am referring

here not only to Chief Justice Rehnquist's fear of prejudice, societal indifference, and coercion, but also to the possibility that some patients would come to think they had a moral duty to commit suicide. There are two aspects to this concern. First, as Carl Schneider so wisely points out, "law is not just a structure of regulation backed by force. Law also enjoys moral authority."[162] The Justices were surely hesitant to establish moral authority for acts as irreversible and ethically complex as ending life. Second, they may have been particularly concerned about the fragility of autonomy, worried that cultural norms regarding end-of-life decisions could subtly, but powerfully, influence individuals' judgment. If so, the vulnerable whom they wished to protect may include more than the mentally incompetent, but may to some degree include all of us. In matters as significant as death and dying, each of the Justices might rightly be concerned about profoundly changing social norms and attitudes by constitutionalizing assisted suicide, however sympathetic they are to the plight of the suffering.

In the end, the *Glucksberg* and *Quill* opinions reveal a Court struggling with complex constitutional, ethical, medical, sociological, and deeply personal issues that touch virtually all of us. One sympathizes with the Justices as they take on the enormous task of trying to address these issues with humanity, judicial restraint, integrity, and limited data. The Court sensed, as it always must, the far-reaching sociological, political, and moral implications of its decision. It ultimately chose to maintain the legal status quo with respect to physician-assisted suicide, even as it expressed provocative views about other important end-of-life interests, such as the interest in palliative care. While the Court might not have changed the legal landscape, one senses a great deal of turbulence beneath the terrain. Rumblings of ambivalence are reflected in the Court's attempts to achieve unanimity and to struggle with the perplexities of assisted suicide and other troublesome and forbidding constitutional issues. The Court might have been ambivalently unanimous, but it was also unanimous in its ambivalence.

NOTES

1. 117 S Ct 2258 (1997).
2. 117 S Ct 2293 (1997).
3. See, for example, *Planned Parenthood of South Eastern Pennsylvania v Casey,* 505 US 833 (1992); *Romer v Evans,* 517 US 620 (1996).
4. "[P]olls of the general population have repeatedly shown that about 60% of the American public favour legal reforms allowing for physician assisted suicide to end the suffering of competent patients." Larry R.

Churchill & Nancy M. P. King, *Physician Assisted Suicide, Euthanasia, or Withdrawal of Treatment: Distinguishing Between Them Clarifies Moral, Legal, and Practical Positions,* 315 British Medical Journal 137, 138 (1997). Of course, these data tell us little about whether the majority believe that there should be a constitutional instead of a statutory right. Moreover, as Ezekiel Emanuel has argued, most of these polls are uninformative, since they so often rely on vaguely worded questions. Ezekiel Emanuel, *Whose Right to Die? America Should Think Again Before Pressing Ahead with the Legalization of Physician-Assisted Suicide and Voluntary Euthanasia,* 279 Atlantic Monthly 73, 74 (1997). Even when they use narrowly worded questions, the most they show is that a "significant majority of Americans oppose physician-assisted suicide and euthanasia *except* in the limited case of a terminally ill patient with uncontrollable pain." Ibid. at 75.

5. *Glucksberg,* 117 S Ct at 2302 (Stevens, J., concurring).
6. Ibid. at 2275.
7. 497 US 261 (1990).
8. 505 US 833 (1992).
9. *Casey,* 505 US at 846; *United States v Salerno,* 481 US 739, 746 (1987).
10. *Daniels v Williams,* 474 US 327, 331 (1986).
11. *Cruzan,* 497 US at 261.
12. Ibid. at 279.
13. *Reno v Flores,* 507 US 292, 301–02 (1993).
14. *Glucksberg,* 117 S Ct at 2271. Recently, the Court has been divided over the appropriate standard of review for state interference with constitutionally protected liberty interests. For example, in *Casey,* the Justices disagreed about the appropriate standard for evaluating abortion regulations. Justices O'Connor, Kennedy, and Souter argued that the appropriate way to reconcile the state's interests with the woman's constitutionally protected liberty interest is to apply the "undue burden" standard. In other words, "a provision of law is invalid, if its purpose or effect is to place a substantial obstacle in the path of a woman seeking an abortion before the fetus attains viability." 505 US at 878. Jus-

tice Blackmun, however, advocated retaining strict constitutional scrutiny, noting that no "other approach has gained a majority, and no other is more protective of the woman's fundamental right." Ibid. at 930, 934. Finally, while disagreeing with strict scrutiny analysis of abortion regulations, Justices White, Scalia, and Thomas nevertheless noted that the strict-scrutiny standard, unlike the "undue burden" standard has "a recognized basis in constitutional law." Moreover, they pointed out, the "undue burden" standard "does not command the support of a majority of this Court." Ibid. at 964. The appropriate standard of analysis for abortion regulations, they concluded, is the rational basis test. Ibid. at 966.

15. *Romer v Evans,* 517 US 620, 631 (1996).
16. *San Antonio Independent School Dist.,* 411 US 1, 16 (1973).
17. *Compassion in Dying v Washington,* 79 F3d 790, 793–94 (9th Cir 1996).
18. *Glucksberg,* 117 S Ct at 2268.
19. Ibid. (quoting *Moore v East Cleveland,* 431 US 494, 503 (1977) (plurality opinion)).
20. Ibid. (quoting *Palko v Connecticut,* 302 US 319, 325, 326 (1937)).
21. Although Chief Justice Rehnquist claimed that the Court "'has always been reluctant to expand the concept of substantive due process,'" ibid. at 2267 (quoting *Collins v Harker Heights,* 503 US 115, 125 (1992)), he implied that the Court has not always been sufficiently reluctant, and he seemed primarily motivated by a desire to move the Court toward more restrained and predictable substantive due process analysis. His repeated emphasis on restraint evokes the image of the Chief Justice "reining in" an overly expansive approach to substantive due process.

22. Ibid. at 2270.
23. Ibid. at 2271.
24. Ibid. at 2262.
25. Ibid. at 2271.
26. Ibid. at 2274.
27. Ibid. at 2275.
28. *Quill v Vacco,* 80 F3d 716 (2d Cir 1996).
29. *Quill,* 117 S Ct at 2298.
30. Ibid.
31. Ibid. at 2299 (quoting Assisted Suicide in the United States, Hearing before the Subcommittee on the Constitution of the House Committee on the Judiciary, 104th Congress, 2d Sess 367 (1996) (testimony of Dr. Leon R. Kass)).
32. Ibid. at 2298. While the medical profession and others have long relied on such distinctions, they have an artificial and unpersuasive quality. For a nice discussion of some of these difficulties, see Rebecca Dresser, *The Supreme Court and End-of-Life Care: Principled Distinctions or Slippery Slope?* and Howard Brody, *Physician-Assisted Suicide in the Courts: Moral Equivalence, Double Effect, and Clinical Practice,* both in this volume; Lawrence O. Gostin, *Deciding Life and Death in the Courtroom: From Quinlan to Cruzan, Glucksberg, and Vacco—A Brief History and Analysis of Constitutional Protection of the "Right to Die,"* 278 Journal of the American Medical Association 1523 (Nov 12, 1997). The Chief Justice was not unaware of the problematic aspects of these arguments, however, for he noted that the line between refusing lifesaving treatment and assisted suicide may not always be clear. *Quill,* 117 S Ct at 2302.
33. Ibid. at 2297–98.
34. Ibid. at 2298 (citing *Personnel Administrator of Massachusetts v Feeny,* 442 US 256, 272 (1979)).
35. Ibid. at 2296.
36. Michael C. Dorf, *Facial Challenges to State and Federal Statutes,* 46 Stanford Law Review 235, 235 (1994).
37. Under a facial challenge, a statute would be unconstitutional only if "no set of circumstances exists under which [it] would be valid." *United States v Salerno,* 481 US 739, 745 (1987).
38. As I discuss later, however, the statutes would not necessarily be fully proof against every further challenge. To uphold the statutes as applied to the terminally ill, mentally competent patient would reveal little about the interests of the terminally ill person suffering from untreatable pain.
39. Brief for Respondents at 45, *Washington v Glucksberg,* 117 S Ct 2258 (1997) (No. 96–110).
40. *Glucksberg,* 117 S Ct at 2269. (Quoting Wash Rev Cod § 9A.36.060(1) (1994)).
41. Ibid. at 2269. One might argue that the phrase "asserted right" is simply shorthand for the particularized right described by the plaintiffs. Yet, as I discuss, in conjunction with the rest of the opinion and the language of the other Justices, this language is ambiguous and confusing at best.
42. Ibid. at 2303 (Stevens, J., concurring).
43. Ibid. at 2304 (Stevens, J., concurring) (citing *Compassion in Dying,* 79 F3d at 798).
44. Ibid. The three terminally ill plaintiffs died after the district court found that the statute placed an undue burden on the right to commit physician-assisted suicide. Ibid.
45. Ibid. at 2305 (Stevens, J., concurring) (citing Court opinion at 2269).
46. Ibid. at 2304 (Stevens, J., concurring).
47. Ibid. at 2311 (Breyer, J., concurring) (quoting Court opinion at 2265).

48. Ibid. at 2310 (Breyer, J., concurring).
49. Ibid. at 2275 n2 (Souter, J., concurring).
50. Ibid. at 2275 (Souter, J., concurring).
51. See, e.g., ibid. at 2262 (emphasis added) (citing *Compassion in Dying,* 79 F3d at 836, 837); ibid. at 2274 ("The Court of Appeals struck down Washington's assisted-suicide ban only '*as applied* to competent, terminally ill adults who wish to hasten their deaths by obtaining medication prescribed by their doctors.'") (emphasis added) (citing *Compassion in Dying,* 79 F3d at 838).
52. Ibid. at 2262 n6 (emphasis added) (citing *Compassion in Dying,* 79 F3d at 797–98 and nn8–9).
53. Ibid. at 2275 (emphasis added); see also ibid. at 2275 n24 ("we emphasize that we today reject the Court of Appeals' specific holding that the statute is unconstitutional *as applied* to a particular class") (emphasis added).
54. Ibid. at 2276 n2 (Souter, J., concurring) ("As I will indicate in some detail below, I see the challenge to the statute not as facial but as-applied. . . .").
55. Ibid. at 2290 (Souter, J., concurring) (emphasis added).
56. Ibid. at 2275 (Souter, J., concurring) (emphasis added).
57. Yale Kamisar, *On the Meaning and Impact of the Physician-Assisted Suicide Cases,* in this volume.
58. Yale Kamisar, *The Physician-Assisted Suicide Cases: What Did the Court Hold? What Questions Did it Leave Open?,* U.S. Law Week's 19th Annual Constitutional Law Conference 13 (Sept 5, 1997). Unfortunately, the oral arguments shed little light on this point, since there was no discussion regarding the applied/facial distinction.
59. See note 68.
60. *Glucksberg,* 117 S Ct at 2269.
61. Ibid. at 2271.
62. Brief for Respondents at 45, *Washington v Glucksberg,* 117 S Ct 2258 (1997) (No. 96–110).
63. *Glucksberg,* 117 S Ct at 2269.
64. See Kamisar, cited in note 57 (interpreting this reformulation as an expression of annoyance at what the Chief Justice apparently considered "sloppy and emotive language").
65. Ibid. at 2275 (citing *Compassion in Dying,* 79 F3d at 838 n24).
66. Ibid. at 2303 (O'Connor, J., concurring) (emphasis added).
67. Ibid. As noted above, she concluded that the Court need not address that "narrower question" because it dealt with a facial challenge.
68. Ibid. at 2305 (Stevens, J., concurring) (quoting Court opinion at 2269). Justices Stevens and O'Connor seemed to address opposite sides of the same coin. Justice Stevens focused on the procedural issue—that is, whether the challenge was facial or as applied, whereas Justice O'Connor focused on the nature of the interest—that is, whether it is a generalized interest in suicide or one limited to a particular class of individuals in particular circumstances.
69. Ibid. at 2310 (Breyer, J., concurring) (quoting ibid. at 2269).
70. Ibid. (noting that he does not agree with the Court's "formulation of the claimed 'liberty' interest").
71. Ibid. at 2311(Breyer, J., concurring). One can only assume that he accepts Justice O'Connor's view that the claim is a facial one since he states that he joins her opinion "except insofar as it joins the Majority." Ibid. at 2310.
72. Ibid. at 2311 (Breyer, J., concurring).
73. See ibid. at 2284 (Souter, J., concurring) ("Exact analysis and characterization of any due process claim is critical to the method and to the re-

sult, . . . the broader the attack the less likely it is to succeed.").

74. Ibid. at 2286 (Souter, J., concurring).

75. Ibid. at 2286 (Souter, J., concurring).

76. If the Court definitely treated the challenge as not only facial, but also as as applied, then one could presume that the Court held that no such liberty interest existed.

77. *Glucksberg,* 117 S Ct at 2271.

78. Ibid. at 2275 n24 (citing ibid. at 2304 (Stevens, J., concurring)).

79. See Dresser, cited in note 32; Robert A. Burt, *The Supreme Court Speaks: Not Assisted Suicide but a Constitutional Right to Palliative Care,* 337 New England Journal Medicine 1234, 1234 (1997).

80. See *Glucksberg,* 117 S Ct at 2312 (Breyer, J., concurring).

81. *Vacco v Quill,* No. 95–1858, United States Supreme Court Official Transcript *36–37 (Jan. 8, 1997) (Laurence H. Tribe).

82. "Death will be different for each of us. For many, the last day will be spent in physical pain and perhaps the despair that accompanies physical deterioration and a loss of control of basic bodily and mental functions." *Glucksberg,* 117 S Ct at 2303 (O'Connor, J., concurring).

83. Ibid. at 2303 (O'Connor, J., concurring) (emphasis added).

84. Ibid. at 2303 (O'Connor, J., concurring) (emphasis added).

85. Ibid.

86. See Burt, 337 New England Journal of Medicine at 1234 (cited in note 79); Dresser, cited in note 32; Kamisar, cited in note 57 (finding "reason to think that at least five members of the Court are likely to resist state legislative efforts to reject or to modify the double effect principle if such action would *force some dying people to endure severe pain*").

87. Indeed, Stevens began his opinion by making "it clear that there is room for further debate about the limits that the Constitution places on the power of the States to punish the practice" of physician-assisted suicide. *Glucksberg,* 117 S Ct at 2304 (Stevens, J., concurring).

88. Ibid. at 2305 (Stevens, J., concurring).

89. Ibid. at 2306 (Stevens, J., concurring).

90. Ibid. at 2306 (Stevens, J., concurring).

91. Ibid. at 2307 (Stevens, J., concurring).

92. For Justice Stevens, the state's interest in preserving life "is not a collective interest that should always outweigh the interests of a person who because of pain, incapacity, or sedation finds her life intolerable, but rather, an aspect of individual freedom." Ibid. at 2307–08 (Stevens, J., concurring).

93. Justice Stevens concluded his opinion by stating that "it is clear that the so-called 'unqualified interest in the preservation of life' . . . is not itself sufficient to outweigh the interest in liberty that may justify the only possible means of preserving a dying patient's dignity and alleviating her intolerable suffering." Ibid. at 2310 (Stevens, J., concurring) (quoting *Cruzan,* 497 US at 282).

94. Justice Stevens did not address the real issue here. The concern was not that truly rational and mentally competent people will be coerced into deciding to commit assisted suicide, but that by constitutionalizing or legalizing physician-assisted suicide, those who are not rational or competent will be vulnerable to coercion or even involuntary euthanasia.

95. *Glucksberg,* 117 S Ct at 2309 (Stevens, J., concurring).

96. Ibid. at 2309 (Stevens, J., concurring). Instead he simply stated that he "would not say as a categorical matter" that the state's interests are invalid. Ibid.

97. Ibid.

98. One might justify Justice Stevens's approach by pointing out that he was appropriately exercising judicial restraint in failing to decide issues that need not be resolved. Since he viewed the challenge as facial, he did not have to decide the issues he discussed. The fact, however, that he went to such great lengths to describe the nature of the liberty interest and the weightiness of the state's interests is somewhat inconsistent with such circumspection. One senses that he tried to go as far as possible, without actually resolving issues that did not need to be resolved.

99. He bases his approach largely on Justice Harlan's dissent in *Poe v Ullman,* 367 US 497, 543 (1961).

100. *Glucksberg,* 117 S Ct at 2284 (Souter, J., concurring). Under his view, the Due Process Clause protects not only those rights that have been recognized historically, but also the "'basic values' that are revealed when we interpret those rights to see which more general principles of political morality they represent." Ronald Dworkin, *Assisted Suicide: What the Court Really Said,* New York Review of Books 40 (Sept 25, 1997). Justice Souter viewed the tradition of our nation, not as static, but as "a living thing." *Glucksberg,* 117 S Ct at 2282 (Souter, J., concurring). He therefore challenged Chief Justice Rehnquist's approach, which he implied is a form of "legal petrification." Ibid. at 2284 (Souter, J., concurring).

101. Ibid. at 2284 (Souter, J., concurring).

102. Justice Souter suggested that this approach circumvents the very pitfalls that have made substantive due process so politically suspect because it "avoids the absolutist failing of many older cases without embracing the opposite pole of equating reasonableness with past practice described at a very specific level." Ibid. at 2281 (Souter, J., concurring).

103. Ibid. at 2283 (Souter, J., concurring). Justice Souter's methodology is reminiscent of what Norm Daniels calls "wide reflective equilibrium," a reasoning process to solve ethical dilemmas by working back and forth between the case (the ethical issue) and the ethical principle that applies to the case so that each shapes our understanding of the other. The goal is to revise both our principles and judgments about cases until we reach an equilibrium between "the texture of the case and our moral beliefs about it and the qualifications we need on the principle. . . ." Norm Daniels, "Wide Reflective Equilibrium in Practice" in *Philosophical Perspectives on Bioethics* 96, 101 (L. Wayne Sumner and Joseph Boyle, eds., University of Toronto Press 1996). The process is intended to enliven and enrich our understanding of both the principle and the dilemma we face. Justice Souter's substantive due process methodology suggests a similar back and forth analysis between legal cases and legal principles. By examining potentially vague principles, which offer little guidance in specific cases, in light of concrete issues, these approaches breathe life into the principles. Similarly, they deepen our understanding of the issues by shaping them in terms of the guiding principles.

104. Justice Souter was very attentive to the importance of framing the issue narrowly, for he noted that the "breadth of expression that a litigant or a judge selects in stating the competing principles will have much to do with the outcome and may be dispositive." Ibid. at 2284 (Souter, J., concurring).

105. Ibid. at 2287 (Souter, J., concurring).

106. Ibid. at 2288 (Souter, J., concurring).

107. Ibid. at 2288 (Souter, J., concurring).

108. Ibid. at 2288–89 (Souter, J., concurring) ("Just as the decision about abortion is not directed to correcting some pathology, so the decision in which a dying patient seeks help is not so limited.").

109. Ibid. at 2290 (Souter, J., concurring).

110. Ibid. (Souter, J., concurring).

111. Ibid. While the experience in Holland offers some glimpse as to how such regulations might affect practice, Justice Souter concluded that there was not sufficient consensus that those guidelines adequately protect patients from involuntary euthanasia. The data continue to be mixed regarding the effects of laws regulating physician-assisted suicide. One study revealed that there is "no evidence that the poor, uneducated, mentally ill or socially isolated are disproportionately seeking—or getting—lethal prescriptions of drugs under [the United States'] only legal program for physician-assisted suicide." David Brown, "A Picture of Assisted Suicide," Washington Post, Feb 24, 2000, at A3. Another study from the Netherlands, however, painted a less positive picture: "[N]early 20 percent of cases of assisted suicide effectively became cases of euthanasia when the intended assisted suicide went awry and the physician had to participate actively in the patients' deaths." Ibid.

112. Ibid. at 2292 (Souter, J., concurring). While some factual disagreements might be resolved through courtroom litigation, Justice Souter was convinced that the very substantial "factual disagreement" over the evidence from Holland is exactly the kind of controversy that cannot be resolved well judicially. Ibid. at 2292. As he noted, a court cannot adequately conduct an "independent front-line investigation into the facts of a foreign country's legal administration," especially when the only available data are in an embryonic state, as in the literature on the Dutch experience. Ibid. In contrast, a legislature is much better suited for resolving just this kind of controversy because it can move "forward and pull[] back as facts emerge within" the various jurisdictions. Ibid. at 2293.

113. Ibid. at 2290 (Souter, J., concurring).

114. Ibid. at 2293 (Souter, J., concurring).

115. If the respondents' interests only *slightly* outweighed the state's interests, the legislature's balancing of the interests would not be arbitrary, and therefore he would still uphold the statute.

116. At that point, one imagines, the scales would tip decidedly in favor of the interests of the terminally ill and prohibitions on assisted suicide might then seem arbitrary and unreasonable. See also *Washington v Glucksberg*, No. 96–110, United States Supreme Court Official Transcript *44 (Jan 8, 1997) (Justice Souter questioning whether the impossibility "for a court to assess [the risks of physician-assisted suicide] for a long time until there is more experience out in the

world . . . [is] a reason for saying that [the Court is] not in a position either to weight the liberty interest, although [it] may recognize that there is one, or to weight the countervailing claim of the state").

117. *Glucksberg,* 117 S Ct at 2311 (Breyer, J., concurring).

118. Ibid. (Breyer, J., concurring).

119. Ibid. (Breyer, J., concurring).

120. Ibid. at 2312 (Breyer, J., concurring).

121. Ibid. (Breyer, J., concurring).

122. See Yale Kamisar, *"Assisted Suicide and Euthanasia: An Exchange,"* New York Review of Books 68 (Nov 6, 1997).

123. See text accompanying notes 145–159.

124. For the opposite perspective, see George J. Annas, *The Bell Tolls for a Constitutional Right to Physician-Assisted Suicide,* 337 New England Journal of Medicine 1098 (Oct 9, 1997).

125. *Glucksberg,* 117 S Ct at 2312 (Breyer, J., concurring).

126. 410 US 113 (1973). See also Kamisar, *On the Meaning and Impact of the Physician-Assisted Suicide Cases,* and Carl E. Schneider, *Concluding Thoughts: Bioethics in the Language of the Law,* both in this volume.

127. 505 US 833 (1992).

128. *Casey,* 505 US at 851. See also Kamisar, cited in note 126.

129. *Glucksberg,* 117 S Ct at 2270.

130. Ibid. at 2307 (Stevens, J., concurring) (quoting *Casey,* 505 US at 851).

131. See ibid. at 2284 (Souter, J., concurring).

132. See ibid. at 2270.

133. Ibid. at 2306 (Stevens, J., concurring).

134. Ibid. at 2305 (Stevens, J., concurring).

135. Ibid. at 2307 (Stevens, J., concurring).

136. Ibid. at 2306 (Stevens, J., concurring).

137. Ibid. at 2311 (Breyer, J., concurring).

138. Ibid. at 2303 (O'Connor, J., concurring).

139. Ibid. at 2286 (Souter, J., concurring).

140. Much of the time allotted for oral arguments was spent addressing concerns regarding line drawing and "doctrinal slippage." See, generally, *Washington v Glucksberg,* No. 96–110, United States Supreme Court Official Transcript (Jan 8, 1997).

141. Schneider, *Concluding Thoughts,* cited in note 126.

142. *Washington v Glucksberg,* No. 96–110, United States Supreme Court Official Transcript (Jan 8, 1997), at *28; see also ibid. at *31 (questioning the line drawn between people suffering from physical pain and those suffering from emotional pain). Justice Ginsburg made similar points, noting that many people, not just the terminally ill, desire relief from "unwanted pain and suffering." Ibid. at *49–50.

143. See, for example, *Glucksberg,* 117 S Ct at 2305 (O'Connor, J., concurring); *Vacco v Quill,* No. 95–1858, United States Supreme Court Official Transcript *42 (Jan 8, 1997) (Justice Breyer noting the difficulty of defining "terminal condition.").

144. See, for example, *Glucksberg,* 117 S Ct at 2303 (O'Connor, J., concurring).

145. Maine voters will decide whether to legalize physician-assisted suicide later in 2000. See David Brown, cited in note 111. Congress is also considering the issue of physician-assisted suicide as it debates the Pain Relief Promotion Act of 1999, a bill that effectively nullifies the Oregon Death With Dignity Act. Nicholas W. Van Aelstyn and Todd G. Glass, "Suffering Under Con-

gress' Orders Pain Relief Promotion Act Discourages States from Debating Appropriate End-of-Life Care," *Legal Times,* Feb 21, 2000, at 68. If enacted, this legislation would raise "serious federalism concerns." Ibid.

146. See *Washington v Glucksberg,* No. 96–110, United States Supreme Court Official Transcript (Jan. 8, 1997) (discussing the appropriateness of leaving these matters to be resolved by the state legislatures).

147. See text accompanying notes 29–32.

148. See Burt, 337 New England Journal of Medicine at 1234 (cited in note 81); Dresser, cited in note 32; Kamisar, cited in note 126.

149. *Quill,* 117 S Ct at 2298–99.

150. Ibid.

151. Ibid. at 2303 n11.

152. Ibid. The Chief Justice's discussion here suggests that he views terminal sedation and the double effect as one and the same. (Discussion with Professor Kamisar.) For many, however, including Justice Stevens, the terms have distinct meanings. See note 157. That the Chief Justice treats these terms as synonymous further highlights the murkiness of these distinctions and definitions.

153. Ibid. at 2311 (Breyer, J., concurring). See also ibid. at 2303 (noting that patients in Washington and New York "can obtain palliative care, even when doing so would hasten their deaths") (O'Connor, J., concurring).

154. I should add, however, that Justice Breyer focused on a negative right, since he noted that the key issue was whether state law *prevents* patients from obtaining relief from suffering. See ibid. at 2310–11 (Breyer, J., concurring).

155. Kamisar, cited in note 126.

156. *Glucksberg,* 117 S Ct at 2274 (Stevens, J., concurring). See Brody, cited in note 32 (noting that the Court merely "rehash[ed] rather stale arguments in favor of moral nonequivalence . . . as if the bioethical debate of the last two decades never occurred").

157. Ibid. at 2310. Justice Stevens and Chief Justice Rehnquist may not be using the phrase "terminal sedation" in precisely the same way. See note 152.

158. Ibid. Stevens pointed out, however, that a doctor may prescribe lethal medications without intending that the patient die and without causing the patient to die. Rather, the doctor may intend to give the patient a sense of control over her fate, and if the patient never takes the medication, her death is not caused by the physician's actions. Ibid. n.15.

159. See Brody, cited in note 32 (noting that Justice Stevens "exhibited a greater understanding of the issues underlying the principle of double effect").

160. See Dresser, cited in note 32; Schneider, *Concluding Thoughts,* cited in note 126 (noting the limitations of the law in "regulating relationships—particularly relationships that are instinct with intimacy").

161. See Brody, cited in note 32 (noting the impact of judicial language on clinical care: "A serious assault on the logic of the principle of double effect could do major violence to the (already reluctant and ill-informed) commitment of most physicians to the goals of palliative care and hospice").

162. Schneider, *Concluding Thoughts,* cited in note 126.

CHAPTER 3

On the Meaning and Impact of the Physician-Assisted Suicide Cases

Yale Kamisar

    I read every newspaper article I could find on the meaning and impact of the U.S. Supreme Court's June 1997 decisions in *Washington v Glucksberg*[1] and *Vacco v Quill*.[2] I came away with the impression that some proponents of physician-assisted suicide (PAS) were unable or unwilling publicly to recognize the magnitude of the setback they suffered when the Court handed down its rulings in the PAS cases.

On Being Given "The Green Light"

The press reported that Barbara Coombs Lee, Executive Director of Compassion in Dying (an organization that counsels people considering PAS and one of the plaintiffs in the *Glucksberg* case), was "really thrilled" that the Supreme Court had given her organization and her allies "a green light" to seek legislation authorizing PAS.[3] But proponents of PAS have *always had* "the green light" to persuade state legislatures to legalize PAS. The issue presented by *Glucksberg* and *Quill* was whether the U.S. Constitution *required* or *compelled* the states to legalize PAS under certain circumstances, not whether the states were *permitted* to do so.

    Early in the oral arguments before the Supreme Court, Justice Stevens asked the attorney representing Washington State whether it was his view that a legislature had "the constitutional authority to authorize assisted suicide" and the answer was an unequivocal "yes."[4] A short time later, Justice Ginsburg asked the attorney representing New York whether he agreed that a legislature was free to legalize PAS and he, too, left no doubt that he believed a legislature was so entitled.[5]

    Nor did lawyers representing the plaintiffs in the PAS cases deny that they had always had the green light to seek legislation authorizing PAS. But they made it clear that they were *not* thrilled about pursuing such a course. Thus, when asked by Justice Breyer why a legislature was not "far more suited" to deal with end-of-life problems than a court interpreting a constitutional provision, Professor Laurence Tribe, the attorney for the respondents in *Quill*, responded that although "in a sense there are 50 laboratories out there," they "are now operating largely with the lights out."[6] And when

This essay originally appeared in 82 Minnesota Law Review 895 (April 1998). Reprinted by permission.

asked a similar question by Justice O'Connor, Kathryn Tucker, the attorney for the respondents in *Glucksberg,* replied that because "ours is a culture of denial of death," she had "some concerns that the political process would not be expected to work in a usual fashion."[7]

That the lawyers for the states, not the lawyers for the respondents, urged the Court to let the state legislatures resolve the difficult issues involved in the PAS cases is hardly surprising. Proponents of PAS have not fared well in the political arena. They did achieve success in 1994 when Oregon voters passed a "death with dignity" act (a vote Oregon reaffirmed three years later), but so far Oregon has been a striking exception.

Washington and California ballot initiatives for "aid-in-dying" both failed in the early 1990s. Moreover, in the last decade bills to legalize PAS have been introduced in more than twenty states and none has passed.[8] Indeed, in 1997 alone seven state legislative attempts to legalize PAS "died outright or . . . languished in committee."[9] On the other hand, bills expressly prohibiting assisted suicide have fared much better. Since 1989, sixteen such bills have been enacted into law.[10]

Some have made much of the fact that five months after the Supreme Court handed down its decisions in the PAS cases, Oregon voters reaffirmed their support for assisted suicide by a much larger margin than the initial 1994 vote. The state legislature had put the initiative (which had initially passed by a 51–49% vote) back on the ballot for an unprecedented second vote. This time the initiative was reaffirmed overwhelmingly, 60–40%. Barbara Coombs Lee hailed the event as "a turning point for the death with dignity movement."[11] David Garrow called the landslide vote "a good indicator of where America may be headed."[12] Still another commentator viewed the lopsided vote as a demonstration of "[h]ow far, and how fast, public opinion is moving on this issue."[13]

I think not. I think the most plausible explanation for the large margin by which Oregon voters rebuffed efforts to repeal the initiative in favor of PAS was their resentment and anger over the fact that the state legislature had forced them to vote on the issue again—the first time in state history that the legislature had tried to repeal a voter-passed initiative. Those running pro-PAS advertisements, we are told by the press, "play[ed] on the perceived anger" generated by the repeal effort itself.[14] It is worth noting that a year after the second vote for assisted suicide in Oregon, a proposal to legalize physician assisted suicide in Michigan was defeated by almost a 3–1 vote.[15]

What, If Anything, Has Changed?

Some consider the long-awaited Supreme Court opinions in the PAS cases anticlimactic.[16] Dr. Robert Brody, a well-known medical ethicist at San Francisco General Hospital and a co-author of recently published guidelines permitting PAS under certain narrow circumstances, has gone so far as to say that the Court's rulings "didn't change a thing."[17] I strongly disagree.

To put the Supreme Court's rulings in the PAS cases in some perspective, let us go back a couple of years. The U.S. Courts of Appeals for the Ninth and Second Circuits may have gladdened the hearts of PAS proponents when they ruled in the spring of 1996 that there was a constitutional right to assisted suicide under certain circumstances,[18] but these decisions stunned many others. Until the two federal courts of appeals had handed down their rulings, within the span of a single month, no American appellate court had ever held that there was a right to assisted suicide under any circumstances.

The decisions by the two courts generated a good deal of momentum in favor of physician-assisted suicide. The fact that the rulings came so close together, that there was no dissent in the Second Circuit case and that the decision of the Ninth Circuit was supported by a lopsided majority (8–3) all contributed to this momentum. So did the directness and forcefulness of the two majority opinions.

For example, the Ninth Circuit disparaged, almost ridiculed, two distinctions long relied on by opponents of PAS: (1) the distinction between "letting die" and actively intervening to promote or to bring about death; (2) the distinction between giving a patient a drug for the purpose of killing her and administering drugs for the purpose of relieving pain, albeit with the knowledge that such palliative care may hasten the patient's death. Observed the Ninth Circuit:

> [W]e do not believe that the state's interest in preventing [PAS] is significantly greater than its interest in preventing the other forms of life-ending medical conduct that doctors now engage in regularly. More specifically, we see little, if any, difference for constitutional or ethical purposes between providing medication with a double effect and providing medication with a single effect, as long as one of the known effects in each case is to hasten the end of the patient's life. Similarly, we see no ethical or constitutionally cognizable difference between a doctors pulling the plug on a respirator and his prescribing drugs which will permit a terminally ill patient to end his own life. In fact, some might argue that pulling the plug is a more culpable and aggressive act on the doctor's part and provides more reason for criminal prosecution. To us, what matters most is that the death of the patient is the intended result as surely in one case as in the other.[19]

Moreover, the Ninth Circuit seemed unwilling to respect still another oft-made distinction, the one between assisted suicide (where the patient herself performs the last death-causing act) and active voluntary euthanasia (where a person other than the patient commits the death-causing act). Although the court noted that there was no need to decide whether there was a constitutional right to, or liberty interest in, active voluntary euthanasia, as well as in PAS, the Ninth Circuit could not resist indicating how it would answer that question if and when the occasion arose: "[F]or present purposes we view the critical line in right-to-die cases as the one between the voluntary and involuntary termination of an individual's life. . . . We consider it less important who administers the medication than who determines whether the terminally ill person's life shall end."[20]

In striking down, on equal protection grounds, New York's criminal prohibition against assisted suicide insofar as it prevented physicians from helping terminally ill, mentally competent patients commit suicide, the Second Circuit, if anything, was more outspoken than the Ninth:

> [T]here is nothing "natural" about causing death by [withdrawing life support]. The withdrawal of nutrition brings on death by starvation, the withdrawal of hydration brings on death by dehydration, and the withdrawal of ventilation brings about respiratory failure. [Withdrawal of life support] is nothing more nor less than assisted suicide. . . .
>
> A finding of unequal treatment does not, of course, end the inquiry, unless it is determined that the inequality is not rationally related to some legitimate state interest. . . . [But] what interest can the state possibly have in requiring the prolongation of a life that is all but ended? . . . [And] what business is it of the state to require the continuation of agony when the result is imminent and inevitable? What concern prompts the state to interfere with a mentally competent patient's "right to define [his] own concept of existence, or meaning, of the universe, and of the mystery of human life," when the patient seeks to have drugs prescribed to end life during the final stages of a terminal illness? The greatly reduced interest of the state in preserving life compels the answers to these questions: "None."[21]

As I hope I have made clear, both the Ninth and Second Circuits employed very strong and very quotable language—language that could be used quite effectively to advance the cause of PAS in editorials, op-ed pieces, talk shows, state legislatures and state courts. But then the U.S. Supreme Court entered the fray. It disagreed with the lower federal courts virtually point by point and, in effect, eradicated all the lower courts' forceful, felicitous, and stirring language (from the viewpoint of a PAS proponent at any rate).

Nor is that all. Now that the Supreme Court has rejected their main constitutional arguments, at least for the near future, I believe that proponents of PAS are in a weaker position than they were before these lawsuits ever commenced. For the constitutional arguments they made without success in the Supreme Court and the policy arguments they have been making, and will continue to make, in the state legislatures or state courts or on the op-ed pages of hundreds of newspapers greatly overlap.

I realize that, although the highest court in the land did not recognize (or is not yet ready to recognize) a constitutional right to PAS, even under narrow circumstances, one may still argue that there is a common law or state constitutional right or a "moral" or "political" right to PAS. Nevertheless, it will be a good deal harder to engage in any kind of "rights talk" after the Supreme Court decisions than before. There are only so many arguments in favor of a "right" to PAS—and almost all of them were addressed by the Supreme Court in the *Glucksberg* and *Quill* cases. The Court, I think it fair to say, did not find any of them convincing. Thus those arguments have lost a considerable amount of credibility and will be easier to rebuff when made again, albeit in a different setting.[22]

Addressing and Rejecting Four Principal Arguments in Favor of a Right to PAS

At this point it may be useful to summarize briefly (1) the main arguments the *Glucksberg* and *Quill* plaintiffs made in assailing a *total* prohibition against PAS and (2) the reasons Chief Justice Rehnquist gave for rejecting each of these arguments (using the Chief Justice's own language wherever possible):

Argument   Withdrawal of life support is nothing more nor less than assisted suicide; there is no significant moral or legal distinction between the two practices. The right to forgo unwanted life-sustaining medical treatment and the right to enlist a physician's assistance in dying by suicide are merely *sub*categories of *the same* broad right or liberty interest—controlling the time and manner of one's death or hastening one's death.

Response   The distinction between assisting suicide and terminating lifesaving treatment is "widely recognized and endorsed in the medical profession and in our legal traditions [and] is both important and logical."[23] The decision to commit suicide with a physician's assistance "may be just as personal and profound as the decision to refuse unwanted medical treatment, but it has never enjoyed similar legal protection. Indeed, the two acts are widely and reasonably regarded as quite distinct."[24]

Argument   There is no significant difference between administering palliative drugs with the knowledge that it is likely to hasten the patient's death and prescribing a lethal dose of drugs for the very purpose of killing the patient. As the Ninth Circuit put it, there is no real distinction between providing medication with a double effect and providing it with a single effect "as long as one of the known effects in each case is to hasten the end of the patient's life."[25]

Response   In some cases, to be sure, "painkilling drugs may hasten a patient's death, but the physician's purpose and intent is, or may be, only to ease his patient's pain. . . . The law has long used actors' intent or purpose to distinguish between two acts that may have the same result. . . . [T]he law distinguishes actions taken 'because of' a given end [dispensing drugs in order to bring about death] from actions taken 'in spite of' their unintended but foreseen consequences [providing aggressive palliative care that may hasten death, or increase its risk.]"[26]

Argument   The 1990 *Cruzan* case is not simply a case about the right to forgo unwanted medical treatment. Considering the facts, it is really a case about personal autonomy and the right to control the time and manner of one's death. *Cruzan's* extension of the right to refuse medical treatment to include the right to forgo life-sustaining nutrition and hydration was "influenced by the profound indignity that would be wrought upon an unconscious patient by the slow atrophy and disintegration of her body [and] can only be understood as a recognition of the liberty, at least in some circumstances, to physician assistance in ending one's life."[27]

Response   *Cruzan* is *not* a suicide or an assisted suicide case. The Court's assumption in that case was not based, as the Second Circuit supposed, "on the proposition that patients have a general and abstract 'right to hasten death,' but on well established, traditional rights to bodily integrity and freedom from unwanted touching."[28] Indeed, "[i]n *Cruzan* itself, we recognized that most States outlawed assisted suicide—and even more do today—and we certainly gave no intimation that the right to refuse unwanted medical treatment could be somehow transmuted into a right to assistance in committing suicide."[29]

Argument   Fourteenth Amendment Due Process protects one's right to make intimate and personal choices, such as those relating to marriage, procreation, child rearing—and the time and manner of one's death. As the Ninth Circuit observed, quoting language from *Planned Parenthood v Casey:* "Like the decision of whether or not to have an abortion, the decision how and when to die is one of 'the most intimate and personal choices a person may make in a lifetime,' a choice 'central to personal dignity and autonomy.'"[30]

Response   The capacious, one might even say majestic, language in *Casey*—observing that "the right to define one's own concept of existence . . . and of the mystery of human life" is "at the heart of liberty"[31] and noting that some important precedents in this area dealt with matters "involving the most intimate and personal choices a person may make in a lifetime, choices central to personal dignity and autonomy"[32]—simply "described, in a general way and in light of our prior cases, those personal activities and decisions that this Court has identified as so deeply rooted in our history and traditions, or so fundamental to our concept of constitutionally ordered liberty, that they are protected by the Fourteenth Amendment."[33] However, the fact that many of the rights and liberties protected by due process "sound in personal autonomy does not warrant the sweeping conclusion that any and all important, intimate, and personal decisions are so protected, and *Casey* did not suggest otherwise."[34]

Justice O'Connor's Concurring Opinion

I am well aware that in both *Glucksberg* and *Quill* Justice O'Connor provided the fifth vote (along with Justices Scalia, Kennedy, and Thomas) to
make the Chief Justice's opinions the opinions of the Court—by stating that
she joined Rehnquist's opinion, yet writing separately. I am aware, too, that
in large measure two other members of the Court, Justices Ginsburg and
Breyer, joined O'Connor's opinion.

However, there is no indication in Justice O'Connor's brief concurring
opinion that she found any of the principal arguments made by PAS proponents any more persuasive than the Chief Justice did. There is no suggestion, for example, that she reads the *Cruzan* opinion any more broadly than
does the Chief Justice or that she interprets the stirring language in *Casey*
any more expansively. Nor is there any suggestion that she has any more difficulty accepting the distinction between forgoing life-sustaining medical
treatment and actively intervening to bring about death. Nor is there any
reason to think that she has more trouble grasping the "double effect" principle (the principle that explains why a doctor forbidden to administer a
lethal dose of drugs for the very purpose of killing a patient may increase the
dosage of medication needed to relieve pain even though the increased
dosage is likely to hasten death or increase its risk).

Indeed, in one respect at least Justice O'Connor may have gone a step
further than the Chief Justice. I think she may be saying—she is certainly
implying—that the "double effect" principle is not only plausible but *necessary*. Her position (and Justice Breyer's as well) seems to be that if, for example, a state were to prohibit the pain relief that a patient desperately
needs when the increased dosage of medication is so likely to hasten death
or cause unconsciousness that, according to the state, the procedure smacks
of assisted suicide or euthanasia,[35] she (presumably along with Justices
Breyer and Ginsburg) would want to revisit the question.

Professor Cass Sunstein reads Justice O'Connor's opinion differently
than I do. He believes that O'Connor "signaled the possible existence of a
right to physician-assisted suicide in compelling circumstances."[36] I think
that is too broad a reading.

Early in her concurring opinion, Justice O'Connor does say that there is
no need to address "the narrower question whether a mentally competent
person who is experiencing great suffering has a constitutionally cognizable
interest in *controlling the circumstances* of his or her imminent death."[37]
That comment would provide some support for Professor Sunstein's view—
if it were all Justice O'Connor had to say on the subject. But it is not. As her
opinion continues, the general question about a constitutionally protected
interest in controlling the circumstances of one's death is put aside and the
opinion turns into a more narrow and more focused discussion about the liberty interest in obtaining needed pain relief or in preventing a state from
erecting legal barriers preventing access to such relief.

This is why, I believe, Justice O'Connor deems it important that the parties and amici agree that the states of Washington and New York have imposed no legal barriers to pain relief.[38] *"In this light,"* she continues, "even assuming" that there is a constitutionally protected interest in controlling the circumstances of one's death, "the State's interests . . . are sufficiently weighty to justify a prohibition against physician-assisted suicide."[39] Moreover, at the end of her opinion, Justice O'Connor describes the "constitutionally cognizable interest" rather narrowly:

> In sum, there is no need to address the question whether suffering patients have a constitutionally cognizable interest *in obtaining relief from the suffering that they may experience in the last days of their lives.* There is no dispute that dying patients in Washington and New York *can obtain* palliative care, *even when doing so would hasten their deaths.*[40]

In isolation, "obtaining relief from suffering" could mean assisted suicide or euthanasia. In context, however, I think it means only a liberty interest in obtaining pain relief. In light of her entire opinion, I believe Justice O'Connor's description of the constitutionally cognizable interest at the end of her opinion is more accurate than the one she refers to at the outset. Justice O'Connor's overall view appears to be that *so long as a state erects no legal barriers to obtaining pain relief* (even when the analgesics may hasten death or cause unconsciousness), the state's interests in protecting those who are not truly competent or whose wish to commit suicide is not truly voluntary (and the difficulties involved in defining "terminal illness" and ascertaining who fits that category) are sufficiently strong to uphold a total ban against PAS.[41]

As best as I can tell, Justice Breyer, who joined Justice O'Connor's opinion (except insofar as her opinion joined the majority) and also wrote separately, took essentially the same position as O'Connor. Even assuming that there is something like a "right to die with dignity," Justice Breyer saw no need to decide whether such a right is "fundamental."[42] Why not? Because, as he saw it, "the avoidance of severe physical pain (connected with death) would have to comprise an essential part of any successful claim"[43] and "as Justice O'Connor points out, the laws before us do not *force* a dying patient to undergo that kind of pain."[44]

"Rather," continued Breyer, the laws of New York and Washington allow physicians to provide patients with pain-relieving drugs "despite the risk that those drugs themselves will kill."[45] *So long as this is the case,* concluded Breyer, laws prohibiting PAS "would overcome any remaining significant interests" making up a "dying with dignity" claim and thus withstand constitutional challenge.[46]

Justice Breyer emphasized that the crucial question is not whether a patient is receiving adequate palliative care but whether *state laws* prevent a patient from obtaining such care: "We [are] . . . told that there are many instances in which patients do not receive the palliative care that, in principle, is available, but that is so for institutional reasons or inadequacies or obstacles, which would seem possible to overcome, and which do not include a *prohibitive set of laws.*"[47]

I believe some passages in Solicitor General Dellinger's amicus brief and some of his remarks during the oral arguments significantly illuminate the views of both Justice O'Connor and Justice Breyer.

Although the Solicitor General denied that "there is a broad liberty interest in deciding the timing and manner of ones death,"[48] he went on to say that the term "liberty" in the Due Process Clause "is broad enough to encompass an interest on the part of terminally ill, mentally competent adults in obtaining relief from the kind of suffering experienced by the plaintiffs in this case."[49] Not only is a liberty interest implicated when a state inflicts severe pain or suffering on someone, continued the Solicitor General, but also when a state "compels a person" to suffer severe pain caused by an illness by "prohibiting access to medication that would alleviate the condition."[50]

During the oral arguments General Dellinger maintained:

> [A] person states a cognizable liberty interest when he or she alleges that the state is imposing severe pain and suffering *or has adopted a rule which prevents someone from the only means of relieving that pain and suffering.* . . .
> . . . [If] one alleges the kind of severe pain and agony that is being suffered here and that *the state is the cause of standing between you and the only method of relieving that,* you have stated a constitutionally cognizable liberty interest. . . .[51]

Kathryn Tucker, the lead lawyer for the plaintiffs in the *Glucksberg* case, addressed the Court immediately after General Dellinger. She was not pleased with the Solicitor General's description of the liberty interest at stake: "[T]he Solicitor General's comment that what were dealing with here is simply a liberty interest in avoiding pain and suffering . . . absolutely trivializes the claim. We have a constellation of interests [including decisional autonomy and the interest in bodily integrity], each of great Constitutional dimension."[52]

It may well be that a liberty interest in obtaining pain relief or not being denied access to such relief is only a "trivialized" version of the liberty interest really at stake.[53] But Justices O'Connor and Breyer (and presumably Justice Ginsburg as well, for she concurred in the judgments in both cases "substantially for the reasons stated by Justice O'Connor"[54]) focused heavily, perhaps exclusively, on that trivialized or down-sized version.

Since Justices Stevens and Souter, who also concurred in the judgments, seem even more receptive than O'Connor, Ginsburg, and Breyer to arguments in favor of a right to PAS, at least in compelling cases,[55] there is reason to think that at least five members of the Court are likely to resist state legislative efforts to reject or to modify the "double effect" principle if such action would force some dying people to endure severe pain.[56] Thus, although "Rehnquist's opinions did not endorse a constitutional right to adequate palliative care but simply rejected the conclusion of the Ninth and Second Circuit Courts of Appeals,"[57] it may well be that "[a] Court majority" (the five concurring Justices in *Glucksberg* and *Quill*) did effectively endorse such a right.[58]

In a sense, the Court's support for the "double effect" principle is a victory for everybody. For whatever position they may take on assisted suicide or euthanasia, surely most people want the dying and severely ill to suffer as little physical pain as possible. And as Howard Brody has observed:

> Clinicians need to believe to some degree in some form of the principle of double effect in order to provide optimal symptom relief at the end of life. . . . A serious assault on the logic of the principle of double effect could do major violence to the (already reluctant and ill-informed) commitment of the mass of physicians to the goals of palliative care and hospice.[59]

In a way, however, the showing of support for the "double effect" principle by the highest court in the land was a special victory for opponents of assisted suicide and euthanasia. For they have long defended the principle. And they did so again in the *Glucksberg* and *Quill* cases.

For example, in an amicus brief supporting the states of New York and Washington, the American Medical Association (AMA), the American Nurses Association, the American Psychiatric Association, and some forty other medical and health care organizations emphasized that a physician's obligation to relieve pain and suffering and to promote the dignity of dying patients "'includes providing palliative treatment even though it may foreseeably hasten death.'"[60] The AMA (and the many other medical organizations that joined it) told the Supreme Court: "[The] recognition that physicians should provide pain medication sufficient to ease their pain, even where that may serve to hasten death, is *vital* to ensuring that no patient suffer from physical pain."[61]

A good number of those favoring the legalization (or constitutionalization) of PAS have sharply criticized the "double effect" principle. They have condemned the supposed hypocrisy in permitting the use of analgesics that hasten death while banning euthanasia. They have further maintained that killing to relieve suffering has already been sanctioned in the context of "risky pain relief."[62]

Moreover, it is worth recalling that it was the 8–3 majority of the U.S. Court of Appeals for the Ninth Circuit that disparaged the "double effect" principle[63]—as Dr. Brody puts it, dismissing the principle as "moral hypocrisy."[64]

A robust version of the "double effect" principle—the view that even when the level of medication is likely to cause death, the "double effect" principle may be constitutionally required—helps *opponents* of PAS, *not* proponents of the practice. For one of the main arguments against the legalization of PAS is that "properly trained health care professionals can effectively meet their patients' needs for compassionate end-of-life care without acceding to requests for suicide."[65] The "double effect" principle eases the task of health care professionals—and eases the plight of their patients—and thus weakens the case for PAS.

Some Final Thoughts on Justice O'Connor's Concurring Opinion

Up to now, I have taken the position that if Justice O'Connor left the door open for future litigation in this area, she only left it open a small crack. But I must say that I find the reason she gave for joining the Chief Justice's opinions quite baffling. At the outset of her concurring opinion she states that she is joining the Rehnquist opinions because she "agree[s] that there is no generalized right to 'commit suicide.'"[66] But nobody claimed that there *was* a "generalized right to commit suicide" or a general right to obtain a physician's assistance in doing so. *Nobody.*[67]

In their Supreme Court brief, the lawyers for the plaintiffs in the Washington case formulated the question presented as "[w]hether the Fourteenth Amendment's guarantee of liberty protects the decision of a mentally competent, *terminally ill* adult to bring about impending death in a certain, humane, and dignified manner."[68] Furthermore, Kathryn Tucker, the lead lawyer for the plaintiffs in the Washington case, *began* her oral argument by telling the Supreme Court that "this case presents the question whether *dying citizens* in full possession of their mental faculties *at the threshold of death due to terminal illness* have the liberty to choose to cross the threshold in a humane and dignified manner."[69] It is hard to see how anyone could emphasize death, dying, and terminal illness any more than that.

Since one of the principal arguments made by opponents of PAS is that once established for terminally ill patients assisted suicide would not remain so limited for very long,[70] it was not surprising that several Justices voiced doubts about whether the claimed right or liberty interest would or could or should be limited to those on the threshold of death.[71] But Ms. Tucker stood her ground.

She told the Court that "we do draw the line at a patient who is confronting death" because, unlike other individuals who wish to die by suicide, one on the threshold of death *no longer* has a choice between living and dying, but "only the choice of *how* to die."[72] She also recognized that a state may prevent a *non*terminally ill person from choosing suicide because one day that person might "rejoice in that," but the same could not be said for the person who is terminally ill—for his or her life is about to end anyhow.[73]

Moreover, when asked to define the liberty interest Dr. Quill and other plaintiffs in the New York case were claiming, Ms. Tucker's co-counsel, Professor Laurence Tribe, told the Court that it "is the liberty, *when facing imminent and inevitable death,* not to be forced by the government to endure . . . pain and suffering"; "the freedom, *at this threshold at the end of life,* not to be a creature of the state but to have some voice in the question of how much pain one is really going through."[74] This caused Justice Scalia to respond, "Why does the voice just [arise] when death is imminent?"[75]

From the outset of the litigation, the lawyers for the plaintiffs in the Washington and New York cases insisted that the right or liberty interest they claimed was limited to the terminally ill because, among other reasons, I think they knew there was no appreciable chance that the courts would establish a general right to assisted suicide. Or, to put it somewhat differently, I think they knew that *the only chance they had of* prevailing in the courts was to ask for a narrowly limited right to PAS, one confined to the terminally ill. They were well aware that such a narrowly limited right would cause less alarm and command more support than a general right to assisted suicide.

In short, if all that the Supreme Court decided last June is that there is no general right to commit suicide, the Court decided virtually nothing—because everybody agreed that there was no such right.

Justice O'Connor observes that "[t]he Court frames the issue in this case as whether the Due Process Clause . . . protects a 'right to commit suicide which itself includes a right to assistance in doing so,' and concludes that our [history and legal traditions] do not support the existence of such a right."[76] But this description of what "The Court" (or Chief Justice Rehnquist) did is incomplete.

In describing the claim at issue in *Glucksberg,* the Ninth Circuit had used such language as "a constitutionally recognized 'right to die,'" "a due process liberty interest in controlling the time and manner of one's death," "a liberty interest in hastening one's own death,"[77] "a strong liberty interest in choosing a dignified and humane death,"[78] and an issue "deeply affect[ing] individuals' right to determine their own destiny."[79] Apparently annoyed at what he apparently considered the Ninth Circuit's sloppy and emotive language, and perhaps displeased that in all its various descriptions of the claim at issue the Ninth Circuit had avoided the term "suicide" (a term that carries strongly negative associations), the Chief Justice maintained that a more careful statement of the question presented than any utilized by the Ninth Circuit would be "whether the 'liberty' specially protected by the Due Process Clause includes a right to commit suicide which itself includes a right to assistance in doing so."[80]

I readily admit that this passage caused a certain amount of confusion. But it should not be forgotten that the Chief Justice pointed out *at least three times* that the Ninth Circuit had held that the challenged law "was unconstitutional '*as applied to terminally ill* competent adults who wish to hasten their death with medication prescribed by their physicians.'"[81] And in the penulti-mate paragraph of his opinion, the Chief Justice concluded: "We therefore hold that [the Washington law] does not violate the Fourteenth Amendment, either on its face or 'as applied to competent, terminally ill adults who wish to hasten their deaths by obtaining medication prescribed by their doctors.'"[82]

The Washington statute was challenged by three terminally ill patients and four physicians who periodically treat terminally ill patients and who wished to help such patients die by suicide. Although the patients died dur-ing the pendency of the case, the physicians remained.

Justice O'Connor did not argue that the physician-plaintiffs "lacked standing" to challenge the constitutionality of the ban against PAS insofar as it applied to competent, terminally ill patients. In contrast, Justice Stevens, who wrote a separate concurring opinion, came close to saying just that. Al-though the Ninth Circuit considered the Washington law *as applied* to ter-minally ill, competent adult patients who wished to hasten their deaths, ob-served Stevens, all the patient-plaintiffs had died by then and therefore the court of appeals' holding "was not limited to a particular set of plaintiffs be-fore it."[83] But Stevens's statement is incomplete.

To be sure, the physician-plaintiffs were not threatened with prosecu-tion for assisting in the suicide of *a particular* patient. As the Ninth Circuit pointed out, however, "they ran a severe risk of prosecution under the Washington statute, which proscribes the very conduct in which they seek to engage."[84] Moreover, although Justice Stevens did not discuss this aspect of the case, both the district court and the court of appeals proceeded on the basis that the physician-plaintiffs had standing to sue on behalf of their ter-minally ill patients as well as on their own behalf.[85] This is hardly surprising; the U.S. Supreme Court has frequently permitted physicians to assert their patients' rights in challenging abortion restrictions.[86] Moreover, it might be said that the Washington statute is aimed more directly at physicians than at their patients. It does not make *committing suicide* with the assistance of another a felony. It makes *aiding another* to commit suicide a felony.

If physicians lacked standing to challenge laws prohibiting assisted sui-cide, how could appellate courts *ever* consider an "as applied to terminally ill patients" challenge? All terminally ill patients *necessarily* will die prior to completion of the litigation. In fact, in the *Glucksberg* case all but one of the patient-plaintiffs had died by the time the district court issued its decision.

What is the most plausible explanation for Justice O'Connor's odd state-ment that she is joining the Chief Justice's opinions in *Glucksberg* and *Quill* because she "agree[s] that there is no generalized right to 'commit sui-cide'"[87] (an odd statement, certainly, in light of the history of the case and against the background of the briefs and the oral arguments)? Although this is a conclusion that I am not eager to reach, I think the reason for Justice O'Connor's statement is a reluctance to rule out the possibility of a right to PAS in every set of circumstances and a desire to "proceed with special cau-tion" in this area.[88]

The Next Time Around

I have to agree with the many Court watchers who say (especially those who were unhappy with the result in the assisted suicide cases) that *Glucksberg* and *Quill* will not be the Court's last word on the subject. But it hardly follows that the next time the Court confronts the issue it will establish a right to assisted suicide in some limited form. There were a number of factors at work when the Supreme Court decided the 1997 PAS cases and most of them will still be operating when the Court addresses the issue a second time.

For one thing, the issue has recently been the subject of intense discussion and vigorous debate and there is no indication this agitation will subside in the foreseeable future. As the Chief Justice observed (and concurring Justice O'Connor agreed), "[p]ublic concern and democratic action are . . . sharply focused on how best to protect dignity and independence at the end of life, with the result that there have been many significant changes in state laws and in the attitudes these laws reflect."[89]

For another thing, the rights of a politically vulnerable group are not at stake—as had been the situation when the Court intervened in prior cases.[90] After all, "[d]ying people are clearly not a discrete and insular minority in the same, sure way as are black people subject to race discrimination laws [or] women subject to abortion restrictions."[91] And when the issue is close and "there is no democratic defect in the underlying political process," courts "should not strike down reasonable legislative judgments."[92]

I think Justice O'Connor put it well when, reiterating a point she made during the oral arguments,[93] she commented:

> Every one of us at some point may be affected by our own or a family member's terminal illness. There is no reason to think the democratic process will not strike the proper balance between the interests of terminally ill, mentally competent individuals who would seek to end their suffering and the State's interests in protecting those who might seek to end life mistakenly or under pressure.[94]

Another reason, quite likely, for the Court's reluctance to establish a constitutionally protected right to, or liberty interest in, assisted suicide, and one that will apply the next time around as well, is capsuled in the Solicitor General's amicus brief: once an exception to the general prohibition against PAS is mandated by the Court, however heavily circumscribed it might be at first, "there is no obvious stopping point."[95]

For example, the Ninth Circuit invalidated the state's assisted suicide ban "only 'as applied to competent, terminally ill adults who wish to hasten their deaths by obtaining medication prescribed by their doctors.'"[96] After noting Washington State's insistence that the impact of the Ninth Circuit's decision "will not and cannot be so limited,"[97] the Chief Justice observed:

The [Ninth Circuit's] decision, and its expansive reasoning, provide ample support for the State's concerns. The court noted, for example, that the "decision of a duly appointed surrogate decision maker is for all legal purposes the decision of the patient himself," that "in some instances, the patient may be unable to self-administer the drugs and . . . administration by the physician . . . may be the only way the patient may be able to receive them," and that not only physicians, but also family members and loved ones, will inevitably participate in assisting suicide. Thus, it turns out that what is couched as a limited right to "physician-assisted suicide" is likely, in effect, a much broader license, which could prove extremely difficult to solve and contain.[98]

Although concurring Justice Ginsburg neither joined the Chief Justice's opinion nor wrote an opinion of her own,[99] during the oral arguments she voiced skepticism that any right to PAS, no matter how narrowly limited initially, could or would be confined to the terminally ill or could or would stop short of active voluntary euthanasia.

When Kathryn Tucker, lead attorney for the plaintiffs in *Glucksberg,* urged the Court to recognize, or to establish, a constitutionally protected liberty interest "that involves bodily integrity, decisional autonomy, and the right to be free of unwanted pain and suffering,"[100] Justice Ginsburg retorted that "a lot of people would fit [this] category," not just the terminally ill.[101] How, she wondered, do you "leave out the rest of the world who would fit the same standards?"[102] At another point, Justice Ginsburg suggested that the patient who is so helpless or in so much agony that she "is not able to assist in her own suicide," but must have a health professional administer a lethal injection, is "in a more sympathetic situation" than one who is able to commit suicide with the preliminary assistance of a physician.[103]

Still another factor that must have had some impact on at least some members of the Court and is bound to influence at least some of the Justices in future cases, is the strong opposition of the AMA and other medical groups to the constitutionalization or legalization of PAS, regardless of how narrowly limited the constitutional right or the statutory authorization might be. As Linda Greenhouse has pointed out,[104] the amicus brief filed by the AMA in *Glucksberg* and *Quill* sharply contrasted with the one the same organization had filed seven years earlier in the *Cruzan* case.[105] In *Cruzan,* the AMA told the Court that under the circumstances, terminating life support was in keeping with "respecting the patient's autonomy and dignity."[106] In *Glucksberg* and *Quill,* however, the AMA (and more than forty other national and state medical and health care organizations) told the Court that "[t]he ethical prohibition against physician-assisted suicide is a cornerstone of medical ethics"; the AMA had repeatedly "reexamined and reaffirmed" that ethical prohibition, and had done so as recently as the summer of 1996; and that "[p]hysician-assisted suicide remains 'fundamentally incompatible with the physician's role as healer, would be difficult or impossible to control, and would pose serious societal risks.'"[107]

Recent and continuing trends in medical practice may only heighten the AMA's resistance to PAS. The next time the issue is presented, the AMA and other medical groups might well tell the Court, as two commentators have recently argued, that new trends and developments make the need to maintain the absolute prohibition against PAS "more important than ever."[108] It would not be surprising if the next time around the AMA and other medical groups were to tell the Court something like this:

> Given the great pressures threatening medical ethics today—including, among other factors, a more impersonal practice of medicine, the absence of a lifelong relationship with a physician, the push toward managed care, and the financially-based limitation of services—a bright line rule regarding medically-assisted death is a bulwark against disaster.[109]

Finally, another factor at work in the assisted suicide cases, and one that will operate as well the next time the Court confronts the issue, is the Justices' realization that if they were to establish a right to assisted suicide, however limited, the need to enact legislation implementing and regulating any such right would generate many problems—which inevitably would find their way back to the Court.

Whether a regulatory mechanism would be seen as providing patients and physicians with much-needed protection or viewed as unduly burdening the underlying right would be largely in the eye of the beholder.[110] Thus it is not surprising that proponents of PAS even disagree among themselves as to how a particular procedural requirement should be regarded.

For example, three of the nation's most respected proponents of PAS, Franklin Miller, Howard Brody, and Timothy Quill, have questioned the desirability of the fifteen-day waiting period required by the Oregon Death with Dignity Act, a provision designed to ensure that a patient's decision to elect assisted suicide is resolute.[111] According to Miller, Brody and Quill, such an "arbitrary time period . . . may be highly burdensome for patients who are suffering intolerably and may preclude access to assisted death for those who request it at the point when they are imminently dying."[112] The same three commentators also criticize a provision of a Model State Act requiring that the discussion between physician and patient concerning a request for assisted suicide be witnessed by two adults,[113] calling it "unduly intrusive and unlikely to be effective."[114] On the other hand, Miller, Brody, and Quill maintain that an Oregon provision requiring a second medical opinion on the assisted suicide decision is "not a reliable safeguard" because it "does not mandate that the consulting physician be genuinely independent."[115]

Perhaps the most rigorous condition on PAS to be found is the requirement of Compassion in Dying that the approval of all of the would-be suicide's immediate family members be obtained.[116] It is hard to believe that any group favoring PAS would retain such a requirement if the Court were to establish a constitutional right to assisted suicide. But one can be fairly sure that if the Court were to establish such a right, opponents of PAS would fight hard to include a "family approval" provision in any legislation regulating assisted suicide–along with mandatory waiting periods, specified information and procedures to ensure that the decision to choose PAS is "truly informed," and all sorts of notification requirements and bans on the use of public facilities, public employees, and public funds.[117]

Although not insubstantial, the differences among proponents of PAS over the requisite conditions and procedures for carrying out the practice pale compared to the differences likely to exist between those who disagree about legalizing PAS in the first place. In short, in many respects the legislative response to a Supreme Court decision establishing a right to assisted suicide is likely to be a replay of the response to *Roe v Wade,*[118] a specter that did not escape the attention of the Justices last year.

At one point in the oral arguments, the Chief Justice told the lead lawyer for the *Glucksberg* plaintiffs:

> You're not asking that [this Court engage in legislation] now. But surely that's what the next couple of generations are going to have to deal with, what regulations are permissible and what not if we uphold your position here. . . . [Y]ou're going to find the same thing . . . that perhaps has happened with the abortion cases. There are people who are just totally opposed and people who are totally in favor of them. So you're going to have those factions fighting it out in every session of the legislature, how far can we go in regulating this. And that will be a constitutional decision in every case.[119]

Roe v Wade ignited what has aptly been called a "domestic war,"[120] one that, after a quarter-century of tumult, seems finally to have come to an end in the courts. The Court that decided the assisted suicide cases in 1997 was not eager to set off a new domestic war. Neither, I venture to say, will the Court be the next time around.

NOTES

Although my views on assisted suicide and euthanasia are no secret to anyone who has dipped into the literature, I should point out that two days before the Supreme Court heard oral arguments in the physician-assisted suicide cases on January 8, 1997, I was one of nine lawyers and law professors who "moot courted" Dennis Vacco, the Attorney General of New York, who

argued for petitioners in *Vacco v Quill.*

1. 117 S Ct 2258 (1997).
2. 117 S Ct 2293 (1997).
3. See Richard Price & Tony Mauro, "Advocates Promise to Press the Fight," *USA Today,* June 27, 1997, at 4A. Kathryn Tucker, the lead attorney for the plaintiffs in the *Glucksberg* case, also told the press that the Court

had given the states "quite a green light to . . . proceed down the path" that Oregon had taken and enact laws permitting physicians to help their patients commit suicide. John Aloysius Farrell, "No Absolute 'Right to Die,' Supreme Court Rules; Bans Upheld on Assisted Suicide; Issue Is Left Open," *Boston Globe,* June 27, 1997, at A1; see also Tony Mauro, "But States Can Enact New Laws," *USA Today,* June 27,1997, at 1A.

4. Transcript of Oral Argument, *Glucksberg* (No. 96–110), *available in* 1997 WL 13671, at *12 (Jan. 8, 1997).

5. Transcript of Oral Argument, *Quill* (No. 96–1858), *available in* 1997 WL 13672, at *11 (Jan. 8, 1997).

6. Ibid. at *43.

7. Transcript of Oral Argument, *Glucksberg* (No. 96–110), *available in* 1997 WL 13671, at *40 (Jan. 8, 1997).

8. See Timothy Egan, "Assisted Suicide Comes Full Circle, to Oregon," *New York Times,* Oct 26, 1997, § 1, at 1, Ezekiel J. Emanuel & Linda L. Emanuel, "Assisted Suicide? Not in My State," *New York Times,* July 24, 1997, at A15.

9. See Price & Mauro, at 4A (cited in note 3).

10. See Emanuel & Emanuel, at A15 (cited in note 8).

11. Timothy Egan, "In Oregon, Opening a New Front in the World of Medicine," *New York Times,* Nov 6, 1997, at A26.

12. David J. Garrow, "The Oregon Trail," *New York Times,* Nov 6, 1997, at A27.

13. Winifred Gallagher, "Go With the Flow: What We Should Be Doing as We Prepare to Die," *New York Times,* Nov 30, 1997, Book Review, at 17 (reviewing MARILYN WEBB, THE GOOD DEATH: THE NEW AMERICAN SEARCH TO RESHAPE THE END OF LIFE (1997)).

14. See Egan, at 1 (cited in note 8). See also Haya El Nasser & John Ritter,

"Officials: Ore. Suicide Law in Effect," *USA Today,* Nov 6, 1997, at 3A.

15. See the discussion in Yale Kamisar, "Devil in the Detail, Not Money, Defeated Assisted Suicide Plan," *Detroit News,* Nov. 5, 1998, at 12A.

16. See, e.g., Ellen Goodman, "Guidelines for Assisted Suicide," *Boston Sunday Globe,* July 27, 1997, at E7.

17. Ibid.

18. See Compassion in Dying v Washington, 79 F 3d 790 (9th Cir 1996) (en banc), *rev'd sub nom.* Washington v Glucksberg, 117 S Ct 2258 (1997); Quill v Vacco, 80 F 3d 716 (2d Cir 1996), *rev'd,* 117 S Ct 2293 (1997). The Ninth Circuit relied on the Due Process Clause without considering the equal protection issue; the Second Circuit rejected the plaintiffs' due process argument, but found the basis for its decision in the Equal Protection Clause. For strong criticism of the majority opinions in these cases see, for example, John Arras, *Physician-Assisted Suicide: A Tragic View,* 13 Journal of Contemporary Health Law & Policy 361 (1997); Howard Brody, Compassion in Dying v Washington: *Promoting Dangerous Myths in Terminal Care,* BioLaw, July-Aug. 1996, Special Section, at S:154; Robert Burt, *Constitutionalizing Physician-Assisted Suicide: Will Lightning Strike Thrice?,* 35 Duquesne Law Review 159 (1996); Yale Kamisar, *The "Right to Die": On Drawing (And Erasing) Lines,* 35 Duquesne Law Review 481 (1996); Alexander Morgan Capron, *Liberty, Equality, Death!,* 26 Hastings Center Report 23 (May/June 1996).

19. *Compassion in Dying,* 79 F 3d at 824.

20. Ibid. at 832. In the case of voluntary euthanasia, of course, *as well as in* assisted suicide, the patient herself determines whether her life shall end.

21. *Quill,* 80 F 3d at 729–30 (quoting from the principal opinion in Planned Parenthood v Casey, 505 US 833, 851 (1992)).

22. See Charles H. Baron, *Pleading for Physician-Assisted Suicide in the Courts,* 19 Western New England Law Review 371 (1997) (arguing persuasively that proponents of PAS are likely to find a warmer reception in the state courts than in the state legislatures). But the decision in *Krischer v McIver,* 697 So 2d 97 (Fla 1997), indicates that in the post-*Glucksberg,* post-*Quill* era, PAS proponents may meet heavy resistance when they turn to the state courts for relief.

About six months before the U.S. Supreme Court rulings in *Glucksberg* and *Quill,* a Florida trial court held that a terminally ill AIDS patient was entitled, under the Privacy Amendment of the Florida Constitution, to determine the time and manner of his death and that, in order to do so, he had the right to seek and obtain the assistance of his physician in committing suicide. See the discussion in *Krischer v McIver,* 697 So 2d at 99–100. But a few short weeks after the Supreme Courts decisions in *Glucksberg* and *Quill,* the Florida Supreme Court reversed the trial court (6–1). *See* ibid. at 104.

Since Florida's Privacy Amendment establishes a right "much broader in scope than that of the Federal Constitution," Winfield v Division of Pari-Mutuel Wagering, 477 So 2d 544, 548 (Fla. 1985), the Florida Supreme Court could have distinguished *Glucksberg* and *Quill* without much difficulty. But the Florida Supreme Court did not do so. Instead, it quoted at length from Chief Justice Rehnquist's opinion in *Glucksberg* and the New York State Task Force Report on assisted suicide and euthanasia, a report that recommended unanimously that New York's total ban against assisted suicide and euthanasia be maintained. (Chief Justice Rehnquist, too, had relied heavily on the New York report.) After discussing, and balking at, the arguments frequently made by proponents of PAS, Florida's highest court concluded:

> [T]his case should not be decided on the basis of this Court's own assessment of the weight of the competing moral arguments. By broadly construing the privacy amendment to include the right to assisted suicide, we would run the risk of arrogating to ourselves those powers to make social policy that as a constitutional matter belong only to the legislature.
> *Krischer,* 697 So 2d at 104.

23. *Quill,* 117 S Ct at 2298.

24. *Glucksberg,* 117 S Ct at 2270.

25. Compassion in Dying v Washington, 79 F 3d 790, 824 (9th Cir 1996) (en banc), *rev'd sub nom.* Washington v Glucksberg, 117 S Ct 2268 (1997).

26. *Quill,* 117 S Ct at 2298–99.

27. Brief for Respondents at 29, *Quill* (No. 95–1858), *available in* 1996 WL 708912.

28. *Quill,* 117 S Ct at 2301.

29. *Glucksberg,* 117 S Ct at 2270.

30. *Compassion in Dying,* 79 F 3d at 813–14 (quoting Planned Parenthood v Casey, 505 US 833, 851 (1992)).

31. *Casey,* 505 US at 851.

32. Ibid.

33. *Glucksberg,* 117 S Ct at 2271.

34. Ibid. (citation omitted).

35. Many physicians and bioethicists seem to believe that providing risky pain relief is always justifiable, regardless of how certain or probable

the risk of death may be. Recently, however, two law professors have maintained that, as a matter of criminal law, the physician's motive or desire to relieve pain does not automatically or necessarily justify the administration of pain relief. See Norman L. Cantor & George C. Thomas III, *Pain Relief, Acceleration of Death, and Criminal Law,* 6 Kennedy Institute of Ethics Journal 107 (1996). They argue that if, for example, the situation were such that no analgesic dosage could provide pain relief without also causing prompt death (or if under the circumstances it was almost certain that the required analgesic dosage would cause death) the physician who administered the analgesic would be criminally liable for the resulting death even though death was not intended as a result. According to the authors, as defined by the Model Penal Code these deaths would be "knowing" homicides (acting with awareness that one's conduct is "practically certain" to bring about a particular result). See ibid. at 119. Moreover, according to the authors, if it were *highly likely* that the administration of an analgesic would cause prompt death (for example a 75–90% chance), the physician who used the painkillers that caused the death would also be criminally liable (for having acted "recklessly"). See ibid. at 111.

36. Cass R. Sunstein, "Supreme Caution: Once Again, the High Court Takes Only Small Steps," *Washington Post,* July 6, 1997, at C 1.

37. *Glucksberg,* 117 S Ct at 2303 (O'Connor, J., concurring) (emphasis added).

38. See ibid.

39. Ibid. (emphasis added).

40. Ibid. (emphasis added).

41. See ibid.

42. *Glucksberg,* 117 S Ct at 2311.

43. Ibid.

44. Ibid.

45. Ibid.

46. Ibid.

47. Ibid. at 2312. (citations omitted).

48. Brief for United States as Amicus Curiae Supporting Petitioners at 12, *Glucksberg* (No. 96–110), *available in* 1996 WL 663186.

49. Ibid. at 13.

50. Ibid. at 12–13.

51. Transcript of Oral Argument, *Glucksberg* (No. 96–110), *available in* 1997 WL 13671, at *18, *20–21 (Jan. 8, 1997) (emphasis added).

52. Ibid. at *35–36.

53. For the view that the O'Connor-Breyer-Ginsburg position that "any constitutional right [in this area] would be limited to relief from pain . . . seems arbitrary" for a number of reasons, see Ronald Dworkin, "Assisted Suicide: What the Court Really Said," *New York Review of Books,* Sept. 25, 1997, at 40, 42.

54. *Glucksberg,* 117 S Ct at 2303.

55. See Richard H. Fallon, Jr., *The Supreme Court, 1996 Term—Foreword: Implementing the Constitution,* 111 Harvard Law Review 54, 139 n.616 (1997).

56. So far as I know, no state presently prohibits the use of palliative care when it is likely to hasten death. However, warns Dr. Howard Brody in this Symposium, "if it becomes widely known (or alleged) that palliative care techniques sometimes deliberately hasten death, we can expect new laws to be introduced that would hamstring palliative practice." Howard Brody, *Physician-Assisted Suicide in the Courts: Moral Equivalence, Double Effect, and Clinical Practice,* 82 Minnesota Law Review 939, 960 (1998) (citation omitted).

57. Robert A. Burt, *The Supreme Court Speaks—Not Assisted Suicide but a Constitutional Right to Palliative Care,* 337 New England Journal of Medicine 1234, 1234 (1997).

58. Ibid. I recently discovered that, acting independently of each other, Professor Burt and I had reached the same conclusion in this regard. Compare Yale Kamisar, *On the Meaning and Impact of the U.S. Supreme Court's Recent Rulings in the Physician-Assisted Suicide Cases,* Prepared Remarks for the Panel on Physician-Assisted Suicide at the American Bar Association Annual Meeting (Aug. 2, 1997) (transcript on file with the *Harvard Law Review*) *with* Burt (cited in note 57).

59. Brody, at 22 (cited in note 56); see also Burt at 1234 (cited in note 57), (noting that the Second Circuit's ruling in *Quill* had led some New York physicians "to fear the legal consequences of adequately managing symptoms through the use of opioids that are believed to carry a foreseeable risk of hastened death").

60. Brief of the American Medical Association, the American Nurses Association, and the American Psychiatric Association et al. as Amicus Curiae in Support of Petitioners at 4, *Glucksberg* (No. 96–110), *available in* 1996 WL 656263 (citation omitted).

61. Ibid. (emphasis added).

62. See the discussion in Cantor & Thomas, at 109 (cited in note 35). To cite one specific example, Dr. Thomas Preston, a well-known proponent of PAS, and one of the plaintiffs in the *Glucksberg* case, has asserted that "the morphine drip is undeniably euthanasia, hidden by the cosmetics of professional tradition and language." Thomas A. Preston, "Killing Pain, Ending Life," *New York Times,* Nov 1, 1994, at A27.

63. See Compassion in Dying v Washington, 79 F 3d 790, 824 (9th Cir 1996) (en banc), *rev'd sub nom.* Washington v Glucksberg, 117 S Ct 2258 (1997).

64. See Brody, at 13 (cited in note 56).

65. Brief of the American Medical Association, the American Nurses Association, and the American Psychiatric Association et al. as Amicus Curiae in Support of Petitioners at 3, *Glucksberg* (No. 96–110), *available in* 1996 WL 656263.

66. Washington v Glucksberg, 117 S Ct 2303 (1997) (O'Connor, J., concurring).

67. Puzzling, too, was Justice O'Connor's remark that, in the context of the facial challenge to the New York and Washington laws, she saw no need "to address the narrower question whether a mentally competent person who is experiencing great suffering has a constitutionally cognizable interest in controlling the circumstances of his or her imminent death." Ibid. The "narrower question" was *the only* question the parties addressed.

68. Brief for Respondents at i, *Glucksberg* (No. 95–1858), *available in* 1996 WL 708925.

69. Transcript of Oral Argument, *Glucksberg* (No. 96–110), *available in* 1997 WL 13671, at *26–27 (Jan. 8, 1997) (emphasis added).

70. See, e.g., Kamisar, at 502–13 (cited in note 18).

71. See Transcript of Oral Argument, *Glucksberg* (No. 96–110), *available in* 1997 WL 13671, at *27, *29, *33–35, *50–51 (Jan. 8, 1997).

72. Ibid. at *28 (emphasis added).

73. Ibid. at *33–34.

74. Transcript of Oral Argument, *Quill* (No. 95–1858), *available in* 1997 WL 13672, at *55–56 (Jan. 8, 1997).

75. Ibid. at *56.

76. Washington v Glucksberg, 117 S Ct 2303 (1997) (O'Connor, J. concurring).

77. Compassion in Dying v Washington, 79 F 3d 790, 816 (9th Cir 1996) (en banc), *rev'd sub nom.* Washington v Glucksberg, 117 S Ct 2258 (1997); *see also* ibid. at 798–99.

78. Ibid. at 814.

79. Ibid. at 801.

80. *Glucksberg,* 117 S Ct at 2269 (footnote omitted).

81. Ibid. at 2262 & n.6, 2274, 2755 & n.24 (emphasis added).

82. Ibid. at 2275 (emphasis added).

83. Ibid. at 2304 (Stevens, J., concurring in the judgment).

84. *Compassion in Dying,* 79 F 3d at 795–96.

85. See ibid. at 795–96 & 795 n.3.

86. See Singleton v Wulff, 428 US 106, 112–13 (1976); Planned Parenthood v Ashcroft, 462 US 476, 478 (1983); Planned Parenthood v Danforth, 428 US 52, 62 (1976); Doe v Bolton, 410 US 179, 188 (1973).

87. *Glucksberg,* 117 S Ct at 2303.

88. Fallon, at 152 (cited in note 55); *see also The Supreme Court, 1996 Term—Leading Cases,* 111 Harvard Law Review 197, 248 (1997).

89. *Glucksberg,* 117 S Ct at 2265–66. See also concurring Justice O'Connor's comment: "As the Court recognizes, States are presently undertaking extensive and serious evaluation of physician-assisted suicide and other related issues." Ibid. at 2303.

90. At one point in the oral arguments, Justice Souter pointed out that in other cases in which the Court had intervened "[t]here were certain groups who simply did not get a representative fair shake," but "[t]hat's not what we've got here. . . . [In this case], everybody is in the same boat." Transcript of Oral Argument, *Glucksberg* (No. 96–110), *available*
in 1997 WL 13671, at *41 (Jan. 8, 1997).

91. Burt, at 179 (cited in note 18).

92. Cass R. Sunstein, *The Right to Die,* 106 Yale Law Journal 1123, 1146 (1997) (written before the *Glucksberg* and *Quill* cases).

93. Addressing Kathryn Tucker, attorney for the plaintiffs in *Glucksberg,* Justice O'Connor remarked:

> I wanted to ask you whether it should enter the balance of state interests versus the interests of the patient here, that this is an issue that every one of us faces, young or old, male or female, whatever it might be. And all of us who are citizens and authorized to vote can certainly participate through this process in the development of state law in this area.
>
> Does that cause the balance in any way to shift, do you think? We are not dealing perhaps with an unrepresented group, a group of children or a group of women who have no other means to protect themselves, some specific confined group. This is something that affects all of us.
>
> Transcript of Oral Argument, *Glucksberg* (No. 96–110), *available in* 1997 WL 13671, at *39–40 (Jan. 8, 1997).

A moment later Justice Ginsburg added that "most of us have parents or other loved ones and we've lived through a dying experience that forces us to think about these things." Ibid. at *42. The reason age is not considered the same kind of suspect classification as race, continued Justice Ginsburg, is that "[w]e were all once young, we hope we will be old, it's universal." Ibid.

94. Washington v Glucksberg, 117 S Ct 2303, 2303 (1996). Some might argue that in a system formally prohibiting PAS the wealthy and the well connected will still obtain such assistance "underground." But the counterargument is that in a system formally authorizing PAS, the risks of abuse are likely to fall most heavily against members of disadvantaged groups. See generally Yale Kamisar, *Physician-Assisted Suicide: The Problems Presented by the Compelling, Heartwrenching Case*, 88 Journal Criminal Law & Criminology 1121, 1127–33 (1998).

95. *Glucksberg*, 117 S Ct at 2274 n.23 (citation omitted). There is considerable literature on this point. See generally Kamisar, (cited in note 18, and the articles and books quoted or cited therein.

96. *Glucksberg*, 117 S Ct at 2274.

97. Ibid. (quoting Compassion in Dying v Washington, 79 F 3d 790, 838 (9th Cir 1996) (en banc), *rev'd sub nom.* Washington v Glucksberg, 117 S Ct 2258(1997)).

98. Ibid. (citations omitted). During the oral arguments, Justice Scalia repeatedly expressed doubts that any right to PAS should or could be limited to the terminally ill or to those undergoing physical pain, as opposed to those experiencing "emotional suffering" or "emotional pain." See Transcript of Oral Argument, *Glucksberg* (No. 96-110), *available in* 1997 WL 13671, at *27–28, *31–34, *55–56 (Jan. 8, 1997).

99. She said only that she "concur[red] in the Court's judgments in [*Glucksberg* and *Quill*] substantially for the reasons stated by Justice O'Connor in her concurring opinion." *Glucksberg*, 117 S Ct at 2310.

100. Transcript of Oral Argument, *Glucksberg* (No. 96–110), *available*
in 1997 WL 13671, at *49–50 (Jan. 8, 1997).

101. Ibid. at *50.

102. Ibid.

103. Ibid. at *29 (emphasis added).

104. See Linda Greenhouse, "An Issue for a Reluctant High Court," *New York Times,* Oct. 6, 1996, at E3.

105. Cruzan v Director, Missouri Department of Health, 497 US 261 (1990).

106. See Greenhouse, at E3, cited in note 104.

107. Brief of the American Medical Association, the American Nurses Association, and the American Psychiatric Association et al. as Amicus Curiae in Support of Petitioners at 5, *Glucksberg* (No. 96–110), *available in* 1996 WL 656263 (citation omitted).

   I believe that the strong opposition to PAS by the AMA and many other medical groups is significant in itself. But I also believe that the AMA amicus brief makes a number of important points. To give some examples:

(1) Demand for PAS among terminally ill persons is "best understood not as a necessary response to untreatable pain uniquely felt by the dying, but in the broader context of requests for suicide generally" (among all suicides only a small percentage are terminally ill and among all terminally or severely ill patients, only a small percentage attempt or commit suicide). Ibid. at 10.

(2) "[T]he fact that many patients do not receive adequate pain relief or suffer from undiagnosed and untreated depression puts undue pressure on them to seek physician-assisted suicide." Ibid. at 13.

(3) "[P]oor and minority individuals are at the greatest risk for receiving inadequate care and thus may feel the greatest pressure to request physician-assisted suicide." Ibid.

(4) "Were physician-assisted suicide to become a legitimate medical option, then a decision not to select that option would make many patients feel responsible for their own suffering and for the burden they impose on others." Ibid. at 17.

(5) "[T]he unprecedented intrusion into the physician-patient relationship needed independently to regulate [assisted suicide] decisions would be fundamentally inconsistent with the private nature of health care treatment, and all too likely to undermine what progress had been made in decisions to withdraw or withhold life-sustaining treatment and to use effective pain control." Ibid.

108. Leon R. Kass & Nelson Lund, *Physician-Assisted Suicide, Medical Ethics and the Future of the Medical Profession,* 35 Duquesne Law Review 395, 423 (1996).

109. Ibid.

110. Although the drafters of a recently proposed "Model State Act" are convinced that a statute authorizing PAS must contain strong safeguards, they recognize that at a time which is likely to be extremely difficult for both patients and families, both patients and family members will "often quite reasonably view the procedures as a profound invasion of their privacy." Charles H. Baron et al., *A Model State Act to Authorize and Regulate Physician-Assisted Suicide,* 33 Harvard Journal on Legislation 1, 13–14 (1996).

111. Franklin Miller et al., *Can Physician-Assisted Suicide Be Regulated Effectively?,* 24 Journal of Law, Medicine, & Ethics 225, 226 (1996).

112. Ibid. Consider, too, the recent observations of Thomas Preston, a well-known proponent of PAS and one of the plaintiffs in the *Glucksberg* case:

> Under the present legal climate, [any] future legislative or judicial allowance of dying by prescription of lethal drugs will be accompanied by a legal regulatory system so protracted and intrusive on the private decision of doctor and patient that it may render a legal request unworkable. . . . An eminent Seattle physician confided to me that he voted against Washington State Initiative 119 (this initiative, in 1991, would have legalized euthanasia and assisted suicide) because, "If I have a patient who is within days of dying and suffering greatly, I need to act quickly. If the initiative became law I'd have so many hoops to jump through every time I had a patient dying, I could never give the best treatment for the individual case."
>
> Thomas A. Preston, *The Case for Privacy in Dying: A Solution from the Supreme Court,* King County Medical Society Bulletin, Nov 1997, at 9, 12.

113. See Baron et al., at 28 (cited in note 110).

114. Miller et al., at 226 (cited in note 111).

115. Ibid. Thus, this procedural safeguard could be satisfied by "a friend or close colleague of the treating physician, or even by a subordinate physician under the treating physician's supervision." Ibid.

116. See Sylvia A. Law, *Physician-Assisted Death: An Essay on Constitutional Rights and Remedies,* 55 Maryland Law Review 292, 297 n.13 (1996).

117. As noted in *Glucksberg,* two months before the Court decided the PAS cases, President Clinton signed the Federal Assisted Suicide Funding Restriction Act of 1997, Public Law 106–12, 111 Stat. 23 (codified as amended 42 U.S.C. §§ 14401 et seq.) prohibiting the use of federal funds in support of PAS. See *Washington v Glucksberg,* 117 S Ct 2258, 2266 (1997).

118. 410 US 113 (1973).

119. Transcript of Oral Argument, *Glucksberg* (No. 96–110), *available in* 1997 WL 13671, at *38–39 (Jan. 8, 1997). Justice O'Connor added, "I think there is no doubt that [if those challenging the constitutionality of Washington's anti-assisted suicide law were to prevail] it would result in a flow of cases through the court system for heaven knows how long." Ibid. at *39.

120. See David J. Garrow, "All Over but the Legislating: There Was a Genuine War over Abortion, These Writers Think, but the Armistice Appears to Be Durable," *New York Times,* Jan. 26, 1998, Book Review, at 14.

Part III

Judicial Principle and Clinical Practice

The Supreme Court and End-of-Life Care: Principled Distinctions or Slippery Slope?

Rebecca Dresser

In *Vacco v Quill*[1] and *Washington v Glucksberg,*[2] the Supreme Court upheld the constitutionality of state criminal laws prohibiting assisted suicide. According to the Court, competent, terminally ill persons do not have a constitutionally protected right to obtain from a willing physician medication to end their lives with greater comfort and dignity than would otherwise occur.

The Justices were unanimous in agreeing that the laws prohibiting physician-assisted suicide were constitutional. But the majority and four concurring opinions presented different rationales for this position. Taken together, the opinions suggest that terminally ill patients have a constitutionally protected interest in obtaining adequate palliative care, including pain medication that could hasten death, and terminal sedation. By conferring their approval on these practices, the Justices advanced current efforts to lessen the suffering of dying patients.

The Court's position on palliative care has important implications for patients and clinicians. Although proponents of legalized physician-assisted suicide were disappointed by the Court's decisions, the Justices did give patients explicit legal authority to control many dimensions of the dying process. And in granting patients this authority, the Justices also shielded clinicians acting to fulfill patients' choices from legal liability.

What additional interests in patient autonomy remain unrecognized? In other words, which patients, as well as prospective patients, might remain unsatisfied with the constitutional interests the Court acknowledged? On the other hand, what concerns might the Court's opinions trigger among those opposing legalization of physician-assisted suicide and active euthanasia? Has the Court established reasonably clear lines delineating permissible and impermissible conduct in hastening a patient's death, or has it taken a step down the slippery slope toward improper use of death-hastening measures?

In this chapter, I explore the clinical implications of the *Quill* and *Glucksberg* opinions. First, I recount the Justices' statements bearing on end-of-life care. Then I describe in detail practices the Justices included as part of the competent, terminally ill patient's constitutionally protected right to control the dying process, and I note weaknesses in their efforts to distinguish such practices from physician-assisted suicide. Next, I discuss why these practices fail to provide some patients with the sort of death they prefer. Last, I consider whether the end-of-life practices the Court authorized raise concerns about mistaken or coerced decisions similar to those raised in arguments against legalizing physician-assisted suicide. I conclude that because legal restrictions on all forms of end-of-life conduct are rarely enforced, the impact of the Court's decisions remains primarily in the hands of clinicians, patients, and families.

The Supreme Court Opinions

In *Glucksberg* and *Quill,* the Court evaluated whether laws prohibiting physician-assisted suicide for terminally ill patients violated the due process or equal protection doctrines. According to the due process doctrine, the government may not infringe an individual's fundamental rights unless it has a compelling reason to do so. In *Glucksberg,* the question was whether Washington's law prohibiting physician-assisted suicide (1) interfered with a fundamental right of terminally ill adults; and (2) if so, whether the government had a compelling reason to do so. Chief Justice Rehnquist, writing for the majority, found no historical or contemporary justification for considering access to physician-assisted suicide a fundamental right. As a result, Washington had only to offer a rational basis for its law against physician-assisted suicide. And as the opinion noted, Washington had numerous legitimate government interests in maintaining this prohibition.

Quill was an equal protection case. Equal protection doctrine requires the government to treat like cases alike. According to the doctrine, states must have a compelling reason to grant some persons a fundamental right and deny it to others. The plaintiffs in *Quill* argued that New York law violated the equal protection doctrine because the state permitted terminally ill persons dependent on medical interventions to hasten death by forgoing life-sustaining treatment but denied the option of a hastened death to similarly situated persons not dependent on life support. But again, the Court majority found no historical or contemporary support for the existence of a fundamental right to hasten death. The state's decision to give all New Yorkers a right to refuse unwanted treatment, but not a right to obtain physician-assisted suicide, was justified by material differences in the two practices.

In the course of presenting their constitutional analyses, Rehnquist and several other Justices discussed in detail patients' rights to forgo treatment and to receive adequate palliative care. Rehnquist's majority opinion in *Quill* relied on the concepts of causation and intent to explain why the Constitution protects these rights, but not a right to physician-assisted suicide.

The clinical and legal traditions that permit withholding and withdrawing life-sustaining medical interventions but prohibit assisted suicide are "important and logical," Rehnquist wrote. He joined many other judges in calling causation the key to the traditional distinctions. In forgoing treatment, he asserted, the patient's death results from the underlying illness or injury, but in assisted suicide, medication prescribed by the physician is the cause of death.[3]

Differences in causation cannot be invoked to distinguish permissible palliative care from impermissible assisted suicide, however. This is because, as Rehnquist acknowledged, pain-relieving agents sometimes cause patients to die sooner than they otherwise would. Rehnquist turned to the concept of intent to distinguish between risky palliative care and physician-assisted suicide. Physicians and patients participating in physician-assisted suicide, he wrote, act with the primary purpose of ending the patient's life. This purpose to cause death is missing when risky palliative care is administered. In the palliative care case, the physician and patient act with the aim of easing pain, not ending life. The clinician's primary intent is to keep the patient comfortable; the possible consequence of an earlier death is an unintended but unavoidable side effect.[4] It is reasonable, Rehnquist noted, for the state to prohibit acts intended to cause death, while permitting risky acts intended to produce a different and legally permissible end.

The lower appellate courts in *Quill* and *Glucksberg* had joined numerous writers in finding the concepts of causation and intent insufficient to justify differences in how the law regards physician-assisted suicide, forgoing treatment, and aggressive palliative care.[5] At various points in *Quill* and *Glucksberg,* Rehnquist implied or openly admitted that the two concepts do not always supply bright-line distinctions between acceptable and unacceptable end-of-life conduct. In discussing aggressive palliative care, he wrote, "[p]ainkilling drugs may hasten a patient's death, but the physician's purpose and intent is, or *may be,* only to ease his patient's pain."[6] Similarly, he said that the line between physician-assisted suicide and forgoing treatment sometimes "may not be clear."[7] Yet Rehnquist ultimately concluded that the concepts furnish a clear enough line to support the states' decisions to deny terminally ill patients legally protected access to physician-assisted suicide.

Two additional elements of the Rehnquist opinions bear on the decisions' implications for end-of-life care. First, each opinion includes a footnote agreeing with Justice Stevens that the Court's rulings leave open the possibility that a particular application of the laws prohibiting physician-assisted suicide would impermissibly limit a terminally ill patient's constitutionally protected freedom. Rehnquist did not describe such a situation, however. Presumably he included the footnotes so that Justice O'Connor would join and make his the majority opinions.[8] The footnotes, together with O'Connor's concurring opinion discussed later, strengthen the terminally ill patient's right to die free of unwanted pain and discomfort.

The second relevant point is in Rehnquist's *Glucksberg* opinion. After discussing why prior Supreme Court decisions on forgoing treatment and abortion do not justify according terminally ill patients a constitutionally protected interest in physician-assisted suicide, Rehnquist listed five legitimate government interests in prohibiting the practice: (1) a "symbolic and aspirational as well as practical" interest in preserving human life regardless of its quality; (2) an interest in preventing suicide, including the suicide of terminally ill people who are depressed or in pain due to substandard palliative care; (3) an interest in preserving the physician's traditional role of trusted healer; (4) an interest in preventing disadvantaged groups from being pressured into requesting physician-assisted suicide; and (5) an interest in avoiding the first step down a slippery slope toward extending physician-assisted death to patients unable to ingest medication independently and to those incapable of voluntary choice.[9] Later I discuss whether these government interests also exist when life-sustaining treatment is forgone or risky palliative care is administered.

Because they are the majority opinions, Rehnquist's analyses will stand as the Supreme Court's official statements. Yet O'Connor wrote a concurrence qualifying her agreement with the majority opinion. Her opinion, as well as the other concurrences, are likely to influence future legal developments. The concurrences focused on potential constitutional protection for the terminally ill individual's right to a death free from severe pain.

O'Connor joined the majority opinion because state laws prohibiting physician-assisted suicide permitted adequate pain medication for terminally ill patients, including medication "to alleviate . . . suffering, even to the point of causing unconsciousness and hastening death."[10] According to O'Connor, as long as they do not impede patients' access to palliative care, laws against physician-assisted suicide are permissible in light of the "difficulty in defining terminal illness and the risk that a dying patient's request for assistance in ending his or her life might not be truly voluntary. . . ."[11]

Although Stevens found the community's interest in the lives of its members sufficient to defeat the individual's "claim [of] a constitutional entitlement to complete autonomy in making a decision to end . . . life,"[12] he refused to rule out the possibility that in some circumstances a terminally ill patient would have a constitutionally protected interest in assisted suicide. In Stevens's view, a terminally ill person might have a constitutionally protected claim to physician-assisted suicide if lethal medication were the "only possible means of preserving a dying patient's dignity and alleviating her intolerable suffering."[13] According to Stevens, the right to refuse treatment recognized in *Cruzan v Missouri Department of Health* "embraces not merely a person's right to refuse a particular kind of unwanted treatment, but also her interest in dignity, and in determining the character of the memories that will survive long after her death."[14] Moreover, Stevens contended that the practice of terminal sedation illustrates the "illusory character" of the differences in intent and causation Rehnquist invoked. Stevens wrote,

> [T]he purpose of terminal sedation is to ease the suffering of the patient and comply with her wishes, and the actual cause of death is the administration of heavy doses of lethal sedatives. This same intent and

causation may exist when a doctor complies with a patient's request for lethal medication to hasten her death.[15]

Stevens implies that physician-assisted suicide should be permitted when performed with the same intent as terminal sedation.

Justice Souter also was unwilling to foreclose completely the possibility that some dying patients have a constitutionally protected interest in physician-assisted suicide. Souter derived that possibility from the Supreme Court's abortion decisions, state statutes and court decisions recognizing patients' rights to "medical counsel and assistance," and the states' decriminalization of suicide.[16] Souter found it unnecessary to settle this claim, however, because he thought the state's interest in preventing abuses of the right justified a continued criminal ban. Souter said that if physician-assisted suicide were legalized, patients might choose to die in response to financial pressures, and physicians would too often resort to voluntary and involuntary euthanasia to address the suffering of patients unable to give themselves medication or to choose assisted suicide. Souter was convinced that data from the Netherlands, together with New York's and Washington's arguments that regulation would be inadequate to prevent mistakes and abuse, justified the criminal prohibition, at least for now.

Finally, Justice Breyer said he agreed with O'Connor's opinion and the full Court's decision to uphold the laws against assisted suicide. He did not join the majority opinion, however, because he thought the Constitution and legal tradition protect a richer individual interest than Rehnquist's opinion described. He believed the Court's precedents support some form of "'right to die with dignity'" which has "at its core . . . personal control over the manner of death, professional medical assistance, and the avoidance of unnecessary and severe physical suffering combined."[17] Breyer concluded, however, that *Quill* and *Glucksberg* did not require the Court to evaluate the strength of this interest because the challenged laws permitted physicians to provide patients with adequate pain relief, even at the risk of hastening death. As long as the laws allowed terminally ill patients access to medical care to prevent "severe physical pain," Breyer wrote, the laws did not impermissibly restrict the individual's right to a dignified death. Though he acknowledged data indicating that many patients receive inadequate palliative care, he attributed this shortcoming to deficiencies in delivering care rather than to the effects of laws prohibiting assisted suicide.[18]

Permissible End-of-Life Practices

Taken together, the opinions of the Justices in *Quill* and *Glucksberg* elevated to constitutional status terminally ill patients' interests in forgoing life-sustaining treatment and receiving effective but potentially lethal pain medication, including terminal sedation. At a minimum, their opinions indicate that patients' constitutional rights would be violated if physicians forgoing life-sustaining treatment or administering risky palliative care were prosecuted for those actions. But how well did the Court distinguish between permissible and impermissible end-of-life conduct? Can the two categories be clearly divided in theory and in practice?

The Supreme Court joined numerous other courts in finding that competent, terminally ill patients have an unlimited right to refuse unwanted medical treatment, including medical nutrition and hydration. Though Rehnquist labeled the patient's underlying condition the cause of death in treatment refusals, this label cannot be legitimately applied to all such refusals. In many cases, forgoing treatment results in death because the patient's underlying condition means the patient's life depends on interventions such as respirators or tube feeding. In these cases, assigning the legal cause of death to the patient's condition is reasonable and morally defensible.[19] .

Yet a few lower courts have also upheld the right of a competent patient capable of eating to refuse both ordinary and medical nutrition and hydration.[20] In these cases, the patient's death results from a cause physically independent of the illness or injury; indeed, a completely healthy person could choose to die by refusing all forms of nourishment.

The Supreme Court has not addressed this sort of case, and Justice Scalia's opinion in *Cruzan* indicated that he would consider such a case to involve a form of suicide.[21] The Justices writing in *Quill* and *Glucksberg* failed to explain how assisted suicide differs from the clinical assistance provided to a dying cancer patient who chooses to stop all forms of nourishment when oral feeding remains possible. By failing to address this issue, the Justices lent tacit support to the claim that patients have a constitutional right to one (unattractive) form of assisted suicide: the right to assistance in ending life by dehydration or starvation.[22]

The Justices also failed to confront practical difficulties in determining when potentially lethal pain medication is permissible. In discussing the patient's right to adequate pain medication, including medication that could cause the patient to die sooner, the Justices adopted a framework resembling the Roman Catholic doctrine of double effect. This doctrine holds that an action having one good and one bad effect is permissible if it meets the following four criteria:

1. the act itself is either good or morally neutral;
2. the actor intends only the good effect;
3. the act directly causes both effects, as opposed to the bad effect causing the good effect; and
4. the moral importance of producing the good effect is sufficient to justify producing the bad effect (the proportionality condition).

In the clinical setting, these criteria are met when a terminally ill patient experiences pain that can be relieved only by medication that risks hastening death. The double-effect doctrine permits physicians aware of the lethal risk to administer such medication if their purpose is to provide pain relief. The doctrine does not permit physicians to administer a lethal dose of medication so that the patient will die and thereby be relieved of pain.[23]

Application of this doctrine in the clinical setting poses difficulties. To separate permissible from impermissible actions, observers must have accurate information on the physician's mental state. In criminal and other legal contexts, mental-state judgments play an important role in assessing legal responsibility. Yet it is questionable whether such judgments can or will be made accurately in the clinical setting.

For example, physician Timothy Quill has described the complexities in his mental state when he prescribed barbiturates to his patient Diane, who had terminal leukemia. After reading his account, some charged him with intentionally assisting in Diane's suicide, while others declared he had acted primarily to alleviate her suffering. Quill reported that he was "pleased to have my primary intention of alleviating pain and suffering acknowledged." At the same time, he characterized his mental state as more ambiguous than that: "if I did not also intend to ensure that Diane had the option of death should she find her suffering intolerable, why the prescription for barbiturates?"[24]

Quill criticizes a legal and ethical framework that relies on the double-effect doctrine to evaluate palliative care. He contends that this approach creates incentives for clinicians to deceive themselves and others about their true intentions. Moreover, he predicts that if medical ethics and the law "do not acknowledge the inescapable multiplicity of intentions in most double-effect situations, then most physicians will remain too fearful to help patients with these delicate deliberations."[25] Though the actual incidence of such deception and fear is unknown, the situation will not be helped by the Supreme Court's endorsement of a double-effect approach to palliative care.

The opinions by Rehnquist and O'Connor also distinguished terminal sedation from physician-assisted suicide. This practice has been adopted for terminally ill patients whose pain or anxiety about the dying process cannot be relieved by measures that leave them conscious.[26] In some cases, patients are sedated until they die from a complication of their illness or injury. In others, life-sustaining interventions (like mechanical ventilation or tube feeding) are removed. According to clinical accounts of terminal sedation, the patient's death may be caused by an untreatable problem related to the illness or injury, by respiratory depression related to the sedatives, or by the absence of the life-sustaining treatment.[27]

At least some cases of terminal sedation are difficult to distinguish from physician-assisted suicide. When forgoing life-sustaining treatment is part of the arrangement, the patient and physician may intend to cause death. When the arrangement involves withholding nutrition and hydration from a patient still capable of eating, the patient may die from a cause physically independent from the terminal condition. As David Orentlicher has commented, in these cases "it is the physician-created state of diminished consciousness that renders the patient unable to eat, not the patient's underlying disease."[28] According to Orentlicher, terminal sedation should be classified as a form of active euthanasia.[29]

In sum, there are conceptual and practical weaknesses in the distinctions the Court invoked to delineate the content of the terminally ill patient's constitutionally protected interests.[30] As Rehnquist admitted, the distinctions between protected and unprotected conduct are not always clear. Despite the gray areas, most of the Justices found the causation and intent analyses strong enough to justify maintaining a line between physician-assisted suicide and the practices they deemed constitutionally protected. Yet people favoring legalization of assisted suicide and active euthanasia, as well as those who consider certain approved practices equivalent to suicide and euthanasia, undoubtedly will criticize *Quill* and *Glucksberg* for failing to draw bolder lines between permissible and impermissible end-of-life conduct.

The Nature of the Protected Right

The Supreme Court reinforced and extended existing case law in recognizing not only a right to forgo all forms of life-sustaining treatment, but also a right to potentially lethal palliative care, including terminal sedation. Though some state statutes explicitly protect from liability physicians administering potentially lethal medication necessary to relieve pain,[31] to my knowledge no legislation or case law had previously conferred explicit protection on physicians performing terminal sedation.

The Court's pronouncements on palliative care should give some satisfaction to supporters of legalized physician-assisted suicide and active euthanasia who desire to increase patients' autonomy and well-being at the end of life,[32] for *Quill* and *Glucksberg* bolster the campaign to increase terminally ill patients' control and comfort during the dying process. In essence, the Supreme Court conferred high significance on the patient's right to be free of unwanted pain, anxiety, and medical interventions.

Certain patient and advocacy-group objectives are left out of *Quill* and *Glucksberg,* however. In criticizing the Court for disapproving physician-assisted suicide while approving terminal sedation, David Orentlicher wrote:

> Although terminal sedation ensures a painless death, it forces patients
> to accept a dying process that is prolonged as compared with what it
> would be if assisted suicide and euthanasia were performed. Terminal
> sedation requires that patients linger in a state that may profoundly
> compromise their dignity and further distort the memory they leave
> behind. Terminal sedation also prevents patients from retaining some
> control over the timing and circumstances of their death, a control
> that may be critical to their psychological well-being.[33]

More graphically, a *New York Times* editorial on the decisions noted with approval Laurence Tribe's statement that terminal sedation has "the dehumanizing effect of turning the patient into a decaying zombie."[34] Other commentators noted that terminal sedation is unacceptable to patients who see consciousness as central to human dignity; these patients reject the prospect of a prolonged dying without awareness.[35] Terminal sedation denies patients an opportunity to communicate with loved ones during the final stage of life as well.[36] Finally, the intensive clinical attention necessary in terminal sedation may require patients who would rather die at home to die in health-care facilities.[37]

These criticisms build on Ronald Dworkin's concept of the individual's interest in creating a coherent life narrative, one that includes a final chapter in harmony with one's earlier life. According to Dworkin, the state should respect—indeed, encourage—this "ideal of integrity," and part of doing so entails giving terminally ill persons freedom to choose a medication overdose when that best suits their values.[38] For Dworkin and his cosigners of the "Philosophers' Brief" to the Supreme Court, it is not enough to protect patients from pain: "Even if it were possible to eliminate all pain for a dying patient . . . that would not end or even much alleviate the anguish some would feel at remaining alive, but intubated, helpless, and often sedated near oblivion."[39]

Stevens was the sole member of the Supreme Court who expressly endorsed the more robust constitutional interest favored by these commentators,[40] but even he was unwilling to label this interest sufficiently compelling to justify a complete ban on laws prohibiting physician-assisted suicide for terminally ill patients. Souter voiced some sympathy for the broader concept but found competing state interests sufficient to override even an enriched constitutional right. Breyer also supported a general right to die with dignity, but he found that right satisfied by laws permitting patients to avoid severe pain.

Was the Court correct in refusing to recognize this richer notion of a right to die with dignity? Though some critics deem the Court's failure cruel and dismissive of many patients' central concerns, others defend the Court's narrower rights concept. Supporters of this narrower concept contend that giving patients and physicians greater control over dying would be both unwarranted and dangerous.

One notable representative of this group is philosopher Daniel Callahan. According to Callahan, because assisted suicide is outside the physician's professional and moral role, the individual patient has no legitimate claim to it. In *The Troubled Dream of Life,* Callahan writes:

> It is not the purpose of medicine to give us control over our human destiny, or to help us devise a life to our private specifications—and especially the specification most desired these days, that of complete control over death and its circumstances. That is not the role of medi-

cine because it has no competence to manage the meaning of life and death—the deepest and oldest human questions—but only some of the physical and psychological manifestations of those problems.[41]

Callahan contends that authorizing physicians to engage in assisted suicide would not only give them too much power, it would be an inadequate and mistaken social response to the suffering of the dying. Neither law nor ethics should encourage, in his view, the notion that a dignified death is one that we can fully control. According to Callahan, "We evade the full meaning of death if we think it can be redeemed or transformed by control over the details of the dying. . . ."[42]

Others have questioned whether patients actually need explicit legal authorization to commit suicide. These writers have observed that many patients desiring the quicker and simpler death a medication overdose provides can fulfill their wishes without the help of a doctor.[43] Others "with a good and trusting relationship with a compassionate physician [can] achieve their objective within the bounds of a private and discreet relationship, but without the cover and consolation of law."[44] But legalization advocates have responded that criminalizing physician-assisted suicide deprives patients of the skilled medical attention that is sometimes needed to help patients die comfortably from a medication overdose.[45]

Supporters of the Supreme Court decision also argue that the Court's refusal to protect greater individual autonomy over the timing and manner of one's death is justified by state interests in preventing mistaken and coerced requests for physician-assisted suicide. This argument assumes that these dangers are greater for legalized physician-assisted suicide than they are for refusing treatment and seeking aggressive palliative care. In the next section, I consider the validity of this assumption.

Did the Court Avoid the Slippery Slope?

As I said earlier, Rehnquist listed several government interests that justify prohibiting assisted suicide for terminally ill patients. Because the majority recognized no constitutionally protected interest in physician-assisted suicide, New York and Washington had to present merely a rational basis for their criminal prohibitions. But even the Justices inclined to establish a broader constitutionally protected interest for terminally ill patients seemed to agree that the risk of error and abuse would generally support significant restrictions on this interest.

In *Quill* and *Glucksberg,* none of the Justices acknowledged that the end-of-life conduct they deemed constitutionally protected raises concerns about error and abuse similar to those they thought justified the prohibition on physician-assisted suicide. Here the Court joined many opponents of legalized physician-assisted suicide and active euthanasia in assuming that the dangers of mistaken, coerced, and nonvoluntary decisions justify more significant procedural and substantive restrictions on these practices than are applied to permissible end-of-life practices.

Is this a valid assumption? In the absence of solid empirical data, it is difficult to judge. One claim is that the dangers of assisted suicide and active euthanasia are especially great because there are more potential candidates for these measures than for currently accepted practices. Seth Kreimer's assertions are representative:

> [A] right to refuse treatment puts at risk only the lives of those who would die without treatment. While this is a considerable number of people, the approval of active euthanasia or assisted suicide would extend the risk to the entire population. Particularly with the emergence of cost controls and managed care in the United States, the danger of tempting health care providers to persuade chronic patients to minimize costs by ending it all is no fantasy.[46]

Though it is true that fewer people depend on life-sustaining medical care than are seriously ill, terminal sedation could produce death in anyone. Furthermore, if any patient has the right to refuse oral and medical nutrition, then any patient could die by doing so. In short, no patient, indeed, no person, is necessarily disqualified from dying while conscious or unconscious due to lack of nourishment.[47]

One can also question why smaller numbers justify less concern about abuses. If the state values each life and seeks to protect each person from premature death due to financial pressures, depression, mistaken diagnosis, incapacity, or other vulnerability, then it should require effective safeguards against all such deaths. Yet everyone who spends time in hospitals knows such deaths may occur when life-sustaining treatment is forgone or risky palliative care is given.

The Justices joined other writers in worrying that permitting assisted suicide for competent terminally ill persons would lead to assisted suicide and active euthanasia for less seriously ill patients and people incapable of independent choice. Souter wrote: "The case for the slippery slope is fairly made out here . . . because there is a plausible case that the right claimed would not be readily containable by reference to facts about the mind that are difficult matters of judgment, or by gatekeepers of the mind who are subject to temptation, noble or not."[48] Souter believed that in the absence of easily verifiable criteria, physicians would assist in the suicides of persons not truly competent and perform euthanasia on patients perceived to be suffering but physically or mentally incapable of performing the lethal act themselves. But these possibilities also exist when physicians forgo life-sustaining treatment or provide aggressive palliative care and terminal sedation.[49] Concerns about improperly hastening the deaths of vulnerable people arise whenever clinicians' acts or omissions cause patients to die sooner than they otherwise would.[50]

A realist must also admit that banning assisted suicide and active euthanasia has not prevented them; indeed, proponents of legalizing them argue that mistakes and abuse would occur less often if they were permitted, but regulated.[51] This, too, is speculative, since with legalization hidden mistakes and abuses could still occur.[52]

In sum, misuses of all forms of end-of-life conduct are possible and should be troubling. Does this mean that all end-of-life conduct should be prohibited or strictly regulated because the risk of mistake and abuse is too great?[53] Or does the current acceptance of this risk in the context of forgoing life-sustaining treatment and aggressive palliative care mean that the risk should also be accepted for physician-assisted suicide?

Competing values and practical considerations make the first scenario unlikely. Today, hardly anyone would accept the moral and social consequences of prohibiting the practices of forgoing life-sustaining treatment and aggressive palliative care. Moreover, cost considerations and a desire to avoid intrusions on patients and families have kept the law from imposing an external regulatory system to monitor accepted end-of-life practices. A rigorous regulatory approach to such practices would be opposed by patients, families, clinicians, and most of the general public.

The second scenario may come to pass, at least in some states. *Quill* and *Glucksberg* left states free to decide whether the risks of physician-assisted suicide can be adequately managed. Because Oregon has now legalized that practice, we can look forward to empirical data on it.[54] Moreover, one could argue that society already accepts the risk of mistakes and abuse in physician-assisted suicide and active euthanasia, for these practices are to a large extent de facto permitted, though formally prohibited.[55]

The reality is that the legal restrictions on all forms of end-of-life conduct are rarely enforced through regulation or prosecution. Instead, clinicians, patients, and families largely control whether formal legal principles are observed and whether patients die inappropriately.

Conclusion

Did the Supreme Court in *Quill* and *Glucksberg* exhibit surprising sensitivity to the needs of dying patients? Alternatively, did the Justices perpetuate a system of "winks and nods" that allows savvy patients to obtain physician-assisted suicide and leaves other patients vulnerable to mistaken and abusive decisions to hasten death through forgoing treatment and risky palliative care? I believe that either characterization has some validity, but I would prefer to find a different message in the decisions.

In the contemporary United States, decisions on the timing and manner of death depend less on formal law than on the beliefs and attitudes of clinicians and, to a lesser extent, of patients and their families. The hard reality is that many clinicians will not comply with constraints they deem unreasonable or unethical, and those failing to observe legal rules will rarely be detected and yet more rarely held accountable.[56] Some clinicians will provide or administer lethal medication to patients requesting it. Some clinicians will intentionally hasten death under the cover of offering palliative care in response to a patient's or family's request or to their own wish to end the patient's or family's ordeal. Some clinicians will withhold life-sustaining treatment for patients whose treatment refusals are tainted by depression, inadequately treated pain, or economic concerns. Some clinicians will withhold life-prolonging treatment from elderly incompetent patients to relieve families and society of the burdens of caring for such patients.

For better or worse, the most effective way for government officials to influence end-of-life conduct is to support and participate in development of clinical guidelines and education on the care of terminally and seriously ill patients. The need for guidelines on the appropriate use of terminal sedation is particularly pressing, for case reports suggest that clinicians do not always take adequate measures to guard against inappropriate application of this procedure.[57] Although guidelines do exist on forgoing treatment and administering risky pain-relieving medications, empirical studies indicate that implementation is sadly inadequate.[58] Moreover, despite the increasing number of people with Alzheimer's disease and other forms of dementia, many questions remain about end-of-life care for conscious incompetent patients.[59]

For me, *Quill* and *Glucksberg* reinforce the need for policy action at the clinical level. Professional organizations, medical and nursing schools, and health-care facilities will determine whether and how the law is observed. Court decisions and legislation will have much greater impact if they are integrated into clinical guidelines and practice; this integration will occur only if clinicians are persuaded of the merits of the law's positions.[60] Dialogue and cooperation are most likely to lead doctors to protect patients and show them respect and compassion as they die. Now that the Supreme Court has spoken, perhaps we can move to the less glamorous yet more essential task of working through the concrete meaning of a right to die with dignity.

NOTES

1. 117 S Ct 2293 (1997).

2. 117 S Ct 2258 (1997).

3. *Quill,* 117 S Ct at 2298.

4. Ibid. at 2298–99.

5. *Quill v Vacco,* 80 F3d 716, 727–30 (1996); *Compassion in Dying v Washington,* 79 F3d 790, 822–23 (1996); Dan W. Brock, *Voluntary Active Euthanasia,* 22 Hastings Center Report 10 (Mar/Apr 1992).

6. *Quill,* 117 S Ct at 2298–99 (emphasis added).

7. Ibid. at 2302.

8. See Robert A. Burt, *The Supreme Court Speaks: Not Assisted Suicide But a Constitutional Right to Palliative Care,* 337 New England Journal of Medicine 1234 (1997). For discussion of the complexities and uncertainties characterizing

the Justices' views on this possibility, see Sonia M. Suter, *Ambivalent Unanimity: An Analysis of the Supreme Court's Holding,* in this volume.

9. 117 S Ct at 2271–75.

10. 117 S Ct at 2303 (O'Connor, J., concurring).

11. Ibid.

12. Ibid. at 2305 (Stevens, J., concurring in the judgments). For extensive discussion of the community interests implicated in the debate over legalization of physician-assisted suicide, see Peter J. Hammer, *Assisted Suicide and the Challenge of Individually Determined Collective Rationality,* in this volume.

13. 117 S Ct at 2305 (Stevens, J., concurring in the judgments).

14. Ibid. at 2306 (footnote omitted).

15. Ibid. at 2310.

16. Ibid. at 2288–90 (Souter, J., concurring in the judgments).

17. Ibid. at 2311 (Breyer, J., concurring in the judgments).

18. Ibid. at 2312. As Sonia Suter notes, some of the Justices may have been suggesting that the Constitution requires states "to ensure that people are not prevented from receiving adequate palliative care." See Suter, in this volume (cited in note 8). I agree with her that this requirement would raise many questions regarding the nature of this duty, the definition of adequate care, and the requisite level of patient access to such care.

19. Some question the attribution of causation even under these circumstances, however. See, for example, *Quill v Vacco,* 80 F3d at 729; Patrick D. Hopkins, *Why Does Removing Machines Count as "Passive" Euthanasia?* 27 Hastings Center Report 29 (May/June 1997).

20. *Bouvia v Superior Court,* 179 Cal App 3d 1127, 225 Cal Rptr 297 (1986); *Plaza Health and Rehabilitation Center* (NY Sup Ct, Onondaga County, Feb. 2, 1984). See also David Margolick, "Judge Says Ailing Man, 85, May Fast to Death," *New York Times,* Feb 3, 1984, A1 (describing situation in *Plaza Health*). Although the majority opinion in *Bouvia* portrayed the situation as a treatment refusal, a concurring judge wrote that the patient was obviously seeking to commit suicide by starvation and called on the court to acknowledge this and provide immunity to health professionals helping Bouvia to achieve her goal. *Bouvia,* 179 Cal App 3d at 1146, 225 Cal Rptr at 307 (Compton, J., concurring).

21. *Cruzan v Director, Missouri Department of Health,* 110 S Ct 2841, 2861 (Scalia, J., concurring).

22. The Justices' approval of terminal sedation means that patients also have a right to be made unconscious while they end life in this manner.

Some writers endorse refusal of nutrition and hydration as an alternative to taking a lethal dose of medication. See James L. Bernat, Bernard Gert, & R. Peter Mogielnicki, *Patient Refusal of Hydration and Nutrition: An Alternative to Physician-Assisted Suicide or Voluntary Active Euthanasia,* 153 Archives of Internal Medicine 2723 (1993). For a physician's account of his mother's desire for assisted suicide and eventual death following her decision to stop eating and drinking, see David Eddy, *A Conversation With My Mother,* 272 Journal of the American Medical Association 179 (1994).

23. See Timothy Quill, Rebecca Dresser, & Dan Brock, *The Rule of Double Effect: A Critique of Its Role in End-of-Life Decision Making,* 337 New England Journal of Medicine 1768–71 (1997).

24. Timothy Quill, *The Ambiguity of Clinical Intentions,* 329 New England Journal of Medicine 1039 (1993). Some empirical data indicate mixed intentions in end-of-life conduct. For example, in twelve of thirty-three cases studied, physicians reported that hastening death was one of their reasons for ordering sedatives and analgesics in patients whose life-sustaining treatment was withheld or withdrawn. See William C. Wilson, Nicholas G. Smedira, & Carol Fink, *Ordering and Administration of Sedatives and Analgesics During the Withholding and Withdrawal of Life Support for Critically Ill Patients,* 267 Journal of the American Medical Association 949 (1992).

25. Quill, 329 New England Journal of Medicine at 1040 (cited in note 24). Another physician agrees that ethical and legal approval of the double-effect approach encourages dishonesty among physicians. He contends that the commonly provided morphine drip to dying patients "is undeniably euthanasia, hidden by the cosmetics of professional tradition and language." See Thomas A. Preston, "Killing Pain, Ending Life," *New York Times,* Nov 1, 1994, A15.

26. According to one account, some patients can obtain adequate symptom control with "conscious sedation" in which they remain responsive to verbal stimuli. Paul Rousseau, *Terminal Sedation in the Care of Dying Patients,* 156 Archives of Internal Medicine 1785 (1996).

27. See David Orentlicher, *The Supreme Court and Physician-Assisted Suicide: Rejecting Assisted Suicide But Embracing Euthanasia,* 337 New England Journal of Medicine 1236 (1997); Robert Troug et al., *Barbiturates in the Care of the Terminally Ill,* 327 New England Journal of Medicine 1678 (1992).

A 1996 review of the empirical literature found that from 5% to 52% of terminally ill patients studied were sedated for otherwise unrelievable symptoms. Rousseau, 156 Archives of Internal Medicine 1785 (cited in note 26).

28. Orentlicher, 337 New England Journal of Medicine at 1237 (cited in note 27).

29. Some clinicians oppose terminal sedation on grounds that it is a form of physician-assisted suicide. See John Sholl and Sinead Donnelly, Kristine Nelson, & T. Declan Walsh, *Correspondence,* 328 New England Journal of Medicine 1350 (1993).

30. As Arthur Frank points out, ordinary persons may be indifferent to these distinctions as well. Arthur W. Frank, *From Story to Law: Euthanasia and Authenticity,* in this volume.

31. The statutes are described in Norman L. Cantor & George C. Thomas, *Pain Relief, Acceleration of Death, and Criminal Law,* 6 Kennedy Institute of Ethics Journal 102, 123 n3 (1996).

32. Some legalization advocates see improved palliative care as a central concern of their movement. See Diane Gianelli, *Court's Recognition of Assisted Suicide Leaves Door Ajar,* 40 American Medical News 1, 24 (July 14, 1997).

33. Orentlicher, 337 New England Journal of Medicine at 1238 (cited in note 27) (footnote omitted).

34. "Assisted Suicide and the Law," *New York Times,* Jan 6, 1997, A12.

35. Timothy E. Quill, Bernard Lo, & Dan W. Brock, *Palliative Options of Last Resort,* 278 Journal of the American Medical Association 2099, 2100 (1997).

36. See Frank, *From Story to Law: Euthanasia and Authenticity,* in this volume.

37. Quill, Lo, & Brock, 278 Journal of the American Medical Association 2100 (cited in note 35).

38. Ronald Dworkin, *Life's Dominion: An Argument about Abortion, Euthanasia, and Individual Freedom* 208–17 (Knopf, 1993). For additional discussion of this concept, see Frank, *From Story to Law: Euthanasia and Authenticity,* this volume.

39. Ronald Dworkin et al, *Assisted Suicide: The Philosophers' Brief,* New York Review of Books 41, 44 (Mar 27, 1997). Of course, patients objecting to intubation are constitutionally free to have the tubes removed.

   In an introduction to publication of the brief, Ronald Dworkin also suggested that terminal sedation may not provide relief from pain for all patients. As support, he cited an amicus brief of the Coalition of Hospice Professionals, which asserted that lack of pain in patients undergoing terminal sedation cannot be verified. See ibid. at 42 n8.

40. In his *Glucksberg* and *Quill* concurrence, Stevens asserted that the state should recognize the "individual's interest in choosing a final chapter that accords with her life story, rather than one that demeans her values and poisons memories of her."

41. Daniel Callahan, *The Troubled Dream of Life: Living with Mortality* 101 (Simon & Schuster, 1993).

42. Ibid. at 147.

43. See, e.g., John Arras, *News From the Circuit Courts: How Not to Think About Physician-Assisted Suicide,* BioLaw S:171, S:182 (Special Section, July/Aug, 1996).

44. Ibid.

45. Quill et al., 278 Journal of the American Medical Association at 2100 (cited in note 35).

46. Seth F. Kreimer, *Does Pro-Choice Mean Pro-Kevorkian? An Essay on Roe, Casey, and the Right to Die,* 44 American University Law Review 803, 841 (footnote omitted).

47. As David Orentlicher notes, terminal sedation can be performed on persons not seriously ill, depressed persons, and those who fail to consent. See Orentlicher, 337 New England Journal of Medicine at 1238 (cited in note 27).

48. *Glucksberg,* 117 S Ct at 2291 (Souter, J., concurring).

49. For discussion of these possibilities in the context of forgoing treatment, see Mark D. Sullivan & Stuart J. Youngner, *Depression, Competence, and the Right to Refuse Lifesaving Medical Treatment,* 151 American Journal of Psychiatry 971 (1994); David L. Jackson & Stuart J. Youngner, *Patient Autonomy and "Death With Dignity": Some Clinical Caveats,* 301 New England Journal of Medicine 404 (1979). In a newspaper article published soon after the Supreme Court decisions were issued, several physicians described forgoing life-sustaining treatment and administering risky pain medications without explicitly discussing these decisions with patients and their families. Gina Kolata, "'Passive Euthanasia' Is the Norm in Today's Hospitals, Doctors Say," *New York Times,* June 28, 1997, A1.

   In commenting on the Supreme Court decisions, Ronald Dworkin noted that administration of pain medication that could hasten death is not regulated; thus, he claimed, vulnerable patients are more at risk of improperly hastened death in this context than they would be if assisted suicide were permitted but regulated. Ronald Dworkin, *Assisted Suicide: What the Supreme Court Really Said,* New York Review of Books 40 (Sept 25, 1997).

   The medical literature describes cases in which terminal sedation or terminal dehydration was administered in the absence of the patient's contemporaneous or clear prior consent. For a case in which a family authorized terminal sedation without having a clear indication of the patient's wishes, see Truog et al, 327 New England Journal of Medicine at 1679 (cited in note 27). For a case in which a patient with moderate dementia and other serious but not immediately life-threatening health problems died after she began refusing food and her family and physician decided not to intervene, see Louise A. Printz, *Terminal Dehydration, a Compassionate Treatment,* 152 Archives of Internal Medicine 697 (1992).

50. Early in this century, Dr. Harry Haiselden was willing to engage in any form of this conduct in his quest to end the lives of "defective" infants. See Martin S. Pernick, *Eugenic Euthanasia in Early Twentieth-Century America and Medically Assisted Suicide Today: Differences and Similarities,* in this volume.

See also Yale Kamisar, *When Is There a Constitutional "Right to Die"? When Is There No Constitutional "Right to Live"?,* 25 Georgia Law Review 1203, 1216–17 (1991). In discussing the possibilities for abuse in the nontreatment context, Kamisar has argued that active euthanasia may be less subject to abuse than passive, because of the greater "repugnance" felt toward active measures. See also Brock, Hastings Center Report at 22 (cited in note 5). Brock suggests that because the Netherlands gives families less authority to permit nontreatment of incompetent patients, the Dutch may view the U.S. as "*already* on the slippery slope in having given surrogates broad authority to forgo life-sustaining treatment for incompetent persons."

51. See, e.g., Timothy Quill, Christine Cassel & Diane Meier, *Care of the Hopelessly Ill,* 327 New England Journal of Medicine 1380, 1383 (1992). These authors contend that with the current secret practice of assisted suicide, "decisions depend more on the physician's values and willingness to take risks than on the compelling nature of the patient's request."

52. Physician Diane Meier reportedly has suggested that with legalization, physicians now willing to violate the law could become even more liberal in determining which persons should receive assisted suicide and active euthanasia. See Herbert Hendin, *Assisted Suicide and Active Euthanasia: An Exchange,* New York Review of Books 68, 69 (Nov 6, 1997).

53. Some writers fear the debate over legalized physician-assisted suicide and voluntary active euthanasia could trigger increased judicial and legislative scrutiny of and restrictions on forgoing life-sustaining treatment. See, e.g., Susan Wolf, *Holding the Line on Euthanasia,* 19 Hastings Center Report 13 (Jan/Feb, 1989). Although I would oppose significant revisions in the rules governing forgoing life-sustaining treatment, I believe it is important to acknowledge their possible weaknesses and attempt to prevent inappropriate decisions to withhold or withdraw treatment.

54. See *Suicide Aid Prevails in Oregon,* American Medical Association News 2 (Nov 17, 1997).

55. In surveys of physician practices in the 1990s, numerous physicians report granting requests from patients for assisted suicide or active euthanasia. See, e.g., Lee R. Slome, Thomas F. Mitchell, & Edwin Charlebois, *Physician-Assisted Suicide and Patients With Human*

Immunodeficiency Virus Disease, 336 New England Journal of Medicine 417 (1997); Melinda A. Lee, Heidi D. Nelson, & Virginia P. Tilden, *Legalizing Assisted Suicide—Views of Physicians in Oregon,* 334 New England Journal of Medicine 310 (1996); Anthony L. Back et al., *Physician-Assisted Suicide and Euthanasia in Washington State,* 275 Journal of the American Medical Association 919 (1996).

56. For detailed discussion, see Ann Alpers, *Criminal Act or Palliative Care? Prosecutions Involving the Care of the Dying,* 26 Journal of Law, Medicine, & Ethics 308 (1998).

57. See J. Andrew Billings & Susan D. Block, *Slow Euthanasia,* 12 Journal of Palliative Care 21 (1996); cases discussed in note 49. See also Rousseau, 156 Archives of Internal Medicine at 1785 (cited in note 26). This author contends that terminal sedation should be performed only in the "presence of terminal disease with impending death, exhaustion of all other palliative treatments, agreement by patient and family members of the need for sedation, and a current do-not-resuscitate order." It is unclear whether there is general agreement with this position, however.

58. See, e.g., SUPPORT Principal Investigators, *A Controlled Trial to Improve Care for Seriously Ill Hospitalized Patients: The Study to Understand Prognoses and Preferences for Outcomes and Risks of Treatments (SUPPORT),* 274 Journal of the American Medical Association 1591 (1995). This empirical study of care of hospitalized seriously ill patients found that physicians were often unaware of patient and family treatment preferences and many seriously ill patients experienced serious pain.

59. See generally Rebecca Dresser & Peter Whitehouse, *The Incompetent Patient on the Slippery Slope,* 24 Hastings Center Report 6 (July/Aug, 1994).

60. Here I agree with Carl Schneider that judges are unlikely to produce the best biomedical policy. See Carl Schneider, *Making Biomedical Policy through Constitutional Adjudication: The Example of Physician-Assisted Suicide,* in this volume. But I would go further to suggest that legislators and regulators are unlikely to produce good policy in the absence of substantial input and guidance from professional and patient advocacy organizations, health-care institutions, and individual clinicians and patients.

CHAPTER 5 **Physician-Assisted Suicide in the Courts: Moral Equivalence, Double Effect, and Clinical Practice**

Howard Brody

When the U.S. Supreme Court agreed to hear appeals from the rulings of the Second and Ninth Circuit Courts of Appeals[1] on whether laws prohibiting physician-assisted suicide (PAS) were constitutional, it opened the way for a legal debate over two relatively arcane ethical concepts. The *moral equivalence hypothesis* holds that if allowing a patient to die by forgoing life-sustaining medical treatment is moral (or immoral), then PAS or active euthanasia must be moral (or immoral) to the same degree. The *principle of double effect* holds that it is moral to administer high-dose narcotics to dying patients, even though there may be some risk of hastening death, whereas it is not moral to administer an overdose of such drugs deliberately to cause death.

These two ethical constructs can be debated in detail and at length, and the protracted discussion would be of great interest in a graduate seminar on ethical theory; however, it would probably put the average physician or attorney promptly to sleep. Nonetheless, the two ethical constructs have, in an implicit rule-of-thumb fashion, helped to guide routine medical practice for some time. Most physicians have conducted their practices as if the moral equivalence hypothesis were false and the principle of double effect were true.

It was therefore striking when the two federal appellate courts recognized a constitutional liberty interest in PAS on grounds that strongly suggested the moral equivalence hypothesis is true and the principle of double effect amounts to hypocritical rationalization. Admittedly, the average physician does not dissect the detailed reasoning in court decisions and modify her clinical practice accordingly. But it is at least noteworthy, if not actually worrisome, when such a radical disconnect appears between the reasoning of federal judges and of practicing physicians on a highly controversial matter of medical practice.

This Article will summarize the recent history of the two ethical constructs and identify the role they played in the two appellate court rulings. It will then assess the final rulings of the Supreme Court and discuss their possible implications for clinical practice in the future. Although the Article will allude to

This essay originally appeared in 82 Minnesota Law Review 939 (April 1998).
Reprinted by permission.

what ethics scholars and the courts have said about these issues, its principal focus will be upon the ethical "rules of thumb" under which physicians operate in everyday practice. In many ways, the quality of care that patients receive depends more on these crude and under-analyzed rules of thumb than on more elegant and logically consistent theories of ethical and legal behavior.[2]

The Moral Equivalence Hypothesis

A defining moment of sorts occurred in the emerging field of bioethics in 1975 when a philosopher, James Rachels, published a paper on the moral equivalence hypothesis in the *New England Journal of Medicine*.[3] It was quite a new development at the time for a philosopher to presume to instruct physicians on medical ethics, especially when the philosopher was declaring that a widely accepted ethical principle was in fact fatally flawed and when the medical editor of a major journal was granting him the forum to do so. Despite the revolutionary nature of the article, subsequent letters to the editor showed that the average practitioner remained unswayed by the philosophical arguments.[4]

Rachels took direct aim at the American Medical Association's (AMA's) ethical stance that physicians could withdraw or withhold life-prolonging medical therapy, but could never ethically participate in mercy killing.[5] Expressing relative indifference to the question of whether active euthanasia was ethical or unethical, Rachels zeroed in on the conceptual dilemma: Is it consistent to have one ethical judgment about allowing a patient to die and a different ethical judgment about active killing? Rachels agreed that most cases of active killing were indeed morally wrong, while many cases of allowing to die were morally defensible, but that left open the question of whether these different moral judgments arose *because of* what Rachels called the "bare difference" between killing and allowing to die, or for other reasons unique to the individual cases or categories of cases involved.

Rachels proposed to resolve this dilemma through a sort of ethical experiment. He constructed a hypothetical case in which the only difference between two actions was the "bare difference" between killing and allowing to die; all other morally compelling features, such as consequences, motives, and intentions, were held constant. He called this hypothetical case the case of Smith and Jones. Supposedly, Smith and Jones each stand to gain an inheritance at the death of a nephew; each sneaks in while the nephew is taking a bath, fully intending to hold the child's head underwater until he drowns. Smith does exactly that, but Jones happens to enter the bathroom just as the child slips, hits his head on the edge of the tub, and falls unconscious with his face submerged. Jones could easily save the child's life by reaching in and lifting his head above water, but instead he stands and watches as the child drowns.

Rachels wondered whether any reader would judge Smith and Jones *differently,* based on the distinction that one actively killed the nephew while the other "merely" allowed him to die. No one offered a justification for doing anything other than condemning both Smith and Jones to an equal degree. This, to Rachels, proved his point. If we judge the case of killing to be morally worse than the case of letting die, it must be due to some difference in the motives, intentions, or consequences of the act, not any general or principled difference between the two actions per se.

Other philosophers and ethicists have been debating Rachels's conclusions in the twenty-three years since the article's publication, and no single consensus position has emerged.[6] I would, however, defend as the best conclusion a critique of Rachels's basic method. What led Rachels to assume that he could answer the general question of whether forgoing treatment and active euthanasia were morally equivalent merely by devising a pair of hypothetical cases, especially cases that had nothing to do with medical practice? Rachels explained that he could do so to the extent that ethical rules and principles are universally applicable, and are thus largely independent of the real-life context of the individual case.[7] If one begins to challenge this view of ethical reasoning, as has occurred with increasing frequency in the last twenty years,[8] then one is less convinced by Rachels's logic.

Perhaps the most thorough rebuttal of Rachels was suggested by Paul Menzel.[9] Menzel argued that in some medical contexts, there might be a major moral difference between killing and allowing to die; in other medical contexts, the difference might be less or even nonexistent. In the end, he disagreed with both Rachels and the AMA. He disagreed with Rachels by saying that only after exploring in detail the actual case circumstances could one judge whether allowing to die and killing might be morally equivalent. And he disagreed with the AMA by noting that in at least some medical contexts, if allowing to die was acceptable, then the logic of the circumstances would dictate that active euthanasia would be acceptable as well. It is precisely the set of cases where Menzel saw the moral difference between killing and allowing to die approaching zero that we now view as the "best candidate" for permitting PAS: a competent, suffering, terminally ill patient who has exhausted all other means for symptom relief.

I have tried to extend Menzel's general line of argument to show that the killing/letting die distinction fails to do the moral "work" that many expect of it.[10] One might argue that killing is wrong and allowing to die by forgoing treatment is acceptable because in killing, one directly intends and causes death, which is not true of allowing to die. I have tried to show through medical case examples that the degree to which one intends and causes death varies along a spectrum; there is no bright line that separates allowing to die and killing. For example, there are a few cases, admittedly atypical, in which a patient has suicidal impulses for what most would consider irrational reasons, but also happens to be dependent upon medical life support. If such a patient refuses ongoing life support and dies as a consequence, is that PAS or "merely" forgoing life-sustaining therapy? Certainly the patient, if minimally competent, has a legal right to refuse the treatment, even in Jurisdictions where PAS is illegal.

A succinct summary of the validity of the moral equivalence hypothesis was provided a decade ago by Raanan Gillon.[11] He distinguished two arguments: that there is a necessary moral *equivalence* between killing and letting die, and that there is no necessary moral *difference* between killing and letting die. Both, he states, are false; there are a few circumstances in which letting a patient die would be morally equivalent to killing the patient, but there are many more cases in which, due to the specific circumstances, the two acts would be quite morally distinct. The problem, he suggests, is that many seem to conclude from the fact that there is no necessary moral difference that killing and allowing to die must necessarily be morally equivalent. For Gillon, Rachels's thought experiment may have successfully proven that in at least one circumstance there is no necessary moral difference, but it certainly failed to show that there is necessary moral equivalence.

Of late, even staunch defenders of PAS and active euthanasia either have avoided using the moral equivalence hypothesis, or else appeared aware of its difficulties. For example, Dan Brock, in one of the most cogent philosophical defenses of a right to PAS and euthanasia,[12] was careful not to employ the moral equivalence hypothesis in its pure form. He argued not that PAS and forgoing treatment are equivalent moral acts, but rather that *the same reasons* that justify forgoing treatment, such as appeals to patient autonomy and a desire to relieve suffering, are the reasons that can be given in defense of PAS.

Against this backdrop, it seemed somewhat odd when in 1992 a note appeared in the *Harvard Law Review* accepting the moral equivalence hypothesis more or less uncritically as a basis for declaring a fundamental right to PAS.[13] In retrospect, this note indeed presaged the two appellate court rulings of 1996, but when the argument first appeared in print it seemed hardly likely to play in Peoria.

Opinion polls give a crude measure of where practicing physicians stand in this debate. A reasonable summary of polling data from the past decade indicates that while as many as ninety percent of physicians support forgoing life-sustaining treatment as an ethical option, only about half endorse PAS or active euthanasia.[14] It is not clear whether the physicians endorsing PAS do so *because* they believe the moral equivalence hypothesis, or whether some or all of them believe that the act is morally acceptable for other reasons, even though the moral equivalence hypothesis is incorrect. My own suspicion is that most practitioners basically agree with the multitude of state supreme court rulings that followed in the wake of the Karen Quinlan case in New Jersey.[15] In virtually all those rulings, the courts stated that in permitting the withdrawal of life-sustaining treatment, they did not intend to permit either suicide or homicide. In other words, I believe that substantially fewer physicians would be willing to endorse forgoing life-sustaining treatment if they were firmly convinced that that act were the moral equivalent of PAS or active euthanasia.[16]

The Principle of Double Effect

If practitioners generally remain unpersuaded by the moral equivalence hypothesis, they seem traditionally wedded to the principle of double effect, even if few of them could give a detailed explanation of what that principle means.

The principle has a venerable tradition in ethics, particularly within the Roman Catholic tradition, quite apart from its medical applications. One may find a variety of statements of its precise content;[17] for our purposes, the following account will suffice:

1. I perform action A.
2. By performing A, I intend to accomplish outcome X.
3. A and X themselves are morally praiseworthy, or at least morally neutral.
4. By doing A, I know that I will also accomplish, or risk accomplishing, outcome Y.
5. I do not intend Y.
6. There is no alternative action to accomplish X that would not risk causing Y in the process.

The principle of double effect states that even if Y is morally bad, it may be acceptable to do A in order to accomplish X. The essence of the principle is that it is acceptable to do A if Y is a *foreseen but unintended consequence* of an otherwise justifiable act.

The principle of double effect is used by many ethicists, particularly within religious traditions, to analyze a wide variety of acts, both medical and nonmedical. Whether abortion is justifiable to save the life of a mother is just one example. Indeed, in some ways, something akin to the principle of double effect is central to medical practice; without it, surgery, for example, would be ethically unacceptable.

There is one complexity of double effect that is not important for present purposes. The point of distinguishing the *action* A from the *outcomes* X and Y is to make it clear that A causes X and Y, but that Y does not cause X. The classical Roman Catholic account lays special stress on this point because that ethical tradition strongly opposes doing an evil act, even if it might produce a good outcome as a consequence. Otherwise stated, if the "evil" outcome Y *directly* caused the "good" result X, then the action A would be immoral regardless.[18] For the ethicist who is not wedded to this religious tradition, however, applying this rule often seems to lead to disingenuous hairsplitting. For instance, if it is evil to cause a patient's death but good to relieve suffering, and a suffering patient is being kept alive on a ventilator, then it would not be moral to discontinue the ventilator to relieve the suffering because causing the patient to die, the evil outcome, would directly cause the good outcome. If the purpose of removing the ventilator is to remove the burden that mechanical ventilation places on the patient's body and death is a "foreseen but unintended" consequence, however, then the action might be ethically acceptable. Such fine distinctions might be beneficial within a system that opposes consequentialist ethical reasoning[19] and yet wants to allow for consequences making a moral difference, but they are not necessary for the present discussion.

The application of double effect of interest here is the justification for using high doses of narcotic medication in treating the pain of terminal illness. In the formula,

A = prescribing or administering high doses of narcotics,
X = relieving pain, and
Y = the risk of hastening death because of respiratory depression due to the medication.

To show the value, as well as the potential precision, of the principle of double effect, consider a recent commentary by two experts in palliative care, Andrew Billings and Susan Block.[20] They argue for expanding the debate over PAS and euthanasia within palliative care circles because, despite the field's widespread rejection of those practices, some commonly accepted palliative care activities are essentially indistinguishable from euthanasia. One practice they consider to be "slow euthanasia" is increasing the rate of a morphine drip in a terminally ill and often unconscious patient with the unspoken intention of hastening death, either for the patient's benefit or for the relief of those standing by and watching the patient's suffering. This probably occurs more frequently in general hospital practice than in hospice programs, but Billings and Block claim that it is commonplace nonetheless.

With respect to terminal analgesia, it is important to note that there is an unexamined empirical assumption in the statement of double effect. It is assumed that the risk of respiratory depression is substantial when one uses narcotics in needed doses in this setting. This was indeed thought to be the case for many years, as part of the general phobia of opioid drugs within the medical and nursing fields. More recent experience within palliative care has shown that respiratory depression, although theoretically possible and occasionally encountered, very seldom is of practical concern when physicians exercise care in adjusting dosages and observing patients for responses to medication.[21] In practice, the dosage level at which one can achieve pain relief and the level at which respiratory depression might occur are much farther apart than traditionally has been appreciated.

Consequently, two things are likely to happen in general hospital settings where the physicians and nurses are relatively unskilled in palliative care. First, if a patient is in pain, staff will increase the rate of the morphine drip, and sometime thereafter the patient will die. Staff will wrongly believe that the drip hastened the patient's death, when in fact the patient would have died at approximately the same time in any event.[22] Second, staff who indeed wish the patient to die more quickly may accomplish this by increas-

ing the morphine drip rate. To accomplish their end, however, they will have
to raise the dosage level much higher than is necessary for analgesia, and in
the process they will have to ignore fairly clear clinical signs that pain has already been adequately relieved and that breathing is becoming shallower
and less frequent.

There is thus a clear practical difference in most cases between appropriately managing a morphine drip for terminal pain relief and mismanaging
a morphine drip as a form of surreptitious euthanasia, real or imagined. The
ethical difference, as our formula has already made clear, is equally distinct.
If one *intends* to hasten death, one is no longer employing the principle of
double effect, and one can no longer seek shelter under its moral umbrella.

Are we then sliding down a sort of "slippery slope" from the legitimate
employment of the principle of double effect in terminal care to permitting
"slow euthanasia"? After all, we know that euthanasia and PAS occur sur-
reptitiously despite their illegal status.[23] But there is no reason to regard terminal analgesia under the principle of double effect as any more "slippery"
than other practices. We can draw fairly clear distinctions, both conceptually and practically, between use and abuse of this principle. If abuse occurs
on a widespread basis in general hospitals, the blame lies not with the principle but with the level of ignorance of palliative care techniques, a matter to
which I will return in greater detail below.

Despite its venerable tradition among practitioners, the principle of
double effect is not without critics. In a textbook intended for clinicians, for
instance, Bernard Lo argues alongside Tom Beauchamp and James Childress that double effect can easily become a form of rationalization:

> People are held accountable for consequences they should have fore-
> seen, not merely those consequences that they intended. . . . The doc-
> trine of double effect also leads to the implausible conclusion that
> physicians are more justified in administering large doses of narcotics
> if they can put out of mind the possibility that death may be has-
> tened.[24]

I would suggest, however, that the potential for abusing the principle does
not necessarily lead to the conclusion that the principle itself is without merit.

To summarize the previous sections, then, most medical practitioners
in the United States believe they have a general ethical roadmap for end-of-
life care:

1. it is permissible to forgo life-sustaining medical therapy at the informed request of a competent patient, or at the request of the surrogate for an incompetent patient; and
2. it is permissible to provide effective analgesia for pain in terminal illness, even if the dosages required approach levels that might hasten
   death; but
3. it is not permissible to perform PAS or active euthanasia.[25]

If asked why the first is permissible while the third is not, the physician would likely base her conclusion on a rejection of the moral equivalence hypothesis. If asked why the second is permissible and the third is not, she would likely allude to the principle of double effect. If challenged, it is true that the physician would probably be unable to discuss the nuances of either ethical argument; a substantial minority of physicians are perhaps even prepared to argue that the third is outmoded and should be re-evaluated. In general, however, physicians have long assumed that the federal courts were on their side as they followed these general rules of conduct.

The Ninth Circuit

Against this background, the ruling of the Ninth Circuit Court of Appeals seemed to toss conventional medical wisdom into a cocked hat.

The court began by redefining the basic question it was to address. The issue was not, according to the court, whether there is a "constitutional right to aid in killing oneself," as the original three-judge panel had phrased it, but rather "whether there is a liberty interest in determining the time and manner of one's death."[26] This reformulation tended already to beg the question, and to tip the scales in favor of accepting the moral equivalence hypothesis. If the moral equivalence hypothesis is indeed correct, and forgoing treatment is an morally acceptable act, then *both* PAS and forgoing life-sustaining treatment would be morally acceptable ways of determining the time and manner of one's death.

The court explained that it preferred this broader reformulation because it was not sure that "suicide" was the correct label for the sort of action involved in the case:

> [A] competent adult has a liberty interest in refusing to be connected to a respirator or in being disconnected from one, even if he is terminally ill and cannot live without mechanical assistance. The law does not classify the death of a patient that results from the granting of his wish to decline or discontinue treatment as "suicide." Nor does the law label the acts of those who help the patient carry out that wish . . . as assistance in suicide.[27]

The court therefore hinted that it had already judged that the action described in the case was morally equivalent to PAS, and if calling PAS "suicide" implies a moral stigma, then the same moral stigma ought to apply to forgoing treatment. Conversely, if forgoing treatment is not morally stigmatized, then PAS should not be either.

The court argued that the *Cruzan*[28] ruling of the Supreme Court presaged such an expanded liberty interest. The Supreme Court must have recognized that removing Nancy Cruzan's feeding tube would "lead inexorably to her death,"[29] so if there was some liberty interest in having this tube withdrawn, it must have been a "liberty interest in hastening one's own death."[30] In fact, the court explicitly stated that "it was the discontinuance of the provision of food and water, not Cruzan's accident almost eight years earlier, that caused her death."[31] As a further salvo in defense of moral equivalence, the court noted that the same abuses many fear from legalizing PAS, such as exerting pressure on vulnerable patients to die prematurely, could arise just as easily from the lax use of advance directives.

The court then addressed the principle of double effect, finding it essentially devoid of value.[32] The fact that "ethical" physicians are prepared to administer high doses of narcotics in terminal pain management was seen by the court as evidence that many terminally ill patients die from drugs rather than their underlying diseases. This could only mean that medical practitioners are already crossing the bridge from letting die to PAS. The opinion concluded that the language of double effect

> may salve the conscience of the AMA, but it does not change the realities of the practice of medicine or the legal consequences that would normally flow from the commission of an act one has reason to believe will likely result in the death of another. In the case of "double effect" we excuse the act or, to put it more accurately, we find the act acceptable, not because the doctors sugarcoat the facts in order to permit society to say that they couldn't really *know* the consequences of their action, but because the act is medically and ethically appropriate even though the result—the patients death—is both foreseeable and intended.[33]

The court was so dismissive of the very notion of double effect as anything other than moral hypocrisy that it failed to make clear its underlying empirical assumptions. Was the court convinced that many cases of high-dosage narcotic treatment are really cases of what Billings and Block call "slow euthanasia,"[34] and did the court believe that conduct to be morally acceptable? Or did the court believe that the real risk of hastening death, when narcotics are titrated properly toward the goal of adequate pain relief, is extremely high? The first assumption is at least questionable[35] and the second is demonstrably incorrect.[36]

If these empirical assumptions arose simply from an ignorance of the present potential of palliative care, then the court gave ample evidence that it shares the level of ignorance of many members of the medical profession today. In fact, one looks in vain through the entire body of this lengthy ruling for any evidence that there is such a thing as *successful* palliative care. For example, the court mentioned the case of an AIDS patient who requested medication to hasten his impending death after enduring four excruciating months "because he did not wish to die in a hospital in a drug-induced stupor,"[37] as if enduring incredible pain or being rendered stuporous are the only choices available to the average terminally ill patient. Another passage that typifies the court's view reads as follows:

> [T]erminally ill adults who wish to die can only be maintained in a debilitated and deteriorating state, unable to enjoy the presence of family or friends. Not only is the state's interest in preventing such individuals from hastening their deaths of comparatively little weight, but its insistence on frustrating their wishes seems cruel indeed. As Kent said in *King Lear,* when signs of life were seen in the dying monarch:
>
> > "Vex not his ghost: O! let him pass; he hate him / That would upon the rack of this tough world / Stretch him out longer."[38]

The Second Circuit

The narrower reasoning of the Second Circuit Court of Appeals led it to espouse the moral equivalence hypothesis, without addressing the principle of double effect.

The Second Circuit differed from the Ninth in its reluctance to find a new fundamental right to assisted suicide, because it could not be described as "deeply rooted" in the nation's history.[39] Nor was the court "'inclined to take a more expansive view of . . . authority to discover new fundamental rights imbedded in the Due Process Clause.'"[40] Ultimately, however, the court found grounds to overturn the New York statute prohibiting PAS in the Equal Protection Clause of the Fourteenth Amendment. This reasoning required the court to adopt the moral equivalence hypothesis (or at least its legal cousin), because if PAS and forgoing treatment were significantly different ethical actions, it would not violate the Equal Protection Clause to permit terminally ill patients to do the latter but not the former. As the court stated:

> New York does not treat similarly circumstanced persons alike: those in the final stages of terminal illness who are on life support systems are allowed to hasten their deaths by directing the removal of such systems; but those who are similarly situated, except for the previous attachment of life-sustaining equipment, are not allowed to hasten death by self-administering prescribed drugs.[41]

In this case it again appeared that the framing of the "factual" circumstances begged the moral question. The issues in the case were precisely whether two terminally ill patients, one connected to life-support equipment and the other not, are indeed "similarly situated," and whether "hastening death" is indeed the proper moral description of the act of forgoing life-sustaining therapy.[42]

In defense of the moral equivalence hypothesis, the court turned to an ironic source: Justice Scalia's concurring opinion in *Cruzan.* Scalia argued that the action-inaction distinction is irrelevant because "the cause of death in both cases [PAS and forgoing treatment] is the suicide's conscious decision to 'pu[t] an end to his own existence.'"[43] Rather than advocating PAS, however, Scalia's intent in *Cruzan* was to invoke the moral equivalence hypothesis to argue that since PAS is illegal, forgoing therapy should be as well.[44] The Second Circuit used his words to argue the opposite conclusion, namely that since forgoing treatment is recognized as a basic right, the Equal Protection Clause requires that PAS be afforded similar protection in sufficiently similar circumstances. According to the court,

> there is nothing "natural" about causing death by means other than the original illness or its complications. The withdrawal of nutrition brings on death by starvation, the withdrawal of hydration brings on death by dehydration, and the withdrawal of ventilation brings about respiratory failure. By ordering the discontinuance of these artificial life-sustaining processes . . . , a patient hastens his death by means that are not natural in any sense.[45]

Practitioners, therefore, "do not fulfill the role of 'killer' by prescribing drugs to hasten death any more than they do by disconnecting life-support systems."[46]

While the Second Circuit's opinion did not have the same dismissive and occasionally contemptuous tone as the Ninth Circuit's, it amounted to an equally severe assault on conventional medical thinking. The court told physicians, in effect, that just as Moliere's character had been speaking prose all his life but never realized it, doctors had been assisting suicide throughout their careers without realizing it. In essence, the court said that in asking physicians to assist in suicides now, it was merely asking them to do something legally and morally indistinguishable from what they had always done. If that notion seemed radical, it merely illustrated how obtuse the court believed doctors had been in the past. Oddly, neither court seemed to recognize the collision that was certain to occur between their lines of reasoning and accepted medical wisdom on ethical care at the end of life. Had physicians actually accepted the reasoning of the federal courts of appeals, they would not merely have agreed to add PAS to their medical armamentarium; they would have been forced to radically rethink virtually every aspect of providing and forgoing care for dying patients.

The Supreme Court

In reversing the two appellate court rulings and denying the existence of a constitutionally protected right to physician-assisted suicide, the Supreme Court principally employed a historical argument. The Court agreed with the Second Circuit that the Due Process Clause protects only those fundamental rights and liberties "'deeply rooted in this Nation's history and tradition.'"[47] Because the historical record is squarely opposed to any recognition of a right to suicide or suicide assistance, the Court believed that it could not find any such basic liberty interest. According to the Court, the task of balancing the liberty interests of individual citizens with the traditionally recognized state interest in preventing suicide is best left to the legislature; it would be inappropriate for the judicial branch to intervene to elevate individual interests at the expense of the state's concerns.

The Court's mode of argument thus diverged for the two appeals. With respect to the Ninth Circuit's holding, which established a basic right to PAS, the Court did not feel compelled to directly address either the moral equivalence hypothesis or the principle of double effect. It believed that it was sufficient to invoke the historical record on laws opposing suicide and suicide assistance.[48] The Court simply noted in passing that the Ninth Circuit had misunderstood *Cruzan:*

> The decision to commit suicide with the assistance of another may be just as personal and profound as the decision to refuse unwanted medical treatment, but it has never enjoyed similar legal protection. Indeed, the two acts are widely and reasonably regarded as quite distinct.[49]

In other words, the Court felt that given the disconnect between the moral equivalence hypothesis and the legal tradition, all it needed to do in its ruling was invoke history and *assert* (without substantive argument) that PAS and forgoing treatment were morally distinct acts. The principle of double effect could simply be ignored.

By contrast, when it discussed the Second Circuit's decision, the Court had no such "out" because the Second Circuit had not found a fundamental right to PAS in the Constitution. Instead, it had to address the moral equivalence hypothesis in a more direct way:

> Unlike the court of appeals, we think the distinction between assisting suicide and withdrawing life-sustaining treatment, a distinction widely recognized and endorsed in the medical profession and in our legal traditions, is both important and logical; it is certainly rational.[50]

Unfortunately, from an academic standpoint, the Court then proceeded to rehash rather stale arguments in favor of moral nonequivalence: the physician in PAS must intend the patient's death, while the physician withdrawing treatment may merely intend that the patient be freed from unwanted medical interventions; in PAS the physician kills the patient, while in withholding treatment the patient dies of the underlying disease. This was indeed an argument against the moral equivalence hypothesis that more closely comports with the prevailing sentiment in the medical community, but it was conducted as if the bioethical debate of the last two decades never occurred. In a paper for a graduate seminar in bioethics, it would have been lucky to earn a C-minus.[51]

The concurring opinions by individual justices attempted to shed more light on the underlying issues. Justice O'Connor stated:

[T]here is no need to address the question whether suffering patients have a constitutionally cognizable interest in obtaining relief from the suffering that they may experience in the last days of their lives. There is no dispute that dying patients in Washington and New York can obtain palliative care, even when doing so would hasten their deaths.[52]

Here, O'Connor seems to be addressing the principle of double effect as a legal construct, permitting even such palliative measures as terminal sedation and barbiturate coma that undeniably shorten life. It is not clear from this passage, however, whether she was swayed by the reasoning of the Ninth Circuit and believed that shortening life was a *frequent* consequence of routine palliative care. Nor is there any hint that she is aware that in practice, quality palliative care may be difficult to obtain, even absent constitutional barriers. The assumption appears to be that the ready availability of palliative care is itself an argument against creating or recognizing any legal right to PAS.

Justice Stevens, in the "concurring" opinion that most closely resembles a dissent from the majority's reasoning, exhibited a greater understanding of the issues underlying the principle of double effect. He stated, "Encouraging the development and ensuring the availability of adequate pain treatment is of utmost importance; palliative care, however, cannot alleviate all pain and suffering."[53] Thus, unlike Justice O'Connor, Stevens explicitly recognized both that there may be problems with obtaining access to palliative care, and that palliative care by itself is not a definitive argument against allowing PAS. Stevens went on to address both the potential strengths and weaknesses of the moral equivalence hypothesis:

[B]ecause physicians are already involved in making decisions that hasten the death of terminally ill patients—through termination of life support, withholding of medical treatment, and terminal sedation— there is in fact significant tension between the traditional view of the physician's role and the actual practice in a growing number of cases . . . I agree that the distinction between permitting death to ensue from an underlying fatal disease and causing it to occur by the administration of medication or other means provides a constitutionally sufficient basis for the State's classification. Unlike the Court, however, I am not persuaded that in all cases there will in fact be a significant difference between the intent of the physicians, the patients or the families in the two situations.[54]

Here, at long last, one finds legal language consistent with what I take to be the best philosophical analyses of the moral equivalence hypothesis. Instead of the uncritical embracing of the hypothesis by the courts of appeals, or the equally uncritical rejection of the hypothesis by the majority, Justice Stevens offered a nuanced appreciation that whether or not there is a significant difference in causality, intent, and other morally important features between a case of PAS and a case of forgoing treatment will depend in the final analysis on the facts of the particular cases.

Implications for Clinical Practice

If some physicians choose to defend PAS and active euthanasia and call for changes in the law to permit and regulate these practices, then it is important that they rely on the best possible justifications for this view.[55] Defenders of assisted death should not expect to make their case "on the cheap"; in other words, they must do more than simply cite a similar but legally distinct medical practice and argue that if that practice is allowed, PAS should be as well. They should look PAS squarely in the eye, with all its advantages and disadvantages, and argue cogently and forthrightly that the practice should be permitted.

Because the debate over PAS seems destined not to be resolved in the foreseeable future, however, physicians of all persuasions must agree in the meantime how to improve the care of the dying right now. In the face of compelling evidence that the status quo is far below optimal, if not actually scandalous,[56] there is no excuse for debating bioethics rather than focusing on the practical steps needed to improve the current quality of terminal care. The Second and Ninth Circuit opinions were a setback to that clinical goal; the Supreme Court at least wiped the slate clean, but without substituting any superior view.[57]

Clinicians must believe, to some degree, in a form of the principle of double effect in order to provide optimal symptom relief at the end of life.[58] This is so because all physicians ought to be equally committed to palliative goals. Roughly a third of physicians, however, are strongly opposed to PAS or euthanasia on moral grounds. At least that third of physicians must be reassured that if they use the most effective palliative techniques, no one will accuse them of violating their own moral codes and deliberately causing death. A serious assault on the logic of the principle of double effect could do major violence to the (already reluctant and ill-informed) commitment of most physicians to the goals of palliative care and hospice.

It would, of course, be desirable for this general endorsement of double effect to be combined with a sophisticated understanding of the bioethical debate about that principle and its potential abuses. This would prevent physicians from mistakenly concluding that surreptitious or "slow" euthanasia can be carried out under the moral cover of that principle.[59] However, to ask the average physician to attend so carefully and consistently to the rather academic discourse of philosophical bioethicists on this point may be a counsel of perfection.

For a similar reason, it is highly desirable that a rough practical distinction be maintained between both the ethics and the law of forgoing therapy and of PAS or euthanasia. This is necessary if the one-third of physicians strongly opposed to PAS are to accept the rights of patients and their surrogates to refuse life-prolonging care.[60] Perhaps more important, however, is the need to ensure that the current legal protections patients enjoy in making these decisions not be dissipated or reversed. Susan Wolf was probably the first to call attention to the relatively flimsy basis of the present "consensus" in favor of the right to refuse treatment. Her warning that the moral equivalence hypothesis could as easily be used to eliminate the rights of patients to refuse treatment as to support PAS remains pertinent today, despite the Supreme Court rulings in *Cruzan* and the present two cases.[61]

The political power and will of those who would impose their religiously grounded right-to-life perspective upon society through force of law do not seem to have diminished. If, for instance, while PAS remains illegal, there are widespread calls for refusal of nutrition and hydration as the quickest and most painless way to hasten one's death,[62] then there are likely to be efforts made to reverse the legal position that refusing food and water is protected to the same degree as refusing a ventilator. Similarly, if it becomes widely known (or alleged) that palliative care techniques sometimes deliberately hasten death,[63] we can expect new laws to be introduced that would hamstring palliative practice.[64] In at least some states, such laws would likely pass, and it is not at all clear that they would be reversed upon court challenge, considering the current prevalence of conservative judges in the court system.

Even if the more general right to refuse "extraordinary" medical therapy remains untouched by such laws, they could exert a highly pernicious chilling effect upon physician practices in terminal care, and upon patient perceptions that they retain some control over medical decisions.[65] Ironically, the net result of this scenario is likely to be an increase in surreptitious PAS, despite the fact that those who would champion these changes in social policy will use the fear of a "slippery slope" toward PAS as one of their rallying cries.

While a rule-of-thumb distinction between forgoing treatment and PAS or active euthanasia is highly desirable for purposes of public policy, one would wish that physicians had a deeper understanding of the clinical difficulties in defining these categories. One would like physicians to attain the level of understanding suggested by Justice Stevens, namely that in particular cases of forgoing treatment or administering palliative care, physician intent and the degree of causation of death might be virtually indistinguishable from that in cases of PAS or euthanasia. The public policy distinction works precisely because many cases fit nicely within the general categories, but there are also going to be messy cases which sit on the fences.[66]

A serious policy question with regard to the fence-sitting cases is how health care professionals will explain them to the public. Thus far, the tendency has been for organized medicine, in its public proclamations, to act as if everything fits within the well-defined category limits, treating the messy cases as an inside secret with which we should not burden the public's delicate sensibilities.[67] I believe this strategy is certain to reduce public trust in medicine in the long run, perhaps ultimately restricting the allowable amount of physician discretion in managing terminal care. We must find better ways to make the public and policymakers understand that fence-sitting cases do exist, and that these cases present a multitude of problems.[68]

Conclusion

Patients with terminal illnesses will receive the best care when physicians and other health professionals adhere to certain general rules of thumb for ethical practice. For some years, a rough consensus on these rules of thumb had been evolving. The decisions of the Second and Ninth Circuits temporarily undermined that evolving ethical consensus. The Supreme Court provided little thoughtful guidance with regard to those ethical principles, but at least restored the status quo ante by overturning the lower court rulings.

Ethical constructs are not sufficient to assure good clinical practice, however; personal and institutional habits, reimbursement incentives, and many other forces may work to reduce the quality of terminal care. While the status of PAS will probably be debated well into the future, some things are certain under the law. Patients have an ethical and legal right to determine whether to accept life-prolonging therapy, and they have an ethical (and legal, according to some Supreme Court Justices) right to adequate pain relief, especially in cases of terminal illness. There is a pressing need today for both physicians who oppose and physicians who support legalization of PAS to put aside those differences and form alliances for enhanced terminal care, so that all patients are provided these treatment options. It is likely that in doing so, they will substantially reduce the number of patients who feel driven to seek PAS.

NOTES

I am grateful to Karla Dingman and Elizabeth Price for research assistance, and to Susan Wolf and Kathryn L. Tucker for helpful comments on an earlier draft.

1. See Compassion in Dying v Washington, 79 F 3d 790 (9th Cir 1996) (en banc), *rev'd sub nom.* Washington v Glucksberg, 117 S Ct 2258 (1997); Quill v Vacco, 80 F 3d 716 (2d Cir 1996), *rev'd,* 117 S Ct 2293 (1997).

2. In the discussion that follows, I will scrutinize the recent court opinions to determine the adequacy with which they deal with the ethical constructs. I agree that the courts are not trying to "get the ethics

right" but rather are interpreting the law. (I am grateful to Susan Wolf for calling my attention to this point.) Nonetheless, the criticisms might be helpful for two reasons: first, if the opinions lack logical coherence, they might be flawed in their legal, as well as ethical, reasoning; second, the message physicians receive from the courts regarding the optimal "rules of thumb" for everyday practice will depend not purely on the law but also on the perceived "fit" between the legal opinions and the widely accepted ethical dictates.

3. James Rachels, *Active and Passive Euthanasia,* 292 New England Journal of Medicine 78 (1975).

4. See Letters, *Euthanasia,* 292 New England Journal of Medicine 863, 863–66 (1975).

5. See Rachels, at 79 (cited in note 3). It is worth noting that the "right to die" debate through the 1970s and 1980s was about allowing to die versus active euthanasia; PAS did not really enter into the discussion until the late 1980s. See, e.g., Sidney H. Wanzer et al., *The Physician's Responsibility Toward Hopelessly Ill Patients: A Second Look,* 320 New England Journal of Medicine 844, 847–48 (1989).

6. For representative replies to Rachels, see Martin Benjamin, *Death, Where Is Thy Cause?,* 16 Hastings Center Report 15 (June 1976); K.D. Clouser, *Allowing or Causing: Another Look,* 87 Annals of Internal Medicine 622 (1977); Jean Davies, *Raping and Making Love Are Different Concepts: So are Killing and Voluntary Euthansasia,* 14 Journal of Medical Ethics 148 (1988); Raymond J. Devettere, *The Imprecise Language of Euthanasia and Causing Death,* 1 Journal of Clinical Ethics 268 (1990); Jeff

McMahan, *Killing, Letting Die, and Withdrawing Aid,* 103 Ethics 250 (1993); Richard L. Trammel, *The Presumption Against Taking Life,* 3 Journal of Medicine & Philosophy 53 (1978).

7. See James Rachels, *The Elements of Moral Philosophy* 139–151 (Temple University Press, 1986).

8. See, e.g., Stanley G. Clark & Evan Simpson eds., *Anti-Theory in Ethics and Moral Conservatism* (State University of New York Press, 1989).

9. See Paul T. Menzel, *Are Killing and Letting Die Morally Different in Medical Contexts?,* 4 Journal of Medicine & Philosophy 269 (1979).

10. See Howard Brody, *Causing, Intending, and Assisting Death,* 4 Journal of Clinical Ethics 112 (1993).

11. See Raanan Gillon, *Euthanasia, Withholding Life-Prolonging Treatment, and Moral Differences Between Killing and Letting Die,* 14 Journal of Medical Ethics 115 (1988).

12. See Dan W. Brock, *Voluntary Active Euthanasia,* 22 Hastings Center Report 10 (March/April 1992).

13. Note, *Physician-Assisted Suicide and the Right to Die with Assistance,* 105 Harvard Law Review 2021, 2040 (1992).

14. See Robert J. Blendon et al., *Should Physicians Aid Their Patients in Dying? The Public Perspective,* 267 Journal of the American Medical Association 2658 (1992); Jerald G. Bachman et al., *Assisted Suicide and Euthanasia in Michigan,* 331 New England Journal of Medicine 812 (1994) (letter to editor); Jonathan S. Cohen et al., *Attitudes Toward Assisted Suicide and Euthanasia Among Physicians in Washington State,* 331 New England Journal of Medicine 89, 90 (1994).

15. See Robert F. Weir & Larry Gostin, *Decisions to Abate Life-Sustaining*

Treatment for Nonautonomous Patients: Ethical Standards and Legal Liability for Physicians After Cruzan, 264 Journal of the American Medical Association 1846 (1990).

16. I have not addressed in this section another possible variant of the moral equivalence hypothesis— that PAS is morally equivalent to active euthanasia, regardless of whether either or both are morally equivalent to forgoing treatment. This point has been occasionally debated in the medical-ethical literature. See, e.g., Glenn C. Graber & Jennifer Chassman, *Assisted Suicide Is Not Voluntary Active Euthanasia, But It's Awfully Close,* 41 Journal of the American Geriatric Society 88 (1993); David T. Watts & Timothy Howell, *Assisted Suicide Is Not Voluntary Active Euthanasia,* 40 Journal of the American Geriatric Society 1043 (1992). For what I am arguing in this article, one may assume that I regard these two acts as morally equivalent, although I have argued for a somewhat different view elsewhere. See Howard Brody, *Assisted Death—A Compassionate Response to a Medical Failure,* 327 New England Journal of Medicine 1384 (1992).

17. See, e.g., Tom L. Beauchamp & James F. Childress, *Principles of Biomedical Ethics* 206–211 (4th ed.; Oxford University Press, 1994); Jorge L.A. Garcia, *Double Effect,* in 2 *Encyclopedia of Bioethics* 636, 636–641 (Simon & Schuster Macmillan, 1995).

18. See Garcia, at 637 (cited in note 17).

19. Consequentialist ethical reasoning states that an action is good or bad depending on whether the consequences that follow from it are good or bad, or on the net balance is good or bad when all the consequences are considered. A nonconsequentialist approach views certain actions, such as causing death, as intrinsically wrong, regardless of the consequences they may produce.

20. See J. Andrew Billings & Susan D. Block, *Slow Euthanasia,* 12:4 Journal of Palliative Care 21 (Winter 1996).

21. See Howard Brody et al., *Withdrawing Intensive Life-Sustaining Treatment—Recommendations for Compassionate Clinical Management,* 336 New England Journal of Medicine 652,652–53 (1997).

22. See William C. Wilson et al., *Ordering and Administration of Sedatives and Analgesics During the Withholding and Withdrawal of Life Support from Critically Ill Patients,* 267 Journal of the American Medical Association 949, 952–53 (1992).

23. See Anthony L. Back et al., *Physician-Assisted Suicide and Euthanasia in Washington State: Patient Requests and Physician Responses,* 275 Journal of the American Medical Association 919, 921 (1996).

24. Bernard Lo, *Resolving Ethical Dilemmas: A Guide for Clinicians* 143 (Williams & Wilkins, 1995).

25. While a narrow majority of physicians support PAS and its legalization, they do not appear to hold this position because they see it as congruent with the "received" medical ethic. Rather, they argue that the received medical ethic needs to be revised and extended.

26. Compassion in Dying v Washington, 79 F 3d 790, 801 (9th Cir 1996) (en banc), *rev'd sub nom.* Washington v Glucksberg, 117 S Ct 2258 (1997).

27. Ibid. at 802.

28. Cruzan v Director, Missouri Department of Health, 497 US 261 (1990).

29. *Compassion in Dying,* 79 F 3d at 816.

30. Ibid.
31. Ibid. at 820 n.91.
32. See ibid. at 821–22.
33. Ibid. at 823 n.95.
34. See Billings & Block (cited in note 20 and accompanying text discussing the similarity between terminal pain management and euthanasia).
35. See Billings & Block; Brody et al.; Wilson et al., (cited in notes 20–23) and accompanying text (describing "slow euthanasia").
36. See Beauchamp & Childress; Garcia (cited in notes 17–18) and accompanying text.
37. *Compassion in Dying,* 79 F 3d at 834.
38. Ibid. at 821 (citations omitted).
39. Quill v Vacco, 80 F 3d 716, 724 (2d Cir 1996), *rev'd,* 117 S Ct 2293 (1997).
40. Ibid. (quoting Bowers v Hardwick, 478 US 186, 194 (1986)).
41. Ibid. at 729.
42. The court assumed, reasonably in my view, that a patient near death who is not attached to life support, but who is suffering enough to contemplate PAS, probably received some form of life-prolonging medical care during an earlier stage of illness to allow the illness to reach such an advanced stage. Thus, the court laid the groundwork for rejecting the idea that forgoing life-sustaining treatment, unlike PAS, *merely* allows the "natural" course of the illness to unfold. The court suggested, along with several philosophers who filed amicus briefs with the Supreme Court, that there is no longer such a thing as the natural course of illness. *See* ibid.; Quill v Vacco (cited in note 45) and accompanying text; see also Ronald Dworkin et al., "Assisted Suicide: The Philosopher's Brief," *New York Review of Books,* Mar. 27, 1997, at 41, 42.
43. Cruzan v Director, Missouri Department of Health, 497 US 261,
296–297 (1990) (Scalia, J., concurring) (quoting 4 WILLIAM BLACKSTONE, COMMENTARIES *189).
44. Hence his use of the loaded term *suicide* to describe both categories of patients.
45. Quill v Vacco, 80 F 3d 716, 729 (2d Cir 1996).
46. Ibid. at 730.
47. Washington v Glucksberg, 117 S Ct 2258, 2268 (1997) (quoting Moore v East Cleveland, 431 US 494, 500 (1977)).
48. See ibid. at 2268–69.
49. Ibid. at 2270.
50. Vacco v Quill, 117 S Ct 2293, 2298 (1997).
51. It may be indicative of the quality of the reasoning that the Court, in its majority opinion, cites only sources widely viewed as opposed to PAS, with no mention of any sources that are either neutral or in sympathy. Apparently Lawrence Gostin agrees with my "C-minus" grade, stating,

> The Supreme Court in *Vacco* found the distinction between assisted suicide and withdrawal of life-sustaining treatment to be "important, logical, rational, and well-established." Yet, its reasons for differentiating between the two practices fly in the face of a body of philosophic literature examining questions of causation and intention in medicine.
> Lawrence O. Gostin, *Deciding Life and Death in the Courtroom,* 278 Journal of the American Medical Association 1523, 1527 (1997) (footnote omitted).

Gostin, in turn, sees a better reason to distinguish between PAS and forgoing treatment in the distinction between negative and positive duties, arguing that a right to forgo treatment places only a negative duty upon the physician (not to interfere with the patient) while a right to PAS would create a positive duty to perform various affirmative acts leading to death. But this in turn seems too simple, since most managements of "withdrawal of treatment" actually entail a mix of doings and omissions on the part of the medical staff. It may be argued that withdrawing life-sustaining treatment, in order to be done compassionately, requires a number of associated medical "doings." See Brody et al., (cited in note 21).

52. *Glucksberg*, 117 S Ct at 2303 (O'Connor, J., concurring).

53. Ibid. at 2308 (Stevens, J., concurring).

54. Ibid. at 2309–10 (Stevens, J., concurring) (citation and footnotes omitted). I will leave to legal analysts the discussion of how wide a door the concurring opinions generally left open for future constitutional challenges to anti-PAS laws, based on the facts of specific cases. The possibility of such future cases is of great interest legally and ethically, but would, I contend, have little impact on clinical practice today. I appreciate Kathryn L. Tucker calling my attention to the importance of this aspect of the decision.

55. See Franklin G. Miller et al., *Regulating Physician-Assisted Death,* 331 New England Journal of Medicine 119 (1994).

56. See generally, Committee on Care at the End of Life, Institute of Medicine, *Approaching Death: Improving Care at the End of Life* (Marilyn J. Field & Christine K. Cassel eds., 1997); Charles S. Cleeland et al., *Pain and Its Treatment in Outpatients with Metastatic Cancer,* 330 New England Journal of Medicine 592 (1994); The SUPPORT Principal Investigators, A *Controlled Trial to Improve Care for Seriously Ill Hospitalized Patients: The Study to Understand Prognoses and Preferences for Outcomes and Risks of Treatment (SUPPORT),* 274 Journal of the American Medical Association 1691 (1995).

57. But compare the view of Robert Burt, who argues that the decision amounts to finding "a constitutional right to palliative care." Robert A. Burt, *The Supreme Court Speaks: Not Assisted Suicide but a Constitutional Right to Palliative Care,* 337 New England Journal of Medicine 1234 (1997). Nor is this to say that the Supreme Court opinions had no value even to physicians who might favor PAS. The Court upheld the permissibility of forgoing life-sustaining treatment, of high-dose pain relief in terminal care, and even of terminal sedation. It encouraged ongoing debate over the issues and state-by-state experimentation with legislation; and indicated that it might hear specific future cases. *But cf. supra* text accompanying note 51 (asserting that the Supreme Court's reasoning was biased against PAS in that the Court relied solely on sources that opposed PAS). For these observations I am indebted to Timothy Quill, one of the appellants in the Second Circuit case. *See generally* Timothy Quill, Address at Michigan State Medical Society Bioethics Conference (Sept. 27, 1997).

58. I am indebted to Franklin G. Miller for the reminder that "some form" of the principle of double effect need not be a form that rejects consequentialist arguments and demands adherence to absolute moral principles; and if so, the new "form" of the principle is so far away from the traditional roots of that mode of moral reasoning to be no longer recogniza-

ble as "double effect." One then simply argues that it is all right to administer high-dose painkillers because of the ratio of benefit to burden (i.e., good consequences to bad consequences); the good intentions of the physician; patient consent; and the lack of better alternatives.

59. I say this with the belief that either euthanasia and PAS should not be performed, or they should be performed openly and regulated appropriately. See Miller et al. (cited in note 55); Franklin G. Miller et al., *Can Physician-Assisted Suicide Be Regulated Effectively?,* 24 Journal of Law, Medicine, & Ethics 225 (1996). If the majority of physicians and patients agree that PAS and euthanasia are moral acts, but the law continues to deny permission and guidance, then many would argue that sub rosa practices such as "slow euthanasia" become the best available safety value under those suboptimal circumstances.

60. Robert A. Burt, analyzing the Supreme Court decisions for the *New England Journal of Medicine* writes, "In the wake of the Second Circuit Court's ruling, some physicians in New York had found new reasons to overrule patients' refusals of life-prolonging treatment and even more reasons to fear the legal consequences of adequately managing symptoms through the use of opioids. . . ." Burt, at 1234 (cited in note 57). However, Burt cites no source for this claim.

61. Susan M. Wolf, *Holding the Line on Euthanasia,* 19 Hastings Center Report S13 (Jan./Feb. 1989).

62. See James L. Bernat et al., *Patient Refusal of Hydration and Nutrition: An Alternative to Physician-Assisted Suicide or Voluntary Active Euthanasia,* 153 Archives of Internal Medicine 2723 (1993); David M. Eddy, *A Conversation with My Mother,* 272 Journal of the American Medical Association 179 (1994).

63. See Billings & Block, *supra* note 20, at 22; David Orentlicher, *The Supreme Court and Physician-Assisted Suicide: Rejecting Assisted Suicide but Embracing Euthanasia,* 337 New England Journal of Medicine 236 (1997).

64. Addressing the flip side of this coin, David Orentlicher argues that by rejecting assisted suicide but apparently accepting terminal sedation and barbiturate coma, the Court actually moved in the direction of "embracing euthanasia." Orentlicher, at 1239 (cited in note 63).

65. A good case in point is Kathryn L. Tucker's article, *Surrogate End of Life Decisionmaking: The Importance of Providing Procedural Due Process, A Case Review,* 72 Washington Law Review 859 (1997), which describes a case in which a flawed decision to remove a feeding tube was made by a family-member surrogate (and reversed upon court review). Tucker then notes that Washington case law precedent permits surrogate decisions to withdraw life-prolonging treatment only for two classes of patients: terminally ill and permanently unconscious. She further argues for "prognosis committees" as a necessary procedural safeguard and seems dismissive of hospital ethics committees, as currently constituted, in that function. Legal questions aside, I agree with Tucker that an unfortunate aspect of the "reverse slippery slope" has been the fact that decisions to withdraw treatment may be made too cavalierly because the spotlight of controversy has shifted over to assisted suicide and euthanasia. That said, I think the legal and procedural solutions she proposes would be

far too restrictive in actual practice and would have the effect of prolonging the suffering of many incurable patients, though the full consideration of this question is beyond the scope of this Article.

66. See Brody, (cited in note 10).

67. In this regard, one of the most worrisome features of the Billings and Block controversy is the note by the editor of the palliative care journal that colleagues had appealed to him to suppress publication of the article. See David J. Roy, *On the Ethics of Euthanasia Discourse,* 12:4 Journal of Palliative Care 3 (Winter 1996) (editorial) (discussing his decision to publish the lead article by J. Andrew Billings and Susan D. Block (cited in note 20)).

68. It is my understanding that there is relatively little established law, either statutory or case law, regarding these "fence-sitting" cases. Because the medical profession has not brought them to public attention, they generally are not addressed by legislators; perhaps surprisingly, few of these cases have been brought to court. In light of the goal of more explicit and open recognition of the problem, however, the Supreme Court's discussion of one fence-sitting category, terminal sedation, is probably a move in the right direction. On this point, see Orentlicher (cited in note 63). Many physicians probably prefer that the law remain silent on these cases and that they be handled in the future by medical discretion; to some extent, this is probably unavoidable. For a discussion of the inability of law to deal effectively with these difficult cases, see J. Griffiths, *The Regulation of Euthanasia and Related Medical Procedures That Shorten Life in the Netherlands,* 1 Medical Law International 137 (1994).

Part IV

Glucksberg and the Institutions of Public Policy

CHAPTER 6

A Part of the Main?
The Physician-Assisted Suicide
Cases and Comparative Law
Methodology in the United States
Supreme Court

Christopher McCrudden

Introduction

The principal focus of this book is on developments in the United States concerning physician-assisted suicide (PAS). The United States has not, however, been alone in seeing pressure for law reform in this area. Since the 1970s there has been a similar movement in several other countries to relax legal prohibitions that render assisting in a suicide a criminal offense. Why there has been a resurgence of the debate at this time is an interesting question in itself, but one that is beyond the bounds of this paper.[1] Whatever the cause, however, reform movements in several countries have concentrated on attempting to change such legal prohibitions through seeking *legislative* changes, and this has led several countries (most notably the United Kingdom and Canada) to establish official committees to examine the issue.[2] In Australia, too, there has been a heated debate on legislative reform both at the national level and at the subnational level.[3] The Northern Territory passed legislation permitting PAS under tightly controlled circumstances,[4] legislation that was upheld by the Supreme Court of the Northern Territory[5] but subsequently overturned by the Australian federal parliament.[6]

There also have been attempts to bring about changes through *judicial* activity in several countries. The judiciary have been involved in two main ways. First, some courts have been asked to decide that such legal prohibitions are contrary to the national constitution, or international human rights norms, or both. This has resulted in several decisions of note, particularly those of the Supreme Court of Canada (in which the Canadian Court upheld a prohibition on assisting in suicide against a challenge under the Canadian Charter of Rights and Freedoms),[7] the European Commission on Human Rights (in which the Commission upheld the equivalent British prohibition against a challenge based on the European Convention of Human Rights),[8] and the Colombian Constitutional Court (in which the Court held that criminal law prohibitions on assisting suicides requested by the patient were unconstitutional).[9]

A second approach has been to attempt to persuade courts to modify existing law, or reinterpret it, or clarify it to make lawful what previously was unlawful or not clearly lawful. In several jurisdictions (Ireland[10] and the United Kingdom,[11] in particular), the issue has arisen indirectly in the context of decisions involving the withdrawal of treatment or nourishment from patients in a permanent vegetative state. The issue has also come to courts in a more direct way, for example, where the court is asked to declare that the administration by a doctor of pain-relief medication would be legal even where it would shorten the patient's life.[12] In the Netherlands, the courts have authorized the nonprosecution of physicians who kill in response to a request by the patient to assist in his or her suicide, provided the doctor follows the court's procedural guidelines.[13]

The controversy over whether to legalize PAS has inspired much comparative analysis, particularly in the United States, Europe, and Australia, by academic writers,[14] official committees,[15] "think tanks" of one sort or another,[16] physicians,[17] and the popular press.[18] Several of these sources, explicitly or implicitly, seek to draw "lessons" from other countries' approaches to the problem. This should cause us little surprise, for it is now relatively common for comparative perspectives to be drawn on in the context of law reform efforts. But how useful are such comparative analyses, and how far is it justified to draw "lessons" for one country from another country's experiences in this area? And if we think that it may be useful, how should we go about doing it?

Here I am particularly interested in this set of questions as applied to *judicial* decision making in the area of individual rights, and especially in the context of decisions on the legality of PAS. This narrower issue has now been given added interest by the approach the U.S. Supreme Court has taken to the comparative experience in *Washington v Glucksberg*[19] and *Vacco v Quill*.[20] At one point in his opinion, Justice Stevens quotes John Donne's observation that "[n]o man is an island."[21] Donne's passage continues: "every man is a piece of the continent, a part of the main."[22] The question this paper addresses is how far the Supreme Court considered that, in deciding these cases, they were part of a larger community beyond the United States—how much they were "part of the main."

In most jurisdictions in which the judiciaries are active in protecting individual rights, there are significant debates about the extent to which they may legitimately or can competently carry out such a role.[23] In part, this debate focuses on whether legal and political approaches to adjudicating rights claims can be distinguished. When a judge interprets an individual-rights provision in a Bill of Rights, for example, is the judge making a legal or a political judgment? This question goes not only to the issue of the independence of the judiciary, but to the larger question of the autonomy of individual-rights law itself and its separateness from political and economic forces. The issue poses a continuing dilemma for judicial adjudication of individual-rights claims. If, on the one hand, judges appear incapable of appreciating the political and economic context in which they operate and in which their decisions will have their effects, they will appear divorced from this reality and will lose their legitimacy. On the other hand, if individual-rights law is not seen as at least relatively autonomous, then the judge interpreting it is acting not as a judge in the traditional sense, but as a politician, and has (in democratic societies) no greater legitimacy or competence in doing so than any other political actor, and arguably a good deal less.

For judges interpreting individual-rights provisions, a continuing concern, therefore, is how to establish their legitimacy and competence. In the United States, this has involved judges in elaborate attempts to justify the legitimacy of their judgments by formulating an acceptable theory of legal interpretation that supports the relative autonomy of law. It has also led them, on occasion, to draw explicitly on empirical and social scientific sources of information as a way of establishing their connectedness with the "real world." But both these attempts at justification of judicial adjudication of individual rights have proved immensely controversial.

As regards the appropriate method of legal interpretation, there is no clearly accepted method by which U.S. judges establish the relative autonomy of individual-rights adjudication. The appropriate sources of authority and the styles of judgment they use in interpretation are the subject of profound disagreement. At the risk of oversimplifying a complex issue, several sources of authority are common, including the authority of the text literally interpreted, the authority of the intention of the founding fathers, the authority of national history and tradition, the authority of contemporary moral or political theory, the authority of legal scholars, the authority of analogy, and the authority of precedent.

As to the last—the use of prior judicial authority—we need to distinguish two different kinds of "authority." Most jurisdictions distinguish binding authority and persuasive authority in judicial interpretation. *Binding authority* refers to authority the judge must apply and follow. It implies that there is a hierarchy of sources of authority some of which the judge must apply and be bound by. *Persuasive authority*, on the other hand, exists when, in addition to binding authority, material is regarded as relevant to the judge's decision but is not binding under the hierarchical rules of authority.[24] Which sources of authority are used is a crucial and often controversial question. So, too, the use of social science evidence has proved immensely controversial from the development of the Brandeis brief,[25] through the use of social-psychological evidence in *Brown v Board of Education*,[26] and more recently.[27]

I am concerned in this chapter with the use of *foreign* judicial decisions as persuasive authority and with the use of *foreign* empirical experience to support conclusions about the socioeconomic context in which law operates. The influence of other jurisdictions on a judge may be general or specific.

But general influences (such as a country's culture of rights) are difficult to pin down and, although important, prone to over- or underestimation. Equally difficult to identify with any certainty are those indirect influences that occur when an idea from one jurisdiction is picked up in a second and then transferred to the third. The continuing influence of the first is indirect but important, palpable but sometimes untraceable. Last, the external influence may be acknowledged or unacknowledged. But where influences are not acknowledged in public papers (like judicial opinions), identifying them is often too speculative to be convincing. More important, as Anne-Marie Slaughter has suggested, it is worthwhile distinguishing courts drawing on the opinions of foreign courts without attribution from courts that directly cite a foreign decision: "In [the latter] cases evidence that a foreign court has reached the same conclusion apparently has independent value, leading the listening court not only to borrow the idea, but to publicize its source."[28]

I have, therefore, mostly confined myself to acknowledged, direct, and specific influences. In general this has involved identifying where judges in one jurisdiction expressly use judicial or other experiences from another jurisdiction.[29] We know that constitutional and human rights *institutions* have often been borrowed, particularly since the end of World War II,[30] but how far do *judges,* in interpreting such individual-rights guarantees, heed or ignore judicial and other experiences in individual-rights issues from another jurisdiction?

This chapter examines the Supreme Court's approaches to these issues in *Glucksberg* and *Quill* and sets it in a discussion of judicial reactions to the utility of comparative experience in judicial decision making in individual-rights policy more generally. The structure of the paper is as follows. In the next section, I consider the U.S. Supreme Court's use of comparative experience in general. In the third section, "The Use of Comparative Material," I discuss the Court's somewhat different use of comparative experience in *Glucksberg.* In the fourth section, "The Growing Worldwide Use of Comparative Experience," I treat the growing use of comparative experience in other countries' courts in "end-of-life" cases and draw some contrasts with the Supreme Court's approach in the PAS cases. In the final section, I address some arguments that may help to explain when recourse is had to comparative experience. I conclude that the combination of the ambiguity of the Supreme Court's view of its relations with the wider judicial world, combined with the failure of comparative law to provide an acceptable methodology of comparison, contributed to the problematic way the Supreme Court approached the issue in *Glucksberg.* Comparative analysis will continue to be used unsystematically, opportunistically, and thus to the detriment of rational, informed, and persuasive judicial decision making in this and other areas if the Supreme Court does not develop a clearer position on its global role and if the academy does not develop an acceptable comparative methodology.

The United States Supreme Court's Previous Use of Comparative Experience

The issue of the use of foreign experience by the U.S. Supreme Court in the area of individual rights is one with an interesting, and largely untold, history.[31] This section will discuss circumstances in which the issue has arisen in the recent past. In general, we shall see that, despite the influence of comparative thinking on the founding fathers,[32] despite extensive citations to U.S. decisions by other courts,[33] despite the Court's heavy use of precedent, despite the Court's being a "common law court," despite America's leadership in the world, despite the Court's history of having done so not infrequently in the past,[34] the Court now seldom cites foreign court decisions or comparative experience in its individual-rights jurisprudence.[35] Some examples, of cases where such decisions or experience might have been thought to be relevant but were not used illustrate the point.

Abortion

During the 1980s, some scholars, most notably Professor Mary Ann Glendon, sought to draw on European experience to argue that the Supreme Court in *Roe v Wade*[36] had erred.[37] She argued that in *Roe* the Supreme Court had preempted the type of political debate leading to legislative compromise that had taken place in Europe and that the emphasis in the United States on rights tended to polarize the citizenry and inhibit political compromise more than in Europe.

Professor Glendon's argument concerning the utility of the European approach to the United States became an issue during the Court's reconsideration of *Roe* in the late 1980s and early 1990s. In *Webster v Reproductive Health Services*,[38] the U.S. government sought to persuade the Court to overrule *Roe,* in part on the basis of the Glendon argument, as did several others who submitted briefs *amicus curiae*. The United States argued, quoting Glendon, that the Court's position on abortion was "out of step" with that of "virtually every other country with which we share a common cultural tradition."[39] This, it was argued, "by itself suggests that the decision ought to be reconsidered."[40] In oral argument, Charles Fried (the Solicitor General) reiterated the point.[41] The International Right to Life Federation produced a detailed brief arguing that *Roe* "has not been persuasive to the international legal and judicial communities" in three respects: first, in making elective abortion a constitutional right; second, in providing no protection for the fetus before viability and very little protection thereafter; and third, in failing to recognize that the fetus is, in their words, "in fact human and alive."[42]

The United States also argued that "[o]ther Western countries have, through the legislative process, reached reasonable accommodations of the competing interests involved in the abortion controversy. There is no reason to believe that American legislatures, if basic decision-making responsibility were returned to them, would not similarly arrive at humane solutions."[43] The brief continued: "[U]nless the American political culture is somehow radically different from that of other countries with which we share a common heritage, it would appear that there is nothing inherent in the abortion controversy, or the sharply conflicting interests and viewpoints in this area, that makes it uniquely resistant to legislative resolution."[44] And the argument by Webster, the Attorney General of Missouri, went further, again drawing on Glendon, predicting: "If the experience of other countries is any guide . . . it is unlikely that widespread criminalization of abortion in early pregnancy will result if *Roe v Wade* is overruled."[45]

Nor were these arguments confined to *Webster*. In *Planned Parenthood of Southeastern Pennsylvania v Casey*[46] the United States returned to the argument that Glendon's work was relevant in demonstrating that *Roe v Wade* was aberrant.[47] In its *Casey* brief, however, the United States tied the comparative argument more tightly into the structure of American constitutional analysis and used it to argue that United States "history and traditions do not establish a fundamental right to abortion."[48]

In the event, the majority of the Court decided to ignore the German and French experience in both *Webster* and *Casey,* or at least not to cite it directly as underpinning its decision. The only exception to this is Chief Justice Rehnquist's dissent in *Casey,* where a one-line footnote[49] refers (for reasons that are not clear) to the first German abortion case[50] and the Canadian decision in *Morgentaler.*[51] The fact that the European experience was not referred to explicitly does not mean, of course, that it was not influential; it may have been, but the point of relevance to my argument is that the Court did not explicitly refer to that experience, even to disagree with or distinguish it.

Sexual Orientation

In *Bowers v Hardwick,*[52] the issue was essentially whether making sodomy criminal unconstitutionally interfered with the right of privacy. Faced with considerable precedent that had gone a substantial way in protecting various activities as private, the Court was forced to reinterpret that precedent to distinguish it in *Bowers*. They did this primarily by interpreting the previous cases not as dealing with a right to liberty in making intimate decisions about sexual activity in private between consenting adults, but rather as primarily having to do with the protection of family, marriage, and procreation. The majority in *Bowers* was not prepared to extend these cases and create a new area of protected activity.

For the court to decide that a new area of protection—particularly that new area—should be created, one of two tests had to be satisfied. One test was whether the fundamental liberty claimed was "implicit in the concept of ordered liberty" such that "neither liberty nor justice would exist if [they] were sacrificed";[53] the second test was whether the liberty claimed was "deeply rooted in this Nation's history and tradition."[54] The majority held that neither test was satisfied. In particular, the Court noted that sodomy had long been criminal and was still a crime in (at the time) twenty-four states. It was only after rejecting this right that the Court asked whether the additional element of privacy involved—the fact that the acts took place in the home—mattered constitutionally. But the argument that it should was rejected on the ground that so broad a right would threaten other criminal law prohibitions, in particular "adultery, incest and other sexual crimes."[55]

The European Court of Human Rights had decided just a few years earlier, in the *Dudgeon* case,[56] that an almost exactly equivalent law in Northern Ireland violated the right of privacy guaranteed under the European Convention on Human Rights, in part because the consensus in favor of such laws had declined in Europe. Significantly, *Dudgeon* was not referred to in any of the opinions in the U.S. Supreme Court. Indeed, only one amicus brief mentioned *Dudgeon*.[57] If the U.S. Supreme Court had focused on *Dudgeon,* it might have considered whether the changing consensus in Europe was relevant, but it was given no opportunity to do so.

Freedom of Speech and Racial Hatred

In *RAV v City of St. Paul, Minnesota,*[58] the U.S. Supreme Court considered the issue of racial hate-speech. Defendants were convicted under a city ordinance of placing a burning cross, the symbol of the Ku Klux Klan, on the property of an African-American neighbor. On appeal, the Minnesota Supreme Court interpreted the ordinance as reaching only conduct that amounted to "fighting words," that is, "conduct that itself inflicts injury or tends to immediate violence," and this interpretation was accepted by the U.S. Supreme Court. Nevertheless, the Court held *unanimously* that the ordinance was unconstitutional under the First Amendment, again without referring to any of the extensive foreign or international approaches to the issue.

For example, the Canadian Supreme Court had extensively considered the equivalent issue under the Canadian Charter just two years previously. In *R. v Keegstra*[59] a teacher was charged under a provision[60] of the Canadian Criminal Code with willfully promoting hatred against an identifiable group (meaning any section of the public distinguished by color, race, religion, or ethnic origin) by making anti-Semitic statements to his students. As Keegstra could establish none of the several statutory defenses, he was convicted after a jury trial. He challenged his conviction on several grounds, the primary one being that the provision under which he was convicted unjustifiably infringed his freedom of expression. The Supreme Court of Canada, by a majority, held the contested provisions did not violate the Charter. Despite its apparent relevance to the issues in *RAV,*[61] *Keegstra*[62] was neither cited to the Court nor referred to in any of its opinions. As David Weissbrodt has written, "[I]f the Court had focused at all on international human rights law [in *RAV*], it would at least have had to consider the balance between freedom of expression and incitements to racial hatred,"[63] an issue noticeably absent from the majority's opinion in the case.

Capital Punishment

The use (or nonuse) of comparative experience in the capital punishment cases is also illuminating. In *Furman*,[64] the Supreme Court's first major decision in its reconstruction of the death penalty, there is an apparent openness to comparative experience, and thus *Furman* seems to represent a divergence from the trend of the cases we have been reviewing. For Justice Marshall, abolishing capital punishment would have enabled the United States to "join the approximately 70 other jurisdictions in the world which celebrate their regard for civilization and humanity by shunning capital punishment."[65] However, for Justice Powell, in dissent, the comparative experience went the other way. Drawing on the English and Canadian experience, he pointed to the advantages of bringing about change legislatively; not only was such change more democratic, it was also open to "revision and change: mistaken judgments may be corrected and refinements perfected."[66] The point can be simply stated: the capital punishment cases begin with an apparent recognition of the comparative experience.

More recently, however, this approach has been explicitly abrogated. The turning point appears to have been in the late 1980s, and the occasion was the issue of the constitutionality of applying the death penalty to juvenile offenders. In *Thompson v Oklahoma*,[67] a majority of the Justices agreed that the Eighth Amendment's prohibition of "cruel and unusual punishment" prevented the execution of a person who was younger than sixteen at the time of his or her offense. In the course of the plurality's judgment, Justice Stevens supported his conclusion that to allow such an execution would offend civilized standards of decency by referring not only to the practice of eighteen states, but also to international experience. Citing the brief of Amnesty International, he wrote, "The conclusion [that it would offend civilized standards] is consistent with the views that have been expressed . . . by other nations that share our Anglo-American heritage, and by the leading members of the Western European community."[68] In dissent, however, Justice Scalia not only disagreed with the conclusion, but also strongly disagreed with the use of the comparative method itself.[69]

Within two years, the issue was revisited in *Stanford v Kentucky*,[70] and Scalia's view became the majority's. The majority upheld the constitutionality of imposing capital punishment on an offender who was seventeen years old when the offense was committed. While the dissent relied in part on comparative experience and international human-rights treaties,[71] Justice Scalia (writing for the majority) emphasized that it is "American conceptions of decency that are dispositive, rejecting the contention of petitioners . . . that the sentencing practices of other countries are relevant. . . ."[72]

In sum, these four sets of cases, which raise some of the most controversial issues in American law and politics, demonstrate the Supreme Court has either not been referred to judicial decisions on similar issues in other jurisdictions (sodomy, racial hatred), or that when referred to them, the majority of justices have either studiously ignored it (abortion) or been hostile to it being seen to be relevant (capital punishment).

The Use of Comparative Material
in the Physician-Assisted Suicide Cases

An Outline of the Decision

In *Vacco v Quill*,[73] the Supreme Court unanimously upheld New York's prohibition on assisting suicide against an attack based on the Equal Protection Clause, and in *Washington v Glucksberg*[74] it unanimously upheld the State of Washington's prohibition on causing or aiding a suicide against an attack based on the Due Process Clause.[75] The separate opinions of the Court in both cases were delivered by Chief Justice Rehnquist. Four other Justices, O'Connor, Scalia, Kennedy, and Thomas, joined both opinions. Justice O'Connor also delivered a separate concurring opinion covering both cases in which Justices Ginsburg and Breyer joined in part. Separate opinions concurring in the judgments but not in the opinions of the Court were written by Justices Stevens, Ginsburg, and Breyer. Justice Souter delivered separate opinions concurring in the judgments in each of the cases.

Regarding the equal protection challenge, the Court said that the New York statutes criminalizing assisted suicide neither infringed fundamental rights nor involved suspect classifications, and the Court therefore applied a relaxed standard of scrutiny. The Court thus rejected the equal protection argument that the distinction between permitting patients to refuse medical treatment (which was legal under state law) and intentionally killing a patient (even with their consent) was arbitrary and irrational. Although the Court agreed that the line between the two acts may not always be clear, logic and contemporary practice justified the distinction. The Court then considered New York's reasons for employing the distinction. These included prohibiting intentional killing and preserving life, preventing suicide, maintaining physicians' role as healers, protecting vulnerable people, and avoiding a slide toward involuntary euthanasia. The Court thought that these were valid and important public interests and that they satisfied the constitutional requirement that the legislative classification bear a rational relationship to some legitimate end.

Regarding the due process argument, the Court held that there was no "right" to assistance in committing suicide that was sufficient to amount to a fundamental liberty interest. The Court thought that the liberty claimed by those challenging the Washington law was unclear. In addition, the Due

Process Clause specially protected those fundamental rights and liberties that were deeply rooted in the nation's history and traditions, and the asserted liberty right did not meet that test. There was a consistent and continuing rejection of such a right, and the argument to the contrary was unpersuasive. The right to refuse medical treatment, which the Court first intimated in *Cruzan v Director, Missouri Department of Health,*[76] was clearly distinguishable. Although both *Cruzan* and *Casey*[77] recognized that personal autonomy was a justification for particular rights protected by the Due Process Clause, it did not follow that any and all important, intimate, personal decisions were protected. Finally, Washington's assisted-suicide law was rationally related to legitimate government interests of the kind the Court had approved in the equal protection analysis previously discussed.

In the concurring opinions, in particular in those of Justices O'Connor, Souter, and Breyer, there is a clear concern that a distinction be recognized between intentionally killing a patient and supplying the patient with pain relief that has the undesired result of shortening the patient's life. Where the patient is suffering severe pain, the Court's opinions should not be read, they argued, as permitting the state to prohibit the doctor from supplying such pain relief. Justice Stevens sought to argue as well that several important issues were not being decided by the Court and that there was room for legitimate debate to continue as to the limits that the Constitution places on the power of the states in this area.

Use of Comparative Experience

In the period before *Glucksberg,* the debate over PAS drew extensively on comparative experience. The campaigns to relax state laws against assisting suicide proceeded on two fronts: attempts to introduce legislative changes at the state level and attempts to modify legal prohibitions on assisted suicide through constitutional challenges.[78] Comparative experience was drawn on fairly extensively in academic commentary before the case,[79] in the decisions in the lower federal courts,[80] in several of the briefs in *Glucksberg* and *Quill,*[81] in congressional hearings on the issue,[82] and in the American press.[83] I shall focus, however, on the use of such evidence in the oral arguments and then on the use to which the Justices put the foreign material in their opinions.

*Discussion of the Foreign Experience
in the Oral Arguments*
In the oral arguments before the Supreme Court,[84] several Justices questioned the lawyers for both sides about the lessons to be learned from the foreign experience, particularly from the Netherlands, but also from England and Australia. So, in the context of an argument by William Williams on behalf of Washington that raised the "slippery-slope" argument, Justice Souter asked what empirical basis there was for evaluating it:

Mr. Williams:	Well, there's no empirical basis in our country, of course, because we do not have a history of recognizing that.
Souter:	Is there anything beyond the references to the Dutch experience?
Mr. Williams:	Well, there's the references to the Dutch experience which are I think important and telling in terms of modern history. And, of course, there is the German experience in the early 1930s.
Ginsburg:	What about the Australian, wasn't there something about Australian law?
Mr. Williams:	The northern territory of Australia, Justice Ginsburg, has authorized by statutory action a form of physician-assisted suicide. And I think a state may legitimately create an exception to its homicide laws for physician-assisted suicide. And if it is subject only to rational basis rule—review, then I think that the line could be maintained at the terminally ill.
Rehnquist:	The Australian proposal was not the result of a judicial decision I take it.
Mr. Williams:	That's my understanding, Mr. Chief Justice.
Ginsburg:	Indeed it was—whatever the legal status of the Netherlands, but what's elsewhere don't have the kind of Constitutional review that we do either. So—
Mr. Williams:	I believe that's correct, Justice Ginsburg.
Ginsburg:	But there has been a lot in the briefs about the Netherlands experience, there is this limited legislation in Australia. Has there been any evidence about what's going on under that legislation?
Mr. Williams:	I think that legislation is so new, my understanding it just became effective in this past year in 1996, that we don't— I'm not aware of any—.[85]

In his rebuttal argument, Mr. Williams returned to the issue:

Mr. Williams:	. . . Justice Souter, I have an opportunity to think a little bit more about your question about what—experience. And I would point out that, in the Netherlands, one of the problems is that, because it's now permitted, it's become institutionalized. And there is—although there is some disagreement about how the data is interpreted, that it appears to be pretty clear that a significant number of the deaths occur in-

voluntarily without any consultation with the patient. The physicians over time believe they know what the patients will want and go ahead at what they think is the appropriate time and administer that.

And I would point out that the Supreme Court of Canada has rejected the notion that there is a Constitutional right under their Article of Freedom, which is very similar to our Due Process Clause. And that the British Government, with the assistance of the British Medical Society, considered this, they rejected the notion on policy grounds.

And of course, the New York State Task Force, which is the most comprehensive report on this subject. So while we can't foretell the future for sure, that's one of the things that a legislature should take into account and we're asking the Court to give the legislature that opportunity.

Ginsburg: Do you know of the—any of the international human rights documents or regional human rights documents, there is recognition of what has been called the right to die or, as described today, for the terminally ill?

Mr. Williams: I'm sorry, Justice Ginsburg. I don't know of any such thing, but I don't want to represent that I have a comprehensive knowledge on that. . . .[86]

In two further brief exchanges, Justices Ginsburg and Breyer returned to the comparative experience. In one intervention, Justice Ginsburg suggested to Dennis Vacco, the Attorney General of New York, that state legislatures were free to decriminalize assisted suicide if they wished.

Ginsburg: But Mr. Vacco, you don't dispute that a legislature in New York or elsewhere could come to the rational judgment that a legislature in Australia or in Oregon or—I don't know how it came about in the Netherlands, but a rational decision could be made the other way, couldn't it?

General Vacco: Yes, Justice Ginsberg [*sic*], indeed we do assert that the State of New York's legislature, if it so choose, could indeed make a judgment in the opposite direction. . . .[87]

Finally, Justice Breyer asked Professor Tribe, who was arguing against New York State, about the implications of the British House of Lords report on the issue.

Breyer: [O]ne of the things that impressed me about looking at that is they said, in Holland, where they have the different line, there were three centers to deal with palliative care, pain removal. And in England, where they have the New York law, there were 185. Do you see the conclusion that they're drawing?[88]

We can see, therefore, that, in a relatively brief set of oral arguments, the foreign experience featured relatively prominently. In previous cases, however, most notably in *Webster* and *Casey,* foreign experience had been referred to in oral argument but been largely ignored in the subsequent opinions of the Justices. Would a similar fate befall the foreign experience in *Glucksberg?* We shall see in the next section that the answer is no.

Use of Foreign Experience in the Opinions
Several uses of the comparative material emerge from the decisions themselves.

1. That material was used by the Chief Justice to argue that there is support from other judiciaries for a legal distinction between withdrawing life-sustaining treatment and assisting suicide. In support of this distinction, he cited the British House of Lords decision in *Airedale N. H. S. Trust v Bland,*[89] a case we shall consider subsequently, although the citation was buried at the end of a footnote mostly taken up with American cases.[90]

2. Foreign experience was used as empirical support for the desirability of this distinction on the theory that retaining it might may contribute to the greater availability of hospices offering pain relief. Thus Justice Breyer, in the course of his argument supporting constitutional protection of the availability of pain relief even where it may shorten life, cited in his opinion, as he did in argument, the British House of Lords Select Committee report, which he said had found that "the number of palliative care centers in the United Kingdom, where physician assisted suicide is illegal, significantly exceeds that in the Netherlands, where such practices are legal."[91]

3. Foreign experience was used to demonstrate that PAS is broadly unacceptable internationally. In his opinion for the Court in *Glucksberg,* Chief Justice Rehnquist used comparative evidence to show that assisting suicide is generally accepted as a crime. "In almost every State," he wrote, "—indeed, in almost every western democracy—it is a crime to assist a suicide."[92] In support of this proposition, he cited the Canadian Supreme Court's decision in *Rodriguez,*[93] which had analyzed the prohibition on assisted suicide in western democracies. So too, Justice Souter referred, without the reference to *Rodriguez,* to the "dominant western legal codes [which] long condemned suicide. . . ."[94]

4. Foreign experience was used to establish that there is considerable international political debate about the issue. Chief Justice Rehnquist pointed to the extent to which other countries are "embroiled in similar debates," citing Canada, the United Kingdom, New Zealand, Australia, and Colombia.[95] By implication, since substantial debate about the issue of PAS continues worldwide, this debate should also be allowed to continue in the United States.

5. Foreign experience was recruited to substantiate the state's argument that laws prohibiting assisted suicide help protect the vulnerable. The Chief Justice drew on comparative empirical evidence heavily in the context of his consideration of the state's argument that permitting assisted suicide "will start it down the path to voluntary and perhaps even involuntary euthanasia."[96] Drawing on several American reports of the Dutch experience, Chief Justice Rehnquist concluded that the state's concern "is further supported by evidence about the practice of euthanasia in the Netherlands."[97] One particular study, he wrote, suggested

> that, despite the existence of various reporting procedures, euthanasia in the Netherlands has not been limited to competent, terminally ill adults who are enduring physical suffering, and that regulation of the practice may not have prevented abuses in cases involving vulnerable persons, including severely disabled neonates and elderly persons suffering from dementia.[98]

He further quoted from the New York Task Force Report, which had cited the Dutch experience, that "assisted suicide and euthanasia are closely linked" and that the "risk of . . . abuse is neither speculative nor distant."[99] "Washington," concluded the Chief Justice, ". . . reasonably ensures against this risk by banning, rather than regulating, assisting suicide."[100]

6. Foreign experience was used to show that we do not know how changes in the law will affect behavior. Justice Souter engaged extensively with the Dutch evidence in considering Washington's slippery-slope argument. Citing Gomez,[101] he observed that the Dutch guidelines require doctors who are asked to assist in a suicide to consult another doctor and to "decide whether the patient's decision is voluntary, well considered, and stable, whether the request to die is enduring and made more than once, and whether the patient's future will involve unacceptable suffering."[102] Unlike the Chief Justice, Justice Souter did not think that the evidence demonstrated that the slippery slope is a problem. Rather, he said there is a controversy over the lessons to be learned from the Dutch experience. On the one hand, Hendin,[103] Keown,[104] and Gomez[105] argue that the evidence shows "that the Dutch guidelines have in practice failed to protect patients from involuntary euthanasia and have been violated with impunity."[106] On the other hand, Posner,[107] Epstein,[108] and a Dutch article (in English),[109] contest that evidence. Justice Souter concludes: "The day may come when we can say with some assurance which side is right, but for now it is the substantiality of the factual disagreement, and the alternatives for resolving it, that matter. They are, for me, dispositive of the due process claim at this time."[110] In brief, Justice Souter argued that the judiciary is not the appropriate body to obtain or assess the facts necessary to decide whether assisted suicide might in practice (and despite good intentions) pose unacceptable risks to the vulnerable. In an important passage (which cites no authority)

he argued against judicial "displacement" of a legislative judgment when the following conditions are met:

> there is a serious factual controversy over the feasibility of recogniz-
> ing the claimed right without at the same time making it impossible
> for the State to engage in an undoubtedly legitimate exercise of power;
> facts necessary to resolve the controversy are not readily ascertainable
> through the judicial process; but they are more readily subject to dis-
> covery through legislative fact-finding and experimentation.[111]

Justice Souter contended that those conditions were met here, because the state's ability to protect the vulnerable under a regime of assisted suicide is "subject to some genuine question, underscored by the responsible dis-agreement over the basic facts of the Dutch experience."[112] This contro-versy, he argued, "is not open to a judicial resolution with any substantial de-gree of assurance at this time."[113]

> The principal enquiry at the moment is into the Dutch experience,
> and I question whether an independent front-line investigation into
> the facts of a foreign country's legal administration can be soundly un-
> dertaken through American courtroom litigation. While an extensive
> literature on any subject can raise the hopes for judicial understand-
> ing, the literature on this subject is only nascent. Since there is little
> experience directly bearing on the issue, the most that can be said is
> that whichever way the Court might rule today, events could overtake
> its assumptions, as experimentation in some jurisdictions confirmed or
> discredited the concerns about progression from assisted suicide to eu-
> thanasia.
>   Legislatures, on the other hand, have superior opportunities to ob-
> tain the facts necessary for a judgment about the present controversy.
>   . . . We therefore have a clear question about which institution, a
> legislature or a court, is relatively more competent to deal with an
> emerging issue as to which facts currently unknown could be disposi-
> tive. The answer has to be . . . that the legislative process is to be pre-
> ferred.[114]

We can see, therefore, that (relatively unusually) foreign experience fea-tured not only in the oral argument but also in the opinions themselves. In the next section I consider some reasons for the apparent difference in this respect between the PAS cases and those we have previously considered.

Analyzing the Use of the Comparative Experience

Three points of difference in the use of comparative material distinguish the PAS cases from the recent individual-rights cases we considered in the sec-ond section of this chapter. First, with the sole exception of abortion, considerably more public attention was paid to foreign experience in the run-up to *Glucksberg* than in other controversial individual-rights cases. Second, the Supreme Court appears to have engaged with comparative material to a much greater extent than it had previously. Third, and as noteworthy, is that, in contrast with these previous cases, there was no articulated objection by any Justice to the use of this comparative material, not even by Justice Scalia who had, as we saw earlier, so vociferously objected to the use of comparative arguments in the capital punishment context.

Some features specific to assisted suicide perhaps suggest why the comparative method was used in *Glucksberg* more than in other recent individual-rights cases. One difference relates to the relative newness of that question as an individual-rights issue. Where an issue is one that (unlike capital punishment, for example) has generated no extensive American jurisprudence, it is not surprising that a court will consult other jurisdictions. A second difference, perhaps, lies simply in the much easier access to global developments than was possible even a few years ago. Computerized databases such as Nexis/Lexis and Westlaw, with their extraordinary range of information on many countries in addition to the United States, considerably simplify finding comparative material. Linked with this is the comparative information available via the Internet, often (as in the case of PAS issues) collected together in various web sites.[115]

Nevertheless, there is substantial continuity of experience in the particular use to which foreign experience is put between *Glucksberg* and the previous cases discussed. Most important, little attention is paid to the comparative experience as a source of persuasive *legal* authority. When foreign experience is discussed, it is largely to support empirical conclusions. I have suggested earlier that the Justices used foreign experience in six places. Of these three (2, 5, and 6) are primarily empirical and use foreign experience to try to understand what would happen in the United States if the experiment of PAS were tried. The empirical uses are much more prominent than the nonempirical uses. Of the three nonempirical uses, only one (3) appears in the text (as opposed to footnotes), and it appears in a six-word parenthetical observation. The three nonempirical uses are generally buried in an avalanche of American examples. Footnote 8 of *Quill* mentions *Bland* only at the end of a long list of American cases; footnote 8 of *Glucksberg* sandwiches its reference to *Rodriguez* between citations to American cases; only footnote 16 of *Glucksberg* pays really substantial attention to foreign experience, and it is appended to a discussion of recent American experience that itself never refers to foreign experiences.

The Growing Worldwide Use of Comparative Experience

Although the Supreme Court in *Glucksberg* proved itself somewhat more open than in the past to comparative experience, its approach remains a far cry from the generally much more substantial and regular use of comparative experience in other countries' courts. It is now commonplace for courts in one jurisdiction to refer extensively to the decision of other courts in interpreting human rights guarantees. David Nelken has observed that "[w]e increasingly have the sense of living in an interdependent global system marked by borrowing and lending across porous cultural boundaries" and that human rights is one of the areas of law with the greatest ability to travel.[116] Mary Ann Glendon describes a "brisk international traffic in ideas about rights" carried on by judges.[117] Anne-Marie Slaughter says: "Courts are talking to one another all over the world."[118] In this section, I explore the increasing use of comparative experience in several other jurisdictions. To illustrate these points in the context of "end-of-life" cases, I will consider two decisions, one by the British House of Lords, the second by the Supreme Court of Canada. These decisions are merely illustrative; decisions in other jurisdictions have much the same features.[119]

The British House of Lords Opinion in *Bland*

In *Airedale NHS Trust v Bland*[120] the British House of Lords considered the question whether it would be lawful to deprive Anthony Bland, who was in a permanent vegetative state (PVS) as a result of a severe accident, of the treatment he needed to stay alive. With the concurrence of his family, the physician in charge of his case, and two independent doctors, the Airedale NHS Trust (which was responsible for the hospital in which Bland was being cared for) applied to the Family Division of the English High Court. The Trust sought declarations that they might "lawfully discontinue all life-sustaining treatment and medical support measures designed to keep [Mr. Bland] alive in his existing persistent vegetative state including the termination of ventilation nutrition and hydration by artificial means," and might "lawfully discontinue and thereafter need not furnish medical treatment to [Mr. Bland] except for the sole purpose of enabling [Mr. Bland] to end his life and die peacefully with the greatest dignity and the least of pain suffering and distress."[121] The House of Lords unanimously upheld this decision. In the absence of a Bill of Rights, the issue was decided under the court's interpretation of common law.

The House of Lords examined comparative judicial consideration of the issue with much care, seeking to draw support from decisions in other jurisdictions. Thus Lord Keith, for example, observed:

> Although this case falls to be decided by the law of England, it is of
> some comfort to observe that in other common law jurisdictions, par-
> ticularly in the United States where there are many cases on the sub-
> ject, the courts have with near unanimity concluded that it is not un-
> lawful to discontinue medical treatment and care, including artificial
> feeding, of PVS patients and others in similar conditions.[122]

Lord Goff also drew explicitly at several points in his opinion, on judicial decisions from the United States, New Zealand, and South Africa, as well as on the European Convention on Human Rights' protection of the right to life in Article 2.[123] For example, he considered the argument that the precedents of some American state courts permitting a substituted judgment to be made on behalf of an incompetent patient were part of English law. He held that they were not, but continued:

> I wish to add however that, like the courts below, I have derived assistance and support from decisions in a number of American jurisdictions to the effect that it is lawful to discontinue life-prolonging treatment in the case of P.V.S. patients where there is no prospect of improvement in their condition. Furthermore, I wish to refer to the section in Working Paper No 28 (1982) on Euthanasia, Aiding Suicide and Cessation of Treatment published by the Law Reform Commission of Canada concerned with cessation of treatment, to which I also wish to express my indebtedness. I believe the legal principles as I have stated them to be broadly consistent with the conclusions summarized [in] . . . the Working Paper. . . . *Indeed, I entertain a strong sense that a community of view on the legal principles applicable in cases of discontinuing life support is in the course of development and acceptance throughout the common law world.*[124]

Lord Mustill asked whether "it is right to terminate the lives of persons in the position of Anthony Bland, and in particular whether it is right that this should be done in the manner proposed."[125] He supported his belief "that adversarial proceedings" are not the "right vehicle" for discussing "this broad and highly contentious moral issue" and his doubt "that the judges are best fitted to carry it out"[126] with a citation to Justice Scalia in *Cruzan*,[127] "where a very similar problem arose in a different constitutional and legal framework."[128] These questions, Lord Mustill argued, are "properly decided by citizens, through their elected representatives, not by the courts."[129] He also drew on comparative experience in considering the distinction between acts and omissions. The difficult question, he thought, is the legal and ethical difference between what the doctors and families (in *Bland*) asked for and a situation in which a person intentionally, and intending to bring about death, withholds nourishment from a person who is helpless because she cannot feed herself and who subsequently dies from starvation. Lord Mustill continued:

> These and kindred questions have given rise to an extensive and understandably contentious literature, and to thoughtful discussions in the courts of the United States, Canada and New Zealand, and no doubt elsewhere. It is impossible to study it all, but the sources placed before the House, supplemented by a few others, have been sufficient to bring out the main lines of the possible arguments. I gratefully acknowledge

the great help which this material has furnished, without thinking it necessary to give any but the barest of citation in what follows.[130]

The Supreme Court of Canada in the *Rodriguez* Case

In *Rodriguez v British Columbia (Attorney-General)*[131] the question the Supreme Court of Canada faced was whether Sue Rodriguez had the right to have help committing suicide. Rodriguez was dying from a progressive disease of the motor neurons that was incurable and commonly gave its victims only about three years to live. She would become bedridden and unable to speak or to care for herself. The disease did not usually affect the patient's mind. Rodriguez sought a declaration that she was entitled to assistance in committing suicide when her condition became unbearable. By that time, she would be unable to commit suicide without help. The Canadian Criminal Code made it an offense to aid or abet a person to commit suicide. Rodriguez's application for a declaration was denied, and her appeal to the Supreme Court of Canada was dismissed (by a majority of five to four).

The Court considered several arguments. The majority held that the Canadian Charter of Rights and Freedoms did not render the prohibition on assisting suicide unconstitutional. The Criminal Code's prohibition did limit Rodriguez's autonomy by depriving her of the ability to end her life when she was no longer able to do so without assistance, and it therefore infringed on the interests protected by section 7 of the Charter.[132] The prohibition was nevertheless consistent with the principles of fundamental justice, and it was therefore constitutional: The prohibition was valid and desirable legislation that fulfilled the government's objectives of preserving life and protecting the vulnerable. This purpose was grounded in the state interest in protecting life and reflected the state's policy that human life should not be depreciated by allowing life to be taken. The active participation by one person in the death of another was morally and legally wrong and there was no certainty that abuses could be prevented by anything less then a complete prohibition. Canada and other western democracies recognized and applied the doctrine of the sanctity of life as a general principle that was subject to limited and narrow exceptions where notions of personal autonomy and dignity must prevail. These societies drew valid distinctions between passive and active intervention in the dying process.

The Court also considered whether the prohibition on assisted suicide violated the guarantee of protection against cruel and unusual treatment or punishment in section 12 of the Charter. Rodriguez argued that the prohibition subjected her to prolonged suffering until her natural death or required that she end her life while she could still do so without help. The majority held, however, that while the provisions of section 12[133] might apply to treatment imposed by the state in contexts other than a penal or quasi-penal nature, a mere prohibition by the state of an act cannot constitute "treatment" under section 12. Rodriguez was simply subject to the requirements of the Criminal Code, as were all other individuals in society. The fact that, because of her personal situation, this prohibition caused her suffering did not subject her to "treatment" at the hands of the state.

Rodriguez also argued that the prohibition of assisted suicide violated the Charter's section 15—which guarantees equality—in that, because of her physical disability, she was deprived of a benefit or subjected to a burden. However, the majority held that, even assuming there was some violation of section 15, the infringement was permissible under the Charter. A desire to protect human life was a pressing and substantial legislative objective, and prohibiting assistance in committing suicide was rationally connected to that purpose.

In his lead opinion for the majority, Justice Sopinka emphasized the comparative experience. He relied heavily on an argument that the consensus of the "western world"[134] was against removing the prohibition on assisting suicide. In contrast to the approach of the U.S. Supreme Court, however, this conclusion resulted from a detailed examination of the legal provisions in several countries. Justice Sopinka's extensive comparative exercise concluded that "the approach taken [elsewhere] is very similar to that which currently exists in Canada. Nowhere is assisted suicide expressly permitted, and most countries have provisions expressly dealing with assisted suicide which are at least as restrictive. . . ."[135] In support, he embarked on a lengthy discussion of Austrian, Spanish, Italian, British, and Australian criminal law.[136] However, he did recognize that some European countries "have mitigated prohibitions on assisted suicide which might render assistance in a case similar to that before us legal in those countries."[137] He thus examined the Dutch experience, together with that of several other countries including Switzerland, Denmark, and France. He also considered the popular referenda in Washington and California (the case was decided before the Oregon referendum). In support of the distinction between active and passive forms of intervention, Justice Sopinka drew extensively on *Bland*.[138] Although there was a common law right of patients to refuse consent to medical treatment (or to demand that treatment, once commenced, be withdrawn or discontinued), the Court should not condone the active assistance of a third party in carrying out a request to die by a terminally-ill patient. Finally, Justice Sopinka invoked the human rights jurisprudence of the European Court of Human Rights. "[I]t is significant," he wrote, "that neither the European Commission of Human Rights nor any other judicial tribunal has ever held that a state is prohibited on constitutional or human rights grounds from criminalizing assisted suicide."[139]

Some Contrasts Between the Judicial Use of Comparative Experience in the Jurisdictions Considered

Three points of contrast between the Canadian and British cases and the U.S. Supreme Court cases emerge with some clarity. The first is that, in contrast with these other courts, American courts seem remarkably insular in their approach to what amounts to persuasive legal authority. The second is that, again in contrast with these other courts, the foreign experience American courts consulted, where it was consulted at all, tends to be of the social scientific type (e.g., empirical evidence of how a law operates in practice). Such evidence appears to be much less frequently drawn on by courts outside the United States. Third, in contrast with the U.S. Supreme Court, equivalent courts, such as the British House of Lords and the Canadian Supreme Court, seem now to regard themselves as engaging in a common enterprise of interpretation of individual rights. It is this issue on which I intend to concentrate in the remainder of this chapter, leaving for another occasion further consideration of the phenomenon of citation of foreign *social scientific* evidence. This is not to deny that the use of such evidence is both problematic and controversial in its own right, nor that this particular issue is central to the PAS cases.[140] It is simply not the issue on which I intend to concentrate.

An American Judicial Dilemma: To Be "Part of the Main" or Not To Be

Interpretation as a Common Enterprise

For a court to be willing to engage in the comparative task, as Anne-Marie Slaughter argues, there needs to be an "awareness of a common enterprise, even if only in the sense of confrontation of common issues or problems."[141] She continues: "Recognition of this commonality does not obviate cultural differences, but it assumes the possibility that generic legal problems such as the balancing of rights and duties, individual and community interests, and the protection of individual expectations, may transcend those differences."[142] In the context of individual-rights jurisprudence, the idea of a common enterprise may be even deeper than this. Patrick Glenn develops the point well.[143] He distinguishes between what he regards as two differing views of the underlying view of law: law as national response, and law as inquiry. Law as national response goes hand in hand with the development of the idea of the nation-state and an idea of legal positivism, which excludes "all but the State itself, and its officers, as sources of law. . . . The idea gains currency that the extent of borrowing of foreign authority is a simple function of the adequacy of local sources and that local sources can be adequate if enough law is produced suitable to local conditions." In contrast is law as inquiry:

> [T]o the extent that the law used by these officers is not definitely made and imposed upon them but is rather chosen by them in an ongoing process, the underlying notion of law is that of enquiry. There is

never a closing of sources, never a declaration of satisfaction with existing knowledge, never a pure process of deduction from a single
given, never an entire commitment to an exclusive paradigm of law. In
general, there is also less assurance as to the role of law and the ongoing commitment to external sources is therefore accompanied by a
certain reticence as to the extension of legislative or judicial jurisdiction.[144]

Anne-Marie Slaughter points in particular to the growth in popularity of this
approach as an explanation of the growing cross-jurisdictional use of human
rights decisions. She suggests that there is now increasing recognition

of a global set of human rights issues to be resolved by courts around
the world in colloquy with one another. Such recognition flows from
the ideology of universal human rights. . . . The premise of universal-
ism, however, does not anoint any one tribunal with universal authority to interpret and apply these rights. Collective judicial deliberation,
through awareness, acknowledgement, and use of decisions rendered
by fellow human rights tribunals, frames a universal process of judicial
deliberation and decision.[145]

In part, what is at issue here is the fundamental (and difficult) question of
what community of respect judges consider themselves to be part of and to
what community they are appealing for approval. Judges, like the rest of us,
want to be seen to do a "good job," but what that involves varies from group
to group. Slaughter argues that "[c]ourts engaged in transjudicial communication . . . conceive of themselves as autonomous actors forging an autonomous relationship with their foreign or supranational counterparts."[146]
To the extent that is so, it would not be surprising if those judges cited the
foreign courts with which they are forging a relationship. Defining the group
with which judges identify will not only affect whether judges refer to foreign
experience, but also *which* foreign experience they regard as appropriate.
Where there is a fundamental dispute within the judiciary or the society as
to which countries are appropriate reference points, judges will be extremely
wary about citing cases from that foreign jurisdiction. If, on the other hand,
the primary audience is domestic popular opinion, then whether to cite foreign courts may well depend on whether such citation is likely to strengthen,
or weaken, its legitimacy with that audience. Where the view is current that
human rights are not subject to international debate, then reference to foreign courts' decisions is much less likely.

International and European Human Rights and PAS

What difference might an approach that viewed the U.S. Supreme Court as
regularly engaged in a common enterprise with other courts have made in

Glucksberg? Justice Ginsburg asked the counsel for Washington: "Do you know [if in] any of the international human rights documents or regional human rights documents . . . there is recognition of what has been called the right to die . . . for the terminally ill?" A recognition of a common enterprise might have caused this question to be treated more systematically and professionally. Had this been done, an intriguing (and somewhat different) light might have been thrown on the Court's choices.

The question whether there is a right to die has been little adjudicated under the International Covenant on Civil and Political Rights.[147] The European Commission on Human Rights, however, was asked to decide this issue in a challenge to a prosecution under an English statute that criminalized assisting in suicide. The applicant argued that his conviction violated his right to respect for private life under Article 8 of the Convention.[148] The Commission disagreed: "While [the English statute] may be thought to touch directly on the private lives of those who sought to commit suicide," held the Commission, "it does not follow that the applicant's rights to privacy are involved. On the contrary, the Commission is of the opinion that the acts . . . are excluded from the concept of privacy by virtue of their trespass on the public interest of protecting life. . . ."[149] The Commission also rejected the applicant's argument that his right to freedom of expression under Article 10[150] was infringed when he was prosecuted for putting people who wanted to commit suicide in touch with his coaccused. The Commission conceded that there had been a prima facie interference with the applicant's right to impart information. However,

> the Commission must take account of the State's legitimate interest in this area in taking measures to protect against criminal behaviour the life of its citizens particularly those who belong to especially vulnerable categories by reason of their age or infirmity. It recognises the right of the State under the Convention to guard against the inevitable criminal abuses that would occur in the absence of legislation against the aiding and abetting of suicide. The fact that in the present case the applicant and his associate appear to have been well intentioned does not, in the Commission's view, alter the justification for the general policy.[151]

In conclusion, therefore, it seems probable that laws prohibiting assistance in suicide are not contrary to international or regional human rights law. However, that does not exhaust the relevant issues. *Glucksberg* is generally understood to leave states free to write or repeal statutes criminalizing assisted suicide. International human rights law may call this freedom into question. Under the International Covenant on Civil and Political Rights, the issue arises primarily under Article 6, which protects the right to life.[152] Under the European Convention on Human Rights, the issue arises under Article 2, which is similar.[153] The relevant part of Article 2 provides: "Everyone's right to life shall be protected by law."[154] A law authorizing the killing of someone against his or her will would plainly violate both articles except in the very limited circumstances explicitly set out in them. Both texts thus embody a requirement by states to take positive measures to protect the right to life. That is, not just must the state forebear from killing; it must also positively protect the right to life against interference by nonstate actors. Beyond that, however, the issue is less clear-cut.

One area of uncertainty relates to the relevance of consent. Would the killing of someone with his or her explicit consent be contrary to these provisions? What of a law that permitted doctors to accelerate death in conformity with the patient's expressed wishes? In other words, is the right to life alienable, held at the will of the individual protected and therefore capable of being "given away"?[155]

No clear answer to these questions appears to have been given by those interpreting the International Covenant on Civil and Political Rights. Somewhat more guidance is available, however, under the European Convention on Human Rights. Harris's view[156] is that "[t]he consent of the patient may be relevant . . . ; it is not clear that Article 2 *requires* that a state's law prohibit active euthanasia (or complicity in suicide generally) at the patient's request. . . . [A] wide margin of appreciation would be allowed if it could be shown that national practice varied a lot."[157] The recent decision of the European Court of Human Rights in *Laskey, Jaggard and Brown v The United Kingdom* appears to support Harris's argument. The issue was whether the criminal conviction in England of a group of men for inflicting injuries on others during consensual sadomasochistic practices was contrary to Article 8 of the Convention, which prohibits interference with the right to respect for private life.[158] The British government, defending the convictions, had argued that the victims' consent was not determinative. The state, it argued, was entitled to punish violence irrespective of consent not only on public health grounds but also because such practices "undermine the respect which human beings should confer upon each other."[159] The Court held that this prosecution and conviction did not violate of the Convention. The Court held, "The determination of the level of harm that should be tolerated by the law in situations where the victim consents is in the first instance a matter for the State concerned since what is at stake is related, on the one hand, to public health considerations and to the general deterrent effect of the criminal law and, on the other, to the personal autonomy of the individual."[160]

The implications of the Court's decision for PAS are uncertain. The decision appears to give considerable discretion to each country to determine how far to permit consent to excuse what would otherwise be criminal. But what does the limitation "in the first instance" mean? It remains to be seen whether this indicates that ultimately the decision is for the Court of Human Rights, and that the Court can envisage circumstances where it would not permit consent to excuse. In principle, however, a country apparently has no absolute duty under international or regional human rights law to prohibit active assistance in suicide where it is requested by the person concerned. This conclusion may well be strengthened by the right embodied in Article 3 of the European Court of Human Rights not to be subject to "inhuman or degrading treatment."[161]

One could envisage circumstances, however, where the discretion of a country could be held to be limited. What if the procedure for policing the dividing line between legal and illegal conduct were such that illegal conduct was common? Or, to bring the issue back to PAS, what if permitting PAS contributed to a situation where the authorities tolerated *involuntary* euthanasia as an unfortunate (but common) side effect? To meet such concerns would surely require an extensive regulatory regime, as was envisaged in the short-lived Northern Territories of Australia legislation. A decision of the European Court of Human Rights appears to support such a regime. In the *McCann* case,[162] the Court held that the United Kingdom violated its duty under Article 2 when three IRA terrorists on an active bombing mission were shot dead by British army special forces in Gibraltar. The Court held that the authorities had placed the special forces in a position that would inevitably lead to loss of life, and other ways of dealing with the threat should have been put in place. In assessing the actions taken by the special forces, the Court considered not only the actions themselves but also such matters as their planning and control. In this, the Court seems to be adopting, albeit indirectly, the type of approach that the Federal Constitutional Court has employed in Germany on the issue of abortion:[163] that the state has a duty to do what it can do to avoid creating circumstances in which a threat to life becomes the only way out of an impossible dilemma.

What are the implications of this? Decriminalization of assisting in suicide brings an increased risk that the poor, for example, might be pressed to "choose" suicide rather than impoverish relatives who would otherwise be called on to pay for long-term palliative care. In the European human rights context, this fear may well translate into an argument that the duty Article 2 imposes on the state to protect life may require it to make available to all persons long-term palliative care and pain relief adequate to reduce the risk that such a dilemma will arise. The issue this raises is the problematic question of how far the right to life in Article 3 (and the equivalent right to life in Article 6 of the International Covenant on Civil and Political Rights)[164] includes a justiciable socioeconomic aspect. Support for such a positive duty in the European human rights context comes from a recent case. In *D. v The United Kingdom,*[165] the Court of Human Rights upheld an argument that the proposed removal of a drug courier dying of AIDS from Britain to his country of origin (St. Kitts in the Caribbean), where he had no accommodation, no family, moral, or financial support, and no access to adequate medical treatment, would be contrary to Article 3 of the Convention, which protects the right not to be subject to inhuman or degrading treatment. The applicant had entered the final stages of his fatal illness and relied on the medical and palliative care he received in Britain. Deporting him would have hastened his death and exposed him to the real risk of dying under the most distressing circumstances. The Court concluded that this would have amounted to inhuman treatment.

How does this apply to the issue of PAS in the United States? In most Western European states of an equivalent national wealth, a welfare state of some kind exists together with a national health service of sorts that is likely to provide palliative care relatively inexpensively. In the United States, all this is, perhaps, more questionable.[166] This may leave some American patients trapped, unable to afford pain relief, unable to cope, but unable to die at their own hand, or anyone else's. A Western European state that permitted PAS yet provided little or no palliative care to those who needed it but could not obtain it elsewhere might thus be seen indirectly to encourage people to "choose" death and thus to violate European human rights law. The absence in the U.S. Supreme Court's approach to PAS of any positive, socioeconomic element to the right to life, is noticeable.

Some Problems of Comparative Method

The brief consideration of a possible international and European human rights perspective on PAS, together with the earlier discussion of the Canadian Supreme Court and House of Lords approaches to the issue can, perhaps, begin to assist us in answering the larger questions: what are the explanations for the differences between jurisdictions in respect of the use of judicial decisions in one jurisdiction as persuasive authority in another? The issue is a complicated one, and it is impossible to do full justice to it in the context of this chapter.[167] The issue I seek to address here, to repeat a point made earlier, is not whether the decisions of the other jurisdictions are regarded as authoritative in a legally binding sense, but rather whether the court regards them as of *persuasive* value when faced with a problematic human rights issue. What, in particular, explains the divergence in approaches between the U.S. Supreme Court and other courts on this issue?

Patrick Glenn provides a useful starting point. He distinguishes between two different kinds of receptions of foreign law: "some are effected in a spirit of deliberate alliance with an external source of law, while others are effected with no particular sense of alliance but in order to draw constructive domestic advantage from the useful characteristics of the external model."[168] In the latter case "foreign law [is] received in the absence of any spirit of alliance simply because it is perceived by the receiving group as useful or desirable. Here the process of reception is more discriminating and particularized and it is perhaps more accurate to speak of 'borrowing' of particular foreign laws than of reception in general. . . . This type of reception is more likely to occur in the absence of overarching political institutions, since the political dimension of reception as alliance will then be absent, and it is the case that this form of reception has occurred principally since the emergence of the Nation State and the decline of larger forms of political structure."[169]

One reason courts may cite other country's human rights decisions, therefore, is that doing so is perceived to be part of a larger project of economic or social integration. Being seen to have regard to these external decisions is thought to be part and parcel of the judiciary's role in bringing about harmonization within the group of countries seeking closer integration. This impulse will be strongest when the integration is set out explicitly as a political program, with institutional characteristics, such as in Europe. As Richards has argued, well expressing this view, "The test for liberal constitutional institutions in Europe, both at the national and European level, will be the degree to which they foster in the lives of their people a national and European identity expressed through respect for human rights, not in antagonism to them. . . . [A]n institutionally enforceable conception of European human rights may be central to such cultural reconstruction."[170]

Similar results may also occur where there is a perception that having regard to other jurisdictions' approaches will encourage important groups within the country to perceive of themselves as members of a larger community, with beneficial results in terms of commitment to democracy and decent treatment. In this case (Israel and South Africa are examples), transnational judicial reception of human rights jurisprudence may be drawn on by the judge as a counterweight or response to isolationist or particularist impulses of which the judge disapproves. As Anne-Marie Slaughter argues, "The court of a fledgling democracy, for instance, might look to the opinions of courts in older and more established democracies as a way of binding its country to this existing community of states."[171] This reasoning may also take on an economic or more self-interested element when the constitutional practice or the Bill of Rights that the court is interpreting has arisen from a need to appeal to outside observers. Where a reason for the form of constitution adopted, or the approach to human rights adopted, is in part to provide a ticket for entry into a desirable trading or political grouping (which it sometimes is[172]), then it is even more likely that comparative experience will be drawn on in its interpretation.

Thus the Canadian Supreme Court's internationalism, and the House of Lords' respect for European Court of Human Rights and Commonwealth court decisions can be seen as examples of judicial recognition of alliances, both economic and political, which the United States has shunned. There is no equivalent to the Council of Europe, or the European Union, or the Commonwealth, which the United States considers themselves *part* of, as opposed to being *leaders* of. Nor does the United States feel the need to gain entry into the community of nations by showing engagement with the judicial opinions of other countries in the human rights context. Rather, the contrary seems to be true. It is difficult to prove, but I think it unchallengeable that many in the United States would regard human rights in the United States as well protected as compared with other countries and believe therefore that other countries can learn from the United States about those rights, rather than the other way round.

But the discussion of possible European responses to PAS prompts an additional set of explanations of why American courts might be uneasy about using foreign approaches. I suggested that had the U.S. Supreme Court considered this it might have been led to wonder how a country's failure to provide adequate medical and palliative care might affect a right to PAS. The absence of the type of developed welfare state that both Canada and most European countries enjoy means that some of the basic shape of American law in this area is going to be significantly different from some of the shape of European human rights law, and thus that European law will fit poorly into American law. Adoption of another legal system's approach may be thought to be inappropriate, then, because of the different social, economic, or political structures of the two societies. If this view is adopted, then there is no "common enterprise" to engage in with other jurisdictions.

Legal concepts may be thought, more broadly, to "fit into clusters of concepts, which together comprise a coherent and consistent set of rules and principles for the regulation of some aspect of social life. One cannot transplant a single foreign concept into domestic law without undermining the coherence of its conceptual scheme, which ultimately causes confusion and inconsistency."[173] We may, then, be unable to fit the foreign concept comprehensively into the "social and economic structure and cultural norms of the [sending] society and the internal logic of its legal system" well enough to be able to "appreciate both how the law works in society and how it fits into a system of legal concepts."[174] Considering oneself engaged in a common enterprise, therefore, needs to be tempered by a realization that there may well be a problem of understanding that has to be overcome before effective engagement is a real possibility.

Where there is disagreement over how to interpret particular foreign experiences and their relevance for the United States, it is not surprising, perhaps, that the U.S. Supreme Court is unwilling to use them as persuasive authority. There is an understandable fear that the Court will "get it wrong" in the sense of misunderstanding what lies behind the foreign decision or not fully appreciating the consequences of the foreign judgment. Nor is this an idle fear. Judges have demonstrated that they can get it wrong, even in much less subtle ways, for example, by citing as persuasive a decision that is not actually apt.[175]

The sophistication of American judges in some respects leads them to be much more punctilious (and therefore more cautious) than their non-American judicial brethren in the use of foreign judicial authority. For the best American judges, the need to place law and judicial decisions in their social, economic, and cultural contexts is second nature. American judges are, in some sense, all legal realists of one kind or another, and that is by no means the case in other jurisdictions. Judges in other jurisdictions perhaps tend toward rather simpleminded citation of foreign judicial decisions for form's sake rather than with any real understanding of what is going on in them. American judicial hesitation in using comparative methodology may therefore be supportable, if it is based on these problems, and may be a healthy spur to the development of a more convincing comparative law methodology in the human rights context.

The challenge it poses to those who wish to see a more universalistic idea of human rights gaining acceptance in national courts is considerable, requiring a reassessment of the theoretical underpinnings of comparative law, in particular the relationship between comparative constitutional law, international human rights, and legal reasoning. Without a comparative law methodology that can appear convincing in theory and workable in practice to a skeptical judiciary, American courts will fail to participate directly in the common judicial enterprise of human rights interpretation and application. It would be a particular pity if comparative law let us down just as it seemed to be coming into its own—at a time when constitutional rights are increasingly taking on a global tinge.

There is, however, a separate concern among some skeptics of such transnational judicial conversations. The idea of national courts getting together and "working things out" on human rights among themselves is somewhat troubling. If we are concerned about the legitimacy of *national* judges making these decisions, isn't the idea of judges making these decisions *transnationally,* in a cozy dialogue with each other, even more worrying? Here is Justice Scalia, dissenting, in *Thompson v Oklahoma,* the death penalty case discussed earlier:

> We must never forget that it is a Constitution for the United States of America that we are expounding. The practices of other nations, particularly other democracies, can be relevant to determining whether a practice uniform among our people is not merely a historical accident, but rather 'so implicit in the concept of ordered liberty' that it occupies a place not merely in our mores but, text permitting, in our Constitution as well. . . . But where there is not first a settled consensus among our own people, the views of other nations, however enlightened the Justices of this Court may think them to be, cannot be imposed upon Americans through the Constitution.[176]

Later, addressing a conference of judges from the Americas, he argued "[W]e judges of the American democracies are servants of our peoples, sworn to apply, without fear or favor, the laws that those peoples deem appropriate. We are not some international priesthood empowered to impose upon our free and independent citizens supra-national values that contradict their own."[177]

To an extent, of course, this concern interestingly echoes at least two of the concerns expressed over globalization generally—that the global will overwhelm the local and that an unelected international elite will subvert elected representatives, with the loss of diversity and a decline in democratic decision making. We return, therefore, by a somewhat circuitous route perhaps, to an underlying issue of several contributors to this book:[178] how far, and in what circumstances, judicial, as opposed to political, decision making is legitimate in this area. Failure to address the democratic concerns about the use of transnational persuasive precedents may end up undermining support for judicial protection for human rights rather than underpinning it. This would be more than a little ironic, given that a principal reason for citing foreign judgments is to *increase* the legitimacy of judicial decision making in the area of human rights. So far, our legal theory seems not to have sufficiently caught up with, and certainly not resolved, this difficulty.

Conclusion

I began this article with a quotation from John Donne and a question: is the Supreme Court becoming "part of the main"? My argument has been that the PAS cases raise interesting issues relating to the use of comparative law methodology. The approaches taken by different Justices in the Supreme Court raise important questions about the place of the U.S. Supreme Court in the trend toward the globalization of human rights interpretation. Should the Supreme Court view itself as part of a continuing conversation with judges in other jurisdictions about appropriate interpretation of apparently common rights? And that question raises, in turn, the question how far, if at all, the rights in issue really should be seen as "common" (impliedly accepting a degree of universality in their meaning and application), or particular and culturally relative. These questions focus attention on how far the "right to die/right to life" debate is one that is so culturally specific as to defy any attempt at a resolution beyond any given national context. They also force us to consider what happens to the principle of democratic government when courts interpret their country's statutes and constitutions in light of supranational standards.

NOTES

1. Zdenkowski has suggested that the debate has been fueled by several developments including the greater availability of artificial methods of prolonging life, landmark cases throughout the world, the increase in the number of those affected by AIDS, the growing number of elderly people, and the declining influence of organized religion. See George Zdenkowski, *The International Covenant on Civil and Political Rights and Euthanasia,* 20 University of New South Wales Law Journal 170, 172 (1997). See also Margaret F.A. Otlowski, *Voluntary Euthanasia and the Common Law* 257–332 (Clarendon, 1997).

2. Senate of Canada, *Of Life and Death, Report of the Special Senate Committee on Euthanasia and Assisted Suicide* (June 1995); House of Lords, Session 1993–1994, *Report of Select Committee on Medical Ethics* (1994);

New York State Task Force on Life and the Law, *When Death Is Sought: Assisted Suicide and Euthanasia in the Medical Context* (May, 1994); House Judiciary Committee, Sub-Committee on the Constitution, *Suicide, Assisted Suicide and Euthanasia,* May 1996; House of Representatives, Commerce Committee, Sub-Committee on Health and Environment, *Assisted Suicide,* March 6, 1997; House Judiciary Committee, *Physician-Assisted Suicide and Euthanasia in the Netherlands, A Report of Chairman Charles T. Canady* (96-H-522–1); Dutch Commission of Inquiry into the Medical Practice concerning Euthanasia, whose commissioned report is published in translation in Health Policy, Special Issue, vol 22/1 and 2, 1992.

3. Roger Magnusson, *The Future of the Euthanasia Debate in Australia,* 20 Melbourne University Law Review 1108 (1996).

4. Northern Territory of Australia, Rights of the Terminally Ill Act 1995.

5. *Wake and Gondarra v Northern Territory of Australia* (1996) 124 FLR 298 (Supreme Court of the Northern Territory).

6. The Euthanasia Laws Act 1997 (Cth). See also "Euthanasia Law Struck Down in Australia," *New York Times,* Mar 27 1997, A15.

7. *Rodriguez v Attorney General of British Columbia,* 107 DLR (4th) 343 (Supreme Court of Canada).

8. *R v United Kingdom,* July 4 1983, DR 33, p 270.

9. Serge F. Kovaleski, "Colombia Debates Court Ruling That Legalizes Mercy Killing," *The Washington Post,* Aug 18, 1997, A15; Tod Robberson, "Legalized Euthanasia Divides Colombia: Catholics Challenge Ruling: Doctors At Odds," *The Dallas Morning News,* Aug 11, 1997, 1A.

10. *In the Matter of a Ward of Court* [1995] 2 ILRM 401 (Irish Supreme Court).

11. *Airedale NHS Trust v Bland* [1993] AC 789 (House of Lords).

12. The English High Court was requested to provide just such an assurance. The case was settled, with the approval of the judge, when it was accepted by all sides that the action would be lawful under English law. Emma Wilkins, "Dying Woman Granted Wish for Dignified End," *The Times,* Oct 29, 1997; Clare Dyer, "Dying Woman Wins Right to End Life in Dignity: Drugs Will Ease Mental Distress," *The Guardian,* Oct 29, 1997.

13. *Office of Public Prosecutions v Chabot* (Supreme Court of the Netherlands, Criminal Chamber, 21 June 1994, nr 96.972, translated and published in The Modern Law Review (March 1995), pp 232–239. See also, Gene Kaufman, *Casenote: State v Chabot: A Euthanasia Case from the Netherlands,* 20 Ohio Northern University Law Review 815 (1994).

14. An incomplete selection includes: Dieter Giesen, *Dilemmas at Life's End: A Comparative Legal Perspective,* in John Keown, ed., *Euthanasia Examined: Ethical, Clinical and Legal Perspectives* 200–224 (Cambridge University Press, 1995); Raphael Cohen-Almagor, *Reflections on the Intriguing Issue of the Right to Die in Dignity,* 29 Israel Law Review 677 (1995); Barney Sneiderman & Marja Verhoef, *Patient Autonomy and the Defence of Medical Necessity: Five Dutch Euthanasia Cases,* XXXIV Alberta Law Review 374 (1996); *Comment, Deference to Doctors in Dutch Euthanasia Law,* 10 Emory International Law Review 255 (1996); John Keown, *Euthanasia in the Netherlands: Sliding Down*

the Slippery Slope?, in John Keown, ed., *Euthanasia Examined: Ethical, Clinical and Legal Perspectives* 261–296 (Cambridge University Press, 1995); Barney Sneiderman & Joseph M. Kaufert, eds., *Euthanasia in the Netherlands: A Model for Canada?* (Legal Research Institute of the University of Manitoba, 1994); Roger S. Magnusson, *The Sanctity of Life and the Right to Die: Social and Jurisprudential Aspects of the Euthanasia Debate in Australia and the United States,* 6 Pacific Rim Law & Policy Journal 1 (1997); Margaret Battin, *Voluntary Euthanasia and the Risks of Abuse: Can We Learn Anything from the Netherlands?* 20 Law, Medicine & Health Care 134 (1992).

15. See sources cited in footnote 2.

16. Luke Gormally, ed., *Euthanasia, Clinical Practice and the Law* (Linacre Centre for Health Care Ethics, London 1994).

17. Carlos F. Gomez, *Regulating Death: Euthanasia and the Case of the Netherlands* (Free Press, 1991); Herbert Hendin, *Seduced by Death: Doctors, Patients, and the Dutch Cure* (Norton, 1996); Herbert Hendin, *Seduced by Death: Doctors, Patients, and the Dutch Cure,* 10 Issues in Law & Medicine 123 (1994); Richard Fenigsen, *Physician-Assisted Death in the Netherlands: Impact on Long-Term Care,* 11 Issues in Law & Medicine 283 (1995); Richard Fenigsen, *Euthanasia in the Netherlands,* 6 Issues in Law & Medicine 229 (1990).

18. See, e.g., Ann Treneman, "Dr. Death Asks Some Painful Questions," *The Independent,* Nov 3, 1997, 15 (English newspaper story about the Australian experience); Sue Woodman, "Death's Doormen," *The Guardian,* July 2, 1997, 12 (English newspaper story about the U.S.'s

Supreme Court decisions in the PAS cases); "Justice Dept: Australian Case Will Not Effect (sic) NL Law," *ANP English News Bulletin* (September 27, 1996) (Dutch article on the Australian debate).

19. 117 S Ct 2258.

20. 117 S Ct 2293.

21. Justice Stevens in *Vacco,* 117 S Ct 2293, 2305.

22. J. Donne, *Meditation No 17,* in *Devotions Upon Emergent Occasions* 86, 87 (A. Raspa ed. 1987).

23. See, e.g., Schneider, *Making Biomedical Policy through Constitutional Adjudication: The Example of Physician-Assisted Suicide,* in this volume.

24. H. Patrick Glenn, *Persuasive Authority,* 32 McGill Law Journal 261, 264 (1987): "Adherence to persuasive authority is therefore a highly sophisticated alternative to notions of binding law and mechanical jurisprudence on the one hand and arbitrary personal licence on the other."

25. *Muller v Oregon,* 278 US 412 (1908). See further Paul L. Rosen, *The Supreme Court and Social Science* 45 (University of Illinois Press, 1972).

26. 347 US 483 (1954).

27. See, for example, the discussions by Dworkin, *Social Sciences and Constitutional Rights—The Consequences of Uncertainty,* 6 Journal of Law & Education 3 (1977); Yudof, *School Desegregation: Legal Realism, Reasoned Elaboration, and Social Science Research in the Supreme Court,* 42 Law & Contemporary Problems 57 (1978).

28. Anne-Marie Slaughter, *A Typology of Transjudicial Communication,* 29 University of Richmond Law Review 99, 118 (1994) .

29. I exclude from consideration situations where judges are acting in a

role different from their ordinary judicial functions, such as chairing committees, etc.

30. Louis Henkin, *Constitutionalism and Rights: The Influence of the United States Constitution Abroad* (Columbia University Press, 1990).

31. I do not include the use by the Supreme Court of *historical* analysis of what the common law in England consisted of prior to the American Revolution.

32. Warren E. Burger, *The Anglo-American Exchange: Our Spiritual Cousinage,* 27 William & Mary Law Review 633, 636 (1986), pointing to the influence of comparative law thinking on the Constitutional Convention in 1787 and the ratification efforts.

33. Anthony Lester, *The Overseas Trade in the American Bill of Rights,* 88 Columbia Law Review 537 (1988).

34. See David S. Clark, *The Use of Comparative Law by American Courts (I),* 42 American Journal of Comparative Law 23, 23 (1994): "Historically, the situation was different." See for example, *International Assn of Machinists v Street,* 367 US 740 (1961), on the issue of whether a union shop agreement that required all employees to join the union and pay union dues was contrary to the First Amendment because an individual was thus compelled to finance political campaigns and views with which he disagreed. In a dissent by Justice Frankfurter there is extensive discussion on the approach to the issue taken in Australia, Canada, and Britain. 367 US at 813: "That Britain, Canada and Australia have no explicit First Amendment is beside the point. For one thing, the freedoms safeguarded in terms in the First Amendment are deeply rooted and respected in the British tradition, and are part of legal presuppositions in Canada and Australia. And in relation to our immediate concern, the British Commonwealth experience establishes the pertinence of political means for realizing basic trade-union interests." *Baldrige v Shapiro,* 455 US 345, 357 (1982), noting that Germany, Great Britain, Italy, Japan, The Netherlands, and Sweden make some provision for the confidentiality of census materials, citing a U.S. Senate Committee report. *Roberts v Louisiana,* 431 US 633 (1977) dissent cites Chief Justice Laskin of the Canadian Supreme Court in *Miller and Cockriell v The Queen,* 70 DLR 3d 324, 337 (1976).

35. Anne-Marie Slaughter, *A Typology of Transjudicial Communication,* 29 University of Richmond Law Review 99 (1994), "The US Supreme Court has not seen fit to reciprocate in kind." Ibid. at 104. Gordon A. Christenson, *Using Human Rights Law to Inform Due Process and Equal Protection Analyses,* 52 Cincinnati Law Review 3, 5 (1983): "I am curious why our courts shun external sources of law—more specifically, contemporary decisions of foreign and international courts . . ." He considers that "most United States courts, both state and federal, show less inclination now than at the beginning of the Republic to use sources of foreign, international and customary law to aid interpretation, especially in constitutional cases. . . . " Ibid. at 6. Richard B. Lillich, *The Constitution and International Human Rights,* 83 American Journal of International Law 851, 855 (1989): "If American constitutionalism has contributed greatly to the development of international human rights law, the reverse, alas, has yet to occur." He argues that this should occur "if the United

States, as well as other countries, is to prosper from it over the long haul." Ibid. at 860.

36. 410 US 113 (1973).

37. Mary Ann Glendon, *Abortion and Divorce in Western Law* (Harvard University Press, 1987).

38. 492 US 490 (1989).

39. Brief, p 23. Note, Planned Parenthood v Casey: *From U.S. "Rights Talk" to Western European "Responsibility Talk,"* 16 Fordham International Law Journal 761, 793 (1992-93): "The Western European example served as a model and guide for the U.S. government's amicus brief for the appellant in *Webster."*

40. Ibid.

41. Oral Argument, p 427.

42. Brief, p 3.

43. Brief of the United States, p 39.

44. Brief, p 24. (Similar arguments were made by the Southern Center for Law and Ethics.)

45. Appellant's reply brief, p 1.

46. 505 US 833 (1992).

47. *Casey* Brief, p 12, n9.

48. Ibid. at 9.

49. 505 US at 833, n1 (Rehnquist, C. J.).

50. 39 B Verf GE 1 (1975).

51. *Morgentaler v The Queen,* 1 SCR 30, 44 DLR 4th 385 (1988).

52. 478 US 186 (1986).

53. 478 US at 191, quoting *Palko v Connecticut,* 302 US 319, 325–26 (1937).

54. 478 US at 191, quoting *Moore v East Cleveland,* 431 US 494, 503 (1977) (opinion of Powell, J.).

55. 478 US at 195.

56. *Dudgeon v United Kingdom* (22 October 1981, European Court of Human Rights), Series A, No. 45, p. 18, (1982) 4 EHRR 149.

57. Amicus Curiae Brief on Behalf of the Respondents by Lamda Legal Defense and Education Fund, Inc., at n10.

58. 505 US 377 (1992).

59. [1990] 3 SCR 697 (Supreme Court of Canada).

60. Section 319(2) of the Criminal Code of Canada, RSC 1985, c. C-46.

61. 505 US 377 (1992).

62. [1990] 3 SCR 697.

63. David Weissbrodt, *Globalization of Constitutional Law and Civil Rights,* 43 Journal of Legal Education 262 (1993).

64. *Furman v Georgia,* 408 US 238 (1972).

65. 408 US at 371.

66. 408 US at 354.

67. 487 US 815 (1987).

68. *Thompson v Oklahoma,* 487 US at 830.

69. 487 US at 869, n4.

70. 492 US 361 (1989).

71. Ibid. at 389.

72. Ibid. at 370, n1.

73. 117 S Ct 2293 (1997).

74. 117 S Ct 2258 (1997).

75. For a more detailed consideration of the cases, see Suter, *Ambivalent Unanimity: An Analysis of the Supreme Court's Holding,* in the volume.

76. 497 US 261 (1990).

77. 505 US 833 (1992).

78. See Nina Clark, *The Politics of Physician Assisted Suicide* (Garland Publishing, 1997).

79. See, e.g., Herbert Hendin, *The Slippery Slope,* 36 Duquesne Law Review 427 (1996); Seth F. Kreimer, *Does Pro-Choice Mean Pro-Kevorkian? An Essay on* Roe, Casey, *and the Right to Die,* 44 American University Law Review 803, 818–19 (1995); Alison C. Hall, *Note, To Die With Dignity: Comparing Physician Assisted Suicide in the United States, Japan and the Netherlands,* 74 Washington University Law Quarterly 803 (1996); David Orentlicher, *The Legalization of Physician Assisted Suicide: A Very Modest Revolution,* 38 Boston College Law Review 443 (1997).

80. *Compassion in Dying v State of Washington,* 79 F3d 790 (9th Cir

1996); *Quill v Vacco,* 80 F3d 716 (2nd Cir 1996).

81. See, e.g., Brief of *Amicus Curiae* Richard Thompson Oakland County Prosecuting Attorney; Brief of *Amicus Curiae* Bioethicists.

82. House Judiciary Committee, *Sub-Committee on the Constitution, Suicide, Assisted Suicide and Euthanasia,* May 1996; House of Representatives, Commerce Committee, Sub-Committee on Health and Environment, *Assisted Suicide,* March 6, 1997; House Judiciary Committee, *Physician-Assisted Suicide and Euthanasia in the Netherlands, A Report of Chairman Charles T. Canady* (96-H-522–1).

83. Charles Krauthammer, "The Dutch Example," *The Washington Post,* Jan 10, 1997, A21; Seth Mydans, "Legal Euthanasia: Australia Faces a Grim Reality," *New York Times,* Feb 2, 1997, A3.

84. The transcript was published in 143:7 *Chicago Daily Law Bulletin* 1 (Jan 10, 1997) ("Justices hear arguments on laws barring physician-assisted suicide").

85. Ibid. at 1.

86. Ibid. at 5.

87. Ibid. at 5.

88. Ibid. at 8.

89. [1993] AC 789 (English House of Lords).

90. 117 S Ct at 2299, n.8.

91. 117 S Ct 2258, 2312 (Breyer, J.).

92. Ibid. at 2258 (Rehnquist, C. J.).

93. *Rodriguez v British Columbia* (Attorney General), 107 DLR 4th 342 (Supreme Court of Canada, 1993).

94. 117 S Ct 2258, 2286 (Souter, J.).

95. Ibid. at 2266, n16 (Rehnquist, C. J.).

96. Ibid. at 2274 (Rehnquist, C. J.).

97. Ibid. at 2274 (Rehnquist, C. J.).

98. Ibid. at 2274 (Rehnquist, C. J.).

99. Ibid. at 2275 (Rehnquist, C. J.).

100. Ibid. at 2275 (Rehnquist, C. J.).

101. Carlos F. Gomez, *Regulating Death: Euthanasia and the Case of the Netherlands* (Free Press, 1991).

102. 117 S Ct 2258 at 2292 (Souter, J.).

103. Herbert Hendin, *Seduced by Death: Doctors, Patients and the Dutch Cure* (Norton, 1997).

104. John Keown, *Euthanasia in the Netherlands: Sliding Down the Slippery Slope?,* in John Keown, ed., *Euthanasia Examined: Ethical, Clinical, and Legal Perspectives* (Cambridge University Press, 1995).

105. Gomez (cited in note 101).

106. 117 S Ct 2258 at 2292 (Souter, J.).

107. Richard Posner, *Aging and Old Age* (University of Chicago Press, 1995)

108. Richard Allen Epstein, *Mortal Peril: Our Inalienable Right to Health Care* (Addison-Wesley, 1997).

109. G. Van der Wal et al, *Euthanasia and Assisted Suicide. II. Do Dutch Family Doctors Act Prudently?,* 9 Family Practice 135 (1992).

110. 117 S Ct 2258 at 2292 (Souter, J.).

111. Ibid. at 2292 (Souter, J.).

112. Ibid. at 2292 (Souter, J.).

113. Ibid. at 2292 (Souter, J.).

114. Ibid. at 2293 (Souter, J.).

115. See for example, http://www .euthanasia.org/contents.html; http://www.rights.org/deathnet /open.html; http://www.iaetf.org /ollib.htm; (Sites visited, May 21, 1999).

116. David Nelken, *Disclosing/Invoking Legal Culture: An Introduction,* 4 Social & Legal Studies 435, 440 (1995).

117. Mary Ann Glendon, *Rights Talk: The Impoverishment of Political Discourse* 158 (Free Press, 1991).

118. Anne-Marie Slaughter, *A Typology of Transjudicial Communication,* 29 University of Richmond Law Review 99, 99 (1994).

119. See, for example, the decision *In the Matter of a Ward of Court by the Irish Supreme Court,* in which there are extensive references to American and British decisions, [1995] 2 ILRM 401, and by the Supreme Court of the Northern Territory of Australia in *Wake and Gondarra v Northern Territory of Australia* (1996) 124 FLR 298 in which the dissent draws on British decisions extensively. In both these cases, however, unlike in *Bland* and *Rodriguez,* there is some expression of reservations on the utility of a comparative approach expressed by one judge, the majority in the Northern Territories decision, and by Denham, J., in the Irish Supreme Court.

120. [1993] AC 789 (House of Lords).

121. Ibid. at 856.

122. Ibid. at 859.

123. Ibid. at 863–65, 867.

124. Ibid. at 872.

125. Ibid. at 890.

126. Ibid.

127. 110 S Ct 2841, 2859 (1990).

128. [1993] AC 789, 890.

129. Ibid.

130. Ibid. at 893–94.

131. 107 DLR 4th 342 (Supreme Court of Canada, 1993).

132. Section 7 provides that "Everyone has the right to life, liberty and security of the person and the right not to be deprived thereof except in accordance with the principles of fundamental justice."

133. Section 12 provides that "Everyone has the right not to be subjected to any cruel or unusual treatment or punishment."

134. 107 DLR 4th at 386.

135. Ibid. at 401 (Sopinka, J.).

136. Ibid. at 401–4 (Sopinka, J.).

137. Ibid. at 402 (Sopinka, J.).

138. [1993] AC 789 (House of Lords).

139. 107 DLR 4th at 402 (Sopinka, J.).

140. The use by the Court in the PAS cases of the Dutch experience has occasioned some debate on similar grounds. In his article on the case in the New York Review of Books, following the decision, Professor Dworkin was critical of Justice Souter's citation of the work of Herbert Hendin, MD, Ronald Dworkin, "Assisted Suicide: What the Court Really Said," *New York Review of Books* 40 (Sept 25, 1997). Dworkin argued that Souter should have been more circumspect in placing any reliance on Hendin's work on the grounds that the author's methodology was suspect. Dworkin particularly objected to the fact that five Dutch doctors interviewed by Hendin had objected to his reports of his interviews with them. Hendin subsequently replied in a letter to the NYRB defending his methodology, and his integrity, Letter to the Editor, Herbert Hendin, MD, *Assisted Suicide and Euthanasia: An Exchange,* New York Review of Books 68–69 (Nov 6, 1997). Dworkin defended his criticism in a published reply to the letter. Reply by Ronald Dworkin, *Assisted Suicide and Euthanasia: An Exchange*, New York Review of Books 69–70 (Nov 6, 1997).

141. Anne-Marie Slaughter, *A Typology of Transjudicial Communication,* 29 University of Richmond Law Review 99, 127 (1994).

142. Ibid. at 127.

143. H. Patrick Glenn, *Persuasive Authority,* 32 McGill Law Journal 261 (1987).

144. Ibid. at 288.

145. Anne-Marie Slaughter, *A Typology of Transjudicial Communication,* 29 University of Richmond Law Review 99, 121–22 (1994).

146. Ibid. at 123.

147. D. McGoldrick, *The Human Rights Committee* 330 (Clarendon Press, 1991).
148. Article 8 provides:

    1. Everyone has the right to respect for his private and family life, his home and his correspondence.
    2. There shall be no interference by a public authority with the exercise of this right except in the interests of national security, public safety or the economic well-being of the country, for the prevention of disorder or crime, for the protection of health or morals, or for the protection of the rights and freedoms of others.

149. *App. No. 10083/82 v United Kingdom,* 6 European Human Rights Review 140, 143–44.
150. Article 10 provides:

    1. Everyone has the right to freedom of expression. This right shall include freedom to hold opinions and to receive and impart information and ideas without interference by public authority and regardless of frontiers. This Article shall not prevent States from requiring the licensing of broadcasting, television or cinema enterprises.
    2. The exercise of these freedoms, since it carries with it duties and responsibilities, may be subject to such formalities, conditions, restrictions or penalties as are prescribed by law and are necessary in a democratic society, in the interests of national security, territorial integrity or public safety, for the prevention of disorder or crime, for the protection of health or morals, for the protection of the reputation or rights of others, for preventing the disclosure of information received in confidence, or for maintaining the authority and impartiality of the judiciary.

151. Ibid. at 144.
152. The relevant part of Article 6, ICCPR provides: "Every human being has the inherent right to life. This right shall be protected by law. No one shall be arbitrarily deprived of his life." An article that collects the main sources relevant for interpreting this article in the context of euthanasia is, George Zdenkowski, *The International Covenant on Civil and Political Rights and Euthanasia,* 20 University of New South Wales Law Journal 170 (1997).
153. See David Harris, *The Right to Life under the European Convention on Human Rights,* 1 Maastricht Journal of European & Comparative Law 122 (1994).
154. Article 2 provides in full:

    1. Everyone's right to life shall be protected by law. No one shall be deprived of his life intentionally save in the execution of a sentence of a court following his conviction of a crime for which this penalty is provided by law.
    2. Deprivation of life shall not be regarded as inflicted in contravention of this Article when it results from the use of force which is no more than absolutely necessary:
        (a) in defence of any person from unlawful violence;
        (b) in order to effect a lawful arrest or to prevent the escape of a person lawfully detained;
        (c) in action lawfully taken for the purpose of quelling a riot or insurrection.

155. A question raised but not determined by P. van Dijk & G. J. H. van Hoof, *Theory and Practice of the*

European Convention on Human Rights 221 (2nd ed, Kluwer, 1990).

156. Widmer v Switzerland, No. 20527/92 (1993), unreported, cited in Harris, O'Boyle, & Warbrick, Law of the European Convention on Human Rights (Butterworths, 1995) at 38, n7.

157. Harris, at 38–39 (cited in note 156). A similar position is taken by P. van Dijk and G. J. H. van Hoof, Theory and Practice of the European Convention on Human Rights 221 (2nd ed, Kluwer, 1990): "there is as yet hardly any standard for a strict review by the Strasbourg organs. . . ."

158. Laskey, Jaggard and Brown v The United Kingdom, Judgment of the European Court of Human Rights, 20 January 1997, (1997) 24 EHRR 39.

159. Ibid. at § 40.

160. Ibid. at §44.

161. P. van Dijk & G. J. H. van Hoof, Theory and Practice of the European Convention on Human Rights 221(2nd ed, Kluwer, 1990).

162. McCann and Others v United Kingdom, Judgment of the European Court of Human Rights, 27 Sept 1995, Series A, No 324, (1996) 21 European Human Rights Review 97.

163. B Verf G, Judgment of 28 May 1993. See Susanne Walther, Thou Shalt Not (But Thou Mayest): Abortion of the German Constitutional Court's 1993 Landmark Decision, 36 German Yearbook of International Law 385 (1993).

164. For a discussion of the issue in the context of Article 6 ICCPR, see S. Joseph, The Right to Life, in D. Harris & S. Joseph, eds., The International Covenant on Civil and Political Rights and United Kingdom Law 155, 174–76 (Clarendon Press, 1995).

165. D. v The United Kingdom, Judgment of the European Court of Human Rights, 2 May 1997.

166. H. Hendin, Suicide and the Request for Assisted Suicide: Meaning and Motivation, 35 Duquesne Law Review 285, 303 (1996): "The United States is the only industrialized democracy that does not guarantee medical care to a large number of its population." Ibid. at 303.

167. I have considered this in greater length elsewhere; Christopher Mc-Crudden, "A Common Law of Human Rights?: Trans-national Judicial Conversations on Human Rights," Oxford Journal of Legal Studies (2000) (forthcoming).

168. H. Patrick Glenn, Persuasive Authority, 32 McGill Law Journal 261, 265 (1987).

169. Ibid. at 274.

170. David A. J. Richards, Comparative Revolutionary Constitutionalism: A Research Agenda for Comparative Law, 26 New York University Journal of International Law & Politics 1, 59 (1993).

171. Anne-Marie Slaughter, A Typology of Transjudicial Communication, 29 University of Richmond Law Review 99, 134 (1994).

172. Rolando Gaete, Rites of Passage into the Global Village, VI Law & Critique 113, 114 (1995): "Human rights have become a banner representing the 'civilising mission' of financial institutions and of the countries that provide most of the funds for these institutions." Gerhard Casper, European Convergence, 58 University of Chicago Law Review 441, 444–45 (1991): "On the whole, Eastern Europe will follow Western European examples. The Eastern Europeans will find this path pragmatically desirable because of their aspirations to join the Council of Europe and, more importantly, the European Community."

173. Hugh Collins, Methods and Aims of Comparative Contract Law, 11 Ox-

ford Journal of Legal Studies 396, 398 (1991).
174. Ibid. at 398.
175. The citation by Justice Breyer in *Gomez v Ruiz,* 117 S Ct 285, 286, n3 of the South African Constitutional Court decision on the death penalty (*Makwanyane,* 1995 (6) BCLR 665 (South African Constitutional Court)) seems an oblique use of the case, to say the least. The main holding in *Makwanyane* was the unconstitutionality of the death penalty under the South African interim constitution. However, Justice Breyer cited the *Makwanyane* case in support of the proposition that delays in the carrying out of capital punishment are unacceptable and that the death penalty should therefore be carried out without further delay. The brief discussion of the case ignores en-

tirely its main holding, a holding that is entirely inconsistent with the trend of recent U.S. Supreme Court decisions on the constitutionality of capital punishment under the U.S. Constitution.
176. *Thompson v Oklahoma,* 487 US at 869, n4 (citations omitted).
177. Antonin Scalia, *Commentary,* 40 Saint Louis University Law Journal 1119, 1122 (1996).
178. See, e.g., Carl E. Schneider, *Making Biomedical Policy through Constitutional Adjudication; The Example of Physician-Assisted Suicide;* Peter Hammer, *Assisted Suicide and the Problem of Individually Determined Collective Rationality;* and Carl E. Schneider, *Concluding Thoughts: Bioethics in the Language of the Law,* all in this volume.

CHAPTER 7

Making Biomedical Policy through Constitutional Adjudication: The Example of Physician-Assisted Suicide

Carl E. Schneider

Introduction

Throughout most of American history no one would have supposed biomedical policy could or should be made through constitutional adjudication. No one would have thought that the Constitution spoke to biomedical issues, that those issues were questions of federal policy, or that judges were competent to handle them. Today, however, the resurgence of substantive due process has swollen the scope of the Fourteenth Amendment, the distinction between federal and state spheres is tattered, and few statutes escape judicial vetting. Furthermore, Abraham Lincoln's wish that the Constitution should "become the political religion of the nation" has been granted. "We now reverently refer to the Supreme Court as the great arbiter of American moral life, as performing a 'prophetic function,' as expressing what 'we stand for as a people.'"[1] Its Justices are invoked as "moral teachers who help to shape the character of our nation."[2] How could our most perplexing ethical issues *not* be confided to such an institution?

My first purpose in this chapter is to consider that question, to ask whether constitutional adjudication is a good way to make biomedical policy. My answer—in its briefest, bluntest form—is no. I believe biomedical policy is generally better made—is better informed, better structured, more responsive, wiser, and more legitimate—when it is made by the whole range of governmental agencies (legislatures, administrative agencies, referenda, courts interpreting statutes and the common law), and semiofficial and nonofficial institutions and individuals (commissions like the New York Task Force on Life and the Law, professional associations like the American Association of Bioethicists and the American Medical Association, voluntary associations like churches, and individuals like scholars, doctors, patients, and families). These actors and agencies will not produce perfect law; they may not even produce good law. But they are likelier to do better than courts acting as interpreters of the Constitution.

My vehicle for this argument is the cases deciding whether there is a constitutional right to assistance in committing suicide, particularly the

Ninth Circuit's decision in *Compassion in Dying v Washington*[3] and the Supreme Court's reversal of that decision in *Washington v Glucksberg*.[4] My principal exhibit will be *Compassion in Dying*. It is the high-water mark of the constitutional claim and the culmination of exceptionally thorough judicial consideration: The District Court found Washington's prohibition of assisted suicide unconstitutional; the Ninth Circuit's three-judge panel reversed; and the Ninth Circuit *en banc* reversed the panel by a vote of eight to three in a long and detailed opinion. *Compassion in Dying,* in short, probably represents as considered a job as a court is likely to achieve in setting biomedical policy through constitutional adjudication. It therefore repays careful inspection.

An obvious objection to the argument against making biomedical policy through constitutional adjudication is that, for better or worse, the Constitution creates rights courts must enforce, that courts thus cannot escape making biomedical policy, and that it is thus not worth asking whether constitutional adjudication will yield sound biomedical policies. I have several answers to this objection. First, I rather quaintly doubt the Fourteenth Amendment creates a constitutional right of privacy of the kind the Court has created. This is a well-worn controversy, and I need only say here that the reasons for my doubts are conventional ones, including the interpretive leap such a right requires, the difficulties the Supreme Court has had articulating and defining that right, and the power the right gives unelected courts. Perhaps somewhat less conventionally, I also believe the problems with constitutional adjudication I will describe are relevant to whether a privacy right should be read into the Constitution.

Second, my arguments should be relevant even to someone who finds a privacy right in the Fourteenth Amendment because they speak to some unresolved issues in the law of substantive due process. For example, even if there is a privacy right, the capacity of courts to handle biomedical questions well should affect our view of the right's scope: The privacy right is a judicial creation; it should be one judges can interpret and implement effectively and intelligently. Furthermore, my arguments speak to a persistent but neglected problem in Fourteenth Amendment analysis—how governmental interests should be evaluated.[5]

Third, I will ask not just whether constitutional adjudication is a good way of making public policy, but also whether, under current constitutional doctrine, statutes that make it a crime to help someone commit suicide are unconstitutional. I will primarily contend that the state's interests are strong enough to make those statutes constitutional even if there is some kind of privacy right to assisted suicide.

In sum, this chapter serves this volume's goals in several ways. First, it asks an important question about any issue of public policy—which institutions are best entrusted with the decision? More particularly, it joins the controversy over the role of courts as an instrument of public policy.[6] Second, it contributes to the debate on the scope of the right of privacy and on how state interests should be treated in Fourteenth Amendment analysis. Third, it comments on the constitutional strength of the state's interests in making it criminal to assist in a suicide. Finally, it speaks to the question whether assisted suicide should be forbidden as a matter of public policy.

Since this chapter is lengthy, let me summarize its argument here. I will not contend that constitutional adjudication must inevitably reach the wrong result in bioethical cases. The Supreme Court in *Glucksberg* reached the right one, even though the Court was divided and several of its members—perhaps a majority—warned that somewhat different facts might have led them to a critically different result. I will argue, rather, that constitutional adjudication is ill-equipped to make good bioethical policy. This is particularly a problem where a court finds that a statute is unconstitutional, for then the court substitutes its judgment for the legislature's and ordinarily attempts to sketch a new policy.

I will argue that there is little reason to prefer a court's judgment and much reason to doubt its ability to craft sound policy. More particularly, I will suggest that the Constitution and constitutional jurisprudence are poor in guidance for making bioethical policy and that judges' training and experience hardly remedy this defect. Worse, litigation commonly fails to furnish judges the information they need for evaluating statutes intelligently. To illustrate this point, I will scrutinize the Ninth Circuit's treatment of the interests the state asserted in *Compassion in Dying*. I will then propose that these judicial handicaps are exacerbated by much in the culture of American law. I will conclude by arguing that other institutions are better placed to make—and indeed are already making—policy governing assisted suicide than are courts.

How Well Equipped Are Judges to Make Policy?

Judges interpreting the Constitution might make good policy for two reasons—because the Constitution states good principles for public policy and provides a good framework for analyzing social issues or because judges' training, experience, and procedures give them insight into what policy should be. Neither of these conditions fits matters of biomedical policy.

First, the absence of any textual commission from the Constitution means the Justices are thrown back on their own resources in making policy. In privacy law, those resources have produced a perfectly worthy desideratum—autonomy. Yet by itself autonomy is no guide to policy. Autonomy, yes. But in what quantities, in what places, and at what costs?[7] The Justices have found no satisfactory way to turn a banality into a workable principle: Autonomy is notoriously a greedy concept, but the Court cannot define its limits. Autonomy is notoriously one good among many, but the Court cannot articulate a sound method for accommodating it to other goods.

Consider the announced principles of Fourteenth Amendment analysis. First, a court decides whether a statute infringes a fundamental right. If it does, it is constitutional only if it is "necessary" to serve a "compelling" state interest. If the statute does not infringe a compelling state interest, it is constitutional if it simply serves a "legitimate" state interest. Much depends, then, on how one decides what rights are fundamental. However, even after several decades of modern substantive due process, that decision remains embarrassingly manipulable. For example, the Court ritually says it begins "by examining our Nation's history, legal traditions, and practices."[8] But everything turns on the specificity of that examination: Define the right narrowly and it will rarely look "fundamental." Justice Scalia was correct in his concurrence in *Cruzan v Director, Missouri Department of Health* when he denied that suicide had ever been thought a right[9] and in his opinion for the plurality in *Michael H. v Gerald D.*[10] when he said Americans had never imagined a right to adultery. But the Court has not always employed Justice Scalia's narrow definition of history and tradition. Had it done so in *Roe v Wade,* for example, it could hardly have derived a fundamental right to abortion.[11] Yet if one broadens one's definition of the right and asks whether there is a history and tradition of protecting autonomy or of a "right to be left alone," virtually any claim may be alchemized into a fundamental right.

This dilemma might lead us into despondency about the history-and-traditions test and toward a more conventional lawyer's approach—inferring principles from precedent and then using the principle to guide decisions. The most celebrated such attempt—one seized on by the Ninth Circuit in *Compassion in Dying*—is from *Planned Parenthood of Southeastern Pennsylvania v Casey:*

> These matters, involving the most intimate and personal choices a person may make in a lifetime, choices central to personal dignity and autonomy, are central to the liberty protected by the Fourteenth Amendment. At the heart of liberty is the right to define one's own concept of existence, of meaning, of the universe, and of the mystery of human life. Beliefs about these matters could not define the attributes of personhood were they formed under compulsion of the State.[12]

Perhaps this rhapsody is inspiring; it is hardly instructive. The Court in *Glucksberg* responded to it sensibly: "That many of the rights and liberties protected by the Due Process Clause sound in personal autonomy does not warrant the sweeping conclusion that any and all important, intimate, and personal decisions are so protected, . . . and Casey did not suggest otherwise."[13] But then what principle *should* be inferred from the cases? The Court does not try to say. And how could it? What consistent principle should be inferred from cases that hold, for instance, that private sexual activities may be criminalized[14] but that most abortions may not be?

Like the formulations for evaluating fundamental rights, the tests for assessing the state's interests are mightily manipulable. A statute that interferes with a "fundamental right" must be "necessary" to promote a "compelling" state interest. What do those Delphic terms mean? The Court never says. "Compelling" languishes in mystery, since the Court rarely uses it to decide cases. "Necessary" has meant first that there is no less offensive way of reaching the statute's goal and second that the statute is neither under- nor overinclusive. Since no statute fully meets either criterion, few statutes that infringe a fundamental right have 'scaped whipping.[15]

As privacy jurisprudence developed, it became clear that the decision whether a fundamental right had been infringed was virtually dispositive. This seemed an embarrassing betrayal of the test the Court had promulgated, and it promoted an impoverished analysis. Gradually, the Court devised an intermediate category of scrutiny less apt to predetermine a statute's fate. This answered some of the criticisms of the old two-tier system, but it has left privacy law even more befogged than before. The Court only intensified these perplexities in *Cruzan,* for there the Court seemed to abandon the language of fundamental rights to adopt the language of "liberty interests." The Court then "balanced" the liberty interest against "the relevant state interests."[16] Justices Brennan and Stevens agreed Cruzan had a fundamental right but not on how to evaluate the state interest. Justice Brennan said that "if a requirement imposed by a State 'significantly interferes with the exercise of a fundamental right, it cannot be upheld unless it is supported by sufficiently important state interests and is closely tailored to effectuate only those interests.'"[17] Justice Stevens said that, at a minimum, the statute must "bear a reasonable relationship to a legitimate state end."[18]

Is this chaos of thought and passion, all confused, merely the product of an early stage in privacy jurisprudence? Perhaps, but there are reasons to think the pattern of undefined terms, multiple tests, and manipulable standards will persist. The problems with which the Court is struggling are bitterly difficult. Autonomy is a core value, but it is so endlessly expansive and has such different costs and benefits in different situations that writing principles to promote it seems to baffle everyone. Furthermore, building doctrine by committee is awkward, particularly where the committee membership changes and the members are fractious and apparently unburdened by any sense of obligation to compromise even enough to provide guidance to lower courts, the bar, and the public. In both *Cruzan* and *Glucksberg,* for example, Justice O'Connor was part of a five-person majority but wrote concurring opinions that cast doubt on the majority's reasoning. And in *Glucksberg* the nine Justices wrote six opinions. Furthermore, the Court constructs constitutional doctrine through a common law process that looks at issues piecemeal. This makes it hard for the Court to assess any doctrine as a whole.

As we will see throughout this chapter, this brief summary hardly does justice to the problems the Court has encountered in stating a defensible autonomy principle and operationalizing it with workable tests. Thus, so much is left to the Justices' discretion that they must draw deeply on their own resources. So how well suited to making sound public policy are those resources?

Little in the training or experience of most judges fits them to make biomedical policy. Law schools primarily teach students to analyze legal documents and doctrines, to derive principles from precedents, and to apply precedents to new cases. Despite decades of criticism, judicial opinions dominate the enterprise. Even statutes are assigned cautiously, resisted by students, and taught gingerly. Students rarely read the social science that public policy should consult and regularly leave law school without encountering a serious analysis of how a legal doctrine actually works. Unhappily, scholars do not write such analyses, law teachers are often uninterested in them,[19] and authors cannot squeeze them into casebooks.

Legal practice hardly remedies these defects of legal training. Lawyers today, particularly elite lawyers, tend to specialize narrowly. And for most lawyers even a general practice is a narrow enterprise. Thus it is possible—it is common—to be appointed to the bench without ever having administered an organization, met a payroll, run a public program, stood for office, or served in a legislature. Judges' social experience is likely to be narrow as well. Most elite judges were born into, and all of them live among, the comfortable classes. As a multimillionaire jurist once lamented to me, "I'm always the poorest man in any room I'm in."[20]

Once anointed, judges become genuine generalists, assigned to resolve a breathtaking range of problems. Legislators may specialize; judges cannot. Legislators serve on specialized committees with expert staffs. Judges have only a few "clerks" who have just graduated from law school, and they cannot consult experts out of court. Some judges even try to limit their social contacts to preserve their dispassion. In their work they lead lives of quiet preparation. In sum, judges suffer the narrowness of the generalist.

All this means judges often know little about the issues of public policy they must resolve and have little experience analyzing public policy issues in any but doctrinal terms. Yet the way courts acquire and analyze information does little to ameliorate this ignorance and inexperience. The only judge who participates in finding facts is the trial judge. But trial judges have little control over what facts are discovered, for it is primarily the lawyers' responsibility to investigate the relevant facts and to introduce them into evidence.

Yet trial lawyers suffer from the same impoverished training and experience judges do. They are specialists at litigation who must educate themselves about every new case. Furthermore, their allegiance is not to the truth, but to the client, so that they typically introduce only evidence favorable to their clients. The range of opinions and information the judge hears thus depends on who the clients are. If they do not represent the full range of interested parties—and they rarely do—relevant positions will go unexplored. (Hospices, for instance, were not litigants in *Glucksberg*.) All this is troublesome enough when the question is only whether some fact occurred. It is crippling when the issue is whether some policy is wise. Such a question requires analyses of complex data that can essentially be introduced only through expert witnesses. In American litigation, these witnesses are ordinarily paid by the parties, and paid to be partisan. Finally, the quantity and quality of the information lawyers introduce depend on the (markedly variable) competence of the lawyers and the wealth of their clients (and on the rules of evidence).

In American law, appellate judges depend on the information trial courts gather. Appellate judges may not make inquiries of their own and in any event have neither time nor taste for doing so. They primarily rely on the parties' briefs and perhaps a joint appendix that reprints a few slivers of the record. (Although judges are entitled to summon the whole record, they rarely do.) Other affected parties may submit *amicus curiae* briefs, although they need not and although judges rarely read them. No judge is polymath enough to be well informed on all the kinds of cases that come before a court. Courts, in other words, make social policy on the basis of "executive summaries."

The result of all this is that appellate courts regularly fail to understand the nature of the institutions and practices for which they make rules, even when those institutions and practices are legal ones. Thus, one fascinating study of the way courts actually deal with criminals concluded that the Supreme Court's decisions "overlook (1) the nature of courts as formal organization; (2) the relationship that the lawyer-regular *actually* has with the court organization; and (3) the character of the lawyer-client relationship in the criminal court (the routine relationships, not those unusual ones that are described in 'heroic' terms in novels, movies, and TV)."[21] As another commentator puts it, "American jurists of criminal law rarely study the reality of the American criminal justice system but potter happily away in an Alice-in-Wonderland world where defendants with competent lawyers go on trial and argue strenuously about *mens rea* or the rules of evidence or the exact weight or implication of the guarantees in the Bill of Rights."[22]

Once again, the contrast with legislators is illuminating. In a well-run legislature, bills are turned over to a specialized committee. Its expert staff prepares reports and interviews witnesses who represent a range of interests and views. At hearings, legislators may ask whatever questions they wish (or are prompted to ask by their staff). Legislators may also interrogate anyone they choose about the controversy. And legislators properly heed public debates and are properly the subject of lobbying (which would be improper ex parte contact were a judge approached).

For all the reasons I have described, then, systematic empirical information rarely intrudes itself into the labors of appellate judges. Even when it does, however, courts all too often dismiss it. As David Faigman says in his extended study of the problem, "Historically, most constitutional fact-finding depended on the Justices' best guess about the matter."[23] Faigman notes, for example, that the Court asked for research on whether excluding jurors who oppose the death penalty biases juries in favor of conviction. Nevertheless, in *Lockhart v McCree,* the Court dismissed the consequent outpouring of research on the ground that it did not meet the Court's high standards of empirical verification, a dismissal Faigman attributes in considerable part to the Court's failure to understand how social science works.[24]

Perhaps my point about the ability of courts to assimilate information may be made more concrete by being made more personal:

> In the Chambers of the justice for whom I clerked, the burden of the Court's work meant that cases were handled like this: The justice would read the parties' briefs in each case; the three clerks divided the argued cases among them. Before oral argument, the clerks and the justice would discuss the cases. The justice would listen to the oral arguments, and the Court would deliberate and vote privately. If my justice was assigned to write the opinion, the clerk who had worked on the case would draft it. He had ten days in which to do so. In that time, he continued to read briefs and to write memoranda to the justice on the petitions to hear cases that kept pouring into the Court. When the clerk was finished drafting the opinion, the justice would read it over and edit it lightly.[25]

In this section, I have been asking whether there are *a priori* reasons to think judges will make good biomedical policy. I have suggested that the Constitution is not a rich source of relevant wisdom, that the Court has not developed constitutional doctrine that provides a cogent and workable analytic framework, that little in the training and experience of judges suits them to make public policy, and that courts are poorly organized to collect the kind of information and analysis on which successful policy ordinarily rests. In short, there are excellent reasons to doubt courts will make good bioethical policy through constitutional adjudication.

Policy Analysis and the State Interests:
The Example of *Compassion in Dying*

I now want to look at one ambitious judicial attempt to make bioethical policy through constitutional adjudication to see how well courts actually succeed at it: by their fruits ye shall know them. My example, of course, is the Ninth Circuit's *en banc* opinion in *Compassion in Dying v Washington.*[26] For brevity's sake, I will ignore the court's arguments about whether Washington's statute infringed some constitutional interest and concentrate on the court's analysis of the interests the state advanced to justify its statute. I will do so because the arguments deriving such a right have already been lengthily criticized while the state-interest arguments have generally been scanted and because the court's treatment of the state's interests exemplifies the judicial incapacities I have been discussing.[27]

In this part, I make two central arguments. The first is that courts typically fail to take states' interests seriously enough.[28] My second central argument is that courts often are poorly informed about the policies they are making. The Ninth Circuit analyzed *Compassion in Dying* at uncommon length. Yet it repeatedly seems to have misunderstood the facts and arguments basic to its decision. To demonstrate this, I will examine the court's treatment of each of the state's principal interests.

The First State Interest: The Unqualified Interest in Life

The Ninth Circuit began by acknowledging what the Supreme Court said in *Cruzan:* "The state may assert an unqualified interest in preserving life in general."[29] The court rejected this interest for two reasons. Its first reason was one that it returned to at several points and that was also the basis for the Second Circuit's decision in *Quill v Vacco:*[30]

> [T]he state of Washington has already decided that its interest in preserving life should ordinarily give way—at least in the case of competent, terminally ill adults who are dependent on medical treatment—to the wishes of the patients. In its Natural Death Act, . . . Washington permits adults to have "life-sustaining treatment withheld or withdrawn in instances of a terminal condition or permanent unconsciousness."[31]

The first problem with this argument is that Washington need not have "decided" its interest in life should give way. Rather, it might only have concluded that the principle of *Cruzan* compelled it to permit people to refuse medical treatment. In other words, the state may have believed people are constitutionally entitled to resist bodily intrusions, even if those intrusions are livesaving. But the state might still have retained an interest in preserving life that it wished to assert in any permissible way.

The second problem with the court's argument lies in its view of doctors' motives: "In disconnecting a respirator, . . . a doctor is unquestionably *committing* an act; he is taking an active role in bringing about the patient's death. In fact, there can be no doubt that in such instances the doctor intends that, as the result of his action, the patient will die an earlier death than he otherwise would."[32] The court is—characteristically—confident, but it is wrong. The doctor need not intend anything of the kind, often will intend nothing of the kind, knows that predictions about disconnecting respirators are perilous (as the case of Karen Ann Quinlan famously demonstrated), and may hope the patient will survive. Nor is it obvious that patients—who often cling to the wispiest hopes—want to die when they refuse treatment.

The court thought it was "not possible to distinguish prohibited from permissible medical conduct" in a second way: "[D]octors have been supplying the causal agent of patients' death for decades. Physicians routinely and openly provide medication to terminally ill patients with the knowledge that it will have a 'double effect.'"[33] The doctrine of double effect is the principle "that a single act having two foreseen effects, one good and one harmful (such as death), is not always morally prohibited if the harmful effect is not intended."[34] The doctrine is commonly invoked to justify providing medication to relieve pain even though the medication is also likely to cause death as long as "the physician's provision of medication . . . [is] intended to relieve grave pain and suffering and [is] not intended to hasten death."[35]

The Ninth Circuit surely was not required to accept the doctrine of double effect. But it was required to understand it and the consequences of rejecting it. Nevertheless, the court rushed headlong from the possibility that a doctor's action may cause death to the certainty that death must be the doctor's goal: "To us, what matters most is that the death of the patient is the intended result as surely in one case as in the other."[36] The court does not seem to grasp that a doctor may know death is a risk without being certain it will happen or wanting it to. The court's misunderstanding may flow partly from its medical naiveté. As one physician (and proponent of assisted suicide) writes, "[C]aregivers experienced in hospice settings know that it is extremely difficult to produce a fatal overdose by increasing the amount of opioid administered to a patient suffering pain. This is especially true when the agent is titrated with care and when the patient has been receiving an opioid long enough to build up tolerance."[37]

Not only does the court misperceive the motives doctors and patients must have in terminating medical treatment or in seeking relief from pain, it seems not to have considered the consequences of equating those acts with suicide. If *any* refusal of treatment that might prolong life is suicide, a person or state that opposes suicide must undergo or demand extremes of treatment no one would think sensible. And if pain relief that runs some risk of causing death were called murder, how many doctors would treat pain adequately? No wonder an observer as sober and serious as John Arras calls the court's rejection of the doctrine of double effect "reckless and counterproductive." He explains, "[M]any physicians would sooner give up their allegiance to adequate pain control than their opposition to assisted suicide and euthanasia. If they are convinced by the judge's reasoning, many will be reluctant to practice adequate pain control techniques on their dying patients."[38]

The court also depreciated the state's general interest in life because that interest "is dramatically diminished if the person it seeks to protect is terminally ill or permanently comatose and has expressed a wish that he be permitted to die without further medical treatment. . . ."[39] But the court failed to explain satisfactorily why the state's interest is diminished by someone's decision to die, and the Supreme Court did not agree that it is: "As we have previously affirmed, the States 'may properly decline to make judgments about the "quality" of life that a particular individual may enjoy . . .'. . . . This remains true, as *Cruzan* makes clear, even for those who are near death."[40]

The court acknowledged that the state might be deterred from permitting assisted suicide by the difficulty of defining "terminally ill." However, the court so confidently assumed a workable definition is easily devised:

> We acknowledge that it is sometimes impossible to predict with certainty the duration of a terminally ill patient's remaining existence, just as it is sometimes impossible to say for certain whether a borderline individual is or is not mentally competent. However, we believe that sufficient safeguards can and will be developed by the state and medical profession . . . to ensure that the possibility of error will ordinarily be remote.[41]

This implies that the problem is that doctors may apply the definition of terminally ill inaccurately. That is certainly a concern, given the relentless uncertainty of medical predictions and the notorious variability of medical practice. But the problem lies not just in applying the definition—it lies in devising it. The court scoffs at the "purported definitional difficulties" on the grounds that they "have repeatedly been surmounted."[42] The court's evidence is that states have enacted definitions of "terminal" into law. But that is no answer if the definitions are bad ones. Unfortunately, there is a reason to doubt the present state of knowledge permits reliable definition. One well-informed study reports that

> every criterion has very serious problems and complexities, even in a population for whom good models for predicting survival is available. The number of long-term survivors increases when more inclusive criteria are applied while the number of very early deaths increases when more restrictive criteria are used. No statistical criterion seems to capture only the population which was really intended.[43]

Thus this study concluded, "Deciding who should be counted 'terminally ill' will pose such severe difficulties that it seems untenable as a criterion for permitting physician-assisted suicide. Allowing physicians (or anyone else) to decide who is terminally ill without standards or guidance will result in uneven application with unjustified variations across diseases, across physicians, and across regions."[44] In short, the Ninth Circuit seems to have been unaware of the evidence that "[h]ighly accurate predictive models of survival are difficult to create, harder to apply, scanty in number, flawed in practice, and impossible in theory."[45]

The Second State Interest:
Preventing Erroneous Decisions

The Ninth Circuit conceded that "the state has a clear interest in preventing anyone, no matter what age, from taking his own life in a fit of desperation, depression, or loneliness or as a result of any other problem, physical or
psychological, which can be significantly ameliorated."[46] However, the court
said that "that interest . . . is substantially diminished in the case of terminally ill, competent adults who wish to die."[47] Here the Ninth Circuit apparently misunderstood both the state's argument and the world of the dying.
The court seemed to think the state was simply trying to prevent suicide. But
the state was arguing that a decision to commit suicide made under the influence of mind-warping pressures is not autonomous.[48] In other words, the
state interest at issue was not a general interest in preventing suicide, but a
more particular interest in preventing suicides that result from "decision defects."[49]

Although its opinion turns on the principle of autonomy, the court is
largely indifferent to the problem of decision defects. Yet that problem is severe for all patients and crucial for terminally ill patients contemplating suicide. Thus Herbert Hendin, a leading student of suicide, writes, "Like other
suicidal individuals, patients who desire an early death during a serious or
terminal illness are usually suffering from a treatable mental illness; most
commonly a depressive condition or alcoholism."[50] Depression is notoriously
unrecognized by its sufferers and those around them, particularly when, as
for the dying, it is easy to identify a reason for sorrow. Worse, "depression is
underdiagnosed and often inadequately treated. Although most people who
kill themselves are under medical care at the time of death, their physicians
often fail to recognize the symptoms of depressive illness or to provide adequate treatment for the illness."[51]

More broadly, the court seems afflicted with a naive view of human motivation, one that does not appreciate how complex, ambiguous, and ambivalent people's motives commonly are. The motives of the seriously ill have
all those characteristics and are further roiled by the fatigue, fear, pressures,
and disorientation disease wreaks on its sufferers.[52] All these problems are
exacerbated by the confrontation with mortality. Thus Hendin writes, "Clinicians and researchers working with patients who request assisted suicide
during an illness have described the patients as having the same intense
emotions, such as hopelessness, despair, anxiety, rage and guilt, seen in suicidal patients without physical illness."[53] These emotions conduce to ill-
considered decisions. Thus Stengel comments that many "suicidal attempts
and quite a few suicides are carried out in the mood 'I don't care whether I
live or die,' rather than with a clear and unambiguous determination to end
life. . . . Most people, in committing a suicidal act, are just as muddled as
they are whenever they do anything of importance under emotional
stress."[54]

In addition, requests for suicide may be motivated by desires that can be less harshly satisfied. Hendin, for instance, suggests that losing their sense of control drives some patients to try to fix the time and circumstances of their deaths.[55] If so, providing them with other kinds of power may satisfy their wish for control.[56] Similarly, Hendin reports, "The vast majority of patients who request assisted suicide or euthanasia are motivated primarily by the dread of what will happen to them in the dying process rather than by their current pain or suffering. . . . When these fears are dealt with by a caring, sensitive physician, the patient's requests for death usually disappear."[57] Hendin also believes patients requesting help committing suicide, "like other suicidal individuals, are often testing the affection and care of others. The overwhelming number of patients drop the request to die, however, if their anxieties are dealt with sensitively and effectively."[58]

If these are the kinds of reasons patients request help committing suicide, it is unsurprising that the "desire for death is variable over time even for patients who are terminally ill. This is true even among the small number of terminally ill patients expressing a persistent wish to die. When interviewed two weeks later, two-thirds of these patients show a significant decrease in the extent of the desire to die."[59] It is commonly observed that, "once patients are confronted with illness, continued life often becomes more precious; given access to appropriate relief from pain and other debilitating symptoms, many of those who consider suicide during the course of a terminal illness abandon their desire for a quicker death in favor of a longer life made more tolerable with effective treatment."[60] Such changes of heart are experienced by patients of all kinds, not just the dying. For example, one patient—Wilfrid Sheed—learned that "cancer, even more than polio, has a disarming way of bargaining downward, beginning with your whole estate and then letting you keep the game warden's cottage or the badminton court; and by the time it has tried to frighten you to death and threatened to take away your very existence, you'd be amazed at how little you're willing to settle for."[61]

In sum, there is much evidence that a disturbing number of terminally ill patients considering suicide are not making truly autonomous decisions. Depression is a predominant motive for seeking assistance in suicide even among the terminally ill. It is generally treatable, but it is often not diagnosed by doctors. People seeking suicide are often in the grip of emotions they do not understand and are pursuing goals that can be met in less drastic ways. The wish to commit suicide is often inconstant. In short, decision defects plague decisions to die. Perhaps all this evidence is not incontrovertible. But it is the kind of evidence a state might reasonably adduce to support the interests it advances. Just such evidence in fact influenced the New York State Task Force on Life and the Law to recommend that assisted suicide not be legally permitted.[62]

Had the court accorded this evidence the respect it warranted, the court would not just have taken the decision-defects argument more seriously. It might also have understood how challenging the state's argument was to the court's view of the case. For the state was not just invoking a paternalistic interest in protecting its citizens. Rather, it was asserting an interest in promoting its citizens' autonomy, in protecting people from being led into making decisions that are not autonomous. In its strongest form, the state's argument was that on balance prohibiting assisted suicide serves autonomy better than permitting it. This would be true if—put crudely—more people would be kept by the prohibition from nonautonomously committing suicide than would autonomously decide to commit suicide were it legal. In short, the court's crucial premise—that the choice was between autonomy and paternalism—was wrong. Rather, the choice was between two views of how to promote autonomous decisions.

But why was the court—which elsewhere in its opinion was shocked at any interference with autonomy—so indifferent to the state's arguments on behalf of it? While the court acknowledged that "many suicides are committed by people who are suffering from treatable mental disorders,"[63] it implied that suicides by the terminally ill are different: "In the case of a terminally ill adult who ends his life in the final stages of an incurable and painful degenerative disease, in order to avoid debilitating pain and a humiliating death, the decision to commit suicide is not senseless. . . ."[64] And the court said that should an error "in medical or legal judgment" occur (a possibility the court thought "remote"[65]), it would be "likely to benefit the individual by permitting a victim of unmanageable pain and suffering to end his life peacefully and with dignity at the time he deems most desirable."[66] Apparently, then, the court thought suicide the rational response to terminal illness.

The court, in other words, appears to espouse the view I suspect many people credit—that suicide is a normal response to terminal illness and that the terminally ill who want to commit suicide thus differ sharply from other suicidal people. This may be a common view, but there is good reason to doubt it (particularly if you do not assume, as the court seems to, that every terminally ill person who wants to commit suicide is in unbearable, untreatable pain). As I have been suggesting, even terminally ill people who consider suicide often change their minds when some of their other problems are ameliorated. And "only a small percentage of terminally ill or severely ill patients attempt or commit suicide."[67]

But even if suicide were the rational response to terminal illness, it would still be surprising that the court could be so unconcerned about decision defects. A standard argument for patient's autonomy is exactly that people's views of rationality differ, and that each person's view should be respected. Is, then, the court concerned for autonomy, or is it animated by a view of how the dying should act?[68]

The Third State Interest: Preventing Undue Influence

The third state interest the Ninth Circuit acknowledged was protecting the dying from arbitrary, unfair, or undue influence. The court dismissed the possibility of two kinds of danger. First, it jeered at the argument that prohibiting assisted suicide is necessary "to protect the disadvantaged."[69] The court, however, hardly bothered to explain why that argument is "disingenuous," "fallacious," and "meretricious," and it rushed on to say "there is far more reason to raise the opposite concern—that the poor would be denied 'the assistance that would allow them to end their lives with a measure of dignity.'"[70] The court expressed itself obscurely, but it apparently reasoned that assisted suicide is a medical service, that the poor get fewer medical services than the rich, and that therefore the poor will have less access to help in committing suicide. The state's argument, however, was that those caring for the poor will be too ready to acquiesce in their suicide because (a) they regard the lives of the poor as less valuable than other lives and (b) helping the poor die is cheaper than keeping them alive. The court never grapples with (a) and seems never to grasp (b).

The court did admit there is reason to worry "that infirm, elderly persons will come under undue pressure to end their lives from callous, financially burdened, or self-interested relatives, or others who have influence over them."[71] The court said it did "not minimize the concern."[72] Perhaps not, but neither did it evince much understanding of it. The concern, of course, is that debilitated and desperate people are suggestible: "[D]emoralization and lack of assertiveness are likely to make the terminally ill patient more vulnerable to the suggestions of others. . . ."[73] The primary point is not (as the court implies) that patients will be hustled off by hard-hearted or grasping doctors and relatives. It is more centrally that "[w]ell-meaning and discreet suggestions, or even unconscious changes in expression, gesture, and tone of voice, can move a dependent and suggestible patient toward a choice for death."[74] It is that families—wearied financially, psychologically, and morally by the trials of caring for someone gravely ill—might yearn for the patient to ease them of their burden. In this light, it is disturbing that, according to one study of the Dutch experience "more euthanasia requests came from the families of patients than the patients themselves. The investigator for the study concluded that the families, the doctors and the nurses were involved in pressuring the patients to request euthanasia."[75]

This is troubling, of course, on autonomy grounds. The rationale for a right to assisted suicide is deference to the patient's choice, but that rationale is defeated where the patient was pressured into committing suicide. But it is troubling on another ground as well, for families' distress can sometimes be satisfied less drastically: "A 1989 Swedish study revealed that when chronically ill patients attempted suicide, their overburdened families often did not want them resuscitated. When social services stepped in and relieved the family's burden by sending in home care helpers, most patients wanted to live and their families wanted them to live as well."[76]

The changing structure of American medical care provides additional reason to worry about pressures to choose death. American health care is being transformed by the rise of managed care and cost containment. We are thus moving from a system in which it was generally in doctors' financial interest to overtreat patients toward one in which doctors have incentives to undertreat them. Both systems have their failings, and it is hardly obvious that the old system was better for patients.[77] But any decision to permit assisted suicide needs to consider that the new system gives doctors direct financial reasons to persuade their patients to die.[78] Once again, however, the Ninth Circuit was either ignorant or indifferent.

The Ninth Circuit did, however, have another string to its bow. Its principal response to concerns that people might be pressured into committing suicide, as to concerns about whether patients might commit suicide improvidently, was that doctors will regulate these decisions. So crucial is this argument that it deserves quoting at length:

> We believe that most, if not all, doctors would not assist a terminally ill patient to hasten his death as long as there were any reasonable chance of alleviating the patient's suffering or enabling him to live under tolerable conditions. We also believe that physicians would not assist a patient to end his life if there were any significant doubt about the patient's true wishes. To do so would be contrary to the physicians' fundamental training, their conservative nature, and the ethics of their profession. In any case, since doctors are highly-regulated professionals, it should not be difficult for the state or the profession itself to establish rules and procedures that will ensure that the occasional negligent or careless recommendation by a licensed physician will not result in an uninformed or erroneous decision by the patient or his family.[79]

It is hard to know where to start analyzing this astonishing statement. Perhaps we may begin by observing that the court does not trouble to provide evidence for it.[80] But evidence is acutely needed, for the court's propositions are, at best, suspect. Even the court's colorable assumption that doctors are "highly-regulated professionals" is dubious. Doctors certainly feel tightly regulated, and bitterly many of them resent it.[81] When doctors talk of assisted suicide, they often assert some kind of entitlement to do what *they* believe is best for their patients and are incredulous when told the law might claim to influence their judgment. But is medicine "highly regulated"? The very definition of a profession is that it is crucially self-regulating, and few professions have been as concerned to preserve that prerogative or as triumphant in doing so as medicine.[82] Law is ordinarily tamely respectful of that prerogative.[83] When it regulates medicine—medical malpractice doctrine is a crucial example—it generally accepts medicine's own standards. Even where the law has powerful reasons to regulate—for example, when disciplining incompetent doctors—it is notoriously feeble. Courts have been particularly loath to be saddled with decisions at the end of life and have preferred to set broad standards rather than adjudicate individual cases.

The Ninth Circuit's assumption that doctors are highly regulated is especially odd in an area where doctors have so flagrantly violated the law with

such impunity. When Timothy Quill admitted in a preeminent medical journal that he had helped a patient commit suicide, he was investigated but
not prosecuted.[84] A few miles down the road from where I write, Jack
Kevorkian's toll has now passed one hundred. He was thrice prosecuted for
assisting with suicides but never convicted.[85] Only when he delivered a tape
of himself in flagrante delicto to *60 Minutes* and stripped himself of legal
counsel was he convicted of murder. Oh law, where is thy sting?

The Ninth Circuit might have recalled that the law's enforcement problem is old and ubiquitous, that people do not obey just because the law commands.[86] The enforcement problem is harshest in cases like those involving
medical decisions—where an activity occurs in private, where the people the
law wants to influence feel the decision is theirs to make,[87] where the only
person keeping records is the person regulated, and where the victim is dead
and cannot complain.[88]

The Ninth Circuit explains its sang-froid about improvident decisions
to commit suicide partly by saying concern about undue influence "is ameliorated in large measure because of the mandatory involvement in the
decision-making process of physicians, who have a strong bias in favor of
preserving life. . . ."[89] Here the court appears to accept an increasingly outmoded version of doctors' attitudes toward treating the dying. It was long re-
gretted that doctors would strive officiously to keep patients alive. But this
criticism is becoming anachronistic. More and more it is doctors who start
discussions of stopping treatment, and understandably.[90] Horribly ill people
who cannot improve are rarely rewarding patients. And the treatments that
keep them alive often distress all concerned.

But the court need not have rested its decision on how much doctors
are regulated or how resolutely they wish to keep patients alive, for there are
many concrete factors it could have consulted and much evidence it might
have evaluated. The court professed to be "aware of the concern that doctors
become hardened to the inevitability of death and to the plight of terminally
ill patients, and that they will treat requests to die in a routine and imper-
sonal manner, rather than affording the careful, thorough, individualized attention that each request deserves."[91] But those concerns are much more
specific and troubling even than this. What the court asks of doctors is more
challenging than the court realizes. For example, "the detection of judgment-
impairing confusion among dying people is surprisingly difficult. . . . [O]ne
researcher concluded that 'our clinical observations miss profound confu-
sional episodes in [20%] of our patients.'"[92] Not only do "physicians and
nurses regularly overstate dying patients' decision-making competence," but
there is currently "inadequate experience or research data to design reliable
safeguards to ensure the lucidity of dying patients who might claim a right to
assisted suicide."[93]

Bluntly phrased, the question the court should have asked was this: If
doctors will supervise suicides so well, why do they so often treat the dying

so badly? As Howard Brody writes, "It has been exhaustively documented that medical management of terminal suffering is currently inadequate."[94] Indeed, he says there is "compelling evidence that the status quo is far below optimal, if not actually scandalous."[95] More specifically, it is notorious that too many doctors are poorly trained to recognize depression, that they often undertreat pain, and communicate badly with patients. And most relevantly, who believes doctors do an exemplary job of learning and heeding the wishes of dying patients? The Ninth Circuit

> apparently assumes that clinicians faithfully adhere to patients' wishes in treatment decisions, including end-of-life care. But there is disturbing evidence that this is not so. . . . [In the] SUPPORT [study,] . . . fewer than one-fourth of treating physicians had ever reviewed the patient's preferences, even when these were explicitly written down in an advance directive. Even when patients' preferences were known, they were frequently simply ignored.[96]

Doctors fail in the duties they already owe dying patients and seem fated to fail as guardians of patients' decisions to die for many—often understandable—reasons. Routine dulls sympathy, as Rousseau knew long ago: "When we have seen a sight it ceases to impress us, use is second nature, what is always before our eyes no longer appeals to the imagination, and it is only through the imagination that we can feel the sorrows of others; this is why priests and doctors who are always beholding death and suffering become so hardened."[97] The frustrations and irritations of unresponsive and unrewarding patients can defeat even dedicated doctors, for "physicians do in fact get tired of treating patients who are hard to cure, who resist their best efforts, who are on their way down—especially when they have had no long-term relationship with them over many years. 'Gorks,' 'gomers,' and 'vegetables' are only some of the less-than-affectionate names such patients receive from the interns and residents."[98] Finally, the delicate decisions the Ninth Circuit wants from doctors are especially elusive when doctors are intensely busy—as many chronically are.

Hardening of sympathies is an unavoidable problem even under good circumstances. But what happens when suicide becomes a right doctors are commanded to respect? The court expects doctors to find the elusive line between honoring the patient's "right to die" and ensuring patients do not make "unfree" decisions. But the lessons of reform are rarely learned in such subtle ways. As I once wrote, "People can usually follow the letter of a new rule, but its spirit is harder to capture."[99] Many doctors learn only crude lessons from bioethics—tell patients the truth (always); accede to patient's decisions to withdraw treatment (always). Doctors who have so long been castigated for their paternalism thus seem likely to err on the side of deferring to assertions of the right to die. The court expects doctors to spot defective decisions because suicide now seems so heterodox. But as it became routine and blessed by the authority of a constitutional right it would become normal and would evoke less anxiety and scrutiny.

Even the most sensitive doctor may be perplexed at the task of supervision the court blithely imposes. For how should a doctor answer when a patient asks for help committing suicide? How hard, if at all, should a doctor try to dissuade the patient? Is dissuasion an improper attempt to manipulate what should be an autonomous decision? A way of helping patients evaluate their situation more intensely and thus of enhancing patients' autonomy? Or is it a way of making sure the patient's decision is free, informed, and irrevocable? And when, if at all, should a doctor propose, or even mention, assisted suicide?[100] Is proposing it a duty commanded by the doctrine of informed consent every time the patient is eligible for it? Is any mention of it inherently a suggestion? What implications would that suggestion have? That the patient's life is not worth living? That the patient is a burden? That the case is hopeless? That the doctor wants to give up? Should the burden always be on the patient to make the first suggestion?

The court's faith that doctors will prevent improvident or pressured decisions to commit suicide ignores yet another problem. Any time the medical profession is made the gatekeeper to something people want and feel entitled to (abortions, draft deferments, letters verifying an employee's disability) a few doctors will be driven by ideology or economics to provide it, often uncritically and even zealously. Only a few such doctors are needed to make the service widely available. Jack Kevorkian is a gruesome example, but Hendin observes, "Although Kevorkian may seem eccentric, it is worth knowing that in the Netherlands, a small number of physicians are attracted to euthanasia and do a great number of cases."[101]

This brings us to our most direct evidence about how well doctors might supervise assisted suicide—Holland. As Hendin notes, "The Dutch model and Dutch guidelines have been accepted as models for the Oregon law and most of the state laws being considered in this country to legalize assisted suicide and euthanasia."[102] Reliable information about the Dutch experiment is elusive, and interpretations of it differ. Nevertheless, there is reason to fear that Dutch doctors regulate these decisions poorly, that "[v]irtually every guideline established by the Dutch, whether it be a voluntary, well-considered, persistent request; intolerable suffering that cannot be relieved; consultation; or the reporting of cases, has failed to protect patients or has been modified or violated with impunity."[103]

One homely test of the doctor's role as supervisor of suicide comes from a model case of assisted suicide—the story of how Timothy Quill helped his patient "Diane" to die.[104] Quill is a prominent exponent of assisted suicide (indeed, he is the Quill of *Quill v Vacco*). His account of Diane's story has widely been thought to exemplify what laudable medical care would be like were assisted suicide legal. That account describes a sorrowful physician yielding to his patient's exercise of her autonomy. Yet in a penetrating and disturbing study of that account, Patricia Wesley shows in some detail how dubious it is. She concludes that "[f]ar from being the neutral reflector and facilitator of Diane's desires that he believes himself to be, Dr. Quill in fact powerfully and directly shapes those desires."[105]

I have been suggesting that one reason the Ninth Circuit was confident doctors could safeguard decisions to commit suicide is that it did not understand what it was asking doctors to do or how they would react. There may be another reason—the court did not have to write the regulations for the new regime. Instead, it could airily say, "Any of several model statutes might serve as an example of how these legitimate and important concerns can be addressed effectively."[106] Perhaps it is only when an institution must actually develop (and administer?) regulations that it realizes their perplexities. The Ninth Circuit could spare itself that burden and hence the trouble of clearer, harder thought.

In sum, the Ninth Circuit would make doctors the guardians of the decision to commit suicide. Why, then, did it not ask the old question, *Quis custodiet ipsos custodes*? We ask that question not because the guardians are untrustworthy (although some will be), but because we recognize the difficulty of their job. It is that difficulty with which the court declines to grapple.

The Fourth State Interest: Protecting the Integrity
of the Medical Profession

The Ninth Circuit did "not believe that the integrity of the medical profession would be threatened in any way by the vindication of the liberty interest at issue here." On the contrary, "it is the existence of a statute that criminalizes the provision of medical assistance to patients in need that could create conflicts with the doctors' professional obligations and make covert criminals out of honorable, dedicated, and compassionate individuals."[107] The court reasoned, "The assertion that the legalization of physician-assisted suicide will erode the commitment of doctors to help their patients rests both on an ignorance of what numbers of doctors have been doing for a considerable time and on a misunderstanding of the proper function of a physician."[108]

The court's reference to what doctors are already doing is a restatement of the court's belief that doctors are helping patients commit suicide (are killing patients?) when they withdraw treatment needed to prolong life. I have already criticized this argument, so we need now say only that this is not what doctors or patients understand doctors to be doing and that those understandings speak to the state's argument about the integrity of the medical profession. For the state's argument is that doctors who think they are assisting in their patients' suicide will regard those patients differently from doctors who believe they would never do so and that patients who believe their doctors would never assist in their suicide can trust their doctors more freely than patients who are denied that confidence.

The court's explanation of "the proper function of a physician" is obscure. Perhaps most mystifying is its statement that "experience shows that most doctors can readily adapt to a changing legal climate. Once the Court held that a woman has a constitutional right to have an abortion, doctors began performing abortions routinely and the ethical integrity of the medical profession remained undiminished."[109] This is mystifying on two levels. First, not everyone would agree that the ethical integrity of the medical profession is undiminished. Kass and Lund, for example, see

> good reasons to argue the contrary. Massive numbers of abortions are now being performed, far beyond what was originally expected, and for reasons not originally regarded as appropriate. Moreover, physician acceptance of abortion may in fact be partly responsible for recent weakenings in the professions's repugnance to cause death. . . . [O]ne of the arguments offered twenty-five years ago against allowing doctors to perform abortions was that it would inevitably lead to doctors performing euthanasia.[110]

Second, the question is not whether doctors will "adapt to a changing legal climate." It is whether that changing climate will be regrettable. First, how will patients regard doctors with a license to kill? Ours is an age of distrust. It is also an age when we must trust even strangers. As medical care is bureaucratized, our doctors become such strangers, strangers to whom we confide our health and even our lives. In these circumstances, one assurance patients may value is the knowledge that doctors will not, cannot, kill.

The justice of these fears is suggested by a second concern—that doctors may be disquieted and even corrupted by the power and practice of euthanasia. The Ninth Circuit was sanguine about the effect of assisted suicide on the profession because doctors already participate in their patients' deaths. But this is all the more reason for concern. Conscientious doctors worry deeply about their power, about how it hardens and distances them, about their own motives; bioethicists have warned for years about the arrogance of power. Assisted suicide would inflame such concerns: "One physician who has worked for many years in a hospice caring for dying patients put the matter most convincingly: 'Only because I knew that I could not and would not kill my patients was I able to enter most fully and intimately into caring for them as they lay dying.'"[111] And in this light it is troubling to read Hendin's report:

> A number of Dutch euthanasia advocates have admitted that practicing euthanasia with legal sanction has encouraged doctors to feel that they can make life or death decisions without consulting patients. Dutch euthanasia practitioners ask themselves the following question: Would I want to live if I were the patient? The question not only implies that a physician has a right to make decisions about whose life is

worth living, it also ignores considerable research that has shown that doctor's [*sic*] consistently underestimate patient perceptions as to their quality of life.[112]

The Fifth State Interest: The Slippery Slope

Finally, the Ninth Circuit evaluated the state's slippery-slope argument—the argument that legalizing assisted suicide will lead down a spiral of unintended consequences toward what the court invidiously refers to as "a parade of horribles."[113] The court contemns this suggestion: "This same nihilistic argument can be offered against any constitutionally-protected right or interest. . . . In fact, the Court has *never* refused to recognize a substantive due process liberty right or interest merely because there were difficulties in determining when and how to limit its exercise or because others might someday attempt to use it improperly."[114] It is hard to understand why the slippery-slope argument is "nihilistic." Nihilism is the belief that all arguments are meaningless; people who invoke the slippery slope are saying that one argument is bad and that others are not. Nor is it a compliment to the Supreme Court to say it has been indifferent to slippery slopes. Part of making good policy is considering where a policy might lead and how it might be misused. In addition, concerns about slippery slopes *have* helped lead the Supreme Court to decline to announce a constitutional right.[115] In short, the Ninth Circuit should have asked whether legalizing assisted suicide would cause intolerable slippery-slope problems. That should have led it to examine the three kinds of slippery slopes.

The first slope is the possibility that people who did not qualify for help with suicide would nevertheless receive it. This could happen in two principal ways. First, doctors might try but fail to distinguish between qualified and unqualified candidates. Second, doctors might not try to distinguish among candidates. This is a familiar process. Legislatures once attempted to permit only those abortions necessary to protect a woman's life or health. That line did not hold and in some places was breached almost overnight. Similarly, even judges in a state as Catholic as Massachusetts declined to make the inquiries the Supreme Court contemplated when it established rules in *Bellotti v Baird*[116] governing the ability of minors to obtain abortions.[117] Likewise, states long sought to make divorce available only on fault grounds, but judges widely flouted that rule.[118]

Lines are fragile for many reasons. Not everyone will sympathize with a line, and some who dislike it will breach it. Even people who approve of a rule may find it easier to say yes than no or may find cases at the margin hard to manage. The process of deciding a series of cases tends to shift the line, since the most extreme case decided in the past tends to become the standard for the present. Furthermore, routine domesticates: a case that once seemed uncomfortable soon becomes too familiar to justify attention. The regulations that sustain lines are particularly susceptible when they challenge a constitutional right, for such rights have so much moral force and usually evoke so much judicial solicitude that they are hard to resist. As John Arras remarks, "We have actually seen this script played out before in the context of abortion law. . . . One regulatory constraint that had been placed on women's choice in some jurisdictions was mandatory review by a hospital-based committee. . . . [T]his regulatory mechanism, along with a host of others, was unceremoniously discarded by the Supreme Court. . . ."[119]

In short, there are good reasons to wonder how durable any line limiting assisted suicide would be. And there are special reasons to fear for the line limiting it to competent, terminally ill adults who have made a free and determined decision. These are the reasons we reviewed when we examined the difficulties of defining "terminally ill," of ascertaining whether a patient was competent to make a considered decision, of preventing patients from choosing suicide under undue influence, and of making doctors the guarantors of regularity. To these excellent *a priori* reasons to doubt the line will hold we must add the evidence that in Holland—the only jurisdiction with real experience of such a line—it has been widely breached.

The first slippery-slope problem, then, is that the rules governing assisted suicide might be applied unsoundly. The second slippery slope is the possibility that the principle the court employed to justify assisted suicide will be more capacious than is necessary to accord competent, terminally ill patients a right to the help of a doctor in committing suicide.[120] In other words, we must ask whether the principle of *Compassion in Dying* leads beyond that limit and would justify a constitutional right to voluntary euthanasia, or to nonvoluntary euthanasia, or even to involuntary euthanasia. The answer is all too likely to be yes. As Justice Holmes said, "All rights tend to declare themselves absolute to their logical extreme."[121] And the Ninth Circuit recruits a notoriously "greedy"[122] right, what is broadly if imprecisely called a right to "privacy," a right "whose core principle seems endlessly expansive."[123] What is more, the Ninth Circuit interprets that right aggressively. For example, the court seemed to believe there is a fundamental right to make all "decisions that are highly personal and intimate, as well as of great importance to the individual,"[124] and it invoked the Supreme Court's most rapturous flights of rhetoric—like the celebrated passage from *Casey* I quoted earlier.

In sum, the second kind of slippery-slope argument suggests that the Ninth Circuit's principle was too strong. It is thus strange that the court says, "The question whether that type of physician conduct may be constitutionally prohibited must be answered directly in future cases, and not in this one."[125] Courts may not decide cases not before them, but they should at least peer down the road to see what lies ahead. This, after all, is why the common law uses hypotheticals so lavishly—to accelerate the process of litigation to test a principle's force and valence.[126]

The third kind of slippery slope raises the possibility that as courts interpret a new right, it will expand beyond its original justification. This process operates by small steps, often without judicial recognition that "rights creep" is occurring. It is easy to imagine ways the right to assisted suicide might slide down this slope. First, we would hear that anything that limits the right is improper. In the zeal to prevent that impropriety, the scope of the right itself would swell. Second, there would be equal protection arguments that people not eligible for assisted suicide were just as deserving as those who were.[127] It would be said, for example, that there are only trivial differences between the seriously and the terminally ill, or between the physically ill and those suffering other kinds of miseries. It would be said that people who are terminally ill but unable to kill themselves should not be denied a right other terminally ill people have. It would next be proposed that people who were terminally ill but not mentally competent should have the benefit of the right to commit suicide. If this seems far-fetched, one should recall that in *Cruzan* Justice Brennan argued that if Cruzan could not exercise her "right to die" someone should exercise it for her.[128]

Justice Brennan's position in *Cruzan* and Justice Stevens's as well exemplify how an idea can be unloosed from its moorings and slide in astonishing directions. The "right to die" was born as an expression of autonomism and antipaternalism. But that rationale could be transformed in a blink into paternalism itself. Justice Brennan, for example, wanted to transmute Cruzan's right to make a decision for herself into her family's entitlement to guess what her decision would have been had she made one. And Justice Stevens wanted to transmute Cruzan's right to make a decision into her family's entitlement to do what they thought would be best for her.[129] These may be good policy choices, but *not* because Cruzan had an autonomy right. Stripped of their autonomy language, these two opinions represent arguments for treating Cruzan benevolently, paternalistically.[130]

One might respond to the state's slippery-slope arguments by saying that such arguments are logically dubious. If a first step is right, it is right even though the second step is wrong. If the second step is wrong, it simply should not be taken. But that should not prevent taking the first step, since there is no logical reason the second step must be taken just because the first one was. Indeed, there is a logical reason to stop before reaching the bottom, since the whole argument assumes that the top of the slope is crucially different from the bottom.[131]

Logically, this refutation of the slippery-slope argument seems convincing. But as Justice Holmes famously said, "The life of the law has not been logic; it has been experience." And the American experience of law at the end of life confirms the hazards of the slippery slope. This should not be surprising. First, slippery slopes are dangerous whatever the logic because of the common law's method. The common law reasons from precedents. It asks whether each new case is essentially the same as some precedent. If so, it is decided in the same way. But if you decide a series of cases in the same way because each case is *almost* the same as its predecessor, the end of the series may wind up far distant from the beginning.

Second, slippery slopes operate psychologically, not logically. "[T]hey work partly by domesticating one idea and thus making its nearest neighbor down the slope seem less extreme and unthinkable."[132] Yet a third reason we slide down slippery slopes is that people are pushing us. Some Americans ardently want to change the law at the end of life. They well know that the public is afraid of the bottom of the slope; they have consciously calculated how to move us down it by small steps.

Experience justifies the state's slippery-slope arguments. Over the past few decades, the United States has moved from a reluctance even to withdraw medical treatment to serious proposals for active euthanasia, with assurances all along the way that each step was the last. My colleague Yale Kamisar rightly asks, "If, as has been well said, 'the history of our activities and beliefs concerning the ethics of death and dying is a history of lost distinctions of former significance,' what reason is there to think that the history will end when we sanction assisted suicide for the terminally ill?"[133] Holland's experiment with assisted suicide suggests that the American slide would continue further than we might like: "Over the past two decades, Dutch law and Dutch medicine have evolved from accepting assisted suicide to accepting euthanasia, from euthanasia for terminally ill patients to euthanasia for chronically ill individuals, from euthanasia for physical illness to euthanasia for psychological distress, and from voluntary euthanasia to the practice and conditional acceptance of nonvoluntary and involuntary euthanasia."[134] The Ninth Circuit's opinion itself exemplifies the slippery-slope problem. That court says to Washington, you have slid thus far down the slope, therefore it would be unconstitutional not to go much further. That court refuses to consider just where the end of the slope might be. If the court could not look at our history, or Holland's, it could at least have looked to itself to see why it should not have dismissed the state's slippery-slope argument.

On Collective State Interests

The Ninth Circuit, I have been saying, had trouble with all the state's interests. However, it, like most courts, particularly scanted interests that do not operate in a direct and obvious way on individual people, but that affect people collectively. Indeed, the court said: "If broad general state policies can be used to deprive a terminally ill individual of the right to make that choice, it is hard to envision where the exercise of arbitrary and intrusive power by the state can be halted."[135] This is perverse. Broad and general policies often promote basic and genuine social interests.[136]

The Supreme Court does seem to recognize the importance of such interests. It believes, for example, that states may have "an 'unqualified interest in the preservation of human life,'" an interest which "is symbolic and aspirational as well as practical."[137] Unfortunately, it is not clear what the Court means by a "symbolic and aspirational" interest or why it is important. Let me suggest one possibility. Sometimes law cannot achieve its goals through direct regulations because effective law enforcement is not practicable. Law has "expressive" resources that may then be recruited. Law's expressive function, that is, seeks "not so much to influence behavior by requiring or forbidding people to perform a particular act, but to influence behavior by encouraging people to think in a particular way."[138]

Assisted-suicide statutes exemplify this expressive use of law. Killing cannot be prevented solely through regulation, for people are not always deterred simply by fear of punishment, particularly when they have lively motives for killing. Rather, they must be led to internalize a norm against killing. Given the forces opposing it, that norm must be exigent. The classic example of a deeply internalized, exigent norm is a taboo. A taboo is a prohibition without exception, to which exceptions are unthinkable. Taboos work for that reason. As soon as they are subject to rational analysis, as soon as qualifications and exceptions become permissible, their social, psychological, and perhaps even moral force begins to crumble:

> Taboos do not work rationally; they work by inducing reactions of horror and disgust at the prohibited practice. Rational analysis of taboos is not only likely to miss this point, but even itself to weaken the taboo. Once you begin to think[, for example,] about which kinds of incest-like activities lack particular identifiable harmful consequences for particular identifiable participants, you begin to think about the unthinkable and about why some "incest" is harmless incest. As this process continues, the emotional force of the taboo, its force as a general deterrent, is eroded.[139]

"Thou shalt not kill" is a core taboo. As we begin to consider when it is good deliberately to end a life without even the cloak of the justification that it is the disease that is causing the death or that the death is an inadvertent and undesired side effect of treating pain, the taboo against killing begins to erode. When we begin to say killing is a question of each individual's values, the erosion worsens.

Recent developments have already troubled the borderland between life and death. For example, withdrawing medical treatment is today not only normal, it is becoming virtuous. The rise of abortion as a right has altered views about whether each abortion is some kind of killing. We have redefined death to suit our need for transplantable organs by adopting a brain-death standard. We are beginning to contemplate using higher-brain death. In the midst of such disruptions of our understanding of death, the state may be particularly concerned to preserve the core understanding that killing is not just wrong, but unimaginable.

This taboo is not aimed just at attitudes toward killing oneself and others. It is directed particularly at a group with extraordinary power that resists regulation—doctors. Thus Kass and Lund invoke "a centuries-old taboo against medical killing, a taboo understood by many to be one of the cornerstones of the medical ethic."[140] They explain,

Medical students, interns, and residents are taught—and acquire—a profound repugnance to medical killing, as a major defense against committing—or even contemplating—the worst action to which their arrogance and/or their weaknesses might lead them. At the same time, they are taught not always to oppose death. . . . But in order to be able to keep their balance, physicians have insisted on the absolute distinction between deliberate killing and letting die. Non-medical laymen (including lawyers and judges) may not be impressed with this distinction, but for practicing physicians it is morally crucial.[141]

The state's interest in the taboo against killing, then, helps explain the apparently arbitrary lines between killing and letting die of which the Ninth and Second Circuits complained. Arbitrary they may in some ways be, but they reflect and affirm social understandings on which crucial taboos rest.

The state's "symbolic and aspirational" interest in human life has a second element. The principal problem with suicide is not that a few dying people have trouble committing it, but that many people—particularly young people—commit it who have not made a wise, or even competent, decision.[142] Criminal prohibitions of suicide are so futile they have long since been abandoned, and thus the state's challenge is again to promote a social environment that deters suicide. Dignifying suicide by medicalizing it and calling it a constitutional right seems likely to corrupt that environment.

I would even make—if cautiously—a third argument—that the state has an interest in helping patients respond well to the shock and horror of mortal illness. When people encounter any new and daunting situation, they rarely wish to work out from first principles how to cope with it. Rather, they often wish to consult common practice. As Alan Wolfe writes, "When people make decisions, they tend to look not to a mathematical formula to determine what is to their best advantage, but to what others do, to what they have traditionally done, or to what they think others think they ought to do."[143] The sick particularly need this social assistance in making decisions, not just because their situation is often so unfamiliar, but because it is so frightening. Thus one student of the memoirs people write about illness observes, "Perhaps one reason why the work of dying seems so difficult today is that the individual is expected not only to face his or her death—in itself a task arduous enough—but also create a way of dying out of the fragments of ideologies and religious sentiments that our culture provides us."[144] This does not tell us, of course, which social practices might most comfort and sustain the dying. But I think the state may decide that in general they will benefit most from practices that do not make suicide a standard resort, which encourage the dying to maintain their ties with the living and to seek the rewards life has yet to give them.[145]

Here I do not think the Ninth Circuit is helpful. The right it announced was rooted in the view that dependence must be deplorable and undignified. The court, for instance, says "a terminally ill adult who ends his life in the final stages of an incurable and painful degenerative disease" might do so partly "to avoid . . . a humiliating death."[146] But why must such a death be humiliating? As Callahan acutely says, "What Reinhardt has done, in effect, is to bless a trivial, even demeaning, notion of dignity. What could be more mischievous than a view of dignity that requires we be clean, alert, and able to take care of ourselves?"[147]

The Ninth Circuit might have argued that all three of these state interests are illegitimate because in promoting them the state makes itself directly interested in people's preferences. However, the state is not seeking to override those preferences, only to shape them, or even to shape the forces that shape them. Some of these preferences—like not wanting to kill—the state is not just entitled but is even obliged to shape. But the state may legitimately shape the forces that influence other preferences. We will always be shaped by our environments. We maximize our autonomy by shaping the environments that shape us. But many of those environments—including the hospitals in which American deaths today occur—are virtually impervious to us unless we use that one great tool, government. Seen in this way, government is not just a threat to autonomy, but a device we recruit to protect ourselves from other threats to our autonomy. For example, Kamisar asks, "In a climate in which suicide is the 'rational' thing to do, or at least a 'reasonable' option, will it become the unreasonable thing *not* to do? The noble thing *to* do?"[148] And David Velleman suggests that the dying might sometimes prefer not to have the choice to commit suicide so that they might escape any sense of duty to do so.[149] Since a truly neutral environment seems impossible, citizens may (within important limits) properly employ the state's power to protect themselves from unfavorable environments.

The "collective" state interests extend beyond the expressive function. For example, instituting a right to assisted suicide might well reduce the presently strong incentive to create better ways to help the sick and dying. Consider the hospice movement. It has helped transform palliative care and provide decent and dedicated care for dying patients who have decided to abandon their struggle for a cure. But as Kass and Lund fear, "Because the quick-fix of suicide is easy and cheap, it will in many cases replace the use of hospice and other humanly-engaged forms of palliative care, for there will be much less economic incentive to continue building and supporting social and institutional arrangements for giving humane care to the dying."[150] Hendin believes this has already happened in Holland, where "the easy solution of euthanasia or assisted suicide has led to a third kind of slippage: a diminution in the quality of and pressure for palliative care, which became one of the first casualties of euthanasia. Hospice care has indeed been virtually non-existent in the Netherlands."[151]

Had it thought about what I am calling the state's collective interests, the Ninth Circuit would no doubt have objected to them. It would have said that it is hard for courts to evaluate them because taboos do their work indirectly, because preferences are shaped in labyrinthine ways, because social institutions are born of many forces. No doubt. But these are reasons courts should judge collective interests perceptively and shrewdly, not reject them out of hand. Such state interests matter, and a jurisprudence too crude to respect them is poorly suited for making bioethical policy.

Assessing the State's Interests

In *Compassion in Dying*, Washington asserted a number of interests, none of which struck the Ninth Circuit as weighty. I have suggested that the court was hostile to the state's account of its interests for two reasons: because of the structure of Fourteenth Amendment analysis, which typically scants state interests, and because the court was ill-informed about the bases for the state's claim. I suspect the Fourteenth Amendment tradition of dismissing state interests helps account for the court's abrupt treatment of many of Washington's asserted interests, particularly what I have called collective interests. And in *Compassion in Dying* that abrupt treatment was particularly easy because the court was so poorly informed. The list of its misperceptions is long. The court did not seem to understand: the doctrine of double effect and how doctors and patients regard it; the inescapable imprecision of "terminally ill"; the extent to which depression motivates the suicide even of terminally ill people; the difficulty of diagnosing depression; how doctors and patients interact; how patients make decisions; why terminally ill people want to commit suicide; how the disadvantaged make choices at the end of life; the effects of changes in American health care on decisions to die; the difficulty of writing effective regulations in this area; the modest capacity of doctors to prevent unwise decisions to commit suicide; the Dutch experience; or the probable effects of assisted suicide on doctors.

My point has not been that the state's interests require it to prohibit assisted suicide, for I do not believe they do. Nor is my primary point that the state's interests justify the state's statute, although I believe they do. What I have argued, rather, is that the Ninth Circuit seems to understand the state's interests so poorly and to dismiss them so facilely as to cast doubt on the court's capacity to make good public policy at least for this bioethical issue.

Making Policy by Weighing Rights and Interests

Once the individual rights and the state interests at stake in a case have been surveyed, standard Fourteenth Amendment jurisprudence calls for the court to judge whether the latter are strong enough to justify the statute's infringement of the former. This is surely a necessary step in making wise policy. But it is not one a court is well equipped to take.

The problems begin at the theoretical level. First, the Supreme Court has been unable to specify what standard to use in evaluating competing rights and interests.[152] Its failure is disconcerting but understandable, since the personal right and the state interest are incommensurable. This awkwardness might be avoided if a court only needed to decide if the right and the interests had each attained some specified standard, and this is what the Court for some time tried to require. Its system, however, proved too rigid, and the Court's categories proliferated and now seem to have collapsed. The Ninth Circuit's response to this defeat was to try to "balance" the right and the interests. But this simply returned it to the core problem of incommensurability—that there is no scale on which rights and interests can be weighed. And this revived the old problem of substantive due process—that it requires judges to make so many poorly guided choices that it invites them to read their own policy preferences into constitutional law.

Far from acknowledging these problems, the Ninth Circuit said proudly,

> Weighing and then balancing a constitutionally-protected interest against the state's countervailing interests, while bearing in mind the various consequences of the decision, is quintessentially a judicial role. Despite all of the efforts of generations of courts to categorize and objectify, to create multi-part tests and identify weights to be attached to the various factors, in the end balancing entails the exercise of judicial judgment rather than the application of scientific or mathematical formulae. No legislative body can perform the task for us. Nor can any computer. In the end, . . . we must rely on our judgment, guided by the facts and the law as we perceive them.[153]

This passage seems wrong-headed at every turn. First, far from being "quintessentially a judicial role," weighing and balancing constitutional rights against the state's interests is at the beginning a task the legislature can and should undertake every time its acts implicate a constitutional right.[154] Second, the judicial failure to "categorize and objectify" critically erodes the court's authority to override the legislature's balance. One condition for granting power to unelected courts is that they must explain the source of their authority and the logic of their decision. Third, the court seems to concede at the end of this passage that it is essentially relying on its own "judgment." It never explains what makes its judgment worthier of respect than the legislature's or even why its judgment might yield good policy. On the contrary, the court unnervingly intimates that it can rely first and primarily on its own judgment and only need have that judgment guided by "the facts and the law as we perceive them."

But even a court less insouciant than the Ninth Circuit would face disabling problems balancing rights and interests in a case like *Compassion in Dying*. Consider what it would take to develop a genuinely informed policy about assisted suicide. Historically, courts have been content to announce an individual interest of some specified weight and ask if the state has a countervailing interest of some specified strength. But in making policy, other questions are relevant. First, how many people would want to exercise the right? This matters, since good policy asks what a statute's total benefit and total harm are.

The Ninth Circuit has no idea how many people would actually assert the right. Perhaps swayed by the plaintiffs' stories, the court insistently says "many."[155] But it never tells us what "many" means or how accurate it is. The court needs to answer these questions because "many" may well be wrong. A good estimate should start with everyone who is terminally ill and mentally competent. From this group must be subtracted all those—clearly the huge majority—who do not want to commit suicide.[156] From the remaining patients must be subtracted all those who can die by refusing medical treatment. Then one must subtract those who have been unduly pressured into committing suicide or who have improvidently decided to do so.[157] Then should be subtracted those who could achieve their goals by a means other than suicide—for example, by entering a hospice or securing proper pain medication. From those (few?) who are left must be subtracted those who could commit suicide satisfactorily without help, for what is at issue is not the right to commit suicide (which is nowhere criminal) but the right to help in doing so. As Campbell writes, "Patients already have access to information about how to end their lives, and 'stockpiling' of medications has in many instances given them access to the means to end life."[158] And perhaps one should also subtract those who will have assistance whatever the law says, for "press reports and polls suggest that some physicians already respond to their patients' requests for help by prescribing medication or providing a lethal injection."[159] Finally, one must subtract those patients for whom even physician-assisted suicide would not provide the deliverance they sought.[160] Perhaps this leaves "many" candidates, but a good policy maker would at least be on notice to inquire in some serious way.

So the first thing we would need to know in weighing the costs and benefits of making assisted suicide a right is how many people would want to exercise it. Second, we would want to know how much worse off these people would be were they denied suicide instead of being relegated to their next choice. This is another inquiry the court seems quite uninterested in, even though it is quite possible that the marginal benefits of assisted suicide would turn out to be quite low. Third, we would want to know what collateral benefits suicides might bring (to families relieved of the burden of caring, paying, and sorrowing for their ill; to society saved the costs of medical care; to dying people in general, who might find comfort in knowing they could escape their travail).

Such calculations would begin to give us a sense of the benefits of a right to assisted suicide. We would also, of course, calculate the benefits of prohibiting it. We would ask first how many people would make a nondefective decision to commit suicide, would be deterred by a statute prohibiting it, and would be glad they had been deterred. Second, we would ask how many people would make a defective decision to commit suicide. Third, we would ask how many friends or family members would benefit should a suicide be prevented.

The preceding paragraphs suggest how complex the court's task would be even if it simply tried to specify the numbers of people who might be injured or helped by a regime of assisted suicide. These are not inquiries at which courts are likely to excel or even attempt. Courts specialize in determining what happened in some past event, not in trying to predict who might be affected by a reform that has not even been instituted. Yet even if the court could make these predictions, it would still need some way of assigning a weight to each kind of benefit and burden. And this is without even considering the perplexities of measuring what I have called the state's collective interests, its interests in attitudes and institutions. In short, as Justice Brandeis wrote,

> Merely to acquire the knowledge essential as a basis for the exercise of this multitude of judgments would be a formidable task; and each of the thousands of these judgments would call for some measure of prophecy. Even more serious are the obstacles to success inherent in the demands which execution of the project would make upon human intelligence and upon the character of men. Man is weak and his judgment is at best fallible.[161]

The standard response substantive-due-process jurisprudence makes to these onerous inquiries is to accord precedence to the individual rights at stake. As I once explained:

> Ordinarily, we talk in terms of what I have called the Mill paradigm: "That is, we think in terms of the state's regulation of a person's actions. In such conflicts, we are predisposed to favor the person, out of respect for his moral autonomy and human dignity."[162] That predisposition also rests on our assumption that the state can bear any risks of an incorrect decision better than the individual can.[163]

Such is the Ninth Circuit's approach: "The consequences of rejecting the as-applied challenge would be disastrous for the terminally ill, while the adverse consequences for the state would be of a far lesser order."[164] However, the Mill paradigm works only where the contest is between an individual's rights and the interests of the state. That is not this case. Rather, this is a contest between some individuals who want to commit suicide and other individuals who have an interest in being protected from making a defective and incompetent decision to commit suicide. These interests conflict. We cannot favor the individual against the state, because some individuals will be harmed whatever we do. The Mill paradigm leads us to worry more about limiting individual rights than injuring the state's interests because the state can take its lumps better than individuals. But here individuals will suffer either way, and their autonomy interests will be injured either way. In other words, part of the problem is that the court's categories—individual rights and state interests—obscure the social realities it confronts.

The Ninth Circuit boasts that "balancing" individual rights and the state's interests is "quintessentially a judicial task." In this section, I have suggested that the court's faith in its skill seems to rest on its underestimate of the challenges of that task. The court does not seem to appreciate how many identifiable groups stand to lose or gain from a regime of assisted suicide, how hard it is to predict the number of members of each group, how tricky it is to evaluate their interests (in health, in life, in happiness), how perplexing it is to assign weights to the state's collective interests, and how impossible it therefore is to balance all the interests involved. To be sure, these problems will harass *any* institution that must evaluate assisted suicide. But what makes the court think itself so excellently suited to handle them?

The Culture of the Case

I have suggested that their training, experience, and resources poorly equip judges for making bioethical policy, and I have tried to show how truncated the analysis in even the court's lengthy opinion in *Compassion in Dying* was. I now want to examine these problems from a different angle. American judges and lawyers live in what we may call the culture of the case. That culture makes the case the focal point of law. That view grows out of our common law system (in which law is made by judges in cases) and out of the American legal faith that even statutes and the Constitution find their meaning only when interpreted by courts in cases. American legal education too reflects the culture of the case, for we teach law primarily through books that compile cases. Cases are thus central to American law, and the culture of the case shapes the way courts think and act. It does so in ways that may perhaps promote the efficient settlement of disputes but that impede making wise policy. This is largely because a system developed to resolve disputes between two individuals or enterprises ordinarily promotes neither the attitudes nor the practices that conduce to making good social policy.

First, the culture of the case leads judges to believe they need historical, not social facts. "*Historical facts* are the events that have transpired between the parties to a lawsuit. *Social facts* are the recurrent patterns of behavior on which policy must be based."[165] Courts tend to believe that social facts may be inferred from historical facts, that the litigants before them represent the facts needed to make policy. This is rarely true in cases of social importance. Anyone might become terminally ill, and the circumstances of the dying differ enormously, but lawyers will present to the court only a few litigants whose vivid but unrepresentative stories are virtually intended to mislead the court about the social problem.[166] People who might be injured by a right to assisted suicide, on the other hand, are likely to be invisible to the court. This is partly because they are hard to identify individually, especially in advance. As Arras writes, "The victims of legalization, . . . will be largely hidden from view: they will include the clinically depressed eighty-year-old man who could have lived for another year of good quality [and] . . . the fifty-year-old woman who asks for death because doctors in her financially stretched health maintenance organization cannot or will not effectively treat her unrelenting but mysterious pelvic pain. . . ."[167] Furthermore, the state appears before the court only in the drab person of a government attorney, not as a suffering individual. Thus the court never puts a human face on those who might be rescued from suicide or who might wrongly be led into it. Yet in my experience judges often grow impatient with Brandeis briefs that try to provide systematic information about social facts. As an eminent jurist once said to me when I suggested there might be systematic information on a legal problem: "I know other people live differently from the way I do, and I'm not interested." One result is the superficial treatment of social facts I catalogued earlier in the third section of this chapter.

The second feature of the culture of the case is that it draws judges toward what I call "hyper-rationalism." Hyper-rationalism may be both methodological and substantive. As a method, it "is essentially the substitution of reason for information and analysis. It has two components: first, the belief that reason can reliably be used to infer facts where evidence is unavailable or incomplete, and second, the practice of interpreting facts through a [narrow] set of artificial analytic categories."[168] Hyper-rationalism, in other words, tempts us to believe we can understand how people think and act merely by reasoning, without investigating.

Methodological hyper-rationalism, then, offers a rationale for a way of understanding and writing about social problems. Substantive hyper-rationalism furnishes the assumptions about how people think and act that stand in for the information that might be garnered from empirical work. In bioethics, as in many other areas of human thought, these assumptions tend to see people as operating in remarkably rational ways. They hold that people deliberate explicitly about their situations, that they do so in predominantly rational terms, that they are autonomy maximizers, and that they have well-worked-out agendas that they need autonomy to implement. These assumptions see people primarily as makers of decisions reaching out for control over their lives. Finally, while these assumptions do not entirely abstract people from their social contexts, they tend to simplify those contexts deplorably.[169]

Courts succumb to hyper-rationalism because they share the common belief that things are generally what they seem and because the alternative is a daunting empirical inquiry.[170] Hyper-rationalism is a shortcut that permits judges to cope with their workload. In addition, hyper-rationalism permits courts that have become committed to a result to reach it without having to explain away awkward evidence. It is hard to say which of these motives most influenced the Ninth Circuit, but it is easy to point to examples of its hyper-rationalism. For example, the court wrote airily,

> We believe that most, if not all, doctors would not assist a terminally ill patient to hasten his death as long as there were any reasonable chance of alleviating the patient's suffering or enabling him to live under tolerable conditions. We also believe that physicians would not assist a patient to end his life if there were any significant doubt about the patient's true wishes. To do so would be contrary to the physicians' fundamental training, their conservative nature, and the ethics of their profession.[171]

This passage purports to describe how doctors behave. It does so not by proffering evidence, but rather by positing that doctors have a nature that predictably governs their behavior. Just as boldly, the court assumes that doctors do what they are trained to do and what their professional ethics command. This requires us to believe that the court correctly describes doctors' training, nature, and ethics and—improbably—that doctors will not be subject to forces (like cost-conscious HMOs, or overwork, or importunate patients, laziness, or a bad temper) that lead them to ignore their training, nature, and ethics. The court hardly tries to substantiate its assumptions, and I have argued that many of them are unlikely.

As it has developed, the culture of the case has a third defect. American lawyers tend to see each case as standing for one primary idea. They commonly ask what the holding in a case is, or what its principle is. This is significant for two reasons. First, it implies that sound results can be reached purely through the analysis of principles. Second, it suggests that the core problems of a case can usually be solved by a single principle.[172] The Ninth Circuit, for example, essentially thought that *Compassion in Dying* could be decided by adumbrating the principle of autonomy. Often, however, good policy arises not out of applying a single principle, but by reconciling many conflicting principles. And often the problem is not to derive principles but to understand complex empirical realities.

This leads us to the fourth problem the culture of the case presents in constitutional litigation: it leads to piecemeal resolution of issues that are closely related and that should be resolved together with an eye to the costs and benefits of each choice. As Michael McCann puts it, "judicial authorities are largely bound to episodic case-by-case remedies for complex social problems at odds with the long-term supervisory capacities necessary for effective means-oriented planning."[173] Both the Ninth and Second Circuits centrally argued that since the state permitted people to die by refusing treatment, it must also permit assisted suicide. These courts seemed to feel that if the risks of one were tolerable, so must be the risks of the other.[174] However, good policy would consider the cumulative effects of practices, not the effects of each practice separately. Presumably we must tolerate some improvident decisions to die, but eventually their sum may begin to seem too great.

The culture of the case is problematic in a fifth, related, way. Because courts consider problems one case at a time, they slide easily down slippery slopes. Courts too readily ask what the right result in *this* case is without investigating where the new precedent might lead. Anticipating the future is a problem for all policy makers. But it is particularly a problem for courts, which are commanded to decide only actual cases and controversies. The problem becomes insuperable where courts, like the Ninth Circuit, refuse even to consider what might lie ahead.

The culture of the case has other effects. Not least, it leads courts to ignore questions not framed by the doctrine under which suit was brought and answers that are not doctrinally available. A court, for instance, is unlikely to say that the best response to the desperation of the dying is to improve palliative care, for no constitutional doctrine points in that direction or gives courts good tools for effectuating such a judgment. Furthermore, the culture of the case tempts courts to twist problems into forms for which judicial remedies *are* available. For example, it might for several reasons be desirable to legalize assisted suicide but not to make it a right. However, the only way the Ninth Circuit could legalize assisted suicide was by making it a right, and that was what it tried to do.

Some Institutional Considerations

In the preceding sections, I have argued that courts are poorly equipped to analyze the issues bioethical policy presents. In this section, I contend that a number of institutional considerations make it desirable that courts not become the arbiters of that policy. These considerations speak not just to judicial disadvantages but to the advantages of other governmental and nongovernmental agencies.

First, a clarification. Where the Constitution commands courts to enforce rights, courts must surely do so. There are many areas in which the Constitution is uncontroversially understood to issue just such commands (even if the substance of each decision may be controversial). However, as I argued earlier, assisted suicide is not such a case. And where there is some reason to think affected people have been excluded from democratic institutions, even rights skeptics may want courts to be specially alert for violations of the Fourteenth Amendment. But here there are no "discrete and insular minorities." There is no reason to think some group or some point of view has been barred from the ballot box or the legislature's hall's. On the contrary, *everyone* risks being in the position of the plaintiffs in *Compassion in Dying,* or their families, or their friends.[175]

But even if courts are not constitutionally commanded to act, do they not at least have institutional advantages? Perhaps so, but probably fewer than courts assume. In choosing an institution to make bioethical policy in general and assisted-suicide policy in particular, one criterion should be an institution's flexibility and its ability to promote—or at least tolerate—social experimentation. Experimentation is desirable for two reasons. First, assisted suicide is terra incognita. Much will depend on our ability to regulate it. If we can regulate it well, many of the objections to it will evaporate. However, failures of regulation are likely to reveal themselves only slowly. For example, we are worried about the extent to which routinization will dull the regulatory ardor of physicians, and routine develops gradually. We are worried about slippery slopes, but we slide down them gradually and unwittingly. Not only will pathologies grow slowly, but they will be hard to detect and to measure. All this means we must be free to reverse our course whenever serious problems become evident.

The second reason we should value flexibility is that medicine at the end of life is a dynamic area in which change is constant and in which law must change with change. For example, progress in pain management or treating depression would vitiate the rights claim by weakening the argument that only suicide could offer the patient relief from misery. On the other hand, better techniques for diagnosing depression might calm our worries that the clinically depressed were being inadvertently helped to die. Similarly relevant are the seismic shifts in the structure and financing of American medical care. Even apparently fundamental professional attitudes may change. For instance, it used to be a commonplace that doctors were too eager to keep patients alive, that they were so determined to keep metabolism going, so enthusiastic about technology, and so loath to fail that they would prolong life even at the cost of kindness. Today, doctors' attitudes have altered strikingly, and the visitor to the ICU will often see doctors counseling patients and families to begin to consider withdrawing treatment.[176]

If flexibility is our goal, constitutional adjudication should not be our tool. For one thing, constitutional rights inhibit the experimentation our federal system is supposed to promote. Justice Brandeis's statement of the point is not just familiar, it is right: "It is one of the happy incidents of the federal system that a single courageous state may, if its citizens choose, serve as a laboratory; and try novel social and economic experiments without risk to the rest of the country."[177] Were the Court to make assisted suicide a constitutional right, all the country would have to permit it, and permit it in the specific forms the Court felt were consonant with the right.

Worse, once courts announce a constitutional opinion, they commonly resist changing it. And not without good reason. *Stare decisis* is crucial to a system of case law. Yet courts dislike reconsiderations for less admirable reasons as well. Judges, like the rest of us, resist admitting error. Once we have made up our minds, we usually have a framework of interpretation into which we fit new evidence. With that framework, we can be wonderfully ingenious in interpreting new data to prove that we were right in the first place. As Bacon put it: "The human understanding, once it has adopted opinions, either because they were already accepted and believed, or because it likes them, draws everything else to support and agree with them. And though it may meet a greater number and weight of contrary instances, it will, with great and harmful prejudice, ignore or condemn or exclude them by introducing some distinction, in order that the authority of those earlier assumptions may remain intact and unharmed."[178] Hence the natural conservatism of the decision maker.

What is more, courts, with their contempt power, readily—and to some extent properly—regard resistance as an affront to judicial dignity and to justice itself. Once a court announces not just an order, but a constitutional right, disagreement looks even more like a perfidy that must be met firmly and even sternly. As a matter of judicial psychology, the judge who has announced "the law of the land" tends to become perturbed and then insistent when states persist in resisting. When thwarted, courts tend to ask "How can these people disobey a lawful order of our court?" instead of "Why are people not doing what we expected and wanted?"

This leads to my next point. I have catalogued ways courts are badly equipped to make bioethical policy. But do not judges bring special virtues to their work? Perhaps, but those virtues have their own vices and are too often absent. One of these virtues is that courts—unlike legislatures—must justify their conclusions in principled terms. And so they should. But in *Compassion in Dying* those principled terms often seem ill considered. And Kamisar, a cautious and careful scholar even if a zealous partisan, strikingly invokes the words of Louis Henkin to describe even the Supreme Court's work: "'Some of the Court's unacceptable lines just happen. To avoid difficult questions, to support a result dictated by intuition or sympathy, perhaps to achieve a majority for that result, the Justices seize a rationale that comes to mind, without asking where it leads and whether they are prepared to go there.'"[179]

But I would also argue that sometimes a purely principled resolution is not the best one. Where people deeply disagree over basic principles (as they do about many matters of bioethical policy), there is much to be said for delaying any kind of final decision until there has been a thorough social examination of the issue and the reasons for disagreement about it.[180] And even where such a process has been carried on as long as is fruitful, compromise may be morally legitimate and practically desirable. Where reasonable and decent people vehemently disagree, it is hard to say who is right. And the political and social cost of unresolved disagreement is likely to be painfully high, as *Roe*'s sequelae attest.[181] So a compromise of the conflicting principles may be necessary. Unfortunately, courts often cannot find a legal basis for such a compromise, predict which compromise might work, or commit the antagonists to accepting it.

Assisted suicide seems an attractive case for compromise. Many and perplexing are the moral and practical issues it presents. Good-hearted and thoughtful are the adversaries. Indeed, we may already be moving toward compromises. One developing pattern is to make assisted suicide a crime but not prosecute it. And Kamisar argues that we have already achieved another kind of compromise, since "the line between letting die and actively intervening to bring about death represents a cultural and pragmatic compromise between the desire to let seriously ill people carry out their wishes to end it all and the felt need to protect the weak and the vulnerable."[182]

Detachment and dispassion are also said to be virtues judges have and others lack.[183] Of course, commitment and passion may be good responses to hard problems. But even when detachment and dispassion are desirable, judges too often spurn them. The Ninth Circuit has much to regret on this score, for its opinion is written in strangely extravagant language. For example, the court lauds itself as a barrier to "arbitrary and intrusive" exercises of state power.[184] Perhaps Washington's statute is unwise. Perhaps it is unconstitutional. But it is not arbitrary. It is a kind of statute many states—indeed, many countries—have long had that plausibly attempts to abate undoubted evils. The Ninth Circuit contends the statute balances the competing interests unwisely, but it hardly attempts to show the statute is arbitrary. (And it is odd to call a statute that prohibits a doctor from delivering fatal drugs to a patient intrusive.)

Perhaps we should not repine at such immoderation. But what is surely dismaying is the court's harsh and vituperative spirit. The court characterizes arguments with which it disagrees—even when they are the arguments of other judges—as "disingenuous," "fallacious," "meretricious," "ludicrous," "nihilistic," "inflammatory," and "disastrous." Yet the court is also sanctimonious, self-serving, and self-satisfied. After slurring those impertinent enough to believe the Washington statute is constitutional and jeering at their opinions and arguments, the court piously concludes by saying,

> Given the nature of the judicial process and the complexity of the task of determining the rights and interests comprehended by the Constitution, good faith disagreements within the judiciary should not surprise or disturb anyone who follows the development of the law. For these reasons, we express our hope that whatever debate may accompany the future exploration of the issues we have touched on today will be conducted in an objective, rational, and constructive manner that will increase, not diminish, respect for the Constitution.[185]

Judicial care and caution are missing not just from the language but the substance of *Compassion in Dying,* as many commentators have noted. Arras says that "[w]ithin the blink of an eye, a seemingly unmovable consensus within the medical profession, the judiciary, the bioethics community, and the general public was unceremoniously overturned."[186] Burt writes that "the rulings by the Second and Ninth Circuit overturning state laws explicitly forbidding physician-assisted suicide were not merely novel exercises of constitutional authority. These rulings startlingly impose a legal result that was without precedent in any prior state or federal legislative action."[187] Kamisar concludes that those two cases "shattered a general consensus that withholding or withdrawing life-saving treatment constitutes neither suicide nor assisted suicide nor homicide. . . . '[T]he moral significance of the distinction has been subjected to periodic philosophical challenge,' but the distinction 'has remained a basic tenet of health care law and mainstream medical ethics.'"[188] The Supreme Court itself said, "To hold for respondents [as the Ninth Circuit had done], we would have to reverse centuries of legal doctrine and practice, and strike down the considered policy choice of almost every State."[189]

I have argued that constitutional adjudication is a poor way of making bioethical policy. Is there a better way? I believe so. I would certainly not argue that *any* human institution will reliably produce admirable results, and I would certainly agree that no other branch of government can meet *all* the high standards for making policy against which I have measured courts. But the alternative to constitutional adjudication is not any single institution. Rather, it is the whole set of governmental and nongovernmental organizations that influence policy where they have not been preempted by constitutional adjudication.

The debate over assisted suicide has been conducted in many venues. The issue has perhaps been discussed most profoundly in the private conversations the dying, their doctors, and their families have had.[190] Doctors have pondered it in private conversations and professional meetings, and their professional groups have developed formal opinions about it. Suicide and euthanasia have for years been a staple of debates among bioethicists. Many kinds of private associations, from religious groups to organizations like Compassion in Dying, have become involved. Journalists have covered these activities and many more, and newspaper stories, television reports, magazine articles, and books continue to proliferate. Left to their own devices, these unofficial conversations are likely to contribute to a set of unofficial social practices not inevitably inferior to judicial edict.

Legal institutions of various kinds have likewise been active. Commissions to investigate assisted suicide—notably the New York Task Force—have been appointed and have written thoughtful reports. Legislative hearings and debates have been conducted.[191] Criminal trials and appeals have been held. Five referenda in four states have been placed before the voters. In all these ways the processes of democracy have been vigorously and usefully at work.

Nor is assisted suicide the only bioethical topic democratic and private institutions have handled actively without the benefit of constitutional adjudication. The President's Bioethics Commission drafted a three-volume report that had wide influence, and many state commissions performed similar services. The definition of death was expanded to include brain death in a quiet but effective process in which professional groups presented carefully considered proposals to legislatures to be enacted into law. The legal doctrine of informed consent developed through common law adjudication. Doctors' attitudes toward withdrawing medical treatment have been considerably moderated through purely private, hardly noticed means. Courts deciding end-of-life cases have even moved away from the constitutional reasoning the court used in *Quinlan* in favor of reasoning based on statutes and the common law.

Each of these institutions has advantages as a bioethical policy maker. Together they have many. Most of these institutions have a flexibility courts interpreting the Constitution cannot have, for they are generally not bound by their previous decisions nor by a particular method. Many of them bring expertise to the issue. Commissions are primarily composed of people who are already expert or who become so during their work, and they employ expert staffs. Professional associations are composed of and employ experts. Even legislatures usually can find within their ranks a few specialists and can hire knowledgeable staffs and recruit expert witnesses.

These institutions can also control the timing of their decisions; they can act when the moment is propitious. Courts, on the other hand, must generally act when litigants arrive. For example, one can imagine the Supreme Court reaching a different result in *Glucksberg* had it arisen after several years of a successful experiment in Oregon with assisted suicide. Many institutions can address issues much more broadly than courts. This is partly because some of them command or influence resources that can be used in many ways. A legislature, for example, can allocate funds for many kinds of programs; courts are essentially confined to a few due process remedies.

Not least, these institutions represent, can speak directly to, or can bind the disputants in a way courts cannot. Thus these institutions are better placed to shape a discussion that leads to effective resolutions of disputes. Some of these institutions have been admirably creative in trying to do so. For example, the Michigan legislature passed a statute criminalizing assisted suicide but provided that the statute would have effect only until a commission with broad representation had examined the problem.

In sum, courts have a number of institutional disadvantages in making bioethical policy. Constitutional adjudication tends to inhibit the flexibility policy needs in a dynamic area both by setting a standard states cannot escape and by cementing judges in decisions they have reached. The judicial virtues of principled reasoning, detachment, and dispassion—even when they are useful virtues—are not always practiced assiduously, and certainly were not in *Compassion in Dying*. No single institution does possess all the virtues a good policy maker needs. But the other branches of government, along with the many interested private organizations, are better placed to consider issues expertly and thoroughly, to act at the right moment, to reach compromises, to develop complex answers to complex problems, and to respond flexibly to the continuing course of change.

Conclusion

I have argued that constitutional adjudication is a poor way to make bioethical policy. My reasons have been several. First, little in the training or experience of judges prepares them to make good public policy in most areas, including this one. Second, little in the text or even the history of the Fourteenth Amendment helps judges make good bioethical policy. Nor has the Court been able to develop doctrine that has a convincing rationale or that seems to help it formulate wise policy. Such a doctrine would require that the Court be able to explain the principles it was consulting, would specify the limits on those principles, would state workable tests to employ in applying them, and would use those tests reasonably and predictably. Such a doctrine remains elusive.

Third, constitutional litigation is a poor way to gather the social facts necessary for making good public policy, and many judges even doubt they need them. This has meant courts have not demonstrated that they understand the issues assisted suicide raises. For example, the Ninth Circuit seems not to have grasped how doctors and ethicists have understood the doctrine of double effect nor the consequences of rejecting that doctrine. It seems not to know where the problem in defining "terminally ill" lies nor how hard it is to do so. It appears not to have understood how common depression is among the suicidal, how often it goes undiagnosed, or how treatable it is. It seems to have a naive view of human motivation generally, of the motives of the ill particularly, and yet more particularly, of the motives of the suicidal. It seems not to realize why people worry about the disadvantaged in a world where assisted suicide is a constitutional right. It does not seem to perceive the ways new economic concerns and new organizational structures create new incentives to hasten the dying along their way. It seems oddly optimistic about how well doctors might regulate the process of suicide. The court seems ignorant of the contemporary ethos of medicine, of the way medical decisions are made, of how doctors deal with patients, of the reasons for the origins of bioethics, and of the regulatory problems Holland has yet to solve. Nor does much in the court's information prepare it to speculate intelligently about how a new regime will work out in practice.

What is more, judicial formulas systematically underweight the state's interests. Some of those interests, as I just said, courts seem not to understand. Less concrete but still important factors—the state's "collective" interests—courts abruptly dismiss. And courts are not equipped to evaluate the cumulative costs of the rights it and other institutions create. Furthermore, the Court has found no principled way to gauge the heft of the individual's right or the state interests so as to weigh the two against each other. On the contrary, the balance is unduly weighed in favor of the individual's rights by the judicial tendency to apply the Mill paradigm, to treat every contest as one between the individual and the state rather than as a conflict among individuals with divergent interests.

In the end, it should not be surprising that courts are so limited as an agency of public policy. They are the institution ultimately responsible for allocating power among the branches of the federal government and the states; defining free speech; structuring religious liberty; setting the boundaries of criminal procedure; deciding when regulations exceed the government's power to take property without compensation; specifying the minimal procedural rights governmental agencies must accord clients; writing some of the basic rules for resolving problems of race; interpreting every federal statute; and much, much more. Responsible for so much, courts can understand only a little. The government of courts must be the government of amateurs.

In sum, the institutions of democracy—public, semipublic, and private—have been working together to shape our policies toward assisted suicide. They are reaching plausible conclusions. Together, they are placed to make better bioethical policy than a court acting as the interpreter of the Fourteenth Amendment. Together they are actually writing better policy than the federal courts when they have tried to write it. (The Supreme Court's success was to decline the invitation.) These institutions have yet another advantage. They are the voice of democracy. That voice is not pure; it is not unflawed; it is not infallible. But assisted suicide is an issue that can affect anyone, that everyone can speak to. In fact, it is an issue as to which an exceptionally large proportion of the population has an opinion.[192] We value democratic government partly because it allows the people affected by a decision to help make it. When courts take decisions away from democratic institutions, courts should be able to advance convincing reasons and to assure us that their job will be done well. I have argued that courts can offer no such assurances when they take bioethical policy into their own hands.

NOTES

I am grateful to Yale Kamisar and Marc Spindelman for their characteristically acute readings of an earlier version of this chapter.

1. Carl E. Schneider, *Bioethics in the Language of the Law,* 24 Hastings Center Report 16, 16 (July/Aug 1994). As McCann puts it, "Courts are to a large extent educational bodies, some activists suggest, and judges the teachers throughout the government and society." Michael W. McCann, *Taking Reform Seriously: Perspectives on Public Interest*

Liberalism 120 (Cornell University Press, 1986).

2. M. Cathleen Kaveny, *Assisted Suicide, the Supreme Court, and the Constitutive Function of the Law,* 27 Hastings Center Report 29, 29 (Sept/Oct 1997).

3. 79 F3d 790 (1996).

4. 117 S Ct 2258 (1997). For a description and analysis of that case, see Sonia M. Suter, *Ambivalent Unanimity: An Analysis of the Supreme Court's Holding,* in this volume.

5. For attempts to redress the neglect, see Carl E. Schneider, *State-Interest Analysis in Fourteenth Amendment "Privacy" Law: An Essay on the Constitutionalization of Social Issues,* 51 Law & Contemporary Problems 79 (Winter 1988); Carl E. Schneider, *The Channelling Function in Family Law,* 20 Hofstra Law Review 495 (1992); Carl E. Schneider, *State-Interest Analysis and the Channeling Function in Privacy Law,* in Stephen E. Gottlieb, ed., *Public Values in Constitutional Law* (University of Michigan Press, 1993).

6. Two landmarks in that controversy are Donald L. Horowitz, *The Courts and Social Policy* (Brookings, 1977), and Gerald N. Rosenberg, *The Hollow Hope: Can Courts Bring About Social Change?* (University of Chicago Press, 1991).

7. For a detailed examination of the problems with making autonomy the preeminent principle of biocthical policy, see Carl E. Schneider, *The Practice of Autonomy: Patients, Doctors, and Medical Decisions* (Oxford University Press, 1998).

8. *Glucksberg,* 117 S Ct at 2262 (citations omitted).

9. 497 US 261, 293 (1990).

10. 491 US 110 (1989).

11. Justice Blackmun did try to mount a kind of historical argument, but the fact remained that abortion had long been regulated through the criminal law and that at the time of *Roe* most states still criminalized abortion.

12. 505 US 833, 851 (1992).

13. 117 S Ct at 2271 (citations omitted).

14. Bowers v Hardwick, 478 US 186 (1986).

15. For criticisms of this and other "technical" deficiencies of state-interest analysis, see Schneider, *State-Interest Analysis,* L & Contemporary Problems at 82–96 (cited in note 5); Robert F. Nagel, Note, *Legislative Purpose, Rationality, and Equal Protection,* 82 Yale Law Journal 123 (1972).

16. 497 US at 278–79, 280–84.

17. Ibid. at 303 (Brennan, J., dissenting) (citation omitted).

18. Ibid. at 344 (Stevens, J., dissenting) (citations omitted).

19. For a deplorable example of this attitude, see Carl E. Schneider, *Definition, Generalization, and Theory in American Family Law,* 18 University of Michigan Journal of Law Reform 1039 (1985). For a recantation, see Carl E. Schneider, *On the Duties and Rights of Parents,* 81 Virginia Law Review 2477 (1995). For a full-scale analysis of the attitude, see Carl E. Schneider & Lee E. Teitelbaum, *Life's Golden Tree: The Case for Empirical Scholarship in American Law* (unpublished manuscript).

20. To which I replied, "Not here you're not." He was not amused.

21. Abraham S. Blumberg, *The Practice of Law as Confidence Game: Organizational Cooptation of a Profession,* 1 Law & Society Review 15, 38–39 (June 1967).

22. Graham Hughes, *The Great American Legal Scholarship Bazaar,* 33 Journal of Legal Education 424, 429 (1983).

23. David L. Faigman, *"Normative Constitutional Fact-Finding": Exploring the Empirical Component of Constitutional Interpretation,* 139 U Pennsylvania L Rev 541, 545 (1991).

24. See ibid. at 589–95 for criticism of the Court's approach.

25. Carl E. Schneider, *Making Sausage,* 27 Hastings Center Report 27, 27–28 (Jan/Feb 1997).

26. 79 F3d 790 (1996).

27. My views about the constitutional right asserted in these cases are well captured by, e.g., Yale Kamisar, *Are Laws against Assisted Suicide Un-*

constitutional?, 23 Hastings Center Report 32 (May/June 1993); Yale Kamisar, *When Is There a Constitutional "Right to Die"? When Is There No Constitutional "Right to Live"?*, 25 Georgia Law Review 1203 (1991). Some of my own views are expressed in Cruzan *and the Constitutionalization of American Life*, 17 Journal of Medicine & Philosophy 589 (1992).

28. It is hard to know how seriously the Supreme Court took the state interests in *Glucksberg*, since the Court's conclusion that there was no fundamental right to assisted suicide meant that the state had to meet only a light burden of proof.

29. 79 F3d at 817.

30. 80 F3d 716 (1996).

31. *Compassion in Dying*, 79 F3d at 817. This argument may reflect a common strategy among courts evaluating state-interest claims—to imply that the state actually does not believe in all the interests it asserts, that the state is being hypocritical. But states do not think. Furthermore, the state is not a human being, and it is not capable of hypocrisy. Hypocrisy is thinking one thing and doing something else. But the state may act in ways that seem to be conflicting without hypocrisy exactly because ours is a system of divided powers in which policy is supposed to change with elections. In addition, of course, hypocrisy is in the eye of the beholder. The Ninth Circuit may think it hypocritical to permit patients to refuse medical treatment but to deny them the help of a doctor in committing suicide; most commentators do not.

32. 79 F3d at 822.

33. 79 F3d at 823.

34. Tom L. Beauchamp & James F. Childress, *Principles of Biomedical Ethics* 206 (4th ed., Oxford University Press, 1994) (footnote omitted).

35. Ibid. at 206–7.

36. 79 F3d at 824.

37. Howard Brody, Compassion in Dying v Washington: *Promoting Dangerous Myths in Terminal Care*, 2 BioLaw S:154, S:156 (Special Section, July/Aug, 1996).

38. John Arras, *News from the Circuit Courts: How Not to Think About Physician-Assisted Suicide*, 2 BioLaw S:171, S:187, n23 (Special Section, July/Aug, 1996).

39. 79 F3d at 820.

40. *Glucksberg*, 117 S Ct at 2272.

41. 79 F3d at 824 (footnote omitted).

42. Ibid. at 831.

43. Joanne Lynn et al, for the SUPPORT Investigators, *Defining the "Terminally Ill:" Insights from SUPPORT*, 35 Duquesne Law Review 311, 322 (1996).

44. Ibid. at 334.

45. Eric Chevlen, *The Limits of Prognostication*, 35 Duquesne Law Review 337, 353–54 (1996).

46. 79 F3d at 820.

47. Ibid.

48. As one standard definition puts it, an autonomous decision is one in which "a patient . . . with substantial *understanding* and in substantial *absence of control* by others *intentionally authorizes* a professional to do something." Tom L. Beauchamp & James F. Childress, *Principles of Biomedical Ethics* 76 (cited in note 34).

49. On which, see Peter Hammer, *Assisted Suicide and the Challenge of Individually Determined Collective Rationality*, in this volume.

50. *Suicide and the Request for Assisted Suicide: Meaning and Motivation*, 35 Duquesne Law Review 285, 286 (1996).

51. Ibid. at 288 (footnotes omitted). "In one study . . . fewer than 15 percent of depressed residents had correctly been diagnosed by the nursing home physician. . . . [Another] study noted that only 15 percent of the alert and

oriented patients with depression received treatment." New York State Task Force on Life and the Law, *When Death Is Sought: Assisted Suicide and Euthanasia in the Medical Context* 32–33 (no publisher, 1994).

52. See Carl E. Schneider, *The Practice of Autonomy: Patients, Doctors, and Medical Decisions* (Oxford University Press, 1998), particularly ch 3.

53. Hendin, 35 Duquesne Law Review at 296 (footnote omitted).

54. Quoted ibid. at 291.

55. Ibid. at 290–91.

56. See Schneider, *The Practice of Autonomy,* particularly ch 4 (cited in note 52).

57. Hendin, 35 Duquesne Law Review at 290 (footnote omitted).

58. Ibid. at 293 (footnote omitted).

59. Ibid. at 293 (footnote omitted).

60. New York State Task Force on Life and the Law, *When Death Is Sought: Assisted Suicide and Euthanasia in the Medical Context* xiv (no publisher, 1994).

61. *In Love with Daylight: A Memoir of Recovery* 14 (Simon & Schuster, 1995). On the ways people adjust to distressing circumstances, see Philip Brickman, Dan Coates, & Ronnie Janoff-Bulman, *Lottery Winners and Accident Victims: Is Happiness Relative?,* 36 Journal of Personality & Social Psychology 917 (1978).

62. *When Death Is Sought: Assisted Suicide and Euthanasia in the Medical Context* (no publisher, 1994).

63. *Compassion in Dying,* 79 F3d at 820.

64. Ibid. at 820–21.

65. Ibid. at 824.

66. Ibid.

67. New York State Task Force on Life and the Law, *When Death Is Sought: Assisted Suicide and Euthanasia in the Medical Context* 9 (no publisher, 1994).

68. For the argument that substantive reforms are often cloaked in the language of autonomy, see Carl E.

Schneider, *The Practice of Autonomy: Patients, Doctors, and Medical Decisions* (Oxford University Press, 1998), especially ch 6.

69. 79 F3d at 825.

70. Ibid.

71. Ibid. at 826.

72. Ibid.

73. Hendin, 35 Duquesne Law Review at 288.

74. Leon R. Kass & Nelson Lund, *Physician-Assisted Suicide, Medical Ethics and the Future of the Medical Profession,* 35 Duquesne Law Review 395, 407 (1996) (footnote omitted).

75. Herbert Hendin, *The Slippery Slope: The Dutch Example,* 35 Duquesne Law Review 427, 428 (1996) (footnotes omitted).

76. Hendin, 35 Duquesne Law Review at 300–301 (1996) (footnotes omitted).

77. For a careful study of many of these issues, see Bradford H. Gray, *The Profit Motive and Patient Care: The Changing Accountability of Doctors and Hospitals* (Harvard University Press, 1991).

78. This argument is extensively developed in Susan M. Wolf, *Physician-Assisted Suicide in the Context of Managed Care,* 35 Duquesne Law Review 455 (1996).

79. 79 F3d at 827.

80. Indeed, in the entire section on unduly influenced decisions to commit suicide there is only one footnote, and it proffers only more assumptions, not evidence.

81. See, e.g., Grace Budrys, *When Doctors Join Unions* (Cornell University Press, 1997).

82. See, e.g., Eliot Freidson, *Medical Work in America* 178–205 (Yale University Press, 1989).

83. See, for example, *Roe v Wade,* 410 US 113, 163 (1973), where the Court becomes so confused about whose rights it is protecting that it

says that "the attending physician, in consultation with his patient, is free to determine, without regulation by the state, that, in his medical judgment, the patient's pregnancy should be terminated."

84. Timothy E. Quill, *Death and Dignity: Making Choices and Taking Charge* 9–22 (W. W. Norton, 1993).

85. Yet "[i]n some of Kevorkian's cases, the push for the patient's death came from relatives; in others no medical pathology was found upon autopsy, and in virtually no case were any possible alternatives to assisted suicide adequately explored." Hendin, *The Slippery Slope: The Dutch Example,* 35 Duquesne Law Review at 441 (1996). This difficulty obtaining convictions is not a recent development. It appears that "eleven physicians have faced criminal charges in connection with the killing of a patient or family member, but none has yet been imprisoned." Judith F. Daar, *Direct Democracy and Bioethical Choices: Voting Life and Death at the Ballot Box,* 28 University of Michigan Journal of Law Reform 799, [825] (1995). It also appears that "[t]here have been no reported convictions to date [for assisting in a suicide of a terminally ill patient], despite the fact that physician-assisted suicide is known to occur in practice." T. Howard Stone & William J. Winslade, *Physician-Assisted Suicide and Euthanasia in the United States,* 16 Journal of Legal Medicine 481, 507 (1995).

86. See Carl E. Schneider & Margaret F. Brinig, *An Invitation to Family Law: Principles, Process, and Perspectives* 148–50, 1157–58 (West, 1996).

87. A typical opinion comes from one of the physician-plaintiffs in *Glucksberg:*

> Although medical professionals must be accountable for their practices, most physicians believe medical decisions and

practices are an intensely private matter in which the state does not and should not intrude. Physicians are likely to dislike or detest state regulation of end-of-life practices because of deeply held professional and philosophical views, as well as pragmatically seeing it as limiting patient options and subverting optimal patient care.

> Thomas A. Preston, *The Case for Privacy in Dying: A Solution from the Supreme Court,* 76 King County Medical Society 9, 13 (Nov 1997).

88. It is often argued that regulation would actually be easier if assisted suicide were legal. Perhaps. But it is hardly reassuring that, "[d]espite changes in the law that ensure Dutch doctors will not be prosecuted if they follow guidelines, 50% of Dutch doctors do not report their euthanasia cases. Further, 20% of the doctors say that they will not do so under any circumstances." Hendin, *The Slippery Slope: The Dutch Example,* 35 Duquesne Law Review at 430 (1996) (footnotes omitted).

89. 79 F3d at 837.

90. See note 176 and accompanying text.

91. 79 F3d at 826–27.

92. Robert A. Burt, *Constitutionalizing Physician-Assisted Suicide: Will Lightning Strike Thrice?,* 35 Duquesne Law Review 159, 172 (1996) (footnote omitted).

93. Ibid. at 174.

94. Compassion in Dying v Washington: *Promoting Dangerous Myths in Terminal Care,* 2 BioLaw S:154, S:155 (Special Section, July/Aug, 1996) (footnotes omitted). "Numerous barriers hamper the delivery of pain relief and palliative care, including a lack of professional knowledge and training, unjustified fears about ad-

diction among both patients and health care professionals, inattention to pain assessment, and pharmacy practices." New York State Task Force on Life and the Law, *When Death Is Sought: Assisted Suicide and Euthanasia in the Medical Context* 35 (no publisher, 1994).

95. *Physician-Assisted Suicide in the Courts: Moral Equivalence, Double Effect, and Clinical Practice,* in this volume.

96. Margot White & Marc Spindelman, *Ninth Circuit Ignores Medical Experience at Our Peril,* 2 BioLaw S:159, S:167 (Special Section, July/Aug, 1996) (footnote omitted). See Support Principal Investigators, *A Controlled Trial to Improve Care for Seriously Ill Hospitalized Patients: the Study to Understand Prognoses and Preferences for Outcomes and Risks of Treatment (SUPPORT),* 247 Journal of the American Medical Association 1591 (1995), and *Dying Well in the Hospital: The Lessons of SUPPORT,* a special supplement in the Hastings Center Report of Nov/Dec 1995.

97. Jean Jacques Rousseau, *Émile* 192 (E. P. Dutton, 1950).

98. Leon R. Kass & Nelson Lund, *Physician-Assisted Suicide, Medical Ethics and the Future of the Medical Profession,* 35 Duquesne Law Review 395, 418 (1996).

99. Carl E. Schneider, *The Practice of Autonomy: Patients, Doctors, and Medical Decisions* 185 (Oxford University Press, 1998).

100. Hendin reports that "more than half of Dutch physicians consider it appropriate to introduce the subject of euthanasia to their patients." *The Slippery Slope: The Dutch Example,* 35 Duquesne Law Review at 428 (footnote omitted).

101. Ibid. at 441.

102. Ibid. at 440.

103. Hendin, *The Slippery Slope,* 35 Duquesne Law Review at 428. Criticisms along these lines are also reported in Herbert Hendin, *Seduced by Death: Doctors, Patients, and the Dutch Cure* 23 (W. W. Norton, 1997); John Keown, *Euthanasia in the Netherlands: Sliding Down the Slippery Slope?,* in John Keown, ed., *Euthanasia Examined: Ethical, Clinical and Legal Perspectives* 261 (Cambridge University Press, 1995); Carlos F. Gomez, *Regulating Death: Euthanasia and the Case of the Netherlands* (Free Press, 1991).

104. The article is reprinted in Timothy E. Quill, *Death and Dignity: Making Choices and Taking Charge* 9–16 (W. W. Norton, 1993).

105. Patricia Wesley, *Dying Safely,* 8 Issues in Law & Medicine 467, 480 (1993). To like effect, see Herbert Hendin, *Seduced by Death: Doctors, Patients and the Dutch Cure* 26–30 (W. W. Norton, 1997).

106. 79 F3d at 833 (footnote omitted).

107. 79 F3d at 827.

108. 79 F3d at 827–28.

109. 79 F3d at 829–30. It is a little hard to see this as an example of adapting to a changed legal climate, since "[b]y 1967 [six years before *Roe*], . . . some 87 percent of American physicians favored a liberalization of the country's anti-abortion policies." James C. Mohr, *Abortion in America: The Origins and Evolution of National Policy* 256 (Oxford University Press, 1978).

110. Leon R. Kass & Nelson Lund, *Physician-Assisted Suicide, Medical Ethics and the Future of the Medical Profession,* 35 Duquesne Law Review 395, 403–4 (1996) (footnotes omitted).

111. Kass & Lund, 35 Duquesne Law Review at 418 (footnote omitted).

112. Herbert Hendin, *The Slippery Slope: The Dutch Example,* 35 Duquesne Law Review 427, 436 (1996) (footnote omitted).
113. 79 F3d at 830.
114. Ibid. at 830–31.
115. See, e.g., *Bowers v Hardwick,* 478 US 186 (1986), and *Michael H. v Gerald D.,* 491 US 110 (1989).
116. 443 US 622 (1979).
117. Robert H. Mnookin et al., *In the Interest of Children: Advocacy, Law Reform, and Public Policy* 149–264 (W. H. Freeman, 1985).
118. See Herbert Jacob, *A Silent Revolution: Routine Policy Making and the Transformation of Divorce Law in the United States* (Chicago University Press, 1988).
119. John Arras, *News from the Circuit Courts: How Not to Think About Physician-Assisted Suicide,* 2 Bio-Law S:171, S:179–80 (Special Section, July/Aug, 1996).
120. Whether this is technically a slippery-slope argument is difficult to say because there is no technical definition of that kind of argument. At least, however, it shares with a slippery-slope argument the danger that a rule contended for may lead further than was anticipated.
121. *Hudson County Water Co. v McCarter,* 209 US 349, 355 (1908).
122. Paul Freund, *Privacy: One Concept or Many,* in J. Roland Pennock & John W. Chapman, eds., *Privacy* (Nomos XIII) (Atherton Press, 1971).
123. Carl E. Schneider, *State-Interest Analysis in Fourteenth Amendment "Privacy" Law: An Essay on the Constitutionalization of Social Issues,* 51 Law & Contemporary Problems 79, 87 (Winter 1988).
124. 79 F3d at 813 (footnote omitted).
125. 79 F3d at 831.
126. It was a similar failure that led Kamisar to say, "With all defer-ence, this author finds it hard to believe that the *Quill* [*v Vacco*] court thought through where its rationale would lead and whether it was prepared to go there." *The "Right to Die": On Drawing (and Erasing) Lines,* 35 Duquesne Law Review 481, 487 (1996).
127. As Kamisar notes, "What the *Quill* Court did, in effect, was to lubricate the 'slippery slope' with the Equal Protection Clause." Ibid. at 487.
128. See *Cruzan,* 497 US at 328. As Kass and Lund observe, "the vast majority of candidates who 'merit' an earlier death cannot request it for themselves. Persons in a so-called persistent vegetative state; those suffering from severe depression, senility, mental illness, or Alzheimer's disease; infants who are deformed; and retarded or dying children—all are incapable of requesting death, but are equally deserving of the new humane 'aid-in-dying.'" Leon R. Kass & Nelson Lund, *Physician-Assisted Suicide, Medical Ethics and the Future of the Medical Profession,* 35 Duquesne Law Review 395, 412 (1996).
129. See *Cruzan,* 497 US at 331.
130. Similarly, Hendin reports a case proffered by an attorney for the Dutch Euthanasia Society as an illustration of why it was often necessary for doctors to end the lives of competent patients without discussion with them. The attorney spoke of a doctor who had terminated the life of a nun a few days before the nun would have died, because the nun was in excruciating pain and her religious convictions did not permit her to ask for death. Herbert Hendin, *The Slippery Slope: The Dutch Example,* 35 Duquesne Law Review 427, 435–36 (1996).

131. For a careful analysis of slippery-slope arguments, see Frederick Schauer, *Slippery Slopes*, 99 Harvard Law Review 361 (1985).

132. Carl E. Schneider, *Rights Discourse and Neonatal Euthanasia*, 76 California Law Review 151, 168 (1988).

133. *Are Laws Against Assisted Suicide Unconstitutional?* Hastings Center Report 32, 40 (May/June 1993), citing Thomas Mayo, *Constitutionalizing the "Right to Die,"* 49 Maryland Law Review 103, 144 (1990).

134. Herbert Hendin, *The Slippery Slope: The Dutch Example*, 35 Duquesne Law Review 427, 427 (1996).

135. 79 F3d at 837.

136. I develop this argument at some length in Carl E. Schneider, *State-Interest Analysis and the Channelling Function in Privacy Law*, in Stephen E. Gottlieb, ed., *Public Values in Constitutional Law* 97 (University of Michigan Press, 1993).

137. 117 S Ct 2272 (1997) (footnote omitted).

138. Carl E. Schneider & Margaret F. Brinig, *An Invitation to Family Law: Principles, Process, and Perspectives* 161 (West, 1996).

139. Carl E. Schneider, *State-Interest Analysis in Fourteenth Amendment "Privacy" Law: An Essay on the Constitutionalization of Social Issues*, 51 Law & Contemporary Problems 79, 98 (Winter 1988). I develop this argument at greater length ibid. at 97–106. See also Guido Calabresi, *Reflections on Medical Experimentation in Humans*, 98 Daedalus 387 (1969).

140. Leon R. Kass & Nelson Lund, *Physician-Assisted Suicide, Medical Ethics and the Future of the Medical Profession*, 35 Duquesne Law Review 395, 401 (1996).

141. Ibid. at 419–20. Lest these fears seem too timorous, we should recall the evidence that for years doctors orchestrated the deaths of newborns whose lives they regarded as not worth living. See, e.g., Raymond S. Duff & A. G. M. Campbell, *Moral and Ethical Dilemmas in the Special-Care Nursery*, 289 New England Journal of Medicine 890 (1973). Cf. Martin S. Pernick, *Eugenic Euthanasia in Early Twentieth-Century America and Medically Assisted Suicide Today: Similarities and Differences*, in this volume.

142. "The major studies all agree in showing that the fraction of suicide victims struggling with a terminal illness at the time of their death is in the range of 2% to 4%." David C. Clark, *"Rational" Suicide and People with Terminal Conditions or Disabilities*, 8 Issues in Law & Medicine 147, 151 (1992).

143. *Whose Keeper? Social Science and Moral Obligation* 43 (University of California Press, 1989).

144. Anne Hunsaker Hawkins, *Reconstructing Illness: Studies in Pathography* 124 (Purdue University Press, 1993).

145. For a defense of this kind of argument in constitutional terms, see Carl E. Schneider, *State-Interest Analysis and the Channeling Function in Privacy Law*, in Stephen E. Gottlieb, ed., *Public Values in Constitutional Law* (University of Michigan Press, 1993).

146. 79 F3d at 821.

147. Daniel Callahan, *Assisted Suicide Is a Power Too Far*, 2 BioLaw S:125, S:126 (Special Section, July/Aug, 1996). I discuss this problem at some length in ch 5 of Carl E. Schneider, *The Practice of Autonomy: Patients, Doctors, and*

Medical Decisions (Oxford University Press, 1998).

148. Yale Kamisar, *Are Laws Against Assisted Suicide Unconstitutional?*, 23 Hastings Center Report 32, 39 (May/June 1993).

149. J. David Velleman, *Against the Right to Die,* 17 Journal of Medicine & Philosophy 664 (1992).

150. Leon R. Kass & Nelson Lund, *Physician-Assisted Suicide, Medical Ethics and the Future of the Medical Profession,* 35 Duquesne Law Review 395, 406 (1996). See also Courtney S. Campbell, Jan Hare, & Pam Matthews, *Conflicts of Conscience: Hospice and Assisted Suicide,* 25 Hastings Center Report 36 (May/June 1995).

151. Herbert Hendin, *The Slippery Slope: The Dutch Example,* 35 Duquesne Law Review 427, 430 (1996) (footnotes omitted).

152. On the Court's confusion, see Carl E. Schneider, *State-Interest Analysis in Fourteenth Amendment "Privacy" Law: An Essay on the Constitutionalization of Social Issues,* 51 Law & Contemporary Problems 79, 82–95 (Winter 1988).

153. 79 F3d at 836.

154. As Cardozo wrote,

> If you ask how [the judge] is to know when one interest outweighs another, I can only answer that he must get his knowledge just as the legislator gets it, from experience and study and reflection; in brief, from life itself. Here, indeed, is the point of contact between the legislator's work and his. The choice of methods, the appraisement of values, must in the end be guided by like considerations for the one as for the other. Each indeed is legislating within the limits of his competence.
>
> Benjamin N. Cardozo, *The Nature of the Judicial Process*

113 (Yale University Press, 1975). It is worth noting that here Cardozo was speaking of a court exercising common law authority.

155. E.g., "By prohibiting physician assistance, it bars what for many terminally ill patients is the only palatable, and only practical, way to end their lives. Physically frail, confined to wheelchairs or beds, many terminally ill patients do not have the means or ability to kill themselves in the multitude of ways that healthy individuals can. Often, for example, they cannot even secure the medication or devices they would need to carry out their wishes." 79 F3d at 832. "The testimony produced by the plaintiffs shows that many terminally ill patients who wish to die with dignity are forced to resort to gruesome alternatives because of the unavailability of physician assistance." Ibid. at 834. "Next, the plaintiffs produced testimony showing that many terminally ill patients are physically or psychologically unable to take their lives by the violent means that are almost always their only alternatives in the absence of assistance from a physician." Ibid. at 835.

156. "Studies indicate that for many patients with severe pain, disfigurement, or disability, the vast majority do not desire suicide. In one study of terminally ill patients, of those who expressed a wish to die, all met diagnostic criteria for major depression." New York State Task Force on Life and the Law, *When Death Is Sought: Assisted Suicide and Euthanasia in the Medical Context* 13 (no publisher, 1994). "Among older persons, for whom chronic painful illnesses are not uncommon, only 0.5% of male deaths and 0.2%

of female deaths are attributable to suicide." David C. Clark, *"Rational" Suicide and People with Terminal Conditions or Disabilities,* 8 Issues in Law & Medicine 147, 160–61 (1992).

157. "The wish to end life by killing oneself is almost always a serious symptom arising from a temporary psychiatric illness." David C. Clark, *"Rational" Suicide and People with Terminal Conditions or Disabilities,* 8 Issues in Law & Medicine 147, 163 (1992).

158. Courtney Campbell, *Sanitizing Suicide in the Culture of Death: "So, Go Back, Jack, Do It Again,"* 2 BioLaw S:121, S:122 (Special Section, July/Aug, 1996). White and Spindelman even write, "Most would-be suicides are quite capable of concocting or consuming a death-inducing potion, or of otherwise ending their lives without a doctor's assistance." Margot White & Marc Spindelman, *Ninth Circuit Ignores Medical Experience at Our Peril,* 2 BioLaw S:159, S:162 (Special Section, July/Aug, 1996).

159. New York State Task Force on Life and the Law, *When Death Is Sought: Assisted Suicide and Euthanasia in the Medical Context* 4 (no publisher, 1994).

160. There is evidence, for example, that Dutch doctors have found that "even if a physician knows the proper drugs and dosage, in one out of four cases, prescribed use does not result in a quick, efficient death, but instead induces a coma that lingers for several days." Courtney Campbell, *Sanitizing Suicide in the Culture of Death: "So, Go Back, Jack, Do It Again,"* 2 BioLaw S:121, S:124 (Special Section, July/Aug, 1996).

161. *New State Ice Co. v Liebmann,* 285 US 262, 310 (dissenting).

162. Schneider, *Rights Discourse and Neonatal Euthanasia,* 76 California Law Review at 157 (cited in note 132).

163. Carl E. Schneider, *Bioethics and the Family: The Cautionary View from Family Law,* 1992 Utah Law Review 819, 838.

164. 79 F3d at 837.

165. Donald L. Horowitz, *The Courts and Social Policy* 45 (Brookings, 1977) (footnote omitted).

166. On the ways people are misled about the likelihood of events by vivid recent experiences, see Richard Nisbett & Lee Ross, *Human Inference: Strategies and Shortcomings of Social Judgment* 17–62 (Prentice-Hall, 1980).

167. John Arras, *News from the Circuit Courts: How Not to Think About Physician-Assisted Suicide,* 2 BioLaw S:171, S:184–85 (Special Section, July/Aug, 1996).

168. Carl E. Schneider, *Lawyers and Children: Wisdom and Legitimacy in Family Policy,* 84 Michigan Law Review 919, 932 (1986).

169. These two paragraphs are roughly borrowed from Carl E. Schneider, *The Practice of Autonomy: Patients, Doctors, and Medical Decisions* (Oxford University Press, 1998), ch 1 of which discusses hyper-rationalism at some length.

170. Law schools should not escape their share of the blame. Not only is their teaching done through cases, but the cases are appellate cases, where the facts have already been winnowed and sifted and cannot be challenged. Complicated cases with complex facts are either not presented (because such cases are pedagogically awkward) or are edited so severely that the complexity seeps away. Legal scholars, who ought to be doing empirical research, resist it, even though it has been persuasively advocated for

most of this century. See Carl E.
Schneider & Lee E. Teitelbaum,
*Life's Golden Tree: The Case for
Empirical Scholarship in American
Law* (in manuscript).

171. 79 F3d at 827.

172. Of course, this is not a necessary
attribute of a common law system;
it is just the way ours has evolved.

173. Michael W. McCann, *Taking Re-
form Seriously: Perspectives on
Public Interest Liberalism* 226
(Cornell University Press, 1986).

174. E.g., "Given the possibility of undue
influence that already exists, the
recognition of the right to physician-
assisted suicide would not increase
that risk unduly." *Compassion in
Dying,* 79 F3d at 826.

175. At oral argument, counsel for the
respondents in *Glucksberg* argued
that because "ours is a culture of
denial of death," she had "some
concern that the political process
would not be expected to work in a
usual fashion." Quoted in Yale
Kamisar, *On the Meaning and Impact of the Physician-Assisted Suicide Cases,* in this volume. It is difficult to know whether to take this
argument seriously. For one thing,
the cliché that "ours is a culture of
denial of death" seems to me simply wrong. Death is honored by its
own section at Border's Books &
Music, books on it become best-
sellers, and death has become an
academic subculture. More to the
point, our supposed denial of death
has not in fact kept "the political
process" from prolonged and vigorous discussion of assisted suicide.

176. See Robert Zussman, *Intensive
Care: Medical Ethics and the Medical Profession* 104–15 (University
of Chicago Press, 1992); New York
State Task Force on Life and the
Law, *When Death Is Sought: Assisted Suicide and Euthanasia in

the Medical Context 4 (no publisher, 1994). Thus one study reports that "family members tended
to err on the side of providing re-
suscitation for the patient whereas
physicians tended to err on the side
of not providing the intervention."
Allison B. Seckler et al., *Substituted Judgment: How Accurate Are
Proxy Predictions?,* 115 Annals of
Internal Medicine 92, 95 (July
1991).

177. *New State Ice Co. v Liebmann,* 285
US 262, 311 (dissenting).

178. Francis Bacon, *Novum Organum,*
Peter Urbach & John Gibson,
translators & eds., 57 (Open Court,
1994).

179. Yale Kamisar, *The "Right to Die":
On Drawing (and Erasing) Lines,*
35 Duquesne Law Review 481, 481
(1996), quoting Louis Henkin,
Foreword: On Drawing Lines, 82
Harvard Law Review 63, 65–66
(1968).

180. For this argument applied specifically to bioethics, see Amy Gutman
& Dennis Thompson, *Deliberating
About Bioethics,* 27 Hastings Center Report 38 (May/June 1997).

181. For an argument that abortion was
the kind of issue that could best
have been resolved through political compromise, see Carl E.
Schneider, *State-Interest Analysis
in Fourteenth Amendment "Privacy" Law: An Essay on the Constitutionalization of Social Issues,* 51
Law & Contemporary Problems 79,
113–14 (Winter 1988).

182. Yale Kamisar, *In Defense of the Distinction Between Terminating Life
Support and Actively Intervening
to Promote or to Bring about Death,*
2 BioLaw S:145, S:148 (Special
Section, July/Aug, 1996).

183. Describing the views of what he
calls "public interest liberals," Mc-
Cann writes, "Judges, above all

else, are praised as independent, neutral, and impartial in ways that bureaucrats cannot be." Michael W. McCann, *Taking Reform Seriously: Perspectives on Public Interest Liberalism* 117–18 (Cornell University Press, 1986).

184. 79 F3d at 837, 839.

185. 79 F3d at 838–39.

186. John Arras, *News From the Circuit Courts: How Not to Think About Physician-Assisted Suicide,* 2 Bio-Law S:171, S:171 (1996).

187. Robert A. Burt, *Constitutionalizing Physician-Assisted Suicide: Will Lightning Strike Thrice?,* 35 Duquesne Law Review 159, 163 (1996).

188. Yale Kamisar, *The "Right to Die": On Drawing (and Erasing) Lines,* 35 Duquesne Law Review 481, 490 (1996) (footnote omitted).

189. 117 S Ct at 2269 (citations omitted).

190. See Arthur Frank, *From Story to Law: Euthanasia and Authenticity,* in this volume.

191. Professor Kamisar reports "that in the last decade bills to legalize PAS have been introduced in more than twenty states" but not enacted and that in that period sixteen bills prohibiting it have been enacted. Yale Kamisar, *On the Meaning and Impact of the Physician-Assisted Suicide Cases,* in this volume. Recently, the flood has continued unabated. See Susan M. Wolf, *Physician-Assisted Suicide: Facing Death After* Glucksberg *and* Quill, 82 Minnesota Law Review 885, 890 n32. Even the federal government has entered the fray to prohibit the use of federal funds for assisted suicide. Federal Assisted Suicide Funding Restriction Act of 1997, Pub L 105–12, 111 Stat 23 (codified as amended 42 USC §§ 14401 et seq). This activity is described in some detail in Henry R. Glick, *The Right to Die: Policy Innovation and Its Consequences* (Columbia University Press, 1992).

192. Henry R. Glick, *The Right to Die: Policy Innovation and Its Consequences* 56 (Columbia University Press, 1992).

Part V

Formulating Principles and Making Policy

CHAPTER 8   Eugenic Euthanasia in Early
            Twentieth-Century America and
            Medically Assisted Suicide Today:
            Differences and Similarities

Martin S. Pernick

Introduction

From 1915 to 1918, Chicago surgeon Harry Haiselden electrified the nation by allowing or accelerating the deaths of at least six infants he diagnosed as "defectives." Seeking publicity for his efforts to eliminate the "unfit," he displayed the dying infants and their mothers to journalists (Fig. 1) and wrote a serialized book about them for the Hearst newspapers. His campaign was front-page news for weeks at a time (Fig. 2) and won endorsements from hundreds of prominent Americans.[1]

Haiselden also wrote and starred in a commercial motion picture, *The Black Stork,* an hour-long melodrama based on his actual cases. In the film, Claude, who has an unnamed inherited disease, ignores graphic warnings from his doctor (played by Haiselden) and marries Anne. Their baby is born "defective" and needs immediate surgery to save its life, but the doctor refuses to operate (Fig. 3). After God provides a horrific vision of the child's future of misery and crime, Anne agrees to withhold treatment, and the baby's soul leaps into the arms of a waiting Jesus. The film was shown around the country in several editions from 1916 to at least 1928, and perhaps as late as 1942.[2]

These events are important for more than their novelty and drama. They are a unique record documenting the now almost completely forgotten fact that Americans ever died because their doctors judged them genetically unfit. These events also illuminate a defining moment in the history of euthanasia and its relationship to the controversial social movement known as eugenics.

Euthanasia was often defined as "merciful death" and *eugenics* as "improving human heredity," but their specific meanings and the links between them were only starting to take shape in 1915. Until late in the nineteenth century, euthanasia had meant efforts to ease the sufferings of the dying without hastening their death, but it soon came to include both passively withholding life-prolonging treatment and active "mercy killing" as well. The term eugenics was first popularized by Charles Darwin's cousin Sir Francis

Galton, who defined it as the science of improving human heredity. Eugenicists pursued a diverse range of activities, from statistically sophisticated analyses of human pedigrees to "better baby contests" modeled on rural livestock shows, compulsory sterilization of criminals and the retarded, and selective ethnic restrictions on immigration.[3]

In this chapter, I do not try to trace the complete history of euthanasia or of medically assisted suicide. Rather, I use Dr. Haiselden's brief, long-forgotten moment in that history to illuminate the similarities and differences between past and present efforts to answer four key questions:

1. Can the incurably sick be distinguished from the socially unwanted?
2. What is the relation between euthanasia and eugenics?
3. Who if anyone should make life-and-death choices, and for whose benefit?
4. How do the mass media, and individual crusading physician-provocateurs, influence both the meaning and the memory of euthanasia?

Fig. 1. Reporters interviewed and photographed the mothers of the babies Dr. Haiselden permitted to die. (*Chicago Tribune,* November 17, 1915 at 7.)

The Sick and the Unwanted: Values and the Meaning of Disease

Social categories like race, class, and ethnicity deeply and notoriously molded eugenic concepts of the "unfit." Yet the relationship between science and social prejudice remains the least understood and most controversial part of eugenics. Haiselden's example helps us understand the interrelation of science and social values in constructing eugenic concepts of disease and in defining the candidates for euthanasia. (When I use words like *defective* or *unfit,* I'm quoting what eugenicists believed to be purely objective technical terms. But I'm doing so in order to examine their value content, not to endorse those values or their claims of objectivity.)

Many of Haiselden's supporters were among the leading popularizers of racial eugenics. The classic text of eugenic race-theory, Madison Grant's *The Passing of the Great Race,* which was published a few months after Haiselden's first case, endorsed "the elimination of defective infants" as the first step in "the obliteration of the unfit," a process Grant hoped to extend "ultimately to worthless race types."[4]

Fig. 2. Dr. Haiselden's cases received banner headline coverage. (*Chicago Tribune,* November 18, 1915.)

The Black Stork links class, ethnicity, and race to hereditary defects. The 1916 version traces a baby's impairments to his grandfather's liaison with "a slave—a vile filthy creature who was suffering from a loathsome disease." The film shows closeups of a severely handicapped black child, while the title itself links blackness with genetic deficiency.[5]

But Haiselden and eugenics held no monopoly on racism in early twentieth-century America. Scientific justifications for racial slavery long predated Darwin, and the most violent white supremacists of Haiselden's time rejected eugenics as unscriptural. Furthermore, Haiselden's racism was neither consistent nor extreme for his day. Haiselden hired a black physician (as well as several immigrant Jews) to work in his hospital, at a time when only one other Chicago hospital had an integrated staff.[6]

By describing heredity as the engine of human progress, eugenics emphasized the importance of ancestry and race. But the specific racial hierarchies adopted did not originate with eugenics. Instead, they reflected broader cultural biases about what counts as "good" heredity.

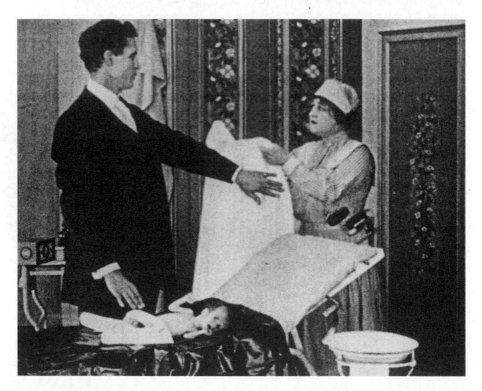

Fig. 3. Dr. Haiselden re-enacts his refusal to operate on a "defective" newborn in his film *The Black Stork*. (University of Michigan Historical Health Film Collection, used with permission of John E. Allen.)

Successive versions of *The Black Stork* provide two graphic illustrations of how easily eugenics absorbed the changing ethnic prejudices of the surrounding society. First, following the bitter controversy over D. W. Griffith's offensive portrait of blacks in *Birth of a Nation,* theater owners demanded removal of all reference to race-mixing in *The Black Stork.* So around 1918 a white servant was substituted for the diseased slave, changing the source of contamination from race to class.[7]

Second, for Haiselden in 1916, Germans were the hereditary elite among immigrants. Thus, in his original film, the innocent girl who married Claude had the phonetically spelled German name Annye (Anja) Schultz. But in February 1917, as war with Germany became a clear possibility, her name was changed to the more Americanized Anne Schultz. And following America's entry into the war, the character became fully naturalized as Anne Smith.[8]

These changes do more than simply illustrate the linguistic war in which sauerkraut was renamed "liberty cabbage." The switch from black to white servant and the Americanization of Annye Schultz illustrate how responsive eugenic assessments of good and bad heredity could be to even rapid fluctuations in the tide of social prejudices.

But eugenicists did not simply absorb passively whatever judgments of human worth they found in their culture. Rather, the movement's leadership selectively attracted middle-class white professionals who brought with them very particular value judgments that they aggressively promoted as the "eugenic" definitions of health and disease. Eugenics did not simply endorse existing cultural preferences, but actively attempted to "improve" current standards. Yale Professor Irving Fisher explained that careful propaganda was needed to "unconsciously favorably modif[y] the individual taste . . . in mate-choosing."[9] *The Black Stork* was part of this effort to mold society's racial and other preferences. The film's black and poor characters were photographed as repulsive defectives (Fig. 4), and Haiselden repeatedly linked "blackness" with "ugliness."[10] Portraying "other" races as ugly was central to labeling them defective, while diagnosing "other" races as diseased reinforced the perception of them as repulsive.

The benefit of hindsight makes it easy for us to see the eugenicists' circularity and subjectivity, but they insisted that their diagnoses were based entirely on objective science. Even Helen Keller, the famed reformer who had become blind and deaf in childhood, believed objective science could determine which impaired infants should be eliminated. In support of Dr. Haiselden, Keller wrote, "A jury of physicians considering the case of an idiot would be exact and scientific. Their findings would be free from the prejudice and inaccuracy of untrained observation."[11]

Like any other field of medicine, eugenics unavoidably required some value judgments to define which human differences were diseases. But their faith in the objectivity of their science left eugenicists particularly blind to the subjectivity of their own values, while it delegitimated opponents whose criticisms were based on explicitly political or ethical concerns.

Euthanasia As a Eugenic Method

Almost no one now remembers that Americans ever died in the name of eugenics, much less that such deaths were highly publicized and broadly supported in the late 1910s. Perhaps the single most important reason for studying these events is to document that eugenic euthanasia took place in America.

How did euthanasia become linked with eugenics? Most early euthanasia advocates focused on cases of painfully and terminally ill adults who voluntarily chose to die. But ever since the earliest proposals to speed death, at least some supporters used "euthanasia" to mean not only "mercy killing" but any "painless killing," whether voluntary and benevolent or not. Anthony Trollope's 1882 satirical novel *The Fixed Period* used "euthanasia" to describe compulsory elimination of the elderly. In 1905, this usage gained enormous notoriety in the United States when the eminent Dr. William

Fig. 4. The Black Stork linked blackness with physical impairments and portrayed diseased African Americans as ugly and menacing. (University of Michigan Historical Health Film Collection, used with permission of John E. Allen.)

Osler appeared to endorse Trollope's idea. Herbert Spencer described his new device for humanely executing stray dogs and criminals as a "euthanasia" machine.[12] During 1906 legislative debates on proposed euthanasia laws in Iowa and Ohio, a well-known psychiatrist—Dr. Walter Kempster—urged that any such legislation apply to "lunatics and idiots," and Dr. R. H. Gregory proposed requiring that "hideously deformed or idiotic children should be put out of existence."[13]

Likewise, a few prominent evolutionary scientists, such as German zoologist Ernst Haeckel, urged death for the unfit as early as 1868. But prior to Dr. Haiselden's crusade such ideas rarely won public endorsement from eugenic leaders.[14] Most advocated selective breeding, not the death of those already born with defects. Charles Davenport, perhaps the foremost American eugenic researcher of the period, insisted in 1911 that eugenics did "not imply the destruction of the unfit either before or after birth." Irving Fisher echoed Karl Pearson's "fundamental doctrine . . . that everyone, being born, has the right to live," but not the right "to reproduce."[15]

Yet when Haiselden moved the issue from theory to practice, these same leaders proclaimed him a eugenic pioneer. Fisher now wrote to "emphatically approve" Haiselden's action. "I hope the time may come when it will be a commonplace that . . . defective babies be allowed to die." Davenport urged doctors not to "unduly restrict the operation of what is one of Nature's greatest racial blessings—death" and warned that by preventing the death of defectives, doctors "may conceivably destroy the race."[16]

Haiselden's attention-grabbing actions were a calculated effort to radicalize the eugenic leadership, a strategy anarchists of the time popularized as "propaganda of the deed."[17] Haiselden was only one doctor, but by gaining extensive media coverage of his dramatic acts, he was able to shift the spectrum of what was considered "mainstream" eugenics and successfully prod the official movement leaders to publicly accept euthanasia as a legitimate method of eugenics.

Initially, Haiselden and his supporters emphasized that he withheld life-saving treatment but did not actively kill.[18] But from the start he blurred the line between the two. Even in his first publicized case, he anticipated that passive euthanasia would lead to active killing and left the clear impression he regarded the distinction as a question of tactics rather than of ethics. "I did not kill Baby Bollinger. That day is not yet."[19]

In that first case, Haiselden also raised the possibility he might administer opiates for pain relief in doses large enough to prove fatal. His subsequent cases further muddied the distinction between killing and letting die. Only a few weeks later, he performed a fatal operation on a baby after agreeing with the parents the child should be either cured or killed.[20] In 1917 he actively removed another baby's umbilical ligature, and the infant reportedly bled to death.[21] And in yet another 1917 case, he prescribed potentially lethal doses of opiates for a microcephalic infant who was taking longer than expected to die.[22]

In defending these increasingly active measures, Haiselden discarded his previous distinction between active and passive methods and increasingly emphasized his intentions. If an act caused both good and harmful consequences, he argued, it should be judged by which effect was intended. The opiates he gave were intended to fight pain, not to kill, Haiselden explained, and this good intention justified the drug's risk to the infant's life.[23]

This doctrine of double effect had long provided a theological rationale for taking the risks inevitably involved in treating the sick. It enabled doctors to use dangerous drugs without committing the sin of murder and without invoking utilitarian trade-offs that could undermine the imperative against killing.[24] But the argument was devised for judging souls, not crimes. It presupposed an omniscient Judge who knows people's true motives. In the mundane setting, a road paved with allegedly good intentions can lead anywhere you want to go. When opponents attempted to block his opiate prescriptions Haiselden responded by threatening to kill the baby surgically, "I may then perform an operation that will relieve the child's suffering—and remove from the world a child doomed to idiocy."[25] Haiselden's justifications highlighted the difficulty of drawing sharp, objective distinctions between active and passive methods, between intended and unintended effects.

Power

Who would benefit from permitting euthanasia? Haiselden presented euthanasia as helping two different groups at once: relieving the suffering of afflicted individuals and protecting society against costly and menacing defectives. Many historians and philosophers who have studied the links between eugenics and euthanasia point to this blurring of social and individual benefits as a critical logical error in ethical reasoning.[26]

But the interests of society and the individual, while logically distinct, and potentially in conflict, are not necessarily incompatible. Often they do coincide.[27] Haiselden focused on those cases in which euthanasia might end individual suffering and cut social costs at the same time, rather than trying to choose among these goals in cases where they conflicted. "By the weeding out of our undesirables," Haiselden explained, "we decrease their burden and ours."[28]

Further, both sides in the debate claimed to be protecting both society and individuals. Like Haiselden, many of his critics also combined individual with collective concerns. The Catholic New Orleans *Morning Star* blasted Haiselden for arguing that defectives posed a "burden upon society" instead of emphasizing the unique value of their individual lives. Yet the paper simultaneously warned that Haiselden's actions posed great dangers "to society at large."[29] Such critics prided themselves on their refusal to sacrifice individuals for the collective welfare. But their "slippery-slope" arguments that portrayed euthanasia as the opening wedge to murder meant that individuals whose sufferings might be helped by euthanasia had to continue suffering in order to protect society at large against worse consequences.[30]

Haiselden's justifications for euthanasia thus did not combine logically incompatible goals, nor was the mixture of individual and social goals unique to his side in the debate. But Haiselden's rhetoric did mix jarringly opposite emotions—compassion and hatred. *The Black Stork* appealed to the audience's empathy with the deformed child's future life of suffering and ostracism and even drew upon religious imagery to portray euthanasia as merciful and humane. Haiselden insisted he allowed defectives to die "because he loves them."[31]

But Haiselden also preached loathing for what he termed "lives of no value."[32] "We have been invaded." "Our streets are infested with an Army of the Unfit—a dangerous, vicious army of death and dread." "Horrid semi-humans drag themselves along all of our streets. . . . What are you going to do about it?"[33] Supporter Clarence Darrow's comments revealingly captured the emotional ambiguity of this appeal. "Chloroform unfit children. Show them the same mercy that is shown beasts that are no longer fit to live."[34] Eugenic euthanasia could combine such contradictory feelings because its advocates believed they were being entirely rational, that all their emotional responses were derived from objective science.

Mass Culture and Medical Crusaders

Mass culture played a key role both in promoting the power of objective science and in enabling one physician to reshape the relation between eugenics and euthanasia. Ironically, mass culture also contributed to the almost total erasure of Haiselden's crusade from later memory.

Most doctors and other professionals, even those who supported death for the unfit, opposed publicizing the issue. "I think all monstrosities should be permitted to die," wrote university president Frank H. H. Roberts, "but I do condemn the physician for making such a public ado about the matter." Three official investigations upheld Haiselden's right not to treat impaired infants, but the Chicago Medical Society expelled him for making movies about it.[35]

Mass culture played an important role in the expansion of professional power during the Progressive era,[36] and many in the media deferred to the professional desire for secrecy. In an editorial about Haiselden entitled "He Forgets Silence Is Golden," the *New York Times* endorsed Haiselden's right to let infants die, but denounced his use of media publicity. "If he is wise, as most doctors are, he settles the question for himself . . . and the incident does not become a subject of public discussion."[37]

The film industry had other reasons for repressing coverage of Haiselden's crusade as well. While Haiselden sought to make disabled people look repulsive, many viewers instead interpreted such scenes as making his film itself "repellent" and "revolting." Even critics who lavishly praised the film's ideas found it esthetically unacceptable: "grim," "depressing and unpleasant," "repulsive."[38] Louella Parsons complained that it was "neither a pretty nor a pleasant picture," because "it shows poor, misshapen bodies of miserable little children."[39]

These unintended esthetic responses were one important reason films about euthanasia or eugenics were often banned. *The Black Stork* helped provoke, and became one of the first casualties of, a movement to censor films for their esthetic content. By the 1920s, film censors went far beyond policing sexual morality to include what I term "esthetic censorship," much of which was aimed at eliminating unpleasant medical topics from theaters. From the perspective of the new esthetic censors, both pro- and antieugenics films were unacceptably ugly. In 1918, the Pennsylvania film board specifically added "eugenics" and "race suicide" to their list of "unduly distressing" topics prohibited from commercial theaters. The powerful New York state film board banned both Haiselden's film and *Tomorrow's Children,* an antisterilization melodrama, because eugenics was too "disgusting" a topic.[40]

Media deference to professional secrecy, combined with the growth of esthetic censorship, drastically curtailed coverage of Haiselden's activities. By 1918, Haiselden's last reported euthanasia case received only a single column-inch buried deep inside the *Chicago Tribune,* a paper that had supported him editorially and given front-page coverage to all his previous cases.[41] Media preoccupation with novelty and impatience with complex issues clearly played a role in this change, as did Haiselden's death in 1919 from a brain hemorrhage at the age of forty-eight.[42] But the sudden silence also reflects the conclusion by both medical and media leaders that eugenic euthanasia was unfit to discuss in public. And, as soon as the media attention flagged, eugenic leaders like Fisher and Davenport resumed their prior claims to oppose euthanasia, as if Haiselden had never existed.[43]

Thus, Haiselden and his cases were not simply forgotten but intentionally erased from history. Both his initial success and his eventual erasure were products of the struggle to shape mass culture's representations of eugenics and euthanasia.

Past and Present

In the 1990s, both euthanasia and human genetics once again became front-page news. How similar are today's events to those of Dr. Haiselden's era?

Many ethicists, scientists, and historians emphasize two key differences. First, the strong contemporary commitment to individual autonomy and "informed consent" in medical decision making supposedly marks a sharp break from the past. On this view, past abuses resulted from compulsory measures for the collective good, defined and imposed by the state. So long as individual parents and patients can choose whether and how to use medical knowledge, modern genetics and modern euthanasia will each promote humane health care without the danger of repeating the past. From this perspective, the economic and legal barriers that deny patients access to medical assistance in suicide and to genetic technology are more serious problems than any risks these voluntary practices might pose.

A second frequently asserted difference from the past is that history has shown the dangers of mixing science and ideology. By rigorously isolating contemporary medicine from social and political influences, euthanasia may be limited to those with objectively hopeless diagnoses and genetic therapies confined to people with objectively defined diseases. On this view, if only they could be kept value-free, euthanasia and gene therapy could be as uncontroversial as setting a broken bone.[44]

Such differences are certainly significant. Yet, in comparing Haiselden's era with the present, I also find important continuities. First, while the professed commitment to individual autonomy is more explicit and elaborated today than ever before, such ideas are neither as new nor as powerful as they seem. A therapeutic rationale for honoring many patient choices and a deep-seated repugnance for state-dictated medicine were both firm components of American law and medicine long before the advent of eugenics,[45] but these traditions were swept aside by the unprecedented deference to professional expertise in Haiselden's era. And today, despite the increased solicitude for personal autonomy, many studies indicate that patient choices are still honored more in theory than in daily medical practice. Some doctors read informed consent forms the way some cops read Miranda warning cards.[46]

Furthermore, although informed consent may protect patients against government or medical force, it does nothing about the many cultural and economic pressures that limited individual freedom in Haiselden's era and that remain important today. Haiselden did not rely on state power to compel the deaths of his patients, but they and their parents were hardly unconstrained in their choices. A working-class family struggling to make ends meet does not have the same freedom to choose to raise a handicapped child as a wealthy family does. And the choices made by one generation can curtail the options of their descendants. That was the logic behind Madison Grant's proposal to gradually expand eugenic targets. Protection from direct coercion is important, but it hardly eliminates all the other barriers to meaningful individual choice.[47]

Second, the racial and other hatreds that converted past eugenic euthanasia into a rationale for genocide are not simply history. The effort to devise rules to keep medical genetics and medically aided euthanasia "objective" is in part a well-meaning recognition of the continued danger from such lethal values. But comparison with Haiselden's era indicates this well-intentioned attempt to keep medicine value-free may itself be re-creating one of the most dangerous aspects of Haiselden's era. Racism became part of eugenics and euthanasia in Haiselden's time not just because racism was prevalent in his culture, but because his culture shared a faith in the objective truth of scientific values.

Past medical racism was based on values most thoughtful people today detest. However, the problem was not that past medicine *had* values, but that it had *bad* values. However appealing complete medical objectivity may seem, defining health and disease has never been a purely objective technical question. Such definitions have always required evaluative judgments.

Haiselden's eugenic euthanasia was neither *uniquely* value-laden nor *peculiarly* influenced by mass culture. Rather, this history is valuable because it makes so dramatically visible the cultural values that have always been part of defining any human difference as a disease or advocating any treatment. Such values may be so taken for granted that they escape notice unless they are examined historically. But even when everyone has agreed on the existence and consequences of a particular human difference, calling the difference a "disease" has meant judging it a "bad" thing to have, and "bad" is a value judgment.[48] Thus, trying to make medical science purely objective only repeats the most flawed aspect of Haiselden's eugenics. It permits subjective values to claim the moral authority of scientific truth, while delegitimating the kinds of political and ethical scrutiny that alone can enable a culture to debate and evaluate value judgments intelligently.[49]

Comparisons between past and present are also central to modern concerns that voluntary euthanasia of the painfully ill will lead to involuntary killing of the unwanted. Such slippery-slope arguments claim that no clear lines can distinguish between: the diseased and the outcast, the dying and the living, voluntary and imposed decisions, passive and active methods, intended and inadvertent effects, authorized and unauthorized practitioners. Dr. Haiselden's example shows that these concerns are not simply hypothetical nor limited to Nazi Germany. Americans died in the name of eugenics, and there were no purely objective bright lines to distinguish when the process had gone "too far."

But that history does not mean that any form of euthanasia must lead to genocide.[50] Meaningful distinctions, such as those between the sick and the unwanted, are not logically impossible. However, they require an explicitly value-based social consensus, not technical factors alone.

Of course, recognizing the values involved might not help us draw workable distinctions. But neither must it always be an admission of futility or a recipe for gridlock.[51] While there may be no purely technical way to distinguish the sick from the unwanted, it has often been possible to reach objective agreement on the values necessary to draw such lines. Those human differences most widely recognized as diseases have that status because of an implicit value consensus, that, for example, dying prematurely in great pain is bad. The badness of such deaths is a value judgment that cannot be proven in a laboratory, but to the extent such values are shared, there can be objective agreement that conditions which cause painful early deaths are diseases.[52]

Finally, there are striking similarities between Dr. Haiselden in the 1910s and Dr. Jack Kevorkian today in their use of the mass media. In both cases, a single doctor outside the official genetics and euthanasia movements made a strategic decision to practice euthanasia publicly. Both successfully used media coverage of their dramatic actions to win support from previously uncommitted or closet supporters, to push the movement leaders to become more radical, and to recast the spectrum of public debate, making formerly radical positions seem more mainstream by comparison to themselves. Both were criticized as much or more for seeking publicity than for practicing euthanasia. But by getting their critics to concentrate on their personalities, they successfully diverted much criticism from their ideas. Both succeeded in their larger goals by getting people to say, "that guy is a dangerous nut, but he raises some good issues."

Yet, if the mass media made Dr. Haiselden, they also unmade him, and there are clear signs the same fate may befall Dr. Kevorkian. Increasingly relegated to the inside local pages even in Michigan, shut out of the recent Supreme Court right-to-die cases, denounced or ignored by both sides in Oregon, Kevorkian soon may be as forgotten as Haiselden was, whether or not the movement he dramatically helped advance wins or loses.

NOTES

Unless otherwise noted, all newspaper articles cited begin on page 1.

Research for this essay was supported by the National Library of Medicine, National Endowment for the Humanities, Spencer Foundation, and the University of Michigan.

1. The long-forgotten story of eugenic euthanasia in America is documented in Martin S. Pernick, *The Black Stork: Eugenics and the Death of "Defective" Babies in American Medicine and Motion Pictures Since 1915* (Oxford University Press, 1996). This essay is largely drawn from the sections of that book dealing with euthanasia. For other comparisons between past and present, see Martin S. Pernick, *Eugenics and Public Health in American History,* 87 American Journal of Public Health, 1767–73 (Nov 1997).

 Haiselden's cases were covered extensively in newspapers nationwide, especially in the Midwest and East. See Nov 12–Dec 30, 1915, and Feb 5–7 and March 14–16, 1916 (for

Bollinger, Roberts, Werder, and Grimshaw cases); July 22–27 and Nov 12–20, 1917 (for Meter and Hodzima cases); Jan 25–30, 1918 (for Stanke case); and June 18–20, 1919 (obituaries).

2. I found and restored the only viewable print of the 1927 version titled *Are You Fit to Marry?* in the garage of film collector John Allen. It is available for research use at the University of Michigan Historical Health Film Collection. An unprojectable fragmentary paper print of the 1916 version is at the Library of Congress Motion Picture, Broadcasting and Recorded Sound Division, Washington DC (hereafter LCMBRS), #LU-9978, Box 110. The library is considering plans to reanimate this version electronically.

3. The literature on eugenics is vast. For a recent introduction to American eugenics, see Diane Paul, *Controlling Human Heredity 1865 to the Present* (Humanities Press, 1995). To place America in comparative context, see Daniel Kevles, *In the*

Name of Eugenics (University of California Press, 1985). For Galton's definition, see *Eugenics, Its Definition, Scope, and Aims,* in his *Essays in Eugenics* at 35 (Garland, 1985 [orig. 1909]).

Euthanasia has received far less attention from academic historians. The best study of the American movement remains Stephen Louis Kuepper, *Euthanasia in America, 1890–1960,* Ph.D. dissertation, Rutgers University, 1981. See also I. van der Sluis, *The Movement for Euthanasia* 1875–1975, 66 Janus 131–72 (1979); W. Bruce Fye, *Active Euthanasia: An Historical Survey of Its Conceptual Origins and Introduction to Medical Thought,* 52 Bulletin of the History of Medicine 492–502 (1979); C. W. & S. D. Triche, *The Euthanasia Controversy 1812–1974, A Bibliography* (Whitston, 1975).

4. Madison Grant, *The Passing of the Great Race* 45, 47 (C. Scribner's Sons, 1916).

5. *Chicago American* (hereafter *C.A.*), Nov 24, 1915. See also ibid., Nov 30, 1915, at 2; ibid., Dec 1, 1915, at 3; ibid., Dec 2, 1915, at 2. For other similarities between race and physical handicap, see Leonard Kriegel, *Uncle Tom and Tiny Tim: Reflections on the Cripple as Negro,* 38 American Scholar 412–30 (Summer 1969).

6. Haiselden hired Carl Roberts as an "extern." See Martin Kaufman, Stuart Galishoff, & Todd L. Savitt, eds., 2 Dictionary of American Medical Biography 641 (Greenwood Press, 1984). The other integrated hospital was Provident. On pre-Darwinian scientific views of race see especially William Stanton, *The Leopard's Spots* (University of Chicago Press, 1960).

7. Quote is from paper print of December 1916 version, LCMBRS, #LU-9978, Box 110. See Moving Picture World (hereafter M.P.W.), 1211 (Feb 24, 1917); Motion Picture News (hereafter M.P.N.), 1256 (Feb 24, 1917); Commissioner to H. J. Brooks, Apr 4, 1923, Motion Picture Division Scripts, New York State Archives, Albany, NY (hereafter NYSA-MPD), Box 2565, Folder 383. In response to *Birth of a Nation* in 1917 Illinois banned any film or publication that incited race hatred, Allan Spear, *Black Chicago* at 191 (University of Chicago Press, 1967).

8. Exhibitors' Trade Review (hereafter Ex.Tr.R.), 836 (Feb 24, 1917); *Are You Fit to Marry?,* Historical Health Film Collection, University of Michigan. Mrs. Bollinger, an Irish woman married to a German man, was named Anna, New York Medical Journal (hereafter N.Y.M.J.) at 1132 (Dec 4, 1915).

9. Irving Fisher & Eugene Lyman Fisk, *How to Live* at 322 (12th ed., Funk & Wagnalls, 1917).

10. *C.A.,* Nov 24, 1915; ibid., Nov 30, 1915, at 2.

11. Keller, *Physicians' Juries for Defective Babies,* The New Republic (hereafter T.N.R.), 173–74 (Dec 18, 1915).

12. The usage may have begun in veterinary practice. For one early example, see Laurence Turnbull, *The Advantages and Accidents of Artificial Anaesthesia* at 262 (2nd ed., Lindsay & Blakiston, 1885).

Anthony Trollope, *The Fixed Period* (University of Michigan Press, 1990 reprint); Herbert Spencer, *Facts and Comments,* at 231–33 (D. Appleton & Co., 1902); William Osler, *The Fixed Period,* in *Aequanimitas; With Other Addresses,* at 391–411 (H. K. Lewis, 1906).

Modern advocates of euthanasia insist the term properly applies only to voluntary death, e.g., Olive Ruth Russell, *Freedom to Die* at 19–20

(Human Sciences Press, 1975); Derek Humphry, *The Right to Die* (Harper & Row, 1986). Whatever validity that claim has today, that is not the only way the term has been used since the 1870s.

13. For Kempster, *New York Times* (hereafter *N.Y.T.*), Jan 26, 1906; for Gregory, Van der Sluis, *Euthanasia,* at 135 (cited in note 3). A similar plan had been debated in the Michigan Legislature three years earlier, *Detroit News* (hereafter *D.N.*), May 22, 1903.

14. Ernst Haeckel, *The Wonders of Life* 114–20 (Harper & Brothers, 1905); Haeckel, 1 *The History of Creation* 170–71 (D. Appleton, 1876 [orig. 1868]); van der Sluis, *Euthanasia* 134–37; Daniel Gasman, *The Scientific Origins of National Socialism* 91 (American Elsevier, 1971). On Haeckel's follower Ploetz, see Stephen Trombley, *The Right to Reproduce: A History of Coercive Sterilization* 71 (Weidenfeld & Nicolson, 1988).

15. Kuepper, *Euthanasia in America* 62 (cited in note 3); National Conference on Race Betterment, 1 Proceedings 500–501 (1914); 2 (1915) 89–90, addenda slip at 61. For others with same point at the conference see: C. W. Saleeby, 1 (1914), 477; Irving Fisher, 1 (1914), 472, 475.

16. Both quoted in *Independent,* Jan 3, 1916, at 23. The same article also contained an endorsement from eugenicist Raymond Pearl.

17. *Boston American* (hereafter *B.A.*), Dec 10, 1915, at 16; George Woodcock, *Anarchism* 328, 336, 462 (Meridian Books, 1962).

18. For example, *New York Call* (hereafter *Call*), Nov 28, 1915, at 6.

19. *C.A.*, Dec 1, 1915, at 3.

20. *Call,* Nov 17, 1915, at 1–2. On operation, *C.A.*, Dec 28, 1915, magazine page; *Call,* Dec 13, 1915.

21. *Chicago Tribune* (hereafter *C.T.*), Nov 17, 1915, at 7; *Chicago Herald* (hereafter *C.H.*), July 24, 1917, at 14.

22. *N.Y.T.*, Nov 13, 1917, at 12; ibid., Nov 16, 1917, at 4.

23. *Call,* Nov 17, 1915, at 1–2. A Catholic bishop denied that the double effect doctrine applied to such cases, without explaining why, *New World* (Dec 24, 1915).

24. In general, see K. Danner Clouser, *Allowing or Causing: Another Look,* 87 Annals of Internal Medicine 622–24 (1977). For the history of ethical debate over medical risk, and the gradual mid-nineteenth-century acceptance of cost-benefit approaches, see Martin S. Pernick, *A Calculus of Suffering* ch 5 (Columbia University Press, 1985).

25. *C.H.*, Nov 19, 1917, at 5.

26. Robert Proctor, *Racial Hygiene: Medicine Under the Nazis* 178 (Harvard University Press, 1988). The nineteenth-century roots of this connection between utilitarianism and humanitarianism are explored in Pernick, *Calculus of Suffering.* Modern advocates of mercy killing insist on distinguishing the two motives, Russell, *Freedom to Die,* at 19–20; Humphry, *Right to Die* (both cited in note 12).

27. For progressivism as the "via media" of "rational benevolence" see James T. Kloppenberg, *Uncertain Victory,* Part One (Oxford University Press, 1986).

28. *Washington Post* (hereafter *W.P.*), Nov 19, 1915; *Washington Star,* Nov 18, 1915, at 13.

29. *Morning Star,* Nov 20, 1915, at 4. For another striking example see P. Smith, quoted in *Independent,* Jan 3, 1916, at 27.

30. The utilitarianism of slippery slopes in a modern context was explained by Tom L. Beauchamp, *A Reply to Rachels on Active and Passive Euthanasia,* in Tom Beauchamp &

Seymour Perlin, eds., *Ethical Issues in Death and Dying* 246–58 (Prentice-Hall, 1984).

31. *Call,* Nov 20, 1915. For one mother's agreement, see *Call,* Nov 27, 1915, at 5.

32. *C.A.,* afternoon ed, Nov 12, 1917, at 1.

33. Ibid. magazine page (Dec 8, 1915); ibid. magazine page (Dec 7, 1915); *W.P.,* Nov 14, 1917, at 2; *C.A.,* Nov 26, 1915, at 2; ibid. magazine page (Dec 30, 1915).

34. Quoted in *W.P.,* Nov 18, 1915, and many other newspapers.

35. The quote is from *Independent,* Jan 3, 1916, at 26. On Haiselden's expulsion, see *N.Y.T.,* Mar 15, 1916, at 5. See also *N.Y.T.,* Dec 14, 1915, at 4. In a Nov 18, 1915 editorial, the Socialist *Call* claimed the root of most criticism was in Haiselden's "widespread discussion of the case, not in the case itself." *Call* at 6.

36. Pernick, *Black Stork;* Pernick, *Thomas Edison's Tuberculosis Films: Mass Media and Health Propaganda,* 8 Hastings Center Report 21–27 (June 1978).

   Occupational health pioneer Dr. Alice Hamilton noted the irony that mass culture demanded expanding the power of the profession: "Curiously enough it is not the medical profession which is seeking an extension of its rights; it is the laity which is trying to force upon physicians a power over life and death which they themselves shrink from." Survey 266 (Dec 4, 1915). But popular support for giving doctors this particular power itself depended on a broader progressive-era faith in the methods of science, a faith which was actively promoted by medical and eugenic leaders through the mass media.

37. *N.Y.T.,* July 26, 1917, at 10. Although the *Times* shifted its position on nontreatment from arguing that any policy other than an absolute commitment to life would lead to abuses, to declaring that the question was "insoluble," to endorsing nontreatment at the doctor's discretion, from first to last the editors insisted that the "wise" physician should make such decisions silently. A Nov 29, 1915, editorial noted with approval a medical article that the *Times* (inaccurately) summarized as saying that Haiselden "should have used his own judgment and said nothing." *N.Y.T.,* Nov 18, 1915, at 8; ibid., Nov 22, 1915, at 14; ibid., Nov 29, 1915, pt 2 at 10.

38. Ex.Tr.R. 836 (Feb 24, 1917); Motography 424 (Feb 24, 1917); Wid's Film Daily 220–21 (Apr 5, 1917).

39. Rival critic Kitty Kelly called it the "most repellent picture" she had ever seen.

   Parsons in *C.H.,* Apr 2, 1917, at 11; Kelly in *Chicago Examiner* (hereafter *C.E.*), Apr 4, 1917, at 8. The *Chicago Tribune* admitted the "ideas may be all right," but found the film "as pleasant to look at as a running sore." Pursuing such clinical metaphors to the limit, Photoplay called Lait's screenplay "so slimy that it reminds us of nothing save the residue of a capital operation." *C.T.,* Apr 2, 1917, at 18; 12 Photoplay 155 (June 1917).

40. Pennsylvania State Board of Censors, Rules and Standards, at 15–17 (J.L.L. Kuhn, 1918). The first Production Code of the Motion Picture Producers and Distributors of America (1930), which synthesized this and similar state lists of forbidden topics, labeled "surgical operations" a "repellent subject," and included a catchall restriction on all other "disgusting, unpleasant, though not necessarily evil, subjects," that was used to eliminate most other graphic or

unpleasant depictions of medical issues.

Garth Jowett, *Film: The Democratic Art* chs 5, 7, 10 (Little, Brown, 1976); the Code of 1930 is reprinted at 468–72. On precode films and the rise of censorship see also Francis Couvares, *Hollywood, Main Street, and the Church: Trying to Censor the Movies Before the Production Code,* 44 American Quarterly 584–615 (Dec 1992); Stephen Vaughn, *Morality and Entertainment: The Origins of the Motion Picture Production Code,* 77 Journal of American History 39–65 (June 1990); Edward De Grazia & Roger K. Newman, *Banned Films: Movies, Censors and the First Amendment* (Bowker, 1982).

Similarly, euthanasia films were censored both for showing murder and for not being "cheerful," Pernick, *Black Stork* at 139–41, 161.

For censorship history of *The Black Stork,* see National Board of Review of Motion Pictures Records (hereafter NBRMP), New York Public Library Rare Books and Manuscripts Division, Box 103; NYSA-MPD Box 2565 Folder 383 and 12,421. Quotations are from letter of disapproval, Commissioner to H. J. Brooks, April 4, 1923, NYSA-MPD, Box 2565, Folder 383.

In a private straw poll of community leaders from across the country conducted by a film industry voluntary rating agency, the National Board of Review of Motion Pictures, nine of the fifty-two respondents explicitly cited esthetic objections as a major reason for not approving *The Black Stork,* NBRMP Box 103.

On *Tomorrow's Children* see Memo on Behalf of the Motion Picture Division to the Commissioner of Education, at 4; and Court of Appeals Brief for the Respondent, at 6, both in NYSA-MPD Box 333, Folder 28,361.

For the role of VD and sex education films in the growth of film censorship, see de Grazia and Newman, *Banned Films;* and Annette Kuhn, *Cinema, Censorship and Sexuality 1909–1925* (Routledge, 1988).

41. *C.T.,* Jan 28, 1918, at 12.
42. Ibid., June 20, 1919.
43. Fisher & Fisk, *How to Live* at 294 (12th ed., 1917) (cited in note 9). Even Dr. William J. Robinson, one of Haiselden's most vigorous supporters in 1915–16, wrote in 1917 that "no eugenic considerations will induce us to adopt Spartan-like methods and to neglect or kill off the weak and puny. . . . Every child that is born . . . is entitled to the very best of care." William J. Robinson, *Eugenics and Marriage* 138 (Critic & Guide Co., 1917), see also ibid. at 73–76.
44. LeRoy Walters, *Human Gene Therapy: Ethics and Public Policy,* 2 Human Gene Therapy 115–22 (Summer 1991); Daniel Kevles, *Is the Past Prologue?: Eugenics and the Human Genome Project,* 2 Contention 21–37 (Spring 1993). For an important critique see Peter Weingart, *Science Abused: Challenging a Legend,* 6 Science in Context 555–67 (Autumn 1993).
45. Martin S. Pernick, *The Patient's Role in Medical Decisionmaking: A Social History of Informed Consent in Medical Therapy,* in 3 Making Health Care Decisions: Studies on the Foundations of Informed Consent, President's Commission for the Study of Ethical Problems in Medicine, at 1–35 (1982).
46. On limitations of modern commitment to autonomy in practice see Carl E. Schneider, *Bioethics with a*

Human Face, 69 Indiana Law Journal 1075–1104 (Fall 1994); Alan Meisel & Loren H. Roth, *Toward an Informed Discussion of Informed Consent,* 25 Arizona Law Review 265 (1983).

47. This criticism is stated most forcefully by Ruth Hubbard, *The Politics of Women's Biology* (Rutgers University Press, 1990), and Troy Duster, *Backdoor to Eugenics* (Routledge, 1990).

48. Disease has sometimes been seen as the lesser of two bad things. And it has been seen as conferring secondary compensations, ranging from spiritual insight to insurance payments. But even in such cases, calling a condition a disease has meant judging some aspect of it to be bad.

49. Peter Steinfels, *Introduction,* issue on The Concept of Health, 1 Hastings Center Studies 3–88 (1973); Charles Rosenberg, *Framing Disease,* in Charles Rosenberg & Janet Golden, eds., *Framing Disease* xiii–xxvi (Rutgers University Press, 1992); H. Tristram Engelhardt, *The Languages of Medicalization,* in *The Foundations of Bioethics* 157–201 (Oxford University Press, 1986); Sander Gilman, *Difference and Pathology* (Cornell University Press, 1985).

The role of values in the specific issue of diagnosing impaired newborns has been stressed by Robert Veatch and others; see Warren T. Reich & David E. Ost, *Ethical Perspectives on the Care of Infants,* 2 Encyclopedia of Bioethics 726 (1st ed., Free Press, 1978); Charles Krauthammer, *What to Do About 'Baby Doe,'* T.N.R. 18 (Sept 2, 1985).

The basic claim that all medical knowledge is value-laden was first developed by Robert Veatch in *Death, Dying and the Biological Revolution* (Yale University Press, 1976), drawing inspiration from Thomas Kuhn, *The Structure of Scientific Revolutions* (University of Chicago Press, 1962). See also Robert Proctor, *Value-Free Science* (Harvard University Press, 1991).

Early eugenicists did not claim to have "value-free" definitions of disease and health, but did claim that their values had been proven objectively true by value-free scientific methods.

50. Prior to the 1930s, the more common metaphor was "entering wedge" rather than "slippery slope." There is a subtle difference between the two. Driving in a wedge makes it easier for subsequent blows to split the wood, but someone still has to strike the subsequent blows. On a slippery slope, the first misstep leads to an inevitably accelerating fall. Slippery-slope metaphors raised the stakes, implying that the first step makes the bad outcome not just more likely but inevitable.

51. For an analogous argument about an even more contentious debate, see Roger Rosenblatt, *Life Itself: Abortion in the American Mind* (Random House, 1992).

52. I am not claiming that disease is nothing but a value judgment, nor that anything a culture dislikes is a disease, nor that there is no physical reality in disease. But calling something a disease involves making a value judgment about physical reality; it is not an intrinsic feature of that reality.

CHAPTER 9   **Assisted Suicide and the Challenge of Individually Determined Collective Rationality**

Peter J. Hammer

Introduction

Assisted suicide is hard to discuss. The subject is simultaneously particular and universal, rife with tensions between the individual and the community and between the personal and policy. While frequently cloaked in a rhetoric of autonomy and individual rights, end-of-life decisions—including assisted suicide—have broader communal implications. The individual makes these decisions as a member of a community, and the community, in turn, is affected by the individual's choices. Similarly, while end-of-life decisions are deeply personal, the rules governing them must pass through the filter of professional ethics, legislation, or judicial decision. Filtering the personal into policy necessarily requires considering the effects rules will have on other members of society, as well as the effect the policies will have on policymakers themselves as a collective act of self-definition.

This debate is emotionally charged. Assisted suicide triggers strong and conflicting personal reactions: an instinctual will-to-live; a fear of death and the unknown; a shrinking from pain, suffering, and incapacitation; and allegiance to family, loved ones, and the community. At the same time, assisted suicide implicates strong and conflicting social values: respect for individual autonomy; reverence for life; and compassion in the face of suffering. In resolving these tensions, we unavoidably make constitutive decisions. At stake are not simply choices about life and death, but choices about personal autonomy and collective obligation, social norms and self-determination, and the relationship between the individual and the state.

Given these many concerns, it is useful to discuss assisted suicide in terms of the various conversations at play. The first is a personal conversation in which the individual struggles with her own emotions, beliefs, and needs. The second is a conversation on a societal level that considers collective needs, obligations, and values. The third reflects an interplay between the first two and can be viewed as a conversation between the individual and society (or between our atomistic and social selves) over personal and collective concerns. In the next section of this chapter, "A Matrix of Individual and Social Rationality," I propose a framework in which individuals and society attempt in parallel ways to resolve the tensions between what is good for the individual and what is good for society as a whole. I will suggest that individuals are of two minds. In one mind, they ask what they want for themselves. For simplicity's sake, I call this "I-for-me" thinking. In the other mind, they ask what would be good for society ("I-for-us" thinking). Similarly, society has two minds. In one mind, it asks what is good for it as a collectivity ("we-for-us" thinking). In the other, it asks what is good for its members as individuals ("we-for-me" thinking). Understanding these perspectives and their implications for the development of social norms can help mediate some of the conflicting tensions in the assisted-suicide debate.

The third section, entitled "Arguments Surrounding Assisting Suicide," frames the arguments in support of and in opposition to assisted suicide in terms of these categories. Arguments for recognizing an individual right to physician-assisted suicide emphasize both the importance of individual autonomy and the reasons a terminally ill person might plausibly decide to end his or her life—I-for-me reasoning. The arguments most persuasive to the Court in *Glucksberg*[1] and *Quill*[2] consisted of various forms of we-for-me reasoning. The Court was concerned about potential deficiencies in the way people make decisions that might undermine their ability to act in their own best interest. The Court was also concerned about numerous slippery-slope possibilities—that is, arguments examining the adverse effects that recognizing a right to assisted suicide might have on noncompetent and non-terminally ill persons. Scanted in the Supreme Court's opinions and much of the surrounding debate, however, are the concerns reflected in we-for-us and I-for-us reasoning. Do concerns over the sanctity of life justify a social norm prohibiting assisted suicide? Does the individual have any collectively based obligation to refrain from assisted suicide, regardless of whether it might be atomistically rational?

To answer these questions, we will step back from the debate over assisted suicide and scrutinize the relationship between individual and state. The fourth chapter section outlines a vision of society as an effort to shape a vibrant collective identity while simultaneously cultivating authentic individual efforts at self-definition and self-perfection. Reconciling the apparently contradictory goals of individual and society requires constant mediation between I-for-me and we-for-us reasoning. I will argue that the doctrine of substantive due process and the category of I-for-us rationality are uniquely suited to this mediating role and can help govern the formation of social norms.

The final chapter section returns to the assisted-suicide debate and explores how the positions for and against assisted suicide might be made more harmonious as a matter of policy and practice. Alternating consideration of the four perspectives in the matrix can promote the convergence of views at both an individual and a social level. This final section reexamines the reasons terminally ill people consider suicide and uncovers numerous communal as well as individual concerns. It explores the limitations of addressing the problems raised by assisted suicide solely in terms of individual autonomy or in terms of decision defects and slippery slopes. Finally, this last section reevaluates arguments concerning the sanctity of life and asks how norms predicated upon the value of life might be formed without sacrificing the dignity and decency of individual lives. While I cannot resolve all these issues, I hope to suggest a framework and a process that might introduce new approaches to a perduring problem.

A Matrix of Individual and Social Rationality

There are many parallels between the individual and society. Both face choices and corresponding responsibilities. Both are concerned with issues of reproduction, transition, and generational change. Both must confront the fact and meaning of death. Although I do not intend to anthropomorphize the state, the state's struggle with individual and collective rationality and the individual's struggle with the same concepts have important similarities. There are symmetries between the state's ability to effectively meet collective needs while respecting individual integrity and the individual's ability to develop a definition of self that embraces communal values. The individual and societal processes rely heavily upon a common set of principles and introspective skills. Society's ability truly to act in the best interest of the individual and the individual's ability to authentically define her social obligations depend on a capacity for empathy, compassion, and a recognition of social interconnectedness.

At the risk of oversimplifying, we may envision the individual as internally divided and having two minds. The person faces a realm of choices that are or can be atomistically rational (I-for-me thinking). Similarly, the individual faces a realm of choices that are or can be collectively rational (I-for-us reasoning). In the same way, society has two minds. It faces decisions that are or can be made on the basis of collective rationality (we-for-us thinking). Society also faces a realm of choices and decisions that are or can be predicated upon what is perceived to be in the best interest of the individual (we-for-me reasoning). The following matrix sketches these possibilities, placing on the vertical axis the actor (individual or society) and on the horizontal axis the mode of rationality (atomistic or collective).[3]

I-for-me reasoning is the domain of traditional individualism. In it, individuals act freely and rationally to attain their own ends and objectives as they define them. Individual autonomy is emphasized in this domain, as is the centrality of self-interest. Libertarian theories of government could be loosely associated with this category.

We-for-me reasoning is the domain of a particularly well developed form of state action—paternalism. Honestly undertaken, paternalism is among the most benign forms of state action, because it seeks to attain through state policy what individuals would choose for themselves if they could make autonomous choices and if they internalized all the consequences of their actions. In this category, the state tries to see through the

Mode of Rationality	Actor	
	Individual (I)	Society (We)
Atomistic (for me)	Individually determined atomistic rationality (I-for-me)	Socially determined atomistic rationality (we-for-me)
Collective (for us)	Individually determined collective rationality (I-for-us)	Socially determined collective rationality (we-for-us)

eyes of its individual members. There may be differences between what individuals would atomistically choose and the paternalistic prescription, to the extent that the conditions for free choice are not present (because of incapacity, duress, or coercion) or that the individual decision maker does not internalize all the effects (externalities) of the decision. Various forms of liberalism could be loosely associated with this category.

We-for-us reasoning is the domain of traditional state action. The state acts in what it perceives to be the best interest of society as a whole. The state provision of public goods is one example of we-for-us reasoning. There is also a role in this domain for the adoption and enforcement of social norms.[4] While liberals would tend to limit state action to situations where there are defects in the way someone makes decisions or where individual conduct injures third parties (we-for-me justifications for policy action), we-for-us reasoning is not so restricted. The ultimate scope of state authority in this domain depends on one's estimate of the divergence between the dictates of atomistic and collective rationality and the propriety of privileging collective interests. In our society, various forms of democratic statism could be loosely associated with this category.

I-for-us reasoning is the least developed and recognized domain. This is the domain of self-imposed social obligations. Its emphasis is on the sense of social responsibility people feel as members of a community. By adopting a collective perspective, people can transcend the limitations of atomistic rationality and make their self-regarding behavior more other-regarding. Alternatively, just as paternalism can mediate the exercise of state power in a way that seeks to be consistent with individual choice, so I-for-us reasoning can mediate between individual choice and we-for-us state action in the realm of defining social norms. According to this view, legitimate social norms should be capable of passing the filter of I-for-us rationality, meaning that we-for-us norms should reflect principles that community-minded individuals would freely choose to be governed by.

What types of norms would be consistent with I-for-us reasoning? They might include norms against free riding on public goods, norms necessary for the community's existence and survival, and norms designed to facilitate individual development. Providing public goods is one example of state action grounded in we-for-us reasoning. Public goods, however, raise the problem of free riders, of individuals enjoying the benefits of the public good without contributing to its support. Indeed, free riding on public goods is often rational from an atomistic perspective (i.e., consistent with the dictates of I-for-me reasoning). Consequently, social norms designed to prevent free riding are a legitimate area of community action. For example, laws require people to pay for certain public services, and the state wants to encourage norms that discourage people from cheating on taxes. These norms are consistent with the dictates of both we-for-us and I-for-us reasoning.

I-for-us norms may also be directed at preserving and improving the community itself. While similar to norms against free riding to the extent that the state can be seen as a public good, these norms go deeper, to structural concerns over the community's existence and integrity. Norms cultivating patriotism or rules (like the draft) designed to maintain national security are examples. A less obvious example might be rules prohibiting the secession of states from the union. Alternatively, community-based norms may take the form of affirmative obligations, such as rules in many countries mandating community service or requiring citizens to vote. These affirmative norms go beyond mere community survival and encompass acts of communal self-definition around commonly held goals or beliefs.

A third category of norms potentially consistent with the dictates of I-for-us rationality are norms, like compulsory education, that govern the process of individual development. Children must attend school, and the state generally outlines what must be learned. This category can be distinguished from the anti-free-riding norms since public goods analysis takes individual preferences as given and seeks to satisfy those existing preferences. Developmentally based norms, on the other hand, are specifically targeted at experiences or phases in life that are transformative of personal preferences. The case for honoring I-for-me reasoning is particularly weak in those circumstances where the individual's underlying beliefs are unstable or subject to change. Correspondingly, the case for collective rules ostensibly consistent with the likely posttransition preferences of individuals are particularly strong in such stages.

Arguments Surrounding Assisted Suicide

The arguments for and against a right to physician-assisted suicide can be categorized in terms of the matrix developed in the preceding section. I will consider four central claims. First is the contention that a terminally ill person's decision to seek assisted suicide may be reasonable and that the value of individual autonomy requires society to respect and empower that choice. This is an I-for-me argument. Second are "decision-defect" arguments against assisted suicide. These invoke factors like incapacity, depression, and coercion that can corrupt the decision-making process. In essence, while the terminally ill claim they want to die, they may not *really* want to die, and the state should enforce their real desires. This is a we-for-me argument. Third, there are administrative-externality or slippery-slope arguments that focus on the (in)ability to design a regulatory system capable of permitting "legitimate" claims for assisted suicide (claims by terminally ill, mentally competent individuals) but denying "illegitimate" claims. This is another we-for-me argument. Finally, there are arguments predicated upon the intrinsic value of life which attempt to justify a social norm prohibiting assisted suicide. I place this contention in the we-for-us box. Notably, none of these claims is an I-for-us argument. That category, however, may hold insights for mediating between claims for individual autonomy and social norms predicated on the sanctity of life.

I-for-Me Rationality

The domain of I-for-me reasoning gives primacy to the individual as the locus of decisions and envisions only a limited role for the state. Thus, arguments for a right of assisted suicide stress the plausibility of suicide for the terminally ill and the underlying importance of respecting individual autonomy and promoting individual choice. According to this view, the state should interfere as little as possible with these highly personal decisions, or perhaps should even help facilitate the individual's decision to die.

Much of the advocacy in *Glucksberg* and *Quill* was devoted to establishing an empathetic link between the courts and the individual plaintiffs to make the plaintiffs' choices understandable. The plaintiffs' stories are compelling.[5] The district court described *Glucksberg* plaintiff John Doe:

> John Doe is a 44-year-old artist dying of AIDS. Since his diagnosis in 1991, he has experienced two bouts of pneumonia, chronic, severe skin and sinus infections, grand mal seizures and extreme fatigue. He has already lost 70% of his vision to cytomegalovirus retinitis, a degenerative disease which will result in blindness and rob him of his ability to paint. His doctor has indicated that he is in the terminal phase of his illness. John Doe is especially cognizant of the suffering imposed by a lingering terminal illness because he was the primary caregiver for his long-term companion who died of AIDS in June of 1991. . . . Mr. Doe is mentally competent, understands there is no cure for AIDS, and wants his physician to prescribe drugs which he can use to hasten his death.[6]

Quill plaintiff Jane Doe described her own condition:

> I have a large cancerous tumor which is wrapped around the right carotid artery in my neck and is collapsing my esophagus and invading

my voice box. The tumor has significantly reduced my ability to swallow and prevents me from eating anything but very thin liquids in extremely small amounts. The cancer has metastasized to my plural [sic] cavity and it is painful to yawn or cough. . . . In early July 1994 I had the [feeding] tube implanted and have suffered serious problems as a result. . . . I take a variety of medications to manage the pain. . . . It is not possible for me to reduce my pain to an acceptable level of comfort and to retain an alert state. . . . At this time, it is clear to me, based on the advice of my doctors, that I am in the terminal phase of this disease. . . . At the point at which I can no longer endure the pain and suffering associated with my cancer, I want to have drugs available for the purpose of hastening my death in a humane and certain manner. I want to be able to discuss freely with my treating physician my intention of hastening my death through the consumption of drugs prescribed for that purpose.[7]

Each of the plaintiffs in *Glucksberg* and *Quill* wanted to have, if not actually exercise, the option of suicide with the assistance of his or her physician.

Jane Roe is mentally competent and wishes to hasten her death by taking prescribed drugs with the help of plaintiff Compassion in Dying. In keeping with the requirements of that organization, she has made three requests for its members to provide her and her family with counseling, emotional support and any necessary ancillary assistance at the time she takes the drugs.[8]

Mr. Kingsley, a plaintiff in *Quill,* said in his declaration:

At this point it is clear to me, based on the advice of my doctors, that I am in the terminal phase of [AIDS]. . . . It is my desire that my physician prescribe suitable drugs for me to consume for the purpose of hastening my death when and if my suffering becomes intolerable.[9]

Mr. Barth, another AIDS patient, expressed similar sentiments.

For each of these conditions I have undergone a variety of medical treatments, each of which has had significant adverse side effects. . . . While I have tolerated some [nightly intravenous] feedings, I am unwilling to accept this for an extended period of time. . . . I understand that there are no cures. . . . I can no longer endure the pain and suffering . . . and I want to have drugs available for the purpose of hastening my death.[10]

People's motives for seeking assisted suicide are complex. They want to avoid pain and suffering. They want to maintain their dignity and control their dying. They want to be independent, and they fear incapacitation that would make them depend on others for even basic needs. They fear abandonment and loneliness. And, as Justice Stevens writes, they want to shape the memories they leave behind by avoiding a lengthy, painful, and debilitating death.[11]

These fears and concerns resonate in each of us and trigger both deeply personal and deeply political responses. Tapping into these sentiments, proponents of assisted suicide argue against state interference in intimate matters. Whatever the communal dimensions of the individual's life and death, they say, it is still the individual who is dying and the individual whose rights and interests should prevail. As applied to assisted suicide, this libertarian perspective would recognize the individual's interest in deciding to die and would permit individuals to do so with the help of their doctors. This sentiment unites the authors of the Second and Ninth Circuit opinions. Judge Miner on the Second Circuit wrote,

> At oral argument and in its brief, the state's contention has been that its principal interest is in preserving the life of all its citizens at all times and under all conditions. But what interest can the state possibly have in requiring the prolongation of a life that is all but ended? . . . And what business is it of the state to require the continuation of agony when the result is imminent and inevitable?[12]

Similarly, Judge Reinhardt for the Ninth Circuit concluded:

> Those who believe strongly that death must come without physician assistance are free to follow that creed, be they doctors or patients. They are not free, however, to force their views, their religious convictions, or their philosophies on all the other members of a democratic society, and to compel those whose values differ with theirs to die painful, protracted, and agonizing deaths.[13]

In addition to affirmative claims of individual rights and personal autonomy, proponents of a right to assisted suicide invoke the specter of abusive state authority. Protecting individual autonomy not only fosters individual development and self-definition, it also checks state power. Permitting norms and values regarding assisted suicide to be formed "under compulsion of the State"[14] could lead to state interference in other personal matters such as a woman's decision to seek an abortion or in intimate relations between nonmarried people (same sex or otherwise).[15] Ultimately, any system justifying state prohibition of assisted suicide on normative grounds must answer such concerns.

Autonomy-based arguments and libertarian instincts are not without limitations. The focus on the individual masks the social dimensions of the controversy and understates the interests of the community. Moreover, autonomy arguments are vulnerable if defects in people's decision-making undermine their ability to make sound choices. Finally, individually based perspectives are not well suited to address conduct that harms people other than the would-be suicide. Opponents of assisted suicide spend most of their energy exploiting these weaknesses.

We-for-Me Rationality

We-for-me arguments accept the "best interest of the individual" as the appropriate standard for policy-making but doubt that people can always act in their own interests. This skepticism opens the door for state action when there are identifiable defects in the way people make decisions or when those decisions engender externalities that harm others. However, these policy concerns ordinarily justify only limited state action. Decision defects typically call for process-oriented regulation of the decisions of the competent and perhaps substantive regulation of the decisions of the incompetent. Externality concerns, on the other hand, typically justify policies designed either to internalize the decision's effects on the decision maker or to lead the decision maker to do what a hypothetical person who considered all the social costs of her conduct would do.

Individual Decision Defects

I-for-me arguments are persuasive only to the extent that the individual is capable of making free, rational choices. If competent choice is not possible, there is no reason to respect the individual's decision. Rhetorically, defects in decision making are important in the assisted-suicide debate because they make a compelling counterpoint to invocations of the plaintiffs' suffering and the heartwrenching case. While arguments for assisted suicide stress the plight of the terminally ill, opponents emphasize the plight of the vulnerable and the improvident as they ponder the imponderable.

The factors that can warp decisions to die are many.[16] Illness, pain, and medication can all undermine free will. Dementia can cripple the mind. The emotional turmoil surrounding terminal illness can lead to severe depression. These considerations stimulate fears that requests to die may not manifest authentic choice. Worse, people's preferences can change. A decision to continue living today may yield to a decision to die tomorrow, which may itself be replaced by a renewed desire to live. But which of these "wills" should be respected? How can rules be written to deal with these uncertainties?

In addition, numerous external forces impinge on the dying.[17] Dying is often difficult, traumatic, and costly. Its toll upon family members can lead them to exert improper influence on the decision to die. If treatment and extended illness reduce the profitability of the treating institution, an additional set of perverse influences arises. Finally, patients may decide to die to spare friends and family hardship, not because they want to do so. The magnitude of these concerns will be greatly influenced by the context in which the option of assisted suicide is raised and the way the question is framed to patients. In physics we are reminded that measuring an object or recording an observation can change the event being examined. Similarly, simply asking a dying person whether she wants the option of assisted suicide can affect the way she thinks and acts. An unavoidable consequence of according some people the right to assisted suicide may be to force others to confront assisted suicide as an alternative when they would rather not have to consider it at all.[18]

In terms of policy, defects in people's decision making may justify state intervention, but that justification is limited. Decision defects typically justify regulations designed to remedy the problems with individual decision making. These regulations may mandate the disclosure of information so that informed choices are made. They may require counseling. They may establish waiting periods that provide an opportunity for reflection. A competency evaluation might be appropriate, as might efforts to ensure that a suicide request was not motivated by inadequate pain control or treatable depression. Only in extreme cases, however, will decision-defect arguments justify completely prohibiting an activity. As a result, there will probably always remain a core of individuals—arguably people like the plaintiffs in *Glucksberg* and *Quill*—who lack any alleged defect. If these individuals do exist and could be identified through a workable administrative system, their claims would deserve careful consideration. To justify prohibiting assisted suicide, therefore, decision defects must ordinarily be combined with problems presented by various administrative externalities.

Administrative Externalities
Administrative externalities reflect the costs to third persons of adopting and administering a regulatory regime for physician-assisted suicide. These externalities encompass line-drawing problems and slippery-slope concerns. Some of the line-drawing issues were anticipated in our discussion of decision defects. How do we distinguish mentally competent from incompetent individuals? How do we determine whether a preference is the product of inadequate pain control or depression rather than an expression of authentic desire? Which will of the dying person should be respected and how should that will be expressed? How do we distinguish terminally ill patients from those who are not? However sound our regulations, some administrative mistakes and miscalculations are inevitable.

Slippery-slope concerns reflect the inability to cabin a "right" of assisted suicide to the intended beneficiaries—terminally ill, mentally competent individuals.[19] Some of the difficulties are inherent in the I-for-me justifications of assisted suicide. If the right is grounded in principles of free will and autonomy, how can it be denied to patients who are competent and terminally ill, but physically unable to commit suicide? The line between assisted suicide and voluntary euthanasia is the easiest to cross, because it is the least defensible line to draw on autonomy principles. Subsequent lines to be crossed may involve the requirement for contemporaneous personal consent. Thus, advance directives requesting euthanasia might be honored; the judgment of appointed agents might be substituted for the expressed will of the dying person; and finally a *projected best interest* standard based on the judgment of nonappointed agents or health-care providers might be adopted. All these changes would substantially blur the line between voluntary and involuntary euthanasia. Other slippery-slope concerns involve the erosion of the line between terminally ill patients and nonterminally ill patients to include those suffering from debilitating, incurable, but not immediately fatal medical conditions. In sum, a right grounded in self-determination and individual autonomy might turn into a general right to commit suicide.

The state frequently restricts individual conduct if it harms third persons. Legalizing a right of assisted suicide for terminally ill, mentally competent patients might well impair the rights and interests of others. Whether assisted suicide should be completely prohibited based on administrative externalities, however, is a different question. A state should not do so unless it could show that the actual harm to third parties outweighed the benefits of permitting this exercise of individual autonomy. This is a highly contestable empirical question, the answer to which is likely to change with improvements in diagnostic and administrative techniques. Consequently, if a prohibition of assisted suicide is predicated on these grounds, the prohibition would have to be periodically reevaluated. Moreover, if policymakers are truly concerned about decision defects and administrative externalities, the most defensible course of action may be a series of limited experiments that would generate new information.

Justice Souter's concurring opinion in *Glucksberg* is illustrative. Souter rested his decision to uphold the Washington statute prohibiting assisted suicide on the state's interest in avoiding slippery slopes. He thought it unnecessary to examine the state's interest in protecting the sanctity of life or in discouraging suicide generally.[20] Souter reasoned that, given existing information, the state's prohibition was not outside the band of legitimate legislative decisions.[21] He stressed, however, that his conclusion might change if better empirical information became available, and he suggested that state legislators may be obliged to keep searching for data.[22] Souter thus concluded that states may rationally limit people's choices to remedy decision defects or to prevent harm to others, but he acknowledged what a tentative basis for state policy these justifications may provide.

The appeal (and frustration) of slippery-slope arguments is that they can resolve issues as a policy matter regardless of one's views about the merits of the initial question—whether assisted suicide is intrinsically desirable or undesirable.[23] If one believes in the right of persons to assisted suicide but thinks the right cannot be administratively implemented and contained, it is rational to reject claims for assisted suicide when the costs of the administrative externalities exceed the benefits flowing to dying patients. The focus on external effects can be even more compelling than ethical arguments based on the "sanctity of life" because real lives are being compared with real lives; no vague philosophical concepts and theories need be confronted. This aspect of slippery-slope arguments helps explain both the unanimity and the ambivalence of the Court's opinion in *Glucksberg*.[24] While differing about the individual interest at stake, almost all the Justices acknowledged the seriousness of the administrative externalities at issue.

Nevertheless, arguments invoking administrative externalities and decision defects embrace a world of second best. These arguments rest not on some desirable balance of individual and collective rights, but rather on transaction costs and administrative concerns. Even if one ultimately accepts a policy of second best, it is useful to examine the values and concerns underlying the assisted-suicide debate. First, an examination of the normative issues is necessary to help states decide *whether* to experiment with assisted suicide. Second, an appreciation of the underlying claims for and against assisted suicide helps us gauge the magnitude and seriousness of the slippery-slope concerns. Lines do not move by themselves. Lines typically move because lawmakers are trying to maintain boundaries that are forced or artificial.

We-for-Us Rationality

We-for-us reasoning looks to society's needs rather than the individual's as the appropriate criterion for making policy. Its range of justifications for state action is much broader than those of theories grounded in we-for-me or I-for-me reasoning. The state is not limited to simply compensating for decision defects or to protecting third parties. But what are society's interests in the debate surrounding assisted suicide?[25] A number of answers could be given to this question.[26] The historic prohibition against and criminalization of suicide sound potentially as much in theories of property as in morality. Everything in the realm, including the subjects, belonged to the crown. Suicide was a crime against the king, entailing forfeiture of property to the state. Most contemporary opponents of assisted suicide, however, would base their opposition on principles such as the sanctity of life.

A respect for life, both as an affirmative value and as a negative limitation of state power, is an important social principle. The critical question for the assisted-suicide debate, however, is not simply whether the state must respect life, but whether the value attached to the sanctity of life should be symmetrically held—shared equally by individuals with respect to their own lives and the state?[27] Many policies suggest the existence of a symmetrical interest. Although criminal prohibitions against suicide have been repealed, the state may still physically restrain people who are a danger to themselves. Moreover, the state may use force to prevent a suicide, even against the person's wishes and even though it is contrary to the "fundamental" right to be free from bodily interference assumed in *Cruzan*.[28] Indeed, the very concept of mental "competence" is defined largely by the extent to which an individual's actions conform with a symmetrical commitment to the sanctity of life. People can be civilly committed if they represent a threat to *themselves or others*.[29]

What is the basis for a social interest that could curtail an individual's autonomy with respect to an issue so basic and personal as her own continued existence? One set of concerns is paternalistic and mirrors the discussion of decision defects: The state-imposed symmetry is designed to safeguard the individual's own best and real interests. Other considerations are external to the individual and focus on the contributions individuals make to their families and communities:

> The State has an interest in preserving and fostering the benefits that every human being may provide to the community—a community that thrives on the exchange of ideas, expressions of affection, shared memories and humorous incidents as well as material contributions that its members create and support. The value to others of a person's life is far too precious to allow the individual to claim a constitutional entitlement to complete autonomy in making a decision to end that life.[30]

Theoretically, these contributions and the community's utilitarian interest in their continuance could independently justify a state prohibition of suicide.

The utilitarian contribution an individual makes to the community, however, is only part of the community's interest. A more appealing justification may be that society and the individual symmetrically respect the value of individual life because, constitutively, that is the kind of society in which we want to live. Symmetry is essential if the sanctity of life is to be accepted and applied as a universal value. Symbolically, a symmetrical obligation connects the individual to the community in a seamless and continuous way. Society is intimately connected to and comprises its individual members, who in turn have a lasting and unseverable tie to the community. If the intrinsic value of life were not symmetrical, the community could be easily fractured into separate, autonomous cells. In the same sense, we can speak of a collective as a vibrant living being that is enriched (as Justice Stevens argues) by its individual members and is impoverished by the premature loss of one of its parts. From this perspective, suicide is not simply an internal and individual matter, it is also a communal concern. It is a kind of collective self-mutilation as potentially violent and harmful as an affirmative act of euthanasia by the state.

As with most constitutive choices, there are plausible alternatives. Moreover, the persuasiveness of these arguments is largely aspirational in nature. One can certainly imagine a world in which the state was committed to policies based on respect for the intrinsic value of life, but where that value was not symmetrically held. In this setting, individual autonomy would trump a symmetric commitment to life, and the freely exercised will of the person would be respected even with regard to assisted suicide. This view strikes a very different balance between the individual and the community and rests on a different understanding of the relationship between the individual and the state. Indeed, Justice Stevens, while acknowledging the collective's interest in the continuation of its members' lives, concludes that the state's interest in the sanctity of life cannot justify infringing the individual rights of competent, terminally ill people: "Properly viewed, . . . this interest [the sanctity of life] is not a collective interest that should always outweigh the interests of a person who because of pain, incapacity, or sedation finds her life intolerable."[31] Stevens concludes that the interest in the sanctity of life must yield "to the individual's interest in choosing a final chapter that accords with her life story."[32]

A crucial issue is how these constitutive choices should be made. In a constitutional democracy, such choices are ordinarily entrusted to the political process. Statist theories of government differ from libertarianism and liberalism in their willingness to predicate policies upon collectively derived social norms. The state can prohibit individual conduct simply because the democratically expressed will of the majority finds it somehow wrong, inappropriate, or "immoral." Democratic statism permits the prohibition of assisted suicide, so long as the prohibition is the product of a legitimate democratic process. This outcome may seem harsh to some, but *Glucksberg* made it clear that substantive due process (as least as currently understood) will not constitutionally protect the individual from such action. Unfortunately, the Court's opinion offers little practical guidance as to how the tensions between collective and individual interests might be addressed as the problem of assisted suicide is entrusted to the legislative process.

I-for-Us Rationality

At the heart of the assisted-suicide debate are strong tensions between respect for the intrinsic value of life and principles of autonomy and self-determination in deeply personal matters. At one level the choice is between worldviews that make different trade-offs between individuals and collective rights. Simplistically stated, in one view the individual's rights and interests trump collective interests and social norms (state policies are based on I-for-me reasoning). In another other view, the individual is denied the "right" to end her life because of the socially determined primacy of the sanctity of life (state policies are based on we-for-us reasoning). The category of I-for-us thinking challenges both these views and suggests a method of mediating the tensions between individual autonomy and collective social norms.

The challenge of I-for-us reasoning is to frame the issue of assisted suicide so as to acknowledge both its individual and communal aspects. It is not enough to cite polls showing that many people favor legalizing assisted suicide or to demonstrate the atomistic rationality of that option. Nor is it enough to cite laws or traditions that condemn the practice as proof that assisted suicide is irrational or inconsistent with an individual's social obligations. What is needed is an examination of whether the asserted social norm is one affected persons could embrace as a statement of their collective responsibility. Would individuals accept a norm prohibiting assisted suicide if asked to make this determination as a matter of individual choice but in a realm acknowledging their social obligations? Conversely, the challenge to proponents of assisted suicide is to make a persuasive aspirational argument by articulating a vision of the individual's right to die that is consistent with a vibrant understanding of community. A discourse based only in I-for-me reasoning is not equal to the task.

Addressing these questions requires a more detailed investigation into the relationship between the individual and the state. The discussion in the next section steps back from the assisted-suicide debate and looks at the individual and the state within a framework that assumes that the dictates of atomistic and collective rationality are not inherently contradictory. One can thus reconstruct substantive due process as a mechanism to mediate conflicts between individual and collective interests, particularly in the area of establishing social norms. As mentioned earlier, the final chapter section returns to the debate over assisted suicide and reexamines these arguments within this new context.

The Convergence of Atomistic and Collective Rationality: Defining Civilization, Reconstructing Substantive Due Process, and Legislating Social Norms

The Purpose of Civilization: What Is Fundamental?

No one individual exists in isolation. We are all part of an elaborate network of social relations.[33] Thus we must respect the social context in which our decisions are made. Conversely, social decisions must acknowledge and respect our autonomy. Each civilization strives to balance individual values and social norms, individual autonomy and collective obligation. Various forms of communism emphasized the supremacy of the collective identity at the sacrifice of the individual's well-being and soul. Various forms of democratic capitalism have idolized the individual, with resulting excesses of personal freedom and the degradation of communal life. What we need is a vision of society that seeks not to compromise either objective. Since society is a whole composed of its individual parts, it must strive to establish a vibrant collective identity while allowing its members to find unique and individualized meaning in their lives.

Achieving these conflicting goals is not easy. It may be impossible. The vision of autonomous agents seeking individual fulfillment while building a common community is as much a recipe for instability and conflict as for growth and fulfillment. Individually rational behavior often differs, sometimes substantially, from collectively rational behavior. Moreover, what is individually rational for one person may not be rational—may even be irrational—for another person. In spite of these inherent difficulties, the hope that autonomous individuals can further the collective good while pursuing their own objectives is powerful and often irresistible. This hope underlies people's faith in various forms of democracy. A similar hope underlies faith in free-market economics. Either as expressed anecdotally by Adam Smith or as embodied mathematically in the first and second theorems of welfare economics, the (neo)classical economic vision pictures unguided and uncontrolled individuals pursuing their own objectives and in the process maximizing the communal welfare.[34] The appeal of promoting the general good by empowering individuals has preserved faith in democracy and capitalism even at times when the actual functioning of economic and political markets casts doubt on that faith's premises. Perhaps, then, that same faith can animate a meaningful doctrine of substantive due process.

But how? Unfettered individual autonomy can degenerate into irresponsibility, conflict, and confusion. Unfettered state authority can degenerate into capriciousness and tyranny. Economists often ask whether a model will reach an equilibrium state and whether the resulting equilibrium will be stable. One precondition for a stable social equilibrium in a system dominated by autonomous individuals would appear to be the existence of some collective good or collective rationality to which authentically exercised free wills must naturally bend. In other words, whatever the starting point or specific route taken, there must be a convergence of individual free wills, however expressed, into a common center.

By speaking of collective rationality, I do not mean to adopt a utilitarian metric or to suggest any specific substantive understanding of the collective good. By speaking of convergence, I do not mean to suggest a linear thought process, nor to insist that convergence necessarily entails uniformity. Indeed, I take it that convergence must occur without loss of individual identity or uniqueness. The convergence (or consistent coexistence) of individual and collective rationality has more the flavor of a Hegelian synthesis than a mathematical equation: the synthesis does not destroy or alter the reality of the thesis and antithesis. In the same sense, the convergence of individual and collective rationality need not eclipse the individual nor detract from that person's uniqueness.

The convergence between individual and collective rationality may be theoretically possible, but is it empirically plausible? This depends on one's view of human nature. That view will influence both where the balance between the state and individual must originally be struck, as well as how the state might promote individual growth. If one believes individual choices will not yield collectively rational results, then one needs a strong system of state controls. If one believes individuals can act in collectively responsible ways, but that such a collective orientation must be taught, then one wants state involvement in establishing and inculcating social norms. If one believes individuals can act in socially responsible ways, but that such norms are ultimately the product of people's free choice and development, then one wants a social environment conducive to individual development and perhaps sanctions for individuals whose failure to develop manifests itself in antisocial conduct.

Whatever one's belief, the state is necessary. It is the instrumentality that mediates conflicts between individuals and establishes policies and mechanisms to promote the collective good. The state must thus be given certain powers, many of them coercive. The obvious vice of power is abuse, which must be controlled. Many aspects of the American constitutional system, including the doctrine of substantive due process, are designed to do exactly this.

Reconstructing Substantive Due Process: Reconciling Individual and Collective Interests

The doctrine of substantive due process declares a sphere of individual interests that, while not specifically enumerated in the Constitution, nevertheless deserve constitutional protection.[35] Before the state may interfere with one of these fundamental liberty interests, the government must articulate a sufficient justification and must attempt to accommodate the interest of the individual within the realm of the collectively defined need. What is striking about the doctrine, however, is not only what it states, but also the controversy continually surrounding it. There is little agreement as to the justification for substantive due process, the scope of the rights it protects, or the nature of the state interests that can trump those individual rights.

No constitutional system can anticipate all possible contingencies. Given this fact, it is often desirable to have a doctrine capable of correcting mistakes while still implementing the broader objectives of the legal system—in our case, protecting individual integrity while permitting the exercise of legitimate state power. A close analogy can be drawn to the contract doctrine of unconscionability. Section 2–302 of the Uniform Commercial Code (UCC) permits courts to limit or refuse to enforce unconscionable contract provisions. The drafters of the UCC deliberately chose not to define "unconscionability," and the comments to 2–302 speak of it in a decidedly circular fashion.[36] The lack of a precise definition can be frustrating, but it also is a source of strength and flexibility. While courts continue to struggle with the doctrine, most cases focus on the existence of procedural and substantive unconscionability.[37] Importantly, some courts will infer procedural unconscionability from a finding of extreme substantive unconscionability.[38] In essence, these courts assume that there are certain contractual terms no rational person would voluntarily accept. The actual existence of such a term must therefore be evidence of a defect in the bargaining process, whether or not the procedural defect can actually be identified or demonstrated. This approach mixes concerns over the process of contract formation with a substantive evaluation of the contract terms.

While a consensus definition of substantive due process is as elusive as a consensus definition of unconscionability, partial definitions and case holdings cluster in a bipolar distribution. One cluster expresses liberty interests in terms of individual freedom and personal autonomy. The other cluster articulates concepts of liberty in terms of a level of individual freedom that must exist within collective state institutions if those institutions are to be consistent with our historical traditions and our vision of civilization and the state. As I suggested earlier, these articulations of protected liberty interests—one focusing on the individual and one on the collective—are not necessarily inconsistent.

Consider the authorities cited in *Glucksberg*. Chief Justice Rehnquist invokes the substantive due process formulation articulated by Justice Cardozo in *Palko v Connecticut*.[39] Cardozo speaks of interests that are "implicit in the concept of ordered liberty"[40] and of those "fundamental principles of liberty and justice which lie at the base of all our civil and political institutions."[41] Cardozo gives further guidance: Liberty interests are fundamental if "neither liberty nor justice would exist if they were sacrificed"[42] and if its abridgement would inflict "a hardship so acute and shocking that our polity will not endure it."[43] Cardozo appeals to historical traditions, political theories of government and society, and *a collective response to individual hardship*. The focus here starts with the state and proceeds to examine the state's relationship to the individual largely in terms of unspoken traditions and political theories.

In contrast to the state-based approach of Rehnquist and Cardozo, a number of other cases define the liberty interest protected under the Fourteenth Amendment directly in terms of the individual. In *Meyer v Nebraska*,[44] the Court, after listing specific rights pertaining to contracting, engaging in a profession, marriage, and raising children, speaks of "those privileges long recognized at common law as essential to the *orderly pursuit of happiness* by free men."[45] This suggests a right of individuals not simply to exist, but to grow and flourish, albeit within the ordered confines of a community and in ways acknowledged by the common law. A similar sentiment was expressed in by the Court in *Allgeyer v Louisiana*,[46] a case from the era of economic substantive due process that defines a fairly broad realm of personal liberty (economic and otherwise):

> The liberty mentioned in that amendment means not only the right of the citizen to be free from the mere physical restraint of his person, as by incarceration, but the term is deemed to embrace the right of the citizen to be *free in the enjoyment of all his faculties;* to be free to use them in all lawful ways; to live and work where he will; to earn his livelihood by any lawful calling; to pursue any livelihood or avocation,

and for that purpose to enter into all contracts which may be proper, necessary and essential to his carrying out to a successful conclusion the purposes above mentioned.[47]

Perhaps the broadest articulation of the individual-based liberty interest is found in Justice O'Connor's opinion in *Planned Parenthood v Casey*.[48] *Casey* is important because it expressly acknowledges the interior, person-centered aspects of the protected liberty interest—ultimately the individual right of self-definition.

> These matters, involving the most intimate and personal choices a person may make in a lifetime, choices central to personal dignity and autonomy, are central to the liberty protected by the Fourteenth Amendment. At the heart of liberty is the right to define one's own concept of existence, of meaning, of the universe, and of the mystery of human life. Beliefs about these matters could not define the attributes of personhood were they formed under compulsion of the State.[49]

The state is not central to this definition. Indeed, the state is portrayed as an implicit threat to authentic self-actualization, at least when the state attempts to impose any particular worldview onto its citizens or preempts individual self-definition.[50]

The tensions between the conflicting definitions of liberty, like the tensions between individual and collective rationality, are frequently more apparent than real. In view of the vision of civilization I have articulated, the primary objective of substantive due process should be to resolve the tension between the state and the individual in a way that promotes the convergence (or consistent coexistence) of the state and individual interests. A vision of a civilized state respecting personal autonomy and individual self-definition "lies at the base of all our civil and political institutions."[51] Justice Harlan speaks of "the balance which our Nation, built upon postulates of respect for the liberty of the individual, has struck between that liberty and the demands of organized society."[52] The balance, however, need not compromise either objective. If there is an ultimate convergence between individual and collective rationality, then the state-centered approach comes full circle to the individual-centered approach. If one of the primary objectives of the state is to preserve a space for individual self-actualization, then broad prohibitions of state interference with self-definition are consistent with "the concept of ordered liberty."[53] The circle, however, must also be closed in the other direction. Self-actualization and self-definition must lead to a growing personal recognition of communal responsibility and social obligation in the "orderly pursuit of happiness"[54]—I-for-us rationality. In this sense, society reaches its full potential in the flourishing of its individual members, while the growth and development of its members contribute to the completeness and vitality of society.

There is an unfortunate tendency, however, to define fundamental rights and protected liberty interests in the individual-centered cluster of substantive due process strictly in terms of personal autonomy. One of the limitations of focusing exclusively on the individual is that it fails to explain why autonomy is being protected. Moreover, the atomistic focus on individual autonomy fails to establish any unifying symmetry with the state-based cluster of definitions. It is more useful to characterize the individual rights protected by substantive due process in terms of individual development and self-actualization within a communal context, instead of in terms of privacy or autonomy. This approach starts to cabin the doctrine of substantive due process and establish meaningful boundaries. The autonomy-focused right of the individual to define her "own concept of existence, of meaning, of the universe, and the mystery of human life"[55] is limitless. A theory of substantive due process premised upon the convergence of the ends of individual development and the proper functioning of the state, however, provides a framework in which the merits of individual claims and the legitimacy of state interests can both be assessed.

Legislating Social Norms

The greatest tension between individual self-definition and the collective needs of society comes in the area of social norms.[56] What is the proper relationship between the individual and the community in the cultivation and adoption of values and beliefs? Can social values be taught effectively? Is an individual's concept of self derived from her concept of community, or is the individual's concept of community derived from her concept of self? What role ought the state play in this process?

Albert Schweitzer struggles with many of these issues in *The Philosophy of Civilization*.[57] He characterizes attempts to define an individual's life view in terms of, or as deduced from, a larger worldview as seductive, but misguided.[58] Individuals must first struggle to define a life view and through this struggle discover a generalizable worldview. Schweitzer speaks of an introspective process through which the individual will-to-live, rationally reflecting upon itself, leads to the discovery of the universal will-to-live.[59] The individual's self-defined life view provides the foundation for a worldview that is ethical, optimistic, and grounded in reverence for life. Importantly, the individual's solitary journey is a thought-driven process that leads her to a worldview and value system that is communally focused. For Schweitzer, at least, there does exist a collective good or collective rationality to which authentically exercised free wills naturally bend. This description of human development and the relationship between the life view and the worldview is instructive. It suggests that one of the state's missions and perhaps the primary purpose of substantive due process is to create and protect a sphere of individual autonomy that permits people to undertake this internal process of self-discovery and self-definition. This view also supports a presumption in favor of the individual when efforts at self-definition directly conflict with external social norms.

It would be naive, however, to contend that society plays no role in individual self-definition. At some level, it must, for the beliefs that shape this process are socially constructed or, at a minimum, individually constructed within a social context. Healthy individual growth, like successful child development, is no accident. Structure, discipline, and education are required. People are products of their environments, and their environments comprise the material, cultural, and educational resources contributed by parents, families, and communities. These contributions help transfer, inculcate, and reproduce a system of beliefs. In fact, the state's contributions to this material environment may more powerfully influence individual development than state efforts to inculcate particular beliefs or to influence behavior through the expressive voice of its laws. It may well be appropriate for substantive due process to permit the state substantial latitude to affect the material base in which self-definition takes place, even as it strictly limits efforts to directly inculcate values.

The dangers inherent in state efforts to establish social norms are plain: Such efforts not only interfere with individual self-definition, they may permit one segment of society to improperly project its values and beliefs on another. The analysis in this chapter, however, suggests a substantive due process screen capable of protecting individuals from community oppression and yet countenancing appropriate social norms. Norms-based legislation should be required to pass a two-part test. First, the legislated norm should reflect sound we-for-us rationality. Judges can ordinarily presume that democratically enacted legislation expresses the collective will. This presumption can be rebutted by identifying procedural defects with the democratic process. If defects are present, the social norm may no longer be presumed to be an authentic statement of collective desires and should not be a basis for interfering with individual rights. Second, legislation should meet the standard of I-for-us rationality. Would the people directly affected by the legislation willingly embrace the norm as a legitimate expression of their collective responsibility?[60] This analysis focuses on those impacted by the legislation and not the beliefs held by groups advocating the law's adoption.

The second prong of the test assumes that judges can empathetically verify someone else's assessment of collective rationality.[61] This assumption rests on the contention that individual and collective rationality are ultimately reconcilable and that an individual's determination of what is collectively rational (I-for-us reasoning) is a thought-driven process that can be articulated and evaluated.[62] To overrule legislation, the court need only be convinced that the individual has an authentic conception of I-for-us rationality that is irreconcilable with the statement of we-for-us rationality embodied in the law. In this process, judges would be free to assess the legitimacy of the individual's beliefs. The contested individual belief must be consonant with the authentic life views and worldviews held by other members of the community and with other recognized expressions of we-for-us rationality. History and tradition are important, although not exclusive or infallible expressions of such views. Moreover, principles traditionally classified as "compelling state interests" would theoretically lie at the core of we-for-us and hence I-for-us rationality.[63] Individual beliefs that strongly conflict with core tenets of we-for-us rationality may be rejected, as may individual beliefs that reject the concept of a common community or the belief that coexistence of beliefs is possible.

Subjecting individual beliefs to a test of collective authenticity will strike many as dangerous. For one thing, the test is expressly content-based. First Amendment jurisprudence is suspicious of content-based regulation of speech and expressly avoids substantive assessments of religious beliefs.[64] One justification for a content-based substantive due process standard is the unenumerated nature of the rights that doctrine protects. Enumerated rights of speech, assembly, and religion may well enjoy a higher level of protection and be evaluated under a different standard. Another justification is my assumption of the convergence between individual and collective rationality. The requirement that individual assessments of I-for-us rationality be thought-driven and capable of empathetic verification serves as an essential check on the scope of the doctrine. It also ensures that different segments of the community can engage in meaningful dialogue over conflicting beliefs. The assumed convergence and a focus on individual self-definition that leads to a communal orientation provide external benchmarks that make the doctrine workable.

A second objection to my proposed standard is that it lets judges strike down legislation in the absence of identifiable defects in the democratic process.[65] Defects in the democratic process, however, are perhaps even harder to identify and document than procedural defects in the contracting process. Just as extreme substantive unconscionability may be persuasive evidence of procedural unconscionability, so democratic decisions that violate the assumed convergence of collective and atomistic rationality may be persuasive evidence of a breakdown in the democratic process. The democratic process is subject to the additional procedural safeguard of determining whether its dictates are consistent with the authentically held I-for-us convictions of citizens affected by the legislation.

Matrix as Process: Reasoning to Convergence

Courts apply the principles of substantive due process to examine legislation. But those same principles can also help us formulate policy, particularly on contentious social issues. The matrix developed earlier in the chapter suggests a method for moving individuals and society closer together: considering *seriatim* how issues might be resolved from the perspectives of I-for-me, we-for-me, I-for-us, and we-for-us reasoning. The convergence between individual and collective rationality implies that honest, thought-driven struggle and reflection within each perspective should lead one closer to rather than further from the authentically held convictions embedded in each of the other perspectives. The outcome will not necessarily be a system of uniform positions, but rather a network of beliefs that can coexist with one another.

For example, individual contemplation of what is collectively rational can guide a person's growth and development. The individual can strive to understand collective needs by struggling to see them in the social dimension of we-for-us rationality. Similarly, she can better understand her own decisions by examining such choices from the perspective of we-for-me rationality—by asking what social policies would ensure that individuals, generically defined, are acting in their best interest. Similarly, I-for-us rationality involves a journey in which the individual begins to acknowledge and understand her social obligations. A capacity for sympathy matures into a capacity for empathy, which permits individual assessments of self-interest to be modified and informed by the needs of others. A similar dialectic consideration of individual and collective interests can guide social decisions. The objective is to establish policies that are both individually and collectively rational. Differences between the results of I-for-me and we-for-us reasoning identify tensions that must be mediated and addressed. Mediation involves efforts to reconcile different perspectives, not necessarily by trading off competing concerns, but rather by attempting to facilitate the coexistence of legitimate individual and collective needs.[66]

In the wake of *Glucksberg*, the fight over assisted suicide will next be waged through state legislation and referendums. The following section returns to the problem of assisted suicide and asks how the perspectives outlined in the four quadrants of our matrix, together with the assumed convergence of atomistic and collective rationality, can help mediate conflicting individual and social positions regarding assisted suicide.

Reexamining the Assisted-Suicide Debate

In apparent contradiction to the assumed convergence of atomistic and collective rationality, many contentious social issues, including assisted suicide, engender more conflict than harmony. The conflict surrounding end-of-life decisions is symptomatic of a profound disequilibrium in the way we face death and dying. The sources of this imbalance are many.[67] Technology has transformed the physical setting in which dying occurs, forcing us to formulate new understandings of life and death. What it means to be alive or to be dead is no longer clear, nor is the exact moment of passage. The structure of modern medicine further contributes to the imbalance: As health care has become more institutionalized, specialized, and routinized, so has dying. Machines regulate and control life and death, maintaining heartbeats and breaths, reducing a person to a series of vital signs. Life is meted out and measured, regulated and controlled. Quantity, defined in hours, days, and years, often displaces quality as the objective to be pursued.

Grieving and burial have been commodified by a funeral industry committed to masking the real face of death. At the same time, the families and communities responsible for nurturing life and consoling the bereaved have been severely strained. The nuclear and extended families have become more fractured, and our friends and loved ones have become geographically dispersed. As a consequence, death is often faced in a cold, technical environment devoid of family and friends, surrounded by strangers.

The problem of assisted suicide forces us to assess the meaning of death and dying (and by implication of life and living). This assessment is hard because death typically provokes fear and denial. The fear is of the unknown, of pain, suffering, and debility. The denial of death can be motivated as much by a sense of emptiness in life as by an actual fear of dying—or perhaps by a heightened fear of death because of a felt incompleteness in life. Still, death retains a significance that is as profound as it is unavoidable. Dying is a stage in life holding many of its own lessons. Moreover, the way death must be faced can influence the choices we make in life, just as how we live will have implications for the way we die. Death can bring us back to a sense of community, both by coalescing a group that provides support and comfort and by bringing to the fore the legacy we will leave behind, a legacy often defined in terms of the contributions we have made to others.

In our passive acquiescence to the medicalization of death and dying, it is not only death that is being denied. There is a denial of life. There is a denial of the individual as an integrated being. There is a denial of meaning and human dignity. Finally, there is a denial of community. Add to this the reality of individual human suffering, pain, disability, and dementia, and it is easy to see how suicide may look atomistically rational. While substantial attention has been paid to the role of pain in decisions whether to seek physician-assisted suicide, similar attention has not been paid to the role of community. The issue is whether suicide is, for some, an atomistically rational response to death or an atomistically rational response to the way people are presently living and dying. The movement for assisted suicide may be symptomatic of larger problems in society and an indictment of the absence of meaningful community. Ironically, ratifying a right to assisted suicide and recognizing the ascendency of I-for-me rationality at the end of life may be the ultimate step in commodifying life and death and may further shift the balance away from the community and toward the increasingly isolated individual.

As the assisted-suicide debate moves from the courthouse to the statehouse, we must reexamine the arguments outlined in the third part of this chapter to determine which elements are essential and which might bend in establishing a network of coexisting beliefs. There are aspects of the beliefs articulated in each quadrant of the matrix that must be respected by any workable social policy toward end-of-life decisions. The I-for-me perspectives of the plaintiffs in *Glucksberg* and *Quill* highlight the importance of respecting individual autonomy and self-determination, particularly as these qualities relate to engendering an appropriate sense of personal dignity and control in the face of death. Moreover, the reality of the pain and suffering experienced by these individuals must be directly confronted and addressed. The we-for-me arguments of opponents of assisted suicide remind us that the scope of individual autonomy and self-determination is necessarily circumscribed in the presence of defects in individual decision making, and that it is appropriate to place limits on personal choice when those choices injure third persons. The we-for-us perspectives highlight the fact that the community is a collective entity with its own needs and interests. There are times when these collective interests may legitimately trump those of the individual.

While there are positive aspects of the viewpoints examined earlier, each perspective has its shortcomings as well. The plaintiffs' claims in *Glucksberg* and *Quill* are arresting, but they have limitations. If we ask the dying why they consider suicide, they frequently speak of pain and suffering. But a number of other themes also emerge. One is a desire for control, another a desire for dignity. While the desire for control is understandable, the important question is what type of control is appropriate and how that control should be manifested. Proponents of assisted suicide argue for control in the form of individually determining the moment and manner of death. This is the kind of control of a Hollywood director, a film editor, or of Dworkin's author writing her life's last chapter.[68] This is not the only kind of individual control that can be envisioned. Being ill and dying entails an inevitable loss of control. That loss is compounded when doctors expect passive compliance with their expertise and authority. But while many aspects of dying are beyond human control, numerous others are not. Individual control can be manifested in many ways short of assisted suicide.[69] Letting people participate in what they can affect is one way for them to assert control and to assuage feelings of helplessness and anxiety. Participation can help people distinguish those parts of dying that are controllable from those that are not and help them to accept the inevitable loss of control they have over their bodies and existence. Dying must involve an appropriate combination of taking charge and letting go, engagement and resignation.

Just as the desire for control requires a balanced understanding of what can and cannot be influenced, so the desire for dignity requires an understanding and acceptance of different forms of dependence. In our culture, dignity is often defined in terms of independence and self-sufficiency. A common fear among the dying is of becoming dependent upon others. Put bluntly but succinctly—"I want to be able to wipe my own butt."[70] While everyone can empathize with this sentiment, "dignity" need not be understood that way.[71] Infants do not lack dignity because they need their diapers changed, nor must changing them be burdensome. Dignity is inherently a relational concept, defining individuals with respect to their community. Illness and dying are necessarily an assault on self-sufficiency, a reminder of one's vulnerability, weakness, and dependence. As illness physically changes the person it calls for a continual redefinition of one's self and of one's sense of dignity.

Confronting incapacity while retaining a sense of self-worth is like accepting loss of control over the uncontrollable and yet remaining engaged and retaining control of the dying process. A static image of self and concepts of dignity defined solely in terms of strength, independence, and autonomy are ill-suited to prepare a person for a protracted illness or prolonged death. Justice Stevens speaks poignantly about people's interest in influencing the memories they will leave behind,[72] but no life is a snapshot. A life is a complex story, with many chapters and phases. Just as the concern about memories is a concern about how others see us, so the concern over dignity is at its heart a fear that our inability to accept the loss of our independence and our control over our bodies will be shared by others. Feelings of indignity are largely fears of rejection by our community. Such fears not only invite, but demand, a communal response.

It is interesting but not surprising to note how tracing the individual's interest in maintaining personal dignity has necessarily led us from viewing the individual in isolation to understanding the individual as a member of a community. Other emotions and fears surrounding death—such as fears of abandonment and feelings of isolation—confirm that it is impossible to speak of the dying individual without also speaking of the living community. The individual and society are intimately interconnected. The decisions of family, friends, and the community will affect the environment in which death occurs and the levels of fear, anxiety, and meaning that are present. Coming to terms with death requires coming to terms with one's self and one's community. A discourse focusing exclusively on individual autonomy and I-for-me rationality is insufficient unless the concept of self it engenders leads the individual back to a sense of community. The presence, attitudes, and actions of family and friends, of doctors and nurses, and health-care providers will have as much to do with finding dignity and meaning in death as the medical condition of the dying person.

This criticism is not limited to I-for-me perspectives. Similar deficiencies can be found in the we-for-me policy arguments raised by opponents of assisted suicide. Rather than addressing the central issue of the individual's relationship to the community and the community's obligations to its members, opponents focus on decision defects and slippery-slope concerns. These are surely important, but at another level they are simply distractions, for they do not address the human dimension of the dying person's needs or the overall needs of society. Worse, these arguments are frequently a pretext to camouflage a debate that is really about social norms. Those favoring a strong norm in favor of the sanctity of life often invoke substantial and irremediable decision defects and a steep and inescapable slippery slope. Their opponents deprecate these concerns. The failure to address the central conflict between individual and collective rationality is ultimately self-defeating. Decision-defect and slippery-slope arguments involve contested empirical claims. Empirical claims invite empirical resolution. Debate will inevitably drift toward "how" to regulate and not "whether" to regulate. In this process, a right to assisted suicide could too easily be adopted incrementally without openly addressing the underlying normative concerns.

We-for-us arguments face their own challenges and limitations. The concern over the sanctity of life can delegitimate itself if pursued so oppressively that it robs individual lives of their meaning. Any authentic communal value must resonate with the needs of its individual members. The sanctity of life cannot be a wooden or artificial principle. To address this problem, the Ninth Circuit advocated using a sliding scale standard to assess the value of life:

> [E]ven though the protection of life is one of the state's most important functions, the state's interest is dramatically diminished if the person it seeks to protect is terminally ill or permanently comatose and has expressed a wish that he be permitted to die without further medical treatment . . . When patients are no longer able to pursue liberty or happiness and do not wish to pursue life, the state's interest in forcing them to remain alive is clearly less compelling.[73]

Unfortunately, this analysis raises its own slippery-slope concerns. If the socially determined value of a life diminishes as people near death, how will the debates over voluntary and involuntary euthanasia, or the rationing of health care be affected? Eroding the intrinsic value society attaches to the lives of its individual members can have profound and disturbing consequences. The use of a sliding scale in which the value of a life is worth less depending on its objective circumstances explains why many associations of handicapped and disabled people oppose assisted suicide.[74] In fairness to the Ninth Circuit, it tries to make the sliding scale depend on the dying person herself. The distinction between the individual's assessment of her life's value and society's assessment, however, is difficult to maintain as a practical matter and almost impossible to implement as a matter of policy. To be given legal effect, the individual's evaluation must ultimately be ratified by the state.

If the sliding scale valuation of human life is not a good way to prevent a rigid version of the sanctity of life from burdening the dying, how should collective concerns over the intrinsic value of life be tailored to address the needs of the terminally ill? A policy that can answer this question will effectively mediate the tensions between individual and collective rationality that divide camps in the assisted-suicide debate. While I do not claim to have a definitive answer to this question, a satisfactory resolution would seem to include the following elements. First is an acknowledgment that a necessary corollary to the sanctity of life is the value of compassion. A society that claims to respect the intrinsic value of life is obligated to respond compassionately to the physical and emotional needs of its dying members, particularly by providing aggressive palliative care to ameliorate individual pain and suffering. Respect for the sanctity of life, without the corresponding value of compassion, can become a hollow and potentially oppressive principle.

Second, the resolution I imagine would supply a vocabulary to operationalize the principles associated with preserving the sanctity of life in a way that could help guide end-of-life decisions. I prefer speaking of a "reverence for life" rather than the "sanctity" or "intrinsic value" of life and operationalizing it by requiring that individual decisions be life-affirming. Terminology, however, should not obscure the fact that life should remain an end in itself and that end-of-life decisions should honor this principle. The danger in the Ninth Circuit's sliding scale and in other efforts to adopt a "quality of life" rhetoric is that both can too easily slip in directions that fail to respect life as its own end. A rhetoric grounded in reverence for life and a requirement that end-of-life decisions be life-affirming help avoids this trap and yet should be capable of acknowledging that the object of life and medicine is not simply to preserve a series of vital signs.

Third, the resolution should try to help the dying find ways to control their lives and their care within a dominant ethic of reverence for life, including reverence for their own lives. They should be allowed to structure a substantial range of end-of-life alternatives, including options other than dying in an institutionalized medical setting. But I would not include suicide among these alternatives since it is not life-affirming and fails to respect the intrinsic value of life that should be symmetrically held by the individual and society.

Although approaching the problem from a substantially different perspective, these principles are in general accord with the Supreme Court's results in *Cruzan* and *Glucksberg*. People are substantially free to refuse unwanted medical care and yet are also denied the right to assisted suicide. Offering choice in one area and denying it in another may appear contradictory, but it embodies an important paradox. Sometimes individual freedom can be realized only in the presence of external constraints. The freedom is the ability to shape and influence the way death and dying occur. The constraint is the prohibition of suicide. The individual and the community may be better able to negotiate the delicate balances these decisions require if they do so within a setting in which both the individual and the state share a commitment to reverence for human life.

But what of the challenge of I-for-us reasoning? Is a norm prohibiting suicide but expressly acknowledging society's obligation for compassionate palliative care and otherwise permitting individuals considerable freedom in making life-affirming end-of-life decisions consistent with the dictates of I-for-us rationality? Could that norm be embraced by the plaintiffs in *Glucksberg* and *Quill* not as a matter of atomistic rationality, but as part of what they could think collectively rational? Justification for such a norm could come from two sources. First are the aspirational arguments in favor of a symmetric commitment to the sanctity of life as an essential aspect of our definition of society. If these arguments present a persuasive picture of how we conceive of our selves and our community, then a norm prohibiting assisted suicide could fall within the category of I-for-us norms essential to the survival and integrity of the community. The arguments against the sliding scale value of life suggest some of the dangers associated with failing to embrace such a norm.

The second possible justification lies in norms designed to facilitate individual development. A norm against assisted suicide could be justified if dying, like primary education, is an important developmental stage in life— a stage that can transform individual preferences and beliefs. Dying is undeniably an important stage in life, potentially no less significant than other developmental stages such as childhood and adolescence. Death and dying may afford unexpected opportunities and lessons for each of us, lessons that would be lost if the process is short-circuited or denied. This contention is not limited to the lessons inherent in the dying process. Knowledge of how we must face death can filter back and influence decisions throughout our lives. Moreover, it is not only the dying who learn through death. The way we die teaches those around us, particularly members of our family, about life and death.

If these I-for-us arguments are not persuasive, then the issue of assisted suicide is reduced to a set of empirical questions regarding the significance of various we-for-me concerns. Appropriate policy should then be based on the assessments of state legislators about the pervasiveness of individual decision defects and the seriousness of slippery-slope problems. The significance of resolving the debate in this manner, however, should not be lost. Assisted suicide raises important constitutive questions. Rejecting the aspirational arguments in favor of the sanctity of life involves adopting a different set of aspirations that will define us as a society. In making constitutive decisions that will define who we are, we should collectively pause to ponder who we want to be.

NOTES

I am grateful to John Beckerman, Eric Bilsky, Steve Croley, Rick Hills, Peter Jacobson, Marc Spindelman, and Yale Kamisar for their comments and suggestions on earlier drafts of this chapter. I wish to extend particular thanks to Carl Schneider for his comments, patience, and editorial assistance.

1. *Washington v Glucksberg,* 117 S Ct 2258 (1997) (*Glucksberg*).
2. *Vacco v Quill,* 117 S Ct 2293 (1997) (*Quill*).
3. "Determined" in the context of "individually determined collective rationality" or "socially determined atomistic rationality" is intended to mean "decided," "derived" or "selected." I intend to imply the existence of meaningful choice at the individual and societal level, not its absence.
4. The term "social norms" can be used in many different contexts. In legal scholarship, social norms are frequently meant to characterize informal sets of private rules or sanctions which are distinct from public laws. See, e.g., Robert C. Ellickson, *Of Coase and Cattle: Dispute Resolution Among Neighbors in Shasta*

County, 38 Stanford Law Review 623 (1986). I intend the term to refer to rules or laws (formal or informal) that are justified primarily on normative grounds. Individual conduct is regulated in a variety of ways to conform with what the community defines to be appropriate behavior.

5. Consideration of what Yale Kamisar terms the "heartwrenching" case plays an important part in the assisted suicide debate. See Yale Kamisar, *Physician-Assisted Suicide: The Problems Presented by the Compelling, Heartwrenching Case,* 88 Journal of Criminal Law & Criminology 1121 (1998). While the facts of the heartwrenching case should not be allowed to dominate the formation of social policy, neither can the facts of difficult cases be forgotten if a meaningful bridge between the individual and the community is to be constructed.

6. *Compassion in Dying v Washington,* 850 F Supp 1454, 1456–57 (WD Wash 1994) (*Compassion in Dying*), aff'd, 79 F3d 790 (9th Cir 1996) (en banc), rev'd as *Washington v Glucksberg,* 117 S Ct 2258 (1997).

7. *Quill v Vacco,* 80 F3d 716, 720 (2d Cir 1996), rev'd, 117 S Ct 2293 (1997) (ellipses in original).

8. *Compassion in Dying,* 850 F Supp at 1456.

9. *Quill v Vacco,* 80 F3d at 720 (ellipses in original).

10. *Quill v Vacco,* 80 F3d at 720–21 (ellipses in original).

11. *Glucksberg,* 117 S Ct at 2306 (Stevens, J., concurring). See also *Cruzan v Director, Missouri Dept. of Health,* 497 US 261, 344, 353 (Stevens, J., dissenting) (*Cruzan*).

12. *Quill v Vacco,* 80 F3d at 729–30.

13. *Compassion in Dying,* 79 F3d at 839.

14. *Planned Parenthood v Casey,* 505 US 833, 851 (1992) (O'Connor, J.).

15. For discussions of the legal relationship between the "right to die" and a woman's constitutional right to choose, see Marc Spindelman, *Are the Similarities Between a Woman's Right to Choose an Abortion and the Alleged Right to Assisted Suicide Really Compelling?* 29 University of Michigan Journal of Law Reform 775 (1996); Seth F. Kreimer, *Does Pro-Choice Mean Pro-Kevorkian? An Essay on Roe, Casey, and the Right to Die,* 44 American University Law Review 803 (1995).

16. Writers on all sides of the assisted-suicide question agree about the need to be sensitive to defects in individual decision making. Writers differ, however, about the seriousness of the defects and the appropriate policy response. For discussions of the factors that can undermine the integrity of decisions see Carl E. Schneider, *Making Biomedical Policy through Constitutional Adjudication: The Example of Physician-Assisted Suicide,* in this volume, draft at 23–27. See also Carl E. Schneider, *The Practice of Autonomy: Patients, Doctors, and Medial Decisions* (Oxford University Press, 1998); Cass R. Sunstein, *The Right to Die,* 106 Yale Law Journal 1123, 1141–44 (1997); David Orentlicher, *The Legalization of Physician Assisted Suicide: A Very Modest Revolution,* 38 Boston College Law Review 443, 459–60 (1997); and Peter G. Daniels, *An Illinois Physician-Assisted Suicide Act: A Merciful End to a Terminally Ill Criminal Tradition,* 28 Loyola University Chicago Law Journal 763, 778–80 (1997).

17. See Carl E. Schneider, *Making Biomedical Policy through Constitutional Adjudication: The Example of Physician-Assisted Suicide,* in this volume.

18. For a further development of this argument, see J. David Velleman,

Against the Right to Die, 17 Journal of Medicine & Philosophy 665 (1992). Velleman argues that the introduction of certain options like the right to die (or dueling) can produce substantial harm, even in situations where there exist some individuals who would affirmatively benefit from exercising the option. Formally introducing the option excludes the possibility of an individual enjoying the status quo (living) *without choosing it.* The decision not to die (or the decision not to duel) becomes a matter of individual choice, a choice that must be justified and a choice that is subject to external judgment and critique. Ibid. at 671–72, 676.

19. Concerns over the slippery slope are probably the most debated issue in the fight over the legalization of assisted suicide. For a comprehensive discussion of the problem see Yale Kamisar, *The "Right to Die": On Drawing (and Erasing) Lines,* 35 Duquesene Law Review 481 (1996); and Yale Kamisar, *Against Assisted Suicide—Even a Very Limited Form,* 72 University of Detroit Mercy Law Review 735 (1995). For the Supreme Court's treatment of the argument, see *Glucksberg,* 117 S Ct at 2274–75 and *Glucksberg,* 117 S Ct at 2290–92 (Souter, J., concurring). For a discussion of the logical form and limitations of slippery-slope arguments see Carl E. Schneider, *The Road to Glucksberg,* in this volume.

20. *Glucksberg,* 117 S Ct at 2290 (Souter, J., concurring).

21. Ibid. at 2292.

22. Ibid. at 2293.

23. This underscores the fact that not all opponents of physician-assisted suicide believe that assisted suicide is individually wrong. Believers in significant slippery-slope concerns can support a prohibition of assisted suicide without believing that the act is morally objectionable, and independent of concerns about the sanctity of life. My colleague Yale Kamisar would fall into this category. Alternatively, it is possible to believe that decision defects and slippery-slope concerns could be administratively contained and that a right to assisted suicide could be successfully implemented, but to oppose such a right on moral, ethical, or communitarian principles.

24. Sonia M. Suter, *Ambivalent Unanimity: An Analysis of the Supreme Court's Holding,* in this volume.

25. The Court in *Glucksberg* did not examine fully the scope of legitimate state action predicated on we-for-us reasoning. In finding that administrative externalities outweighed the individual interest in committing suicide, Justice Souter (along with Justices O'Connor, Breyer and Ginsberg) did not ask whether a normative case could be built against assisted suicide. The majority opinion acknowledged the state's normative interest in preserving the sanctity of life, but since the majority concluded that no "fundamental" right was at stake, the Court held only that the state's normative interest in preserving the sanctity of life was a "rational" basis for state policy. *Glucksberg,* 117 S Ct at 2271–72, 2275.

26. For an insightful discussion of the collective state interests implicated in the assisted-suicide debate see Carl E. Schneider, *Making Biomedical Policy through Constitutional Adjudication: The Example of Physician-Assisted Suicide,* in this volume. Schneider examines the use of the expressive voice of the law in shaping individual beliefs and behavior, the role of taboos in internalizing

social norms, and the role that clear social values may play in providing individuals guidance in difficult and traumatic times, such as youths contemplating suicide or individuals recently diagnosed with terminal illness.

27. International law provides some interesting perspectives on this question. See Christopher McCrudden, *A Part of the Main? The Physician-Assisted Suicide Cases and Comparative Law Methodology in the United States Supreme Court,* in this volume. Various international legal instruments guarantee individuals a right to life protected by the state. Ibid. draft at 39 (citing Article 6 of the International Covenant on Civil and Political Rights and Article 2 of the European Convention of Human Rights). McCrudden examines international treatment of whether this "right to life" may ever be infringed *with the consent of the individual* or whether the right to life is indeed inalienable (symmetrical).

28. In *Cruzan,* the Court assumed "that the United Stated Constitution would grant a competent person a constitutionally protected right to refuse lifesaving hydration and nutrition." *Cruzan,* 497 US at 279. Justice Scalia argued that nothing in a fundamental right grounded in bodily integrity could implicate the authority of the state or even the right of a private citizen to prevent a suicide, even by force. Ibid. at 298 (Scalia, J., concurring).

29. See, e.g., Mich Statutes Ann § 14.800(401)(a) (defining persons who may be subjected to involuntary medical treatment in terms of people's propensity to physically injure themselves or others).

30. *Glucksberg,* 177 S Ct at 2305 (Stevens, J., concurring).

31. *Glucksberg,* 117 S Ct at 2307–08 (Stevens, J., concurring).

32. Ibid. at 2308 (citing Ronald Dworkin, *Life's Dominion: An Argument about Abortion, Euthanasia, and Individual Freedom,* 213 (Knopf, 1993)).

33. The importance of communal concerns in the assisted-suicide debate has been noted by other scholars. See Martin E. Marty & Ron P. Hamel, *Some Questions and Answers,* in R. Hamel, ed., *Choosing Death: Active Euthanasia, Religion, and the Public Debate* 27, 46 (Trinity Press International, 1991) ("We are not merely a collection of isolated, self-determining individuals. We are social by nature; we are connected to others in many different ways. Because of that interconnectedness and the impact of individual acts of euthanasia upon those others, euthanasia is also a social issue and therefore a matter of public policy."). See also Donald L. Beschle, *Autonomous Decisionmaking and Social Choice: Examining the "Right to Die,"* 77 Kentucky Law Journal 319, 346–58 (1988–89).

34. For a discussion of the power and influence of Adam Smith's metaphor and the theory of competitive equilibrium see J. Eatwell, M. Milgate, & P. Newman, eds., *The New Palgrave: The Invisible Hand* (Macmillan, 1989).

35. For a more detailed discussion of substantive due process see Sonia Suter, *Ambivalent Unanimity: An Analysis of the Supreme Court's Holding,* in this volume, and Carl E. Schneider, *Making Biomedical Policy through Constitutional Adjudication: The Example of Physician-Assisted Suicide,* in this volume.

36. UCC 2–302, Comment 1: "The basic test [for unconscionability] is whether, in light of the general commercial background and the commercial needs of the particular trade

or case, the clauses involved are so one-sided as to be unconscionable."

37. For the classic formulation of this approach, see Judge Skelly Wright's opinion in *Williams v Walker-Thomas Furniture Co.,* 350 F2d 445 (DC Cir 1965).

38. See *Maxwell v Fidelity Fin. Servs.,* 184 Ariz 82, 907 P2d 51, 59 (1995) ("a claim for unconscionability can be established with a showing of substantive unconscionability alone"). Not everyone agrees. See generally James J. White & Robert S. Summers, 1 Uniform Commercial Code, § 4–7 at 230–32 (4th ed., 1995). Many courts, however, mechanically go through the motions of finding both procedural and substantive unconscionability, even if it is clear that only one or the other is really driving the opinion.

39. 302 US 319 (1937), cited in *Glucksberg,* 117 S Ct at 2268.

40. *Palko,* 302 US at 325.

41. Ibid. at 328.

42. Ibid. at 326.

43. Ibid. at 328.

44. 262 US 390 (1923).

45. *Meyers v Nebraska,* 262 US at 399 (emphasis added).

46. 165 US 578 (1897).

47. *Allgeyer v Louisiana,* 165 US at 589 (emphasis added).

48. 505 US 833 (1992).

49. *Casey,* 505 US at 851 (O'Connor, J.).

50. It is difficult to assess how much vitality remains of this passage in *Casey* after *Glucksberg.* See Yale Kamisar, *On the Meaning and Impact of the Physician-Assisted Suicide Cases,* in this volume. The majority opinion, which O'Connor joins, attempts to marginalize the individual-centered cluster and ground substantive due process in a backward-looking focus on history and tradition. The Court states that autonomy may be a necessary but is not a sufficient basis for establishing a "fundamental" liberty interest. "That many of the rights and liberties protected by the Due Process Clause sound in personal autonomy does not warrant the sweeping conclusion that any and all important, intimate, and personal decisions are so protected . . . and *Casey* did not suggest otherwise." *Glucksberg,* 117 S Ct at 2271 (citation omitted). The opinion, however, provides little further guidance as to how the tensions between the state-centered cluster and the individual-centered cluster of definitions of protected interests should be resolved. *Glucksberg* is the latest, but is hardly likely to be the last, word on the subject.

51. *Palko,* 302 US at 328.

52. *Poe v Ullman,* 367 US 497, 542 (1961) (Harlan, J., dissenting).

53. *Palko,* 302 US at 325.

54. *Meyer v Nebraska,* 262 US at 399.

55. *Casey,* 505 US at 851 (O'Connor, J.).

56. Again, by social norms I am referring to state policies controlling individual conduct that are based primarily on normative justifications. The role of moral and communitarian concerns as a basis for legislating individual conduct is a controversial topic. At issue is the legitimate scope of democratic action and the role of the Constitution in protecting individual rights. Readers interested in further discussions of these issues might consult, for example, David L. Fitzgerald, *Let Justice Flow Like Water: The Role of Moral Argument in Constitutional Interpretation,* 65 Fordham Law Review 2103 (1997); Edward O. Correia, *Moral Reasoning and the Due Process Clause,* 3 Southern California Interdisciplinary Law Journal 529 (1994); Steven G. Gey, *The Unfortunate Revival of Civic Republicanism,* 141 University of Pennsylvania Law Review 801

(1993); Pamela S. Karlan & Daniel R. Ortiz, *In a Different Voice: Relational Feminism, Abortion Rights, and the Feminist Legal Agenda,* 87 Northwestern University Law Review 858 (1993); D. Don Welch, *Legitimate Government Purposes and State Enforcement of Morality,* 1993 University of Illinois Law Review 67 (1993); Robin West, *The Ideal of Liberty: A Comment on Michael H. v. Gerald D.,* 139 University of Pennsylvania Law Review 1373 (1991); and Robert Post, *Tradition, the Self, and Substantive Due Process: A Comment on Michael Sandel,* 77 California Law Review 553 (1989).

57. Albert Schweitzer, *The Philosophy of Civilization* (MacMillan, 1949).

58. Ibid. at 76–78, 271–78.

59. Ibid. at 78–79, 281–85.

60. It might be helpful to state how this test differs from Rawls's "veil of ignorance"—see John Rawls, *A Theory of Justice* 136–42 (Harvard University Press, 1981)—and Kant's categorical imperative—see Immanuel Kant, *Grounding for the Metaphysics of Morals,* in *Ethical Philosophy,* at 1, 14 (*402) (J. Ellington, trans., Hackett Pub Co., 1986) ("I should never act except in such a way that I can also will that my maxim should become a universal law"). Substantive due process analysis takes place in a world where all people are aware of their endowments and the endowments of others. People's assessment of I-for-me and I-for-us rationality is conditioned on the actual state of the world and their position in it. There is no ignorance in this regard. Moreover, the vision of society articulated here is potentially much more heterogeneous than might prevail under a strict Kantian regime. The issue is not whether the individual could will all members of society to hold the same belief or act in the same fashion, although such an imperative could well be both atomistically and collectively rational. The issue is whether the individual's conception of I-for-us rationality can consistently coexist with the community's expressions of we-for-us rationality.

61. The type of analysis required by this test is very different from the type of policy-making called for by traditional substantive due process analysis. Carl Schneider makes a number of telling criticisms of the ability of the judiciary to engage in policy-making. See Carl E. Schneider, *Making Biomedical Policy through Constitutional Adjudication: The Example of Physician-Assisted Suicide,* in this volume. My test, however, focuses on the judiciary's capacity to empathetically verify the legitimacy of an individual's beliefs. This calls for introspection, not policy-making. Schneider's criticisms concerning the narrow life experiences and lack of broad-based training for judges still raise serious and legitimate concerns. The claim that the judiciary does not possess a comparative advantage to engage in introspection, however, is less persuasive. The insular structure of the judiciary is particularly well suited to this type of contemplative analysis. The central issue is the authenticity of the individual's beliefs, evidence of which will be fully before the court. This inquiry is more theoretical than empirical in nature. My claim is not that judges can be expected to always get the answer right, but rather that the judiciary is better situated than the legislature to make these types of decisions and that such a role can function as an important safeguard to the potential failings of the legislative process.

62. Courts frequently engage in empathetic examinations of the beliefs of individuals and discrete communities. Courts also have substantial experience attempting to balance and weigh competing individual and collective interests. *Wisconsin v Yoder,* 406 US 205 (1972), is one example. The trial court entertained substantial expert testimony about Amish traditions and the Amish way of life. The Supreme Court's treatment of the Amish parents convicted of violating Wisconsin's compulsory school attendance law by keeping their fourteen- and fifteen-year-old children at home is quite empathetic. *Wisconsin v Yoder,* 406 US at 207–13. Finally, the Court engages in a careful balancing of the interests of the state and the interests of the Amish subcommunity in an effort to facilitate the consistent coexistence of each party's legitimate concerns. *Wisconsin v Yoder,* 406 US at 221–29.

63. Legitimate expressions of we-for-me rationality will ordinarily be a subset of I-for-us rationality, meaning that individual assessments of what is collectively rational must necessarily incorporate decision defects and administrative externalities. This implies that state policies narrowly designed to ameliorate defects in individual decision making or to safeguard third parties from the adverse effects of individual action will not violate substantive due process. Of course, I-for-us and we-for-us reasoning are not limited to these concerns and may embrace additional principles.

64. See, e.g., *Police Dep't of Chicago v Mosley,* 408 US 92, 95 (1972) ("above all else, the First Amendment means that government has no power to restrict expression because of its message, its ideas, its subject matter, or its content."); *Thomas v Review Board of Indiana Employment Sec. Div.,* 450 US 707, 714 (1981) ("religious beliefs need not be acceptable, logical, consistent or comprehensive to others to merit First Amendment Protection").

65. Cass Sunstein and other constitutional scholars concerned about the legitimacy of courts overturning democratic legislation would likely object to this requirement. Specifically, Sunstein argues that defects in the democratic process are unlikely in the context of the assisted-suicide debate and that in the absence of such defects judges should defer to the legislative process. See Cass R. Sunstein, *The Right to Die,* 106 Yale Law Journal 1123, 1149–52 (1997). See also *Glucksberg,* 117 S Ct at 2303, where Justice O'Connor wrote, "There is no reason to think the democratic process will not strike the proper balance between the interests of terminally ill, mentally competent individuals who would seek to end their suffering and the state's interests in protecting those who might seek to end life mistakenly or under pressure."

66. I am struck by the many differences and similarities between my use of the term "mediation" and my assumed convergence of atomistic and collective rationality, and Arthur Frank's intriguing proposal to have people actually mediate end-of-life decisions and his faith that such mediation would produce a workable consensus in individual cases. See Arthur W. Frank, *From Story to Law: Euthanasia and Authenticity,* in this volume. In many respects, Frank's mediation is matrix as process, where the community is operationally defined as the people immediately surrounding the bedside of the dying person.

67. For a discussion of the many social and technological factors that have contributed to this disequilibrium and resulting conflict see Carl E. Schneider, *The Road to* Glucksberg, in this volume.

68. See, e.g., Ronald Dworkin, *Life's Dominion: An Argument about Abortion, Euthanasia, and Individual Freedom* 213–17 (Knopf, 1993).

69. See Carl E. Schneider, *Making Biomedical Policy through Constitutional Adjudication: The Example of Physician-Assisted Suicide,* in this volume.

70. I could have easily attributed this statement to my own grandfather. It is telling how frequently this sentiment emerges in the literature and in the stories of people's lives. See Michael Vitez, "Should Death Be a Matter of Choice?," *News & Record* (Greensboro, NC), Jan 5, 1997, F1 ("It's the indignity of having to be diapered and sedated. People can endure pain. But once their children have to wipe their butts, that's the end. When that dignity is gone, no one wants to live.") (statement of Janet Good); Kay Miller, "Helping End Life Left a Daughter Feeling Bitter," *Star Tribune* (Minneapolis, MN), June 11, 1997, 1A ("'My father very much liked to take care of him-

self,' she said. 'He didn't want at the end of his life that people should have to clean him. He felt it wasn't dignified. He'd always say, I want to wipe my own butt.'") (statement of April Kane); Jack Friedman, *For Close Relatives, a Suicide Can Bring Relief or More Suffering,* People 44 (June 25, 1990) ("I couldn't stand the thought of him ending up in a place like that, unable to wipe his butt") (statement of Louise Dinicolo).

71. See Carl E. Schneider, *Making Biomedical Policy through Constitutional Adjudication: The Example of Physician-Assisted Suicide,* in this volume.

72. *Glucksberg,* 117 S Ct at 2306 n11, 2308.

73. *Compassion in Dying,* 79 F3d at 820.

74. See Evan J. Kemp, "Could You Please Die Now? Disabled People Like Me Have Good Reason to Fear the Push for Assisted Suicide," *Washington Post,* Jan 5, 1997, C1; Tony Mauro, "Disabled Plan Protest Against Assisted Suicide," *USA Today,* Jan 6, 1997, 3A; Sandy Banisky, "Protesters Fear Ruling Could Be Death Sentence, Disabled Urge Upholding Ban on Assisted Suicide," *Baltimore Sun,* Jan 9, 1997, 13A.

CHAPTER 10

From Story to Law: Euthanasia and Authenticity

Arthur W. Frank

The irrelevance I feel pervading the discussion of the *Glucksberg* decision comes to this: I hear little that will make any difference in how people who are dying, with their families and caregivers, negotiate—so far as they are able—dying. Unlike the Justices in *Glucksberg*, I am interested in how the stories of individual deaths unfold. If I were to parody a professional designation for this interest it might be "narratologist": I am a student of people's narratives of illness and suffering. In a hyperbolic phrase he earned because he was dying, Anatole Broyard wrote: "Storytelling seems to be a natural reaction to illness. People bleed stories, and I've become a blood bank of them."[1] Hyperbolic, but also true. Storytelling does seem a natural reaction to illness, and in the last years I have told my own illness story,[2] I have edited others' stories,[3] and I have written a monograph seeking to amplify the importance of ill people's stories.[4] My objective is not to interpret these stories, not to decipher some truth in them that is unknown to their authors, but to enhance society's sense of why these stories matter and how to trust them. I would not call myself a blood bank, but I have tried to be a faithful teller of people's stories.

The narrative view integrates theory and personal experience. Thus I begin this consideration of euthanasia and its place in end-of-life care by reflecting on the personal history—the stories—I bring to this issue. I present my history as an instance of the self-reflection that I think anyone, scholar or layperson, must engage in before pronouncing on these issues. There are so many arguments and so many ways of arguing about euthanasia; I believe that how we argue and which arguments we find compelling are determined not only on theoretical and professional grounds but on the basis of stories of family members and friends whose deaths we have been told about and participated in.

I have never been asked to assist someone in dying. For those who have had this experience, their response and their sense of the outcome are mighty influences on their later lives and views. My friend John Hofsess is president of the Right to Die Society of Canada. Hofsess has said in interviews that his commitment to legalizing assisted suicide began when a terminally ill friend asked his help in ending his life. Hofsess refused, and his friend committed suicide by jumping off a bridge; he could think of no other way to be certain he would end his life. What haunts Hofsess is that the man was afraid of heights: he died alone, in a way that terrified him. Hofsess's refusal is the central story in the larger narrative of his commitment to assisted suicide. I begin by recognizing that if I had lived such a story myself, I would probably think differently about these issues.

Hofsess's story underscores another crucial point. For those who are making end-of-life decisions, what counts are not arguments but relationships. Anyone I have known who participates in euthanasia (as opposed to advocating it as an abstract possibility) speaks not of rights, or autonomy, or beneficence, but of the particular people they have assisted or refused to assist.[5] In the phrase of the philosopher Emmanuel Levinas, they respond to *the face* of the other:

> The proximity of the other is the face's meaning, and it means from the very start in a way that goes beyond those plastic forms which forever try to cover the face like a mask of their presence to perception. But always the face shows through these forms. Prior to any particular expression and beneath all particular expressions, which cover over and protect with an immediately adopted face or countenance, there is the nakedness and destitution of the expression as such, that is to say extreme exposure, defenselessness, vulnerability itself.[6]

Any legal consideration of euthanasia must confront Levinas's subsequent question: "Does not expression resemble more closely this extreme exposure than it does some supposed recourse to a code?"[7] When I listen to people who respond to euthanasia requests, I hear the echoes of Levinas: "the face before me summons me, calls for me, begs for me."[8] To the legal philosopher this phrase may only open up the larger question—summons me to *what?* And beyond that lies the question how I make my response to this summons accountable to the larger community of other faces. Levinas is not denying those questions, but he is calling us to remember what comes first: the primordial demand of the face, the other whom I am called to recognize as my neighbor, and whose claim on me is the foundation of my action and my moral being.

What faces summon me, when I think of euthanasia? Once when I was discussing these issues with my father he startled me by saying that it must affect me to come from a family in which several members had died through what he called euthanasia. By any legal or medical use of that term he misspoke, yet his usage was clearly intended. When I was a teenager I knew that my great-uncle had had colon cancer, had refused surgery, and had died in his sleep at home. I recall no questioning, no discussion within the family of whether his decision was right or wrong; it was simply *his*. He had made his decision and nothing more was asked except how to visit and comfort him during his dying. Years later my uncle died, at an age I rapidly approach, of a heart condition that could have been treated, but again he declined to live in the conditions treatment required. One evening he lay down on his couch in his living room and, suddenly but with full consciousness, died. My grandfather's death also followed this pattern.

These deaths did not involve the withdrawal of any treatment, much less active intervention to hasten death, yet my father called them euthanasia. He might have known more of the causes of death than I have been told—it is hardly unknown in families for some members to have information others lack—but I believe not. He simply speaks in a broader, more common sense than law and medicine allow themselves. For him, *euthanasia* means choosing to die a preventable death, in order to forestall dying in a way that might contradict how the person has lived. The crucial ethical issue to him is accepting a shortened life. The means by which life is shortened—refusal to initiate treatment, withdrawal of treatment, or active intervention in hastening death—are secondary. I take seriously his indifference in these distinctions, and I pose the question what this lay indifference means for medicine and for law.[9]

Of my great-uncle's decision not to have surgery, I still recall (perhaps incorrectly after so many years) my mother saying, "Given the life he has led, he has chosen. . . ." My family narratives, and my family's speech, shape me. These are Levinas's "extreme exposures" that affect me before I have "some supposed recourse to a code." Each of us has encountered faces that have summoned us, and each of us remains summoned by them. Before any more formal ethics is the face and its primordial demand.

Believing all this, when I turn to professional ethicists I am drawn to the writing of Ronald Dworkin because he is sensitive to dying as a narrative act. Dworkin takes seriously the prior sociological question: Why does it matter so much to people how they die? "We must therefore begin by asking," he writes, "how does it matter to the critical success of our whole life how we die?"[10] Answering his own question, Dworkin draws a significant distinction:

> We should distinguish between two different ways that it might matter: because death is the far boundary of life, and every part of our life, including the very last, is important; and because death is special, a peculiarly significant event in the narrative of our lives, like the final scene of a play, with everything about it intensified, under a special spotlight. In the first sense, when we die is important because of what will happen to us if we die later; in the second, how we die matters because it is how we *die*.[11]

Dworkin elaborates this distinction between "people who want to live on . . . in order to do something they believe important to have done" and others who "think they have strong reasons of a comparable kind for *not* staying alive."[12] He substantiates this distinction by quoting from the personal narrative that Philip Roth wrote about his father's death. "Dad," Roth whispers to his father, "I'm going to have to let you go."[13] To interpret Dworkin's quotation through Levinas, when Roth makes the decision to end his father's treatment, he responds not to principles but to his father's face. The certainty of which mattered more—what might still be done during a continuing life or the value of not staying alive—was simply there for him. Roth's certainty that his father benefits more from not staying alive than from what he might still experience by living longer rests on principle but invokes the whole story of who his father was. The decision rests on Roth's faith that he knows his father's story well enough to act in accordance with the volition of that story.

Dworkin does not seem to think, nor do I think, there is any way *in principle* to adjudicate the value of deciding which matters more: what a longer life might still hold, or how the life that has been lived might be degraded by staying alive. Here we reach an impasse. Was it Mr. Roth's good fortune to have caring for him, as a surrogate decision maker, a son who grasped so well the narrative of his life and could create a last act suitable to that narrative? Or, others might ask, did Philip Roth get it wrong in the decision he made when he let his father go? How does he *know,* and how can anyone know, that he decided as his father would have? And even if Mr. Roth had left the clearest of living wills, others might ask what right he had to shorten his own life by refusing treatment, since he could not know what else he might have experienced in his remaining life. These questions end in an extreme sanctity-of-life position, and I have never heard them answered in principle. Any person's answer can only be, that is not the form of life I choose to live. This response seems to introduce a language of *autonomy,* even if that word is never used.

I think the issue is not autonomy, however, but its cousin, *authenticity.* I prefer authenticity because, as I will suggest, it implies a dialogic relation among persons rather than the opposition of my rights to your rights that autonomy talk often lapses into when autonomy counts in practice. In clinical grand rounds I hear autonomy talk as an inevitably dead end, and I seek another word that will allow the dialogue to continue between those who think differently about the same stories.

The preeminent contemporary philosopher of authenticity is Charles Taylor. Here is Taylor describing the version of the self that developed in Romanticism and pervades contemporary self-reflections:

> Herder put forward the idea that each of us has an original way of being human. Each person has his or her own "measure" is his way of putting it. The idea entered very deep into modern consciousness. It is also new. Before the eighteenth century no one thought that the differences between human beings had this kind of moral significance. There is a certain way of being human that is *my* way. I am called upon to live my life in this way, and not in imitation of anyone else's. But this gives a new importance to being true to myself. If I am not, I miss the point of my life, I miss what being human is for *me.*[14]

Taylor underscores the importance that Dworkin notes about *how* we die. Because it is all too possible, in the post-Romantic world, to miss the point of one's life, the decision Dworkin suggests becomes crucial: might the point of my life still be forthcoming and does my life depend on staying alive so that I can grasp this point? Or alternatively, might the manner of my death diminish the point of that life; is it crucial to the point of my life to die a certain way, or at least to avoid dying other ways? For example, my uncle and my grandfather certainly took it to be important to the points of their lives that they died at home rather than in an intensive care unit. Others may feel it necessary to die in the fullest possession of their faculties and able to respond to their loved ones, rather than dying in what palliative-care workers call "terminal sedation." Still others may consider it crucial to live to the last moment medical technology can achieve, in whatever comatose condition technology imposes.[15]

What makes these decisions matters of authenticity rather than autonomy? Taylor goes on to argue that in another respect modernity did not follow Herder, who undervalued people's social being. For Herder, my discovery of "my own original way of being. . . . cannot be socially derived but must be inwardly generated."[16] Taylor proposes that "there is no such thing as inward generation. . . . My discovering my identity doesn't mean that I work it out in isolation but that I negotiate it through dialogue, partly overt, partly internalized, with others."[17] In this description I hear my own experience represented. I have been trying to suggest through my family stories how I have been in dialogue with others about identity and dying since I was fairly young, as I believe many if not most people are. Any of my future decisions between the alternative values Dworkin poses—the value of life to come versus the value of not living that future—will be extensions of that dialogue, in which I now involve my children. The issue in these decisions is not so much my autonomy but this more dialogic quality, my authenticity.

The way I draw the distinction is that autonomy is an a priori value; my autonomy must be respected by virtue of my being human. Authenticity, by contrast, depends on what Taylor calls recognition. Recognition is a perpetual process: "[the self] doesn't enjoy this recognition a priori. It has to win it through exchange, and it can fail."[18] At any point in this process of dialogue, authenticity can fail. Autonomy, being a priori, cannot fail in the same way. Others can refuse to grant me my autonomy, but that denial is an unfortunate contingency of my situation—I've fallen among brutes—not a failure of autonomy per se.

Authenticity constantly risks failing because it always requires others to keep building it up—again, it is not a priori. Taylor emphasizes "how much an original identity needs and is vulnerable to the recognition given or withheld by significant others. It is not surprising that in the culture of authenticity, relationships are seen as the key loci of self-discovery and self-confirmation."[19] Nor is it surprising that many people in this culture of authenticity find their thinking supported and articulated by Levinas. His attention to the primordial importance of the dialogic relation with the other reflects the contemporary self's dependence on and vulnerability to the recognition of others.

So not autonomy but rather authenticity, resting as it does on recognition achieved through dialogue. Dworkin's dramaturgical metaphor of dying as the final scene of a play can now be unpacked and extended. Our dying is "intensified, under a special spotlight," because it is our last occasion for recognition and thus the last, maybe best, affirmation that I truly had an identity. What do these abstractions look like at the bedside of the dying person? The poet and physician Rafael Campo describes one of his patients, dying of AIDS, who is intubated at his own request, and the consequences of that decision:

> As we sedated him (because he still contained so much life at that critical moment that he was able to fight the respirator), I watched his face change. He had lost his language: the endotracheal tube by anatomical necessity passes through the vocal cords in connecting the respirator to the airspaces of the lungs, thereby taking away one's ability to speak.
>
> I am still not sure whether what he needed more during those last few days of his life was to speak or to breathe. The pneumonia that had made it so difficult for him to breathe on his own progressed rapidly. . . . His fever climbed. We had given him a chance to live longer . . . but at the cost of his last words. He died without his last words.[20]

Campo suggests that one way we can miss the point of our lives is to die without our last words and the full participation in dialogue that these words represent. This dying man's family and friends continue to reach out to him in words and gestures, but his crucial participation in what should be a dialogue with them is restricted to nonverbal responses, themselves restricted by sedation. Any recognition this dying man received could only be partial since he could not respond in the speech that is our singular human gift. Perhaps his extended life allowed him to have experiences that redeemed the imposition of silence, but Campo fears that the cost—the imposition of silence—may have been too high. This story would not bear reporting in the "ethics" literature; the intubation went according to all the conventions of informed consent and standard practice. Campo points beyond formalities to a deeper ethical issue: the physician's sense of responsibility to the voice of his patient echoes Levinas's ethical demand of the face of the other.

Because our identities depend on recognition achieved through dialogue, it is not only the dying man's authenticity that is at risk in Campo's story. Equally at risk are the authenticity of his lover and of his family, because they lose what they needed to hear from him as he was dying. Equally at risk is Campo's own authenticity. As the physician who can do so much—tubes can be inserted, antibiotics can be infused—but ultimately so little, he also needs forgiveness and affirmation. His authenticity depends on his patient being able to thank him, to tell him he did his best, that it's all right how it's ending.

I want to suggest two friendly amendments to the account I have derived from Dworkin and Taylor of why *how* we die matters so much. Campo's story illustrates that the culture of authenticity places preeminent importance on the *body* as the site on which conflicts of recognition are enacted. What is at issue is the body of the dying man: the body's respiration, its infections, its speech. To unpack Dworkin's concatenation of terms in his subtitle, in a culture of authenticity it is no coincidence that matters of individual freedom find their flash points where control of the body is most at issue: the pregnant body in the abortion controversy and the dying body in the euthanasia controversy. We negotiate recognition and authenticity about bodies and with bodies. The body is where the inward meets the social. The dialogue through which recognition is achieved is embodied: it is carried out by bodies—their gestures, expressions, and capacities for touch and presence—and its topic and controversy are the proper use of bodies. Dying, as a crisis of recognition and authenticity, is about what we do or refuse to do with our bodies, what we allow or refuse to allow to be done to the bodies of others. Responses to euthanasia requests are not responses of minds to arguments but responses of bodies to bodies.

My second amendment is the suggestion that perhaps, in an increasing proportion of lives, the sort of narrative presupposed by Dworkin and Taylor is too linear. The popular imagination of narrative may well be shifting from causal sequence—one life event follows another in the sense of being sequential to the earlier event—to hypertext.[21] In the computer milieu of hypertext, any textual configuration offers a variety of options for the next site to be visited; the "reader" thus has a new freedom to create the desired narrative by pursuing whichever "links" are chosen. Thus how one got to a particular point in the narrative becomes far less important than the choice of where to go next; that choice is remarkably unconstrained by past choices. The other relevant feature of hypertext is that one travels through the narrative in virtual time, limited only by the speed of the machine. The transitional spaces between sites disappears. Hypertext is the genie that turns wishes into reality, at least virtual reality.

Best guesses are that about 115 million Americans use the Internet, with that number increasing daily. No one could say when the mass of users becomes sufficiently critical for the hypertext environment to enter into ordinary narrative expectation, but I suspect that hypertext—or its simpleminded cousin, television channel-surfing—already affects many people's sense of narrative. Thus we are living increasingly in a hypertext culture of authenticity in which people expect to be able to control the narrative direction in unprecedented ways, and they expect to move from one narrative possibility to another without traversing intermediate stages. Applied to the process of dying, these expectations have significant consequences.

Yet even before Moses came down from the mountain, society was interested in when its citizens shorten each other's lives, and even in a world of hypertext, law and policy are invoked when assistance is sought in dying. Ultimately I want to leave the choice of assistance pretty much to the judgment of those present, as they respond to the face of the dying person. But no one responds in isolation. Those at the bedside are part of a society that tells stories praising some ways of acting, tolerating others, and castigating still others. How people at the bedside will be moved to act is certainly influenced—though never quite determined—by the arguments and principles represented in those stories. I am less interested in regulating action at the end of life than in recommending some stories and principles rather than others.

Before advancing several of the arguments that seem useful, let me qualify the issue of euthanasia. Although advocates of legalized assisted suicide often speak of a "right to die," this is not—or is very rarely—what is actually advocated. What they advocate is the right to seek and receive assistance in dying without the assistant being threatened by legal prosecution. From this minimal starting point, proposals proliferate about who might assist others in dying, what sorts of requests (and from whom) should be allowed, and what safeguards might protect people from unwanted termination of their lives. The advocacy of such proposals usually pays lip service to some notion of "right," but I find talk about rights less often occurs as people actually live through the work of providing assistance in dying.[22] The lived situations proceed through dialogues about whose life means what to whom and negotiations over when that meaning ceases and the time comes to let go. These dialogues exemplify Taylor's ideas about the primacy of recognition and the need to achieve it continually. At their best, they are occasions when each person honors the authenticity of the other most fully.

What arguments can address these situations, and what principles can guide people in them? First, what matters to people making decisions about dying is nicely stated by ethicist Barry Hoffmaster when he writes that people in any illness dilemma "know they have a hard, perhaps tragic decision to make, and they want to do the best or the right thing."[23] The problem people face is deciding what the best thing is; they confront Dworkin's choice (rephrased in Taylor's vocabulary): is the best thing to imagine that the point of one's life could still be forthcoming and thus to preserve life as long as possible lest that experience be missed, or is the point to avoid the pain, degradation, and drain on social resources that diminish a life which has already achieved all it can? End-of-life decisions are made in the same uncertainty that pervades life at any stage, but because this is *the end,* that uncertainty assumes massive, possibly tragic, force. But people must act. Disease and treatments will proceed, and not to intervene in them is itself to act.

Ethicist William May takes Hoffmaster's argument a step further. For May, "The appropriate question is not 'What are we going to do about it?' but 'How does one rise to the occasion?'"[24] People *cannot know* what they or those they love might still experience if life is prolonged, or what suffering prolonged life might inflict. Decisions can never be judged right or wrong, because it can never be known what would have happened otherwise. But those involved in the decision can feel enhanced or diminished by who they became as they participated in the dying person's own story, and as that participation became part of their own stories. Thus the question is not what they *did* but who they *were,* as is well stated in May's idea of rising to the occasion.

Rising to the occasion also emphasizes that people do not make specific decisions around end-of-life issues so much as they enter into processes in which decisions evolve incrementally. In practice, end-of-life decisions are rarely either/or but more often require asking *how much* of life can there be before the oppressions of dying become too much. The subjects of these decisions are people whose lives have already been "artificially" prolonged by modern medicine and who are not deciding whether they will die but, so far as these things can be controlled, when and how. As May writes, making these decisions requires that people rise to the occasion. But Taylor's work requires adding that few people rise to occasions alone. We rise to the occasion in response to others and in dialogue with others. We measure our rising to the occasion by the recognition others offer in response to our participation in decisions we make together. Our sense of doing the right thing depends on others.

Crucial as I think it is to recognize that participating in end-of-life decisions is better described not as making a decision but as rising to the occasion, this recognition offers little guidance on the acceptability of assisted suicide. Instead the moral issue shifts. I am far less troubled by the prospect of legalized euthanasia than I am by the possibility of death becoming mundane. The assimilation of death to institutional routines encourages indifference to death at a moment that requires people to rise to the occasion. This indifference can develop—it *is* developing—equally where assistance in dying is permitted and prohibited.[25] One reason for the demand for assisted suicide is the fear of dying among indifferent strangers; the complementary objection to legalization of assisted suicide is that it will encourage indifference to death.

Rising to the occasion means, first and foremost, holding each person's death as a unique and sacred event. If we fail to treat death with honor and awe, then it seems to matter little whether we actively assist in dying or not. So my first principle is that it matters less whether death occurs by refusal of treatment, withdrawal of treatment, or active assistance. What matters is whether the people involved in that death rise to the occasion, and this rising is a dialogic process, measured in mutual recognition.

The second argument I find relevant to people's actual decisions is that some dying people can feel forced to take their own lives sooner than they wanted if they do not have the assurance of reliable and legal assistance in dying. I ask myself when I might be willing to assist another person in dying, and one answer is when that person could convince me that without the assurance of my help, she or he would die sooner. Many illnesses present people with the prospect of becoming either physically or mentally incapable of taking their own lives by the time they want to do so. I take a lesson from stories of people who, once assured they could get assistance when they needed it, went on to die "natural" deaths.[26]

Complementary to this argument in favor of legalized assisted suicide is the poignant reflection of physician Timothy Quill on his patient "Diane," to whom he prescribed sleeping pills that she eventually used in her suicide. Quill writes:

> [T]he only regret I have about the care which I gave Diane herself is that she was alone in her death. The case [against Quill] was dismissed by the grand jury in part because of this tragic fact. . . . Diane was a brave person who faced death squarely, but it violates every principle of humane care of the dying if she felt she had to be alone at the end because of our laws. As a physician, I make the solemn promise to my dying patients that I will not abandon them no matter where their illness may take them.[27]

People do not rise to the occasion by leaving the dying to commit suicide earlier than they wish in order to be certain they do not die in conditions they fear. Nor do they abandon patients and loved ones to die alone. The fundamental principle here is the human need for mutual *presence* and the care that is expressed by being present to the dying. The challenge to law is not to disrupt that presence, as the law did when Diane felt she had to die alone in order to shield her physician and her family from prosecution.

If my first principle, the need for dying to be a time of rising to the occasion through dialogue and recognition, is neutral toward legal assistance of suicide, then my second principle (about the need for a continuing presence) is permissive. My third principle suggests a caution about legalization. Again I turn to William May, who in his recent work differentiates between the ethics of individual acts of conscience in assisting others to die and the ethics of social policy toward the dying.[28] Against the legalization of assistance in dying May writes: "To put it bluntly, a country has not earned the moral option to kill for mercy in good conscience if it hasn't already sustained and supported life with compassion and mercy. Active euthanasia could become a final solution for handling the problem of the aged poor."[29] I first heard this argument from a physician as we stood in the corridor of a decrepit, overcrowded veterans' hospital on the decaying outskirts of a major American city. In that setting it was all too easy to imagine patients being told that if they did not like their care, they could be helped to die.

May acknowledges that he can "imagine rare circumstances in which I hope I would have the courage to kill for mercy," but he believes that "hard cases do not always make good law." He rejects relaxing current legal prohibitions and asserts personal responsibility, and risk, as the solution to hard cases: "Were I ever to find myself in a situation in which I felt that I must euthanize someone, I would think it best not to seek advance legal protection but to proceed as best I could and eventually throw myself on the mercy of the court."[30] Like most arguments for or against legalization, this one has an easy answer, and an equally easy response to that answer. The answer is to ask what happens to those who want assistance in dying but lack a friend willing to take the risks May might take. The response is that if they lack a friend of May's principles, are they not at the greatest risk of being victimized by a system of more permissive euthanasia? There is no easy exit from that circle of arguments.

If we have not, in either America or Canada, "earned the moral option to kill for mercy in good conscience," is there a way people could ask for help in dying without knowing they were forcing their loved ones and physicians eventually to throw themselves on the mercy of the court? Because if that mercy is not uncertain, then there is no point in having legal prohibitions.

Here I turn finally to law and to the role courts might play in euthanasia decisions. I find it difficult to imagine that legalization of euthanasia, with whatever safeguards, will lead to a more just and compassionate society. As we move toward increasing (because it is already happening) rationing (by whatever euphemism we call it) of health care, this seems a precarious time to throw legalized assisted suicide into the mix. Thus I agree with May that assisted suicide should not be legalized, but that hardly makes the issue go away. On the contrary, in the culture that made *Final Exit* a best-seller and that has brought the assisted-suicide issue to close referendum votes in two states and victory in a third, prohibition can be expected to generate more covert acts of euthanasia, an undesired consequence that hardly benefits patients and families, professionals, or what legal scholars fondly call the "rule of law."

Perhaps because I take May's argument so seriously, I also believe that for the same reasons society has not earned the moral option of mercy killing, it has not earned the right to make a priori judgments on individuals and their families who hasten death as the best way to play out the last act of their lives. Precisely because Canadian and American societies do fail so many tests of compassion, we are poorly placed to judge those who seek their own, most compassionate way to die. As society affords people fewer resources to care for the dying, it has less moral basis for judging how they die. In an age of persistent vegetative states and criteria for brain death, "dying" is increasingly negotiated and incremental. The moment between death and what precipitates death can seem arbitrary indeed; here I refer back to my father's blanket usage of "euthanasia" to refer to deaths including refusal of treatment. As the lines drawn by professionals get finer, people draw their own lines.

If I could design a policy toward euthanasia, it would stop far short of a blanket acceptance of mercy killing yet go further than requiring those who assist another's death to throw themselves on the mercy of the court. What I would develop are possibilities for diversion outside the courts, much as family law matters are sometimes diverted to mediation.[31] I would like to imagine concerned parties—dying persons, their loved ones and friends, and medical caregivers, including hospice workers—being able to present themselves for mediation of a request for assistance in dying. The value of imagining a mediation system has less to do with whether it actually evolves—though I think it might be workable—and more to do with jarring our thinking out of the worn-out dichotomies of legal *versus* illegal, right to die *versus* antieuthanasia, personal autonomy *versus* state interest, and so forth. These dichotomies fail to represent the complexity of these decisions adequately, they suppress people's desire to "rise to the occasion," and they substitute the banal response of taking sides.

The premises and possibilities of mediation would be (a) that all concerned want to do the right thing; that they want to rise to the occasion, but (b) that the occasion presents both legal difficulties and divergent opinions as to what is right, yet (c) that with sufficient and impartial reorientation to the interest of the dying person, a consensus can be reached. Mediation for the dying would be more complicated than divorce or custody mediation because fewer outcomes would be up for discussion and thus there would be fewer openings for parties to compromise on one point in exchange for gaining what they want elsewhere. Nor is it self-evident who ought to be at the table; who participates in the decision making may itself require mediation. Time is also a problem; the onset of pain and the need for treatment might prevent protracted discussion. But mediation would also be simpler because, again, there are fewer issues to resolve. Most consequentially, the presumption of each person's goodwill and everyone's dedication to the common goal of a "good death" for the dying person would more often be justified. Certainly the death of one person can crystallize conflicts among family members, but in general mediators would confront less acrimony and suspicion than couples bring to divorce mediation.

Mediators might come from various professional backgrounds, as divorce mediators currently do. The crucial qualification would be that mediators be open to all options for the dying, so that they could promote what Jürgen Habermas calls communicative action: "making what everyone could want in this situation plausible."[32] What counts in communicative action is that each person be heard without constraint and that the hearing proceed long enough that those who may still disagree could, despite their disagreement, entertain each speaker's view as plausible; each should come to respect the other person's views. For some, rising to the occasion will ultimately mean consenting to a course of action they disagree with because they realize and accept the sincerity of others' feelings.

The crucial point is that mediation would nurture dialogue and minimize adversarial positions. The mediator would keep it before all participants that the decision being made is an unwanted, even a tragic one, but that the situation demands a decision. The objective would be to satisfy the dying person first, then the family, and finally the medical workers. If the eventual decision involved criminal acts, the mediator would ask a court for dispensation from the assisted-suicide laws.

I propose this compromise between the law we now have and the law often proposed by advocates of legalized euthanasia with the hope and expectation that requests for assistance in dying would be rare. Frequent mediation might signal the need for other social changes in the care of the dying, but policymakers would then have the record of past mediations that would provide data to guide reforms.

Mediation could address the objection of hospice workers that every request for assistance in dying is in reality a cry for help and that what is required is better care, not euthanasia.[33] Mediation could make referrals for additional care. If recommended resources were not made available, mediation would be a social forum to provide official notice—and publicity—of that shortfall. But mediation would also be a venue for disagreeing with hospice workers. Not all people want to die a lingering death, possibly heavily sedated, even if the best palliative care is available to them. They and their surrogates could make this case in mediation, with the safeguard that the presence of an impartial and official third party would forestall retribution in the form of withdrawn care.

Mediation would, by intention, be far slower than simply obtaining medical second (or third) opinions attesting to the competence and determination of the person seeking euthanasia. If physicians wanted to participate in a mediation, they would have to find the time to show up and listen to the dying and their families. But physicians are not necessary to the process: various right-to-die societies already have volunteers who, given legal access to appropriate drugs, could assist in dying. Again, mediation would generate a formal record of who participated in assisted-suicide decisions.

Perhaps most important, mediation could recognize that dying is a *process*. Mediation encourages people to change their views as they hear each other, entertain each other's views as plausible, and explore options. Court processes are not set up to encourage parties to recognize the validity—as opposed to the potential effectiveness in court—of each other's positions. Courts may be at their best when the facts of a case are all available and worst when the situation remains in flux. Most important, courts set people apart as adversaries. The goal of mediation would be to nurture the values people share and produce a consensual decision from that shared core, not to declare one party's values right and the other's wrong. The most depressing talk I hear about *Glucksberg* involves references to who "won" and "lost." Nothing is more natural in an adversarial system, but nothing could be more counterproductive in clinical situations where people need care.

The question might be asked when a mediator would *not* be willing to take to a court a recommendation to permit assisted suicide. A simple answer is, when the mediator believes the dying person is being coerced or fails to understand all his or her options for care. But in most instances the question has the wrong emphasis. The reason for mediation is to avoid refusing requests, not because the bias of mediation is to permit euthanasia but because refusals indicate that mediation broke down. If mediation works, either the request for assistance will be withdrawn as new provisions of care are offered, or objections to the request will be withdrawn once the request is made fully plausible to those who objected.

But what if these outcomes are not achieved? Mediators are not paralegal adjudicators; they facilitate communication, not judge people's cases. Mediators do not recommend a decision to the court so much as certify that a process has reached or failed to reach a consensus. I emphasize that in this consensus some participants might still regret what *may* be done, since diseased bodies often go their own way, but each participant agrees to respect others' intentions. The outcome is the participants' own; thus there are no *a priori* criteria for accepting or rejecting requests. Where no consensus is achieved, the mediator would confront two opposing dangers: forcing the dying person to commit suicide prematurely or alone because assistance is denied or sanctioning an assisted suicide that trivializes dying. But only through the accumulation of mediation experience can we understand what sort of processes lead to these unhappy alternatives and what additional resources need to be brought to these situations. Again, a society that does not make these resources available has no right to judge how people evaluate their own circumstances.

To ask when mediators would refuse requests for assistance in dying is to ask how mediation will solve the assisted-suicide problem. Mediation is not a solution because dying is not a problem to be solved. We never know if we have done it right, but we can recognize each other as having been all we could be in the circumstances. Mediation could be a venue for helping people rise to the occasion.

* * *

"Dad," whispered Philip Roth, "I'm going to have to let you go." I was with my wife when she had to say this to her mother. At such moments people truly have to rise to the occasion, and they need others to recognize that what they do honors their own authenticity because it honors the dying person, so far as possible in circumstances everyone would have avoided, if they could.

At such moments the relationships that allow people to rise to the occasion must be nurtured, not fractured. Wherever the illness leads, the presence of loved ones and physicians must be sustained, not withdrawn. Many of us will have to let loved ones go. I hope that in my own future letting go does not involve hastening death, either someone else's or my own. But what "hastening death" means becomes an increasingly troubled question as innovations in medical technology create new variations and complications: what does it mean to hasten death when life has already been artificially prolonged?

It is an easy prediction that as individuals and as a society we will have increasing difficulty finding the balance between sustaining life so long as its point can still be realized and allowing life to end before authenticity is degraded. No one should be forced to act alone in these situations. The issue of euthanasia calls on law to abandon its paradigm of adversarial litigation and learn to facilitate dialogues. What counts is responding to the face of the other: the primordial ethical demand to recognize the suffering person as my neighbor. In responding to the issue of euthanasia, possibly law can reinvent itself, to the benefit not only of the dying but of all society.

NOTES

1. Anatole Broyard, *Intoxicated by My Illness and Other Writings on Life and Death* 20 (Clarkson Potter, 1993).
2. Arthur W. Frank, *At the Will of the Body: Reflections on Illness* (Houghton Mifflin, 1991).
3. The "Case Stories" series published in *Second Opinion: Health, Faith, Ethics* (January 1994 to July 1995) and continued in *Making the Rounds in Health, Faith, and Ethics* (September 25, 1995 to September 23, 1996). A total of fourteen stories were published, along with one story I solicited and commented on before my editorship began (January 1992).
4. Arthur W. Frank, *The Wounded Storyteller: Body, Illness, and Ethics* (University of Chicago Press, 1995).
5. For many examples of this response, and how they originate in a series of personal experiences, see Marilynne Seguin, *A Gentle Death* (Key Porter Books, 1994).
6. Sean Hand, ed., *The Levinas Reader* 82–83 (Blackwell, 1989). For one application of Levinas to issues of health, see Stan van Hooft, *Health and Subjectivity*, 1 Health 23–36 (1997).
7. *The Levinas Reader* at 83.
8. Ibid. at 83.
9. On the contrast between lay and professional discourses of ethics see Arthur W. Frank, *The Language of Principle and the Language of Experience in the Euthanasia Debate,* in Ronald P. Hamel & Edwin R. DuBose, eds., *Must We Suffer Our Way to Death? Cultural and Theological Perspective on Death by Choice* (Southern Methodist University Press, 1996).
10. Ronald Dworkin, *Life's Dominion: An Argument About Abortion, Euthanasia, and Individual Freedom* 209 (Knopf, 1993).
11. Ibid.
12. Ibid.
13. Ibid.
14. Charles Taylor, *The Malaise of Modernity,* 28–29 (Anansi, 1991).
15. For such a case, see Nancy Neveloff Dubler & David Nimmons, *Ethics on Call* 147–51 (Harmony Books, 1992).
16. Taylor, *The Malaise of Modernity* at 47.
17. Ibid.
18. Ibid at 48.
19. Ibid at 49.
20. Rafael Campo, *The Poetry of Healing* 168 (Norton, 1997).
21. I owe my thoughts about hypertext to Martha Faith McLellan, *The Electronic Narrative of Illness.* Ph.D. dissertation, University of Texas Medical Branch at Galveston, December 1997.

22. For an empirical study of assisted suicide in practice, see Lonny Shavelson, *A Chosen Death: The Dying Confront Assisted Suicide* (Simon & Schuster, 1995). Shavelson is a physician and journalist, and he describes five different deaths in which assistance was an issue. His book is also interesting for his telling of the family stories that shaped his choice to write about euthanasia and become deeply involved in these five people's deaths.

23. Barry Hoffmaster, *Can Ethnography Save the Life of Medical Ethics?*, 35 Social Science & Medicine 1426 (1992). See also Richard Zaner, *Troubled Voices: Stories of Illness and Ethics* 1, 148 (Pilgrim Press, 1993).

24. William F. May, *The Patient's Ordeal* 131 (Indiana University Press, 1991); see also ibid. at 4.

25. For a case study of institutional indifference to the dying and euthanasia as a response, see Arthur W. Frank, *Not in Pain, but Still Suffering,* Christian Century, 860–61 (Oct 7, 1992).

26. For one such story see Shavelson, *A Chosen Death* at 35–67 (cited in note 22). Shavelson concludes, "And yet for the majority of people who are dying, it will be sufficient merely to know that assistance is available. They will rest assured of comfort as they progress to their natural deaths, perhaps never needing the fatal dose that is ready." Id. at 66.

27. Timothy E. Quill, *Death and Dignity: Making Choices and Taking Charge* 21–22 (Norton, 1993).

28. William F. May, *Testing the Medical Covenant: Active Euthanasia and Health Care Reform* (Eerdmans, 1996).

29. Ibid. at 28.

30. Ibid. at 48–49.

31. See, among other sources, Jay Folberg & Alison Taylor, *Mediation: A Comprehensive Guide to Resolving Conflicts Without Litigation* (Jossey Bass, 1984); John M. Haynes, *Divorce Mediation: A Practical Guide for Therapists and Counselors* (Springer, 1981); Howard Irving, *Divorce Mediation: The Rational Alternative to the Adversary System* (Personal Library Publishers, 1980); John Allen Lemmon, *Family Mediation Practice* (Free Press, 1985); and Donald T. Saposnek, *Mediating Child Custody Disputes* (Jossey-Bass, 1983).

32. Jürgen Habermas, "Theory and Politics: A Discussion with Herbert Marcuse, Jürgen Habermas, Heinz Lubasz and Telman Spengler," 38 *Telos* 124, 137 (1978).

33. The most recent expression of this argument is Ira Byock, *Dying Well: The Prospect for Growth at the End of Life* (Riverhead Books, 1997). For a response to Byock's earlier statements on the preference of palliative care over euthanasia, see Shavelson, *A Chosen Death* at 217–19 (cited in note 22).

CHAPTER 11   **Concluding Thoughts: Bioethics in the Language of the Law**

Carl E. Schneider

> Scarcely any political question arises in the United States that is not resolved, sooner or later, into a judicial question. Hence all parties are obliged to borrow in their daily controversies, the ideas, and even the language, peculiar to judicial proceedings. . . . The language of the law thus becomes, in some measure, a vulgar tongue; the spirit of the law, which is produced in the schools and courts of justice, gradually penetrates beyond their walls into the bosom of society, where it descends to the lowest classes, so that at last the whole people contract the habits and the tastes of the judicial magistrate.
>
> Alexis de Tocqueville, *Democracy in America*

What happens when the language of the law becomes a vulgar tongue? What happens, more particularly, when parties to bioethical disputes are obliged to borrow in their daily controversies, the ideas, and even the language, peculiar to judicial proceedings? How suited are the habits and tastes and thus the language of the judicial magistrate to the political, and more particularly, the bioethical, questions of our time?

We must ask these questions because, as the incomparable Tocqueville foresaw, it has become American practice to resolve political—and moral—questions into judicial questions. We now reverently refer to the Supreme Court as the great arbiter of American moral life, as performing a "prophetic function," as expressing what "we stand for as a people." Lower courts, as *L.A. Law* wants to teach us, likewise are considered forums for the apotheosis of social and moral reasoning. Certainly bioethical issues in our time have been presented to the public in legal terms, in cases ranging from *Quinlan* to *Cruzan* to *Glucksberg*, in the constitutional principles of *Roe v Wade*, in referenda in Washington, California, Oregon, and Michigan, in the law's travails with Jack Kevorkian, in the tribulations and trials of Baby Doe and Baby M.

Professional and public discourse about bioethics has been primarily concerned, I think, with analyzing the moral issues each bioethical problem presents. Law has contributed to that endeavor by generating vivid and pressing instantiations of many of those issues, by discussing them—in part—in moral terms, and by proffering means of resolving them. I want to

---

This is a slightly adapted version of an article that originally appeared in 24 Hastings Center Report 16 (July/Aug 1994).

explore some of these contributions. But I also want to argue that the law's gifts should be cautiously received. For the law has goals that go beyond the purposes of professional and public debate over bioethical issues, and those goals peculiarly shape the moral terms the law employs and specially alter the direction legal discourse takes.

Law is essentially a device of social regulation. This is its boon and bane as a language of bioethics. As boon, law's attractions are two. First, it provides a highly developed, conceptually fertile, analogically abundant, carefully precise, systematically disciplined language for thinking about bioethical issues, a rich language Holmes called "the witness and external deposit of our moral life."[1] Second, law provides a tool not just for talk, but for action. As bane, law's disadvantages are also two. First, its language is often inapt. Second, it regularly fails to achieve its desired effect, and indeed sometimes seems to have hardly any effect at all.

Let us begin with law's two attractions as a vehicle for considering bioethical issues. First, because law draws on centuries of experience with social regulation, it furnishes a highly articulated method and language for analyzing social problems. The method, in the United States, is the common law process. In it, courts construct legal principles incrementally, by evaluating the facts of one case at a time, and legislatures respond intermittently with reforms and reconsiderations of their own. One might think of the common law method as Rawls's reflective equilibrium in action. It brings to bear long-nurtured principles on emerging problems, and thus is an appealing way of dealing with as new and febrile a field as bioethics. It is also a method particularly congenial to medicine and applied ethics, since, like those fields, it relies centrally on cases.

This almost-dialectical common law method has over the last millennium elaborated a language of social regulation. That language includes a vocabulary not just of terms, but of conceptual, organizing ideas. Three sets of ideas have formed idioms that particularly influence bioethical debate and that will repay our attention: law's dispute-resolution function, its facilitative function, and its rights talk.

One of law's oldest goals is to help resolve disputes among citizens. American law does this partly through the law of torts. When one citizen injures another, the law may—although it does not always do so—offer the remedy of a tort suit. This is the legal remedy when one person strikes another with his fist, runs over another with his car, sells another a defective product, or injures another in the practice of a profession. The tort action provides a means of settling the dispute between the injurer and the victim and of restoring the victim to his prior well-being. But by setting the substantive terms for resolving disputes, tort law also establishes a standard of behavior which—one hopes—may shape future conduct so that injuries are deterred, disputes are forestalled, and, even, citizens are induced to behave better.

The language of torts provides a temptingly convenient framework for thinking about those bioethical issues that arise where one person has injured another. In particular, tort law has in recent decades seemed a promising response where doctors have abused their power over patients. Thus, building on tort doctrines of malpractice, the law of informed consent arose to achieve three bioethical goals: to help resolve disputes over injuries caused by a doctor's failure to inform a patient adequately; to provide a way, however unsatisfactory, of recompensing the injured patient; and—more ambitiously—to improve the way doctors in general treat their patients.

The law tries to conduce good in yet another way—through what I call the facilitative function. The most familiar example of this function is the law of contracts, which allows people not just to reach whatever agreements about their affairs they themselves desire, but to deploy the law's power to make those agreements binding and thus predictable and reliable. The facilitative function also lets individuals recruit the law's force to give binding effect to their personal preferences. Two common examples of this are the will and the power of attorney, documents that permit people to dispose of their property as they wish or to allocate that power to someone else.

As bioethics began to hunt for ways of enhancing the power of patients, the idiom of the facilitative function attractively presented itself. Some people have, for example, sought to improve the relationship between doctors and patients by analyzing it in contractual terms. (This effort has not succeeded because, I think, of a classic problem with contract law: contracts tend to ratify preexisting differences in power.) More successful have been analogies to the law of wills and the law of agency (the law providing for the power of attorney). Out of those analogies have arisen the living will and the durable power of attorney, devices that extend the authority of patients to control their medical treatment when they can no longer think and act for themselves.

Finally, as Cardozo said, "The great ideals of liberty and equality are preserved against the assaults of opportunism, the expediency of the passing hour, the erosion of small encroachments, the scorn and derision of those who have no patience with general principles, by enshrining them in constitutions. . . ."[2] This process calls on the language of rights, a language that has achieved a potence and preeminence in the United States that may be unmatched anywhere in the world. That language is woefully marred by our tendency to muddle moral rights, statutory rights, and constitutional rights. (In *Glucksberg,* the Court held there is no constitutional right to assisted suicide, but in Oregon there is a statutory right to it in some circumstances, and everywhere there may be a moral right.) Nevertheless, constitutional rights are undoubtedly the trump cards of our legal system. Once recognized, they massively prevail against statutes that infringe on them. What is more, they have not just a legal, but also a special social and moral, authority.

Rights discourse has seemed delightfully suited to that engine of bioethical thought, the doctrine of autonomy. Thus proponents of one set of bioethical positions have enlisted the doctrine of constitutional rights with overwhelming effect in the law of reproduction generally and abortion specifically.

Because the debate over that law came to be phrased in rights terms, its language, tone, content, and result have been transformed. And proponents of another bioethical position have similarly labored, with some profit, to transpose the discourse about euthanasia into a debate over a—constitutional—right to die.

In America, then, the language of the law lies easy on the tongue. It abounds in productive principles and illuminating analogies. It provides familiar and powerful tools for treating many social problems, including perhaps most bioethical issues. And to a truly notable extent, bioethical discourse in the United States has been phrased in legal terms, has been conducted in courts and legislatures, and has produced legal reforms. But alluring as the law's language may be, it carries drawbacks and limits that are not always perceived or understood. Like the attractions of that language, these drawbacks arise from law's status as a means of social regulation.

First, the idioms of the law are often inapt. They have grown up in response to needs for social regulation. But the systemic imperatives that have shaped the law are not always a good pattern for bioethical discourse. For example, the law of torts is centrally a way of compensating victims of an injury. But bioethicists, noting that tort law has some broader aims, have hoped that the law of informed consent would not just provide a remedy for specific failures to inform patients, but would fundamentally reform the doctor-patient relationship. Despite its apparent appositeness, however, tort law is poorly suited to this ambitious goal.

For one thing, the language of torts is the language of wrongs. That language states only a minimal level of duties; it is not the language of aspiration. A doctor may meet its requirements through quite mechanical and sadly unsatisfactory routines that mock the solicitous dialogue bioethicists imagine for doctors. Furthermore, the law (generally speaking) penalizes the breach of even those minimal duties only sporadically—when a patient has actually been injured by that breach (and injured enough to justify the expenses and misery of a suit). In short, for these reasons and many others, the law of torts particularly and the law generally are not good at regulating relationships—particularly relationships that are instinct with intimacy. The law that tries most directly to do so—family law—is perhaps the sorriest of law's enterprises. Thus the attempt to improve the relationship between doctor and patient through tort law may be an example of what Judith Shklar disparagingly calls "the structuring of all possible human relations into the form of claims and counterclaims under established rules."[3]

A second important drawback of analyzing bioethical problems in legal terms is that law is a *system* of social regulation, a system whose parts should mesh to form a (reasonably) coherent body of precedent and principle. Jurists have worried for centuries that changing one area will unexpectedly or undesirably affect another area. Such concerns probably help explain the Supreme Court's decision in *Glucksberg*. That case might have been decided differently except for *Roe v Wade*,[4] which is, of course, the case establishing a constitutional right to an abortion. The Court has repeatedly reconsidered *Roe,* and several Justices clearly regret that the Court ever embogged itself in the jurisprudential and political quagmire of abortion and the questions of constitutional interpretation and federalism it raises. Whatever the moral appeal of the plaintiffs' right-to-die argument, accepting it would have reinvigorated *Roe* and its controversial answers to those questions. Thus even a Justice who found much to like in the plaintiffs' argument might have voted against it for fear of its systemic implications.[5]

This point can be put somewhat differently. Every judicial opinion looks forward as well as backward; every opinion is both based on precedent and itself becomes precedent. Yet a court cannot easily anticipate what kind of precedent an opinion will become, for the cases and arguments it will govern are cloaked in the mists of the future. The resulting apprehension about the unforeseen consequences of each legal precedent is one reason slippery-slope arguments are so common and so convincing in law.

Accurately foreseeing consequences is particularly urgent in the context of the "privacy" rights that are at stake in *Glucksberg* and *Roe.* To maintain the vigor of those rights, the Court has made it structurally unlikely for a state to justify a statute that conflicts with them. This has introduced a crucial rigidity in the law: the Court has become reluctant to define interests as "rights" because the consequences of that decision are so severe. The more potent the doctrine of rights, then, the more reluctant the Court must be to employ it.

That reluctance is sharpened by yet another factor: Because a system of law demands a stable base of precedent, the Court will only rarely overrule a decision. And the Court's constitutional decisions are virtually immune to reversal by any other means. This increases the incentive for the Court to act cautiously in finding new constitutional rights.

Seen in this light, *Glucksberg* is not hard to understand. The Court faced several kinds of systemic pressures not to extend the privacy rights it had announced in *Roe,* and it had reason to be apprehensive about the slippery slope down which it might be sliding. In addition, it was dealing with a substantive question—euthanasia—in which the slippery-slope problem had long been acute, as to which thinking had changed with chastening speed, and whose future dimensions were forbiddingly murky. Thus, however the Justices may have assessed the ethical merits of the plaintiffs' position, whatever their views of good public policy, and however seductive the idiom of rights, they confronted strong systemic reasons not to find a right to die.

This leads us to a third limitation of thinking about bioethical problems in legal terms. Law is a system of social regulation, and social regulation is the art of the possible and the necessary. Further, law is a system confided to a specialized set of institutions with specialized capacities. For these reasons, there are often gaps in legal doctrine where those institutions have not dealt with an issue or have lacked the capacity to do so fully.

For example, the law of rights has historically flourished in one paradigmatic situation—where a single individual confronts the power of the state.

"'In such conflicts,'" as I once wrote, "'we are predisposed to favor the person, out of respect for his moral autonomy and human dignity.' That predisposition also rests on our assumption that the state can bear any risks of an incorrect decision better than the individual can."[6] But bioethics abounds in troubling situations where the conflict is not between one person and the state, but between two people, each with a claim against the other and each with a rights claim against the state. In these situations, our legal rights doctrine tells us little about how to choose.

Surrogate-mother contracts exemplify this problem. In the Baby M case, did Mr. Stern have a constitutional right to father a child through such an arrangement? Did Mrs. Whitehead have a constitutional right to raise Melissa, the child she had borne? Did Melissa have a constitutional right to a decision made in her best interests? Little in our blunt and limited doctrine of constitutional rights helps answer those questions.

In sum, in investigating the first advantage of law as a vehicle for bioethical thought, I have observed that bioethicists and the public commonly expect to discuss bioethical issues in primarily moral terms and, to a lesser extent, in terms of public policy. Law provides a language that can enrich that discussion. Yet I have been suggesting courts and legislatures must also employ a language shaped by the special exigencies of a legal system of social regulation.

We move now to study the second advantage of law as a language of bioethical discourse. Perhaps the most delightful thing about that language is that it is not just talk. Law is also a way of actively, directly trying to change the world. It is not the only way, it is not always the best way, but it has conspicuous attractions.

The first of those attractions is that law embodies an already established enforcement structure. Further, that structure is backed, ultimately, by society's fiercest instruments of coercion. For instance, the fear of criminal prosecution even today influences—and on some views, should influence—decisions about terminating medical treatment. And anti-abortionists feel precisely that it is wrong not to use the criminal law to prevent abortions.

But law is not just a structure of regulation backed by force. Law also enjoys moral authority. Laws are often obeyed because people believe they should obey the law. And people are subtly but truly influenced by the law's expressive capacity and by the social force acquired by institutions the law supports. This is, for instance, one defense of the law of informed consent: even though recalcitrant doctors may evade it, it symbolizes society's aspirations for medicine. That symbol over time, and taken with other legal and social measures, may gradually prevail in the minds and methods of doctors.

These concerns may help us understand why legislatures have been reluctant to follow the logic of the principle that patients have a right to refuse treatment toward the principle that patients have a right to the help of a doctor in committing suicide.[7] Even if legislators could see no moral difference between dying by refusing treatment and dying by taking the pills a doctor prescribed, legislators must worry about preserving inviolate in the public and medical mind the unbreachable rule: Thou shalt not kill. A rule embroidered with elaborately qualified and subtly phrased exceptions stands in danger of losing the moral force on which its enforcement relies.

The law is an appealing device for change for yet another reason—there are so many points of access to it. The law can be reached through the instruments of democracy and through litigation, all means available—in principle—to anyone. This helps explain why people trying to challenge, for instance, the institutional authority of medicine and the individual power of doctors have sought to speak in the voice of the law.

Despite these attractions, almost all laymen and too many lawyers grossly overestimate the law's effectiveness. Why does law so often fail to translate hopes into reality?

Once again, it is crucial that law is a system of social regulation. Bioethical reflection generally analyzes each case meticulously to produce the right result for that case. But a system of social regulation cannot trust each decision maker to do justice in each case. Nor can it tolerate the inconsistency and unpredictability of discretionary justice. In fact, a wisely considered and carefully formulated rule may produce the right result in more cases than the ad hoc efforts of individual decision makers. For all these reasons, justice may require that an agency of social regulation write rules.

Considerations of efficiency may lead to the same result. As Whitehead wonderfully wrote,

> It is a profoundly erroneous truism, repeated by copy-books and by eminent people when they are making speeches, that we should cultivate the habit of thinking about what we are doing. The precise opposite is the case. Civilization advances by extending the number of important operations which we can perform without thinking about them. Operations of thought are like cavalry charges in a battle— they are strictly limited in number, they require fresh horses, and must only be made at decisive moments.[8]

But of course, when you adopt a rule, you risk diminishing the chance of doing exact justice in every case, since rules by their nature sweep many cases under a single category. These are the problems the Washington legislature confronted in the statute tested in *Glucksberg*. That statute flatly forbade doctors to help their patients commit suicide. The legislature presumably calculated that allowing scope for discretion in such decisions was likelier to result in more "errors" than the rule it adopted. Similarly, some legislatures have concluded that a rule prohibiting surrogate-mother contracts will produce more good results than a series of discretionary decisions. But the cost of both rules is what might be widely regarded as wrong decisions, as the stories of the plaintiffs in *Glucksberg* suggest.

Rules have another drawback. They must be written clearly and comprehensibly enough that the people who actually need to apply them will be able to do so. This problem has plagued bioethics. It has infected attempts to define death, for example. And, to take another example, doctors have not unreasonably complained that the vague "reasonable patient" standard of tort law tells them deplorably little about their duties of informed consent.

In all these ways, then, the languages of the law have to give up something—and sometimes a great deal—in precision and in sensitivity to the moral and social contexts in which law is actually applied. But there is a further problem. One of the great truths about law is that, with unnerving frequency, it fails to achieve the effects intended for it, and sometimes quite fails to have any effect at all. Some of the most fascinating modern legal scholarship reminds lawyers how removed their talk is from the world's ken. That literature reveals that, to the lawyer's chagrin, businesses resist using contracts, ranchers do not know what rules of liability govern damage done by wandering cattle, suburbanites do not summon the law to resolve neighborhood disputes, engaged couples do not know the law governing how they will own property when they marry, citizens repeatedly reject the due process protections proffered them, and, what is worse, many of these people simply don't care what the law says.

Much the same can be said of a number of the law's recent bioethical reforms. There is evidence that as few as 10 percent of us have made an advance directive, that as few as a quarter of us have signed an organ donor card (despite the swarms of us avowing our desire to donate organs), that even competent patients are not widely consulted when do-not-resuscitate orders are written, that doctors have turned informed-consent principles into one more bureaucratic chore, and that virtually no plaintiff wins an informed-consent suit.

What is going on here? Well, of course, lots of things. But central among them is the fact that the society law tries to regulate is enormously complex. The people the law wants to affect are enticed by many incentives beyond those the law creates. They have their own agendas and, more important, their own normative systems. The law writes rules, but the governed often have the incentives, time, and energy to avoid them.

Consider advance directives. They offer people a surely irresistible way of speaking in one of life's greatest crises. Yet people spurn them. People do so because they have their own lives to lead. Momentous as the issue may be, it will generally not seem pressing until it arrives. People resist thinking about their own mortality. They don't easily understand and heartily dislike legal forms: People find them obscure and darkly imagine how they might be misused. For that matter, people may—reasonably—doubt that they will be used at all. Finally, many people have trouble envisioning their circumstances years into the future and how they would respond to those hypothetical circumstances. In short, advance directives were formulated and promoted by people—bioethicists, lawyers, and doctors, for instance—who know what they want to do through them and keenly want to do it. Much of the public is less clear about what it wants and about whether getting it is worth the costs. In short, while the language of the law may have penetrated into the bosom of society, it must still, in quotidian life, compete with the many other languages that people speak more comfortably, more fluently, and with more conviction.

In this chapter, I have argued that law offers a rewarding language for treating questions of social regulation. But I have also contended that, as a vehicle for morally consequential issues like those in bioethical disputes, that language is momentously limited and often inapt. Law is the language of social regulation and hence responds to systemic imperatives that are irrelevant to and even may conflict with genuine understanding and wise resolution of moral issues. This is why Holmes saw himself "as a judge whose first business is to see that the game is played according to the rules whether I like them or not."[9] It is why Cardozo thought the judge "is not to yield to spasmodic sentiment, to vague and unregulated benevolence. He is to exercise a discretion informed by tradition, methodized by analogy, disciplined by system, and subordinated to 'the primordial necessity of order in the social life.'"[10]

Of course courts and (much more) legislatures sometimes speak in moral terms and always strive to write law that is consistent with moral insight. But that fact must be understood in light of law's task as a system of social regulation: "The law is full of phraseology drawn from morals, and by the mere force of language continually invites us to pass from one domain to the other without perceiving it. . . . Manifestly, therefore, nothing but confusion of thought can result from assuming that the rights of man in a moral sense are equally rights in the sense of the Constitution and the law."[11] *Glucksberg* does not express the Court's opinion about whether the plaintiffs should have been helped to die. *Roe* does not state the Court's view of the desirability of Texas's abortion statute. The law of informed consent does not embody any legislature's whole understanding of the ethical duties of doctors to patients.

The law, then, has evolved to regulate social life, however awkwardly, and its language reflects that purpose. That is its strength. But like any lexicon, law's vocabularies must be handled cautiously. For its idioms rule us in ways we do not always grasp or desire, and they have limits growing out of the ends for which they were created.

NOTES

1. Oliver Wendell Holmes, *The Path of the Law,* in *Collected Legal Papers* 170 (Harcourt, Brace, 1920).
2. Benjamin N. Cardozo, *The Nature of the Judicial Process* 92–93 (Yale University Press, 1921).
3. Judith Shklar, *Legalism: Law, Morals, and Political Trials* 10 (Harvard University Press, 1964).
4. 410 US 113 (1973).
5. For one of several attempts to free the assisted-suicide issue from *Roe,* see Seth F. Kreimer, *Does Pro-Choice Mean Pro-Kevorkian? An*

Essay on Roe, Casey, *and the Right to Die,* 44 American University Law Review 803 (1995).

6. Carl E. Schneider, *Bioethics and the Family: The Cautionary View from Family Law,* 1992 Utah Law Review 819, 838.

7. For a helpful discussion of this problem, see Howard Brody, *Physician-Assisted Suicide in the Courts: Moral Equivalence, Double Effect, and Clinical Practice,* in this volume.

8. Alfred North Whitehead, *An Introduction to Mathematics* 61 (n.d.).

9. Oliver Wendell Holmes, *Ideals and Doubts* in *Collected Legal Papers* 307 (Harcourt, Brace, 1920).

10. Benjamin N. Cardozo, *The Nature of the Judicial Process* 141 (Yale University Press, 1921).

11. Oliver Wendell Holmes, *The Path of the Law,* in *Collected Legal Papers* 171–2 (Harcourt, Brace, 1920).

Appendixes

Court Opinion in:
Compassion in Dying
v.
State of Washington

79 F3d 790
United States Court of Appeals for the Ninth Circuit

REINHARDT, Circuit Judge

I.

This case raises an extraordinarily important and difficult issue. It compels us to address questions to which there are no easy or simple answers, at law or otherwise. It requires us to confront the most basic of human concerns—the mortality of self and loved ones—and to balance the interest in preserving human life against the desire to die peacefully and with dignity. People of good will can and do passionately disagree about the proper result, perhaps even more intensely than they part ways over the constitutionality of restricting a woman's right to have an abortion. Heated though the debate may be, we must determine whether and how the United States Constitution applies to the controversy before us, a controversy that may touch more people more profoundly than any other issue the courts will face in the foreseeable future.

Today, we are required to decide whether a person who is terminally ill has a constitutionally-protected liberty interest in hastening what might otherwise be a protracted, undignified, and extremely painful death. If such an interest exists, we must next decide whether or not the state of Washington may constitutionally restrict its exercise by banning a form of medical assistance that is frequently requested by terminally ill people who wish to die. We first conclude that there is a constitutionally-protected liberty interest in determining the time and manner of one's own death, an interest that must be weighed against the state's legitimate and countervailing interests, especially those that relate to the preservation of human life. After balancing the competing interests, we conclude by answering the narrow question before us: We hold that insofar as the Washington statute prohibits physicians from prescribing life-ending medication for use by terminally ill, competent adults who wish to hasten their own deaths, it violates the Due Process Clause of the Fourteenth Amendment.

II. Preliminary Matters and History of the Case

This is the first right-to-die case that this court or any other federal court of appeals has ever decided. The plaintiffs are four physicians who treat terminally ill patients, three terminally ill patients, and a Washington non-profit organization called Compassion in Dying. The four physicians—Dr. Harold Glucksberg, Dr. Thomas A. Preston, Dr. Abigail Halperin, and Dr. Peter Shalit—are respected doctors whose expertise is recognized by the state. All declare that they periodically treat terminally ill, competent adults who wish to hasten their deaths with help from their physicians. The doctors state that in their professional judgment they should provide that help but are deterred from doing so by a Washington statute that makes it a felony to knowingly aid another person to commit suicide.

Under the Washington statute, aiding a person who wishes to end his life constitutes a criminal act and subjects the aider to the possibility of a lengthy term of imprisonment, even if the recipient of the aid is a terminally ill, competent adult and the aider is a licensed physician who is providing medical assistance at the request of the patient. The Washington statute provides in pertinent part: "A person is guilty of promoting a suicide attempt when he knowingly causes *or aids* another person to attempt suicide." RCW 9A.36.060 (emphasis added). A violation of the statute constitutes a felony punishable by imprisonment for a maximum of five years and a fine of up to $10,000. RCW 9A.36.060(2) and 9A.20.020(1)(c).

On appeal, the four plaintiff-doctors asserted the rights of terminally ill, competent adult patients who wished to hasten their deaths with the help of their physicians so that they might die peacefully and with dignity. That group included the three patient-plaintiffs. The district court described the patient-plaintiffs, each of whom desired to obtain prescription drugs to hasten his death, as follows:

> Jane Roe is a 69-year-old retired pediatrician who has suffered since 1988 from cancer which has now metastasized throughout her skeleton. Although she tried and benefitted temporarily from various treatments including chemotherapy and radiation, she is now in the terminal phase of her disease. In November 1993, her doctor referred her to hospice care. Only patients with a life expectancy of less than six months are eligible for such care.
>
> Jane Roe has been almost completely bedridden since June of 1993 and experiences constant pain, which becomes especially sharp and severe when she moves. The only medical treatment available to her at this time is medication, which cannot fully alleviate her pain. In addition, she suffers from swollen legs, bed sores, poor appetite, nausea and vomiting, impaired vision, incontinence of bowel, and general weakness.
>
> Jane Roe is mentally competent and wishes to hasten her death by taking prescribed drugs with the help of Plaintiff Compassion in Dying. In keeping with the requirements of that organization, she has made three requests for its members to provide her and her family with counseling, emo-

tional support, and any necessary ancillary drug assistance at the time she takes the drugs.

John Doe is a 44-year-old artist dying of AIDS. Since his diagnosis in 1991, he has experienced two bouts of pneumonia, chronic, severe skin and sinus infections, grand mal seizures and extreme fatigue. He has already lost 70% of his vision to cytomegalovirus retinitis, a degenerative disease which will result in blindness and rob him of his ability to paint. His doctor has indicated that he is in the terminal phase of his illness.

John Doe is especially cognizant of the suffering imposed by a lingering terminal illness because he was the primary caregiver for his long-term companion who died of AIDS in June of 1991. He also observed his grandfather's death from diabetes preceded by multiple amputations as well as loss of vision and hearing. Mr. Doe is mentally competent, understands there is no cure for AIDS and wants his physician to prescribe drugs which he can use to hasten his death.

James Poe is a 69-year-old retired sales representative who suffers from emphysema, which causes him a constant sensation of suffocating. He is connected to an oxygen tank at all times, and takes morphine regularly to calm the panic reaction associated with his feeling of suffocation. Mr. Poe also suffers from heart failure related to his pulmonary disease which obstructs the flow of blood to his extremities and causes severe leg pain. There are no cures for his pulmonary and cardiac conditions, and he is in the terminal phase of his illness. Mr. Poe is mentally competent and wishes to commit suicide by taking physician-prescribed drugs.

Compassion in Dying, 850 F.Supp. at 1456–57.

The names of the patients are pseudonymous in order to protect their privacy. All three patients died after the case began. Two had died by the time the District Court issued its decision. *See Compassion in Dying v. State of Washington,* 850 F.Supp. 1454, 1456 n.2 (W.D.Wash.1994). The other died prior to the date of the decision by the three-judge panel of this court. *Compassion in Dying v. State of Washington,* 49 F.3d 586, 588 (9th Cir.1995).

Since the District Court properly granted the physicians standing to assert the rights of their terminally ill patients in general, 850 F.Supp. at 1467, it is clear that this case was not rendered moot by the death of the three named patients. The physicians meet both Article III and jurisprudential standing requirements. *See Singleton v. Wulff,* 428 U.S. 106, 116–17, 96 S.Ct. 2868, 2875–76, 49 L.Ed.2d 826 (1976) (holding that doctors had standing to challenge—on behalf of women patients in general—a Missouri law banning Medicaid reimbursement for abortions that were not medically required). *See also Doe v. Bolton,* 410 U.S. 179, 188, 93 S.Ct. 739, 745, 35 L.Ed.2d 201 (1973) (holding that physicians, asserting the rights of their patients, have standing to challenge the constitutionality of a criminal abortion statute even though "the record does not disclose that any one of them has been prosecuted, or threatened with prosecution, for violation of the State's abortion statutes"); *Planned Parenthood of Cent. Mo. v. Dan-*

forth, 428 U.S. 52, 62, 96 S.Ct. 2831, 2837, 49 L.Ed.2d 788 (1976) (same). Although there is some ambiguity in *Bolton* as to whether the physicians were asserting their own rights or the rights of their patients, the Court in *Singleton,* after discussing *Griswold v. Connecticut,* 381 U.S. 479, 85 S.Ct. 1678, 14 L.Ed.2d 510 (1965), described *Bolton* as a case "where the Court also permitted physicians to assert the rights of their patients."

The doctors in *Bolton* were held to have standing to assert their patients' rights even though the doctors had never been threatened with prosecution. The doctors here also meet the standing requirements because they run a severe risk of prosecution under the Washington statute, which proscribes the very conduct in which they seek to engage. The state has never indicated that it would not prosecute doctors who violate that law. *See Babbitt v. United Farm Workers National Union,* 442 U.S. 289, 99 S.Ct. 2301, 60 L.Ed.2d 895 (1979) (holding that plaintiff does not have to risk arrest or prosecution in order to have standing to challenge the constitutionality of a criminal statute). *See also Planned Parenthood of Cent. Mo.,* 428 U.S. at 62, 96 S.Ct. at 2837; *Bolton,* 410 U.S. at 188, 93 S.Ct. at 745 (saying that the "physician is the one against whom these criminal statutes directly operate" and that the "physician-appellants, therefore, assert a sufficiently direct threat of personal detriment. . . . [and] should not be required to await and undergo a criminal prosecution as the sole means of seeking relief").

We need not decide whether the deaths of the three patient-plaintiffs would negate the ability of their lawyers to continue the challenge that those patients brought while they were still alive. *See Southern Pacific Terminal Co. v. ICC,* 219 U.S. 498, 515, 31 S.Ct. 279, 283, 55 L.Ed. 310 (1911) (holding a case is not moot when the controversy is capable of repetition yet evading review). We note, however, that in invoking the capable-of-repetition-yet-evading-review doctrine in *Roe v. Wade,* 410 U.S. 113, 93 S.Ct. 705, 35 L.Ed.2d 147 (1973), the Court specifically relied, in part, on the fact that *other* women would become pregnant. The Court said:

> [W]hen, as here, pregnancy is a significant fact in the litigation, the normal 266-day human gestation period is so short that the pregnancy will come to term before the usual appellate procedure is complete. If that termination makes a case moot, pregnancy litigation will seldom survive much beyond the trial stage, and appellate review will be effectively denied. *Our law should not be that rigid. Pregnancy often comes more than once to the same woman, and in the general population, if man is to survive, it will always be with us.*

Roe, 410 U.S. at 125, 93 S.Ct. at 713 (emphasis added). So, too, unfortunately, will terminal illness.

The District Court in this case reached only claims asserted by two of the three categories of plaintiffs: the patients' claims that they had a right to receive medical assistance from their physicians and the claims that the physicians asserted on behalf of their patients. It did not address the claim asserted by Compassion in Dying. Nor, correlatively, did it reach the claim by the terminally ill patients that they had a right to receive assistance from organizations such as Compassion in Dying.

Like the District Court, we decide only claims brought by the terminally ill patients and the doctors. We consider those claims to the extent that they relate to the provision of certain medical assistance to terminally ill persons by physicians or persons acting pursuant to their authorization or direction. The claims involving Compassion in Dying are not before us. The district court suggested that it would reach those additional claims at a later stage in the proceedings if Compassion in Dying so desired. We have jurisdiction over this appeal from partial summary judgment because the district court certified the appeal at the request of both parties under Federal Rule of Civil Procedure 54(b).

The plaintiffs do not challenge Washington statute RCW 9A.36.060 in its entirety. Specifically they do not object to the portion of the Washington statute that makes it unlawful for a person knowingly to *cause* another to commit suicide. Rather, they only challenge the statute's *"or aids"* provision. They challenge that provision both on its face and as applied to terminally ill, mentally competent adults who wish to hasten their own deaths with the help of medication prescribed by their doctors. The plaintiffs contend that the provision impermissibly prevents the exercise by terminally ill patients of a constitutionally-protected liberty interest in violation of the Due Process Clause of the Fourteenth Amendment, and also that it impermissibly distinguishes between similarly situated terminally ill patients in violation of the Equal Protection Clause.

In an extremely thoughtful opinion, Chief District Judge Barbara Rothstein held that "a competent, terminally ill adult has a constitutionally guaranteed right under the Fourteenth Amendment to commit physician-assisted suicide." 850 F.Supp. at 1462. Ruling on cross-motions for summary judgment, the District Court concluded that the Washington statute places an undue burden on the exercise of that constitutionally-protected liberty interest. *Id.* at 1465. The District Court held that the Washington law also violates the Equal Protection Clause because it impermissibly treats similarly situated groups of terminally ill patients differently. *Id.* at 1467. Although the scope of the relief the District Judge ordered is not clear, *id.* at 1456, 1459, 1462–1464, 1467, it appears that she declared the statute invalid only insofar as it applies to the prescription of medication to terminally ill competent adults who wish to hasten their deaths— or, to use the district court's precise terminology, only insofar as it applies to "physician-assisted suicide," *id.* at 1467.

On appeal, a three-judge panel of this court voted 2–1 to reverse the district court decision. *Compassion in Dying v. State of Washington,* 49 F.3d 586 (9th Cir. 1995). The majority held that there is no due process liberty interest in physician-assisted suicide. It also concluded that the Washington statute does not violate the Equal Protection Clause. Accordingly, the majority held that the statute is not invalid facially or as applied. Judge Wright dissented and would have held that the statute is invalid as applied to terminally ill, mentally competent adults because it violates their privacy and equal protection rights. *Id.* at 594, 597 (Wright, J., dissenting). Because of the extraordinary importance of this case, we decided to rehear it en banc. *Compassion in Dying v. State of Wash.,* 62 F.3d 299 (9th Cir. 1995).

We now affirm the District Court's decision and clarify the scope of the relief. We hold that the "or aids" provision of Washington statute RCW 9A.36.060, as applied to the prescription of life-ending medication for use by terminally ill, competent adult patients who wish to hasten their deaths, violates the Due Process Clause of the Fourteenth Amendment. Accordingly, we need not resolve the question whether that provision, in conjunction with other Washington laws regulating the treatment of terminally ill patients, also violates the Equal Protection Clause.

III. Overview of Legal Analysis: Is There a Due Process Violation?

In order to answer the question whether the Washington statute violates the Due Process Clause insofar as it prohibits the provision of certain medical assistance to terminally ill, competent adults who wish to hasten their own deaths, we first determine whether there is a liberty interest in choosing the time and manner of one's death—a question sometimes phrased in common parlance as: Is there a right to die? Because we hold that there is, we must then determine whether prohibiting physicians from prescribing life-ending medication for use by terminally ill patients who wish to die violates the patients' due process rights.

The mere recognition of a liberty interest does not mean that a state may not prohibit the exercise of that interest in particular circumstances, nor does it mean that a state may not adopt appropriate regulations governing its exercise. Rather, in cases like the one before us, the courts must apply a balancing test under which we weigh the individual's liberty interests against the relevant state interests in order to determine whether the state's actions are constitutionally permissible. As Chief Justice Rehnquist, writing for the Court, explained in *Cruzan v. Director, Missouri Dept. of Health,* 497 U.S. 261, 110 S.Ct. 2841, 111 L.Ed.2d 224 (1990), the only right-to-die case that the Court has heretofore considered:

> [D]etermining that a person has a "liberty interest" under the Due Process Clause does not end our inquiry; "whether respondent's constitutional rights have been violated must be determined by balancing his liberty interests against the relevant state interests." *Youngberg v. Romeo,* 457 U.S. 307, 321, 102 S.Ct. 2452, 2461, 73 L.Ed.2d 28 (1982); *See also Mills v. Rogers,* 457 U.S. 291, 299, 102 S.Ct. 2442, 2448, 73 L.Ed.2d 16 (1982).

Cruzan, 497 U.S. at 279, 110 S.Ct. at 2851–52 (footnote omitted).

The Court has invoked a balancing test in a number of substantive due process cases, not just in the right-to-die context. For example, as the *Cruzan* Court noted, the Court applied a balancing test in *Youngberg* and *Mills,* liberty interest cases involving the right to refuse medical treatment. *Youngberg* addressed the rights of patients involuntarily committed to state mental institutions. The Court said: "In determining whether a substantive right protected by the Due Process Clause has been violated, it is necessary to balance the liberty of the individual and the demands of organized society." *Youngberg,* 457 U.S. at 320, 102 S.Ct. at 2460 (internal citation and quotation omitted). *Mills* addressed the question of the right of mental patients to refuse treatment with antipsychotic drugs. There, the Court stated explicitly that the "state interests" are "to be balanced against an individual's liberty interests." 457 U.S. at 304, 102 S.Ct. at 2451. As the *Cruzan* Court also noted, the use of a balancing test is deeply rooted in our legal traditions. The Court has been applying a balancing test in substantive due process cases at least since 1905, when in *Jacobson v. Massachusetts,* 197 U.S. 11, 25 S.Ct. 358, 49 L.Ed. 643 (1905), "the Court balanced an individual's liberty interest in declining an unwanted smallpox vaccine against the State's interest in preventing disease." *Cruzan,* 497 U.S. at 278, 110 S.Ct. at 2851.

As Justice O'Connor explained in her concurring opinion in *Cruzan,* the ultimate question is whether sufficient justification exists for the intrusion by the government into the realm of a person's "liberty, dignity, and freedom." *Cruzan,* 497 U.S. at 287, 289, 110 S.Ct. at 2856, 2857 (O'Connor, J., concurring). If the balance favors the state, then the given statute—whether it regulates the exercise of a due process liberty interest or prohibits that exercise to some degree—is constitutional. If the balance favors the individual, then the statute—whatever its justifications—violates the individual's due process liberty rights and must be declared unconstitutional, either on its face or as applied. Here, we conclude unhesitatingly that the balance favors the individual's liberty interest.

IV. Is There a Liberty Interest?

Before beginning our inquiry into whether a liberty interest exists, we reiterate a few fundamental precepts that guide us. The first lies in the Court's cautionary note in *Roe v. Wade,* 410 U.S. 113, 116, 93 S.Ct. 705, 708, 35 L.Ed.2d 147 (1973):

> We forthwith acknowledge our awareness of the sensitive and emotional nature of the . . . controversy, of the vigorous opposing views, even among physicians, and of the deep and seemingly absolute convictions that the subject inspires. One's philosophy, one's experiences, one's exposure to the raw edges of human existence, one's religious training, one's attitude toward life and family and their values, and the moral standards one establishes and seeks to observe, are all likely to influence and to color one's thinking and conclusions. . . .

Like the *Roe* Court, we endeavor to conduct an objective analysis of a most emotionally-charged of topics. In doing so, we bear in mind the second Justice Harlan's admonition in his now-vindicated dissent in *Poe v. Ullman,* 367 U.S. 497, 543, 81 S.Ct. 1752, 1776–77, 6 L.Ed.2d 989 (1961) (Harlan, J., dissenting from dismissal on jurisdictional grounds):

> [T]he full scope of the liberty guaranteed by the Due Process Clause cannot be found in or limited by the precise terms of the specific guarantees elsewhere in the Constitution. This 'liberty' is not a series of isolated points pricked out in terms of the taking of property; the freedom of speech, press,

and religion; the right to keep and bear arms; the freedom from unreasonable searches and seizures; and so on. It is a rational continuum which, broadly speaking, includes a freedom from all substantial arbitrary impositions and purposeless restraints, . . . and which also recognizes, what a reasonable and sensitive judgment must, that certain interests require particularly careful scrutiny of the state needs asserted to justify their abridgment.

Applying Justice Harlan's teaching, we must strive to resist the natural judicial impulse to limit our vision to that which can plainly be observed on the face of the document before us, or even that which we have previously had the wisdom to recognize.

Most important, we undertake our difficult task with a profound respect for the noble objectives of the Constitution, as described by Justice Brandeis in the second most famous dissent in American jurisprudence. In *Olmstead v. United States,* 277 U.S. 438, 48 S.Ct. 564, 72 L.Ed. 944 (1928), Justice Brandeis wrote, and his words have since been quoted in full in several opinions of the Court and in innumerable appellate court decisions:

> The makers of our Constitution undertook to secure conditions favorable to the pursuit of happiness. They recognized the significance of man's spiritual nature, of his feelings and of his intellect. They knew that only a part of the pain, pleasure and satisfaction of life are to be found in material things. They sought to protect Americans in their beliefs, their thoughts, their emotions and their sensations. They conferred, as against the government, the right to be let alone—the most comprehensive of rights, and the right most valued by civilized men.

Id. at 478, 48 S.Ct. at 572 (Brandeis, J., dissenting).

In examining whether a liberty interest exists in determining the time and manner of one's death, we begin with the compelling similarities between right-to-die cases and abortion cases. In the former as in the latter, the relative strength of the competing interests changes as physical, medical, or related circumstances vary. In right-to-die cases the outcome of the balancing test may differ at different points along the life cycle as a person's physical or medical condition deteriorates, just as in abortion cases the permissibility of restrictive state legislation may vary with the progression of the pregnancy. Equally important, both types of cases raise issues of life and death, and both arouse similar religious and moral concerns. Both also present basic questions about an individual's right of choice.

Historical evidence shows that both abortion and assisted suicide were for many years condemned, but that the efforts to prevent people from engaging in the condemned conduct were always at most only partially successful. Even when prohibited, abortions and assisted suicides flourished in back alleys, in small street-side clinics, and in the privacy of the bedroom. Deprived of the right to medical assistance, many pregnant women and terminally ill adults ultimately took matters into their own hands, often with tragic consequences.

Because they present issues of such profound spiritual importance and because they so deeply affect individuals' right to determine their own destiny, the abortion and right-to-die cases have given rise to a highly emotional and divisive debate. In many respects, the legal arguments on both sides are similar, as are the constitutional principles at issue.

In deciding right-to-die cases, we are guided by the Court's approach to the abortion cases. *Casey* in particular provides a powerful precedent, for in that case the Court had the opportunity to evaluate its past decisions and to determine whether to adhere to its original judgment. Although *Casey* was influenced by the doctrine of *stare decisis,* the fundamental message of that case lies in its statements regarding the type of issue that confronts us here: "These matters, involving the most intimate and personal choices a person may make in a lifetime, choices central to personal dignity and autonomy, are central to the liberty protected by the Fourteenth Amendment." *Casey,* 505 U.S. at 851, 112 S.Ct. at 2807.

A. Defining the Liberty Interest and Other Relevant Terms

The majority opinion of the three-judge panel that first heard this case on appeal defined the claimed liberty interest as a "constitutional right to aid in killing oneself." *Compassion in Dying,* 49 F.3d at 591 (emphasis added). However, the subject we must initially examine is not nearly so limited. Properly analyzed, the first issue to be resolved is whether there is a liberty interest in determining the time and manner of one's death. We do not ask simply whether there is a liberty interest in receiving "aid in killing oneself" because such a narrow interest could not exist in the absence of a broader and more important underlying interest— the right to die. In short, it is the end and not the means that defines the liberty interest.

The broader approach we employ in defining the liberty interest is identical to the approach used by the Supreme Court in the abortion cases. In those cases, the Court initially determined whether a general liberty interest existed (an interest in having an abortion), not whether there was an interest in implementing that general liberty interest by a particular means (with medical assistance). Specifically, in *Roe v. Wade,* 410 U.S. 113, 93 S.Ct. 705, 35 L.Ed.2d 147 (1973), the Court determined that women had a liberty interest in securing an abortion, not that women had a liberty interest in obtaining medical assistance for purpose of an abortion. The Court did so even though the Texas statute at issue did not prohibit a woman from inducing her own abortion; nor did it criminalize a woman's conduct in securing an abortion. Rather, the Texas statute, like the Washington statute here, prohibited the rendering of assistance; specifically, the Texas statute prohibited only *assisting* a woman to secure an abortion. *Roe,* 410 U.S. at 151–52, 93 S.Ct. at 725–26. The Court first determined that a woman had a constitutional right to choose an abortion. Only after it did so, did it proceed to the second step: to determine whether the state's prohibition on assistance unconstitutionally restricted the exercise of that liberty interest. Similarly, in *Planned Parenthood v. Casey,* 505 U.S. 833, 112 S.Ct. 2791, 120 L.Ed.2d 674

(1992), the Court first reaffirmed, after extensive analysis, its earlier holding that women have a liberty interest in obtaining an abortion. In determining the *existence* of that liberty interest, the Court did not address the subject of spousal notification. As in *Roe,* only after affirming a woman's right to have an abortion, did the Court proceed to the second step: to examine whether the statutory provision requiring married women to notify their spouses prior to obtaining an abortion posed an undue burden on the exercise of that liberty interest. In this case, our analysis is necessarily the same. First we must determine whether there *is* a liberty interest in determining the time and manner of one's death; if so, we must then examine whether Washington's ban on assisted suicide unconstitutionally restricts the exercise of that liberty interest.

While some people refer to the liberty interest implicated in right-to-die cases as a liberty interest in committing suicide, we do not describe it that way. We use the broader and more accurate terms, "the right to die," "determining the time and manner of one's death," and "hastening one's death" for an important reason. The liberty interest we examine encompasses a whole range of acts that are generally not considered to constitute "suicide." Included within the liberty interest we examine, is for example, the act of refusing or terminating unwanted medical treatment. As we discuss later at pp. 821–822, a competent adult has a liberty interest in refusing to be connected to a respirator or in being disconnected from one, even if he is terminally ill and cannot live without mechanical assistance. The law does not classify the death of a patient that results from the granting of his wish to decline or discontinue treatment as "suicide." Nor does the law label the acts of those who help the patient carry out that wish, whether by physically disconnecting the respirator or by removing an intravenous tube, as assistance in suicide. Accordingly, we believe that the broader terms—"the right to die," "controlling the time and manner of one's death," and "hastening one's death"—more accurately describe the liberty interest at issue here. Moreover, as we discuss later, we have serious doubts that the terms "suicide" and "assisted suicide" are appropriate legal descriptions of the specific conduct at issue here. *See infra* 824.

There is one further definitional matter we should emphasize. Following our g573 determination regarding the existence of a liberty interest in hastening one's death, we examine whether the Washington statute unconstitutionally infringes on that liberty interest. Throughout that examination, we use the term "physician-assisted suicide," a term that does not appear in the Washington statute but is frequently employed in legal and medical discussions involving the type of question before us. For purposes of this opinion, we use physician-assisted suicide as it is used by the parties and district court and as it is most frequently used: the prescribing of medication by a physician for the purpose of enabling a patient to end his life. It is only that conduct that the plaintiffs urge be held constitutionally-protected in this case.

B. The Legal Standard

There is no litmus test for courts to apply when deciding whether or not a liberty interest exists under the Due Process Clause. Our decisions involve difficult judgments regarding the conscience, traditions, and fundamental tenets of our nation. We must sometimes apply those basic principles in light of changing values based on shared experience. Other times we must apply them to new problems arising out of the development and use of new technologies. In all cases, our analysis of the applicability of the protections of the Constitution must be made in light of existing circumstances as well as our historic traditions.

Historically, the Court has classified "fundamental rights" as those that are "implicit in the concept of ordered liberty," *Palko v. Connecticut,* 302 U.S. 319, 325–26, 58 S.Ct. 149, 151–52, 82 L.Ed. 288 (1937). The Court reasserted this historic standard, along with an alternative description, in its highly controversial *Bowers v. Hardwick* opinion, 478 U.S. 186, 191–92, 106 S.Ct. 2841, 2844–45, 92 L.Ed.2d 140 (1986):

> Striving to assure itself and the public that announcing rights not readily identifiable in the Constitution's text involves much more than the imposition of the Justices' own choice of values on the States and the Federal Government, the Court has sought to identify the nature of the rights qualifying for heightened judicial protection. In *Palko v. Connecticut,* 302 U.S. 319, 325, 326, 82 L.Ed. 288, 58 S.Ct. 149 [152] (1937), it was said that this category includes those fundamental liberties that are "implicit in the concept of ordered liberty," such that "neither liberty nor justice would exist if [they] were sacrificed." A different description of fundamental liberties appeared in *Moore v. East Cleveland,* 431 U.S. 494, 503, 97 S.Ct. 1932, 1937, 52 L.Ed.2d 531 (1977) (opinion of POWELL, J.), where they are characterized as those liberties that are "deeply rooted in this Nation's history and tradition." *Id.* at 503, 97 S.Ct. at 1938 (POWELL, J.).

In recent years, the Court has spoken more frequently of substantive due process *interests* than of *fundamental* due process *rights.* Compare *Thornburgh v. American Coll. of Obst.,* 476 U.S. 747, 772, 106 S.Ct. 2169, 2184, 90 L.Ed.2d 779 (1986) (describing "fundamental right" to abortion) and *Akron v. Akron Center for Reproductive Health, Inc.,* 462 U.S. 416, 420 n.1, 103 S.Ct. 2481, 2487 n.1, 76 L.Ed.2d 687 (1983) (same) with *Webster v. Reproductive Health Services,* 492 U.S. 490, 520, 109 S.Ct. 3040, 3057, 106 L.Ed.2d 410 (1989) (plurality opinion) (describing women's entitlement to an abortion as a "liberty interest protected by Due Process Clause"). *See also Cruzan,* 497 U.S. 261, 110 S.Ct. 2841. The Court has also recently expressed a strong reluctance to find new fundamental rights. *Collins v. City of Harker Heights, Tex.,* 503 U.S. 115, 123, 112 S.Ct. 1061, 1068, 117 L.Ed.2d 261 (1992).

The Court's evolving doctrinal approach to substantive due process claims is consistent with the basic truth enunciated by Justice Harlan and later endorsed by the Court in Casey: "the full scope of the liberty guaranteed by the Due Process Clause is a rational continuum which, broadly speaking, includes a freedom from all substantial arbitrary impositions and purposeless restraints . . ." *Casey,* 505 U.S. at 848, 112 S.Ct. at 2806, citing *Poe v. Ullman,* 367 U.S. 497, 543, 81 S.Ct. 1752, 1776–77, 6 L.Ed.2d 989 (1961) (Harlan, J., dissenting from dismissal on jurisdictional grounds). As Justice Harlan noted, some liberty interests are weightier than others. Under the Court's traditional jurisprudence, those classified as fundamental rights cannot be limited except to further a compelling and narrowly tailored state interest. *See Collins,* 503 U.S. at 123, 112 S.Ct. at 1068. Other important interests, such as the liberty interest in refusing unwanted medical treatment, are subject to a balancing test that is less restrictive, but nonetheless requires the state to overcome a substantial hurdle in justifying any significant impairment.

Recent cases, including *Cruzan,* suggest that the Court may be heading towards the formal adoption of the continuum approach, along with a balancing test, in substantive due process cases generally. If so, there would no longer be a two-tier or three-tier set of tests that depends on the classification of the right or interest as fundamental, important, or marginal. Instead, the more important the individual's right or interest, the more persuasive the justifications for infringement would have to be. We see the evolution in the Court's approach more as a recognition of the artificiality of the current classification system than as a fundamental change in the Court's practical approach to specific issues. So long as the liberty interest is an important one, the state must shoulder the burden of justifying any significant limitations it seeks to impose. However, we need not predict the Court's future course in order to decide the case before us. Here, as we have said, even under the Court's traditional mode of analysis, a balancing test is applicable.

Nothing in *Reno v. Flores,* 507 U.S. 292, 113 S.Ct. 1439, 123 L.Ed.2d 1 (1993), the insubstantial reed on which the dissent rests its case—even though the case was not cited by any of the parties or any of the eleven amici who filed briefs before this court—suggests anything to the contrary. In *Flores,* the Court simply declined to find a new fundamental right, and repeated its general reluctance to do so. *Id.* at 302, 113 S.Ct. at 1447. The Court did not, as the dissent implies, purport to establish a new classification system under which all liberty interests other than fundamental rights would be subject to rational basis review. Nor did *Flores* purport to overrule, or even hint at any desire to modify, the Court's ninety-year-old practice of using a balancing test in liberty interest cases that raise important issues of the type before us. In fact, *Flores* did not mention *Cruzan, Youngberg, Mills, Jacobson,* or any other balancing case. While one might legitimately argue either that the liberty interest at issue here rises to the level of a fundamental right or that it is simply an important liberty interest that is subject to a balancing test, one point is absolutely clear: there can be no legitimate argument that rational basis review is applicable, and *nothing* in *Flores* suggests that it is.

Although in determining the existence of important rights or liberty interests, the Court examines our history and experience, it has stated on a number of occasions that the limits of the substantive reach of the Due Process Clause are not frozen at any point in time. In *Casey,* the Court said: "Neither the Bill of Rights nor the specific practices of States at the time of the adoption of the Fourteenth Amendment marks the outer limits of the substantive sphere of liberty which the Fourteenth Amendment protects." 505 U.S. at 848, 112 S.Ct. at 2805. Justice Frankfurter may have put it best when, writing for the Court in *Rochin v. California,* 342 U.S. 165, 171–72, 72 S.Ct. 205, 209, 96 L.Ed. 183 (1952), he declared, "To believe that this judicial exercise of judgment could be avoided by freezing 'due process of law' at some fixed stage in time or thought is to suggest that the most important aspect of constitutional adjudication is a function for inanimate machines and not for judges. . . ." Certainly, it would be difficult to imagine a more felicitous expression of the dynamism of constitutional interpretation. Thus, while historical analysis plays a useful role in any attempt to determine whether a claimed right or liberty interest exists, earlier legislative or judicial recognition of the right or interest is not a *sine qua non*.

In *Casey*, the Court made it clear that the fact that we have previously failed to acknowledge the existence of a particular liberty interest or even that we have previously prohibited its exercise is no barrier to recognizing its existence. In discussing a woman's liberty interest in securing an abortion, the *Casey* Court stated that pregnancy involves "suffering [that] is too intimate and personal for the State to insist, without more, upon its own vision of the woman's role, *however dominant that vision has been in the course of our history and culture.*" *Casey*, 505 U.S. at 852, 112 S.Ct. at 2807 (emphasis added).

In contrast to *Casey*, the majority opinion of the three-judge panel in the case now before us erroneously concluded that a historical analysis alone is sufficient basis for rejecting plaintiffs' claim to a substantive liberty interest or right. *Compassion in Dying*, 49 F.3d at 591. As explained below, we believe that the panel's historical account is misguided, but even if it were indisputably correct, historical evidence alone is not a sufficient basis for rejecting a claimed liberty interest.

Were history our sole guide, the Virginia anti-miscegenation statute that the Court unanimously overturned in *Loving v. Virginia*, 388 U.S. 1, 87 S.Ct. 1817, 18 L.Ed.2d 1010 (1967), as violative of substantive due process and the Equal Protection Clause, would still be in force because such anti-miscegenation laws were commonplace both when the United States was founded and when the Fourteenth Amendment was adopted. The Court explicitly acknowledged as much in *Casey*, 505 U.S. at 847, 112 S.Ct. at 2805, in rejecting the view that substantive due process protects rights or liberties only if they possess a historical pedigree. In *Casey*, the Court said:

> It is . . . tempting . . . to suppose that the Due Process Clause protects only those practices, defined at the most specific level, that were protected against government interference by other rules of law when the Fourteenth Amendment was ratified. . . . But such a view would be inconsistent with our law. It is a promise of the Constitution that there is a realm of personal liberty which the government may not enter. We have vindicated this principle before. Marriage is mentioned nowhere in the Bill of Rights and interracial marriage was illegal in most States in the 19th century, but the Court was no doubt correct in finding it to be an aspect of liberty protected against state interference by the substantive component of the Due Process Clause in *Loving v. Virginia*, 388 U.S. 1, 12, 87 S.Ct. 1817, 1824, 18 L.Ed.2d 1010 (1967), (relying, in an opinion for eight Justices, on the Due Process Clause). Similar examples may be found in *Turner v. Safley*, 482 U.S. 78, 94–99, 107 S.Ct. 2254, 2265–67, 96 L.Ed.2d 64 (1987) [holding

that prisoners have a constitutionally protected right to marry a civilian or other inmate]; in *Carey v. Population Services International,* 431 U.S. 678, 684, 686, 97 S.Ct. 2010, 2015–2017, 52 L.Ed.2d 675 (1977) [holding that the state cannot prohibit the sale of contraceptives to all minors or bar everyone but licensed pharmacists from selling contraceptives to adults]; in *Griswold v. Connecticut,* 381 U.S. 479, 481–82, 85 S.Ct. 1678, 1680–81, 14 L.Ed.2d 510 (1965) [holding that a Connecticut law forbidding the use of contraceptives unconstitutionally intrudes on the right of marital privacy] . . .

Casey, 505 U.S. at 847–48, 112 S.Ct. at 2805. Indeed, if historical evidence of accepted practices at the time the Fourteenth Amendment was enacted were dispositive, the Court would not only have decided *Loving* differently, but it would not have held that women have a right to have an abortion. As the dissent pointed out in *Roe,* more than three-quarters of the existing states (at least 28 out of 37 states), as well as eight territorial legislatures restricted or prohibited abortions in 1868 when the Fourteenth Amendment was adopted. *Roe,* 410 U.S. at 175–76 & n.1, 93 S.Ct. at 737–39 & n.1 (Rehnquist, J., dissenting).

C. Historical Attitudes Toward Suicide

The majority opinion of the three-judge panel claimed that "a constitutional right to aid in killing oneself" was "unknown to the past." *Compassion in Dying,* 49 F.3d at 591. As we have pointed out at p. 803, our inquiry is not so narrow. Nor is our conclusion so facile. The relevant historical record is far more checkered than the majority would have us believe.

Like the Court in *Roe,* we begin with ancient attitudes. In Greek and Roman times, far from being universally prohibited, suicide was often considered commendable in literature, mythology, and practice.

> The first of all literary suicides, that of Oedipus' mother, Jocasta, is made to seem praiseworthy, an honorable way out of an insufferable situation. Homer records self-murder without comment, as something natural and heroic. The legends bear him out. Aegeus threw himself into the sea— which therefore bore his name—when he mistakenly thought his son Theseus had been slain by the Minotaur.

A. Alvarez, The Background, in *Suicide: The Philosophical Issues* 18 (M. Pabst Battin and David J. Mayor, eds. 1980). In Athens, as well as the Greek colonies of Marseilles and Ceos, magistrates kept a supply of hemlock for those who wished to end their lives. The magistrates even supplied those who wished to commit suicide with the means to do so.

> Whoever no longer wishes to live shall state his reasons to the Senate, and after having received permission shall abandon life. If your existence is hateful to you, die; if you are overwhelmed by fate, drink the hemlock. If

you are bowed with grief, abandon life. Let the unhappy man recount his misfortune, let the magistrate supply him with the remedy, and his wretchedness will come to an end.

While Socrates counseled his disciples against committing suicide, he willingly drank the hemlock as he was condemned to do, and his example inspired others to end their lives. *Id.* at 19. Plato, Socrates' most distinguished student, believed suicide was often justifiable.

He suggested that if life itself became immoderate, then suicide became a rational, justifiable act. Painful disease, or intolerable constraint were sufficient reasons to depart. And this when religious superstitions faded was philosophic justification enough. *Id.*

Many contemporaries of Plato were even more inclined to find suicide a legitimate and acceptable act. In *Roe,* while surveying the attitudes of the Greeks toward abortion, the Court stated that "only the Pythagorean school of philosophers frowned on the related act of suicide," 410 U.S. at 131, 93 S.Ct. at 716; it then noted that the Pythagorean school represented a distinctly minority view. *Id.*

The Stoics glorified suicide as an act of pure rational will. Cato, who killed himself to avoid dishonor when Caesar crushed his military aspirations, was the most celebrated of the many suicides among the Stoics. Montaigne wrote of Cato: "This was a man chosen by nature to show the heights which can be attained by human steadfastness and constancy. . . . Such courage is above philosophy."

Like the Greeks, the Romans often considered suicide to be acceptable or even laudable.

To live nobly also meant to die nobly and at the right time. Everything depended on a dominant will and a rational choice.

This attitude was reinforced by Roman law. . . . According to Justinian's Digest, suicide of a private citizen was not punishable if it was caused by "impatience of pain or sickness, or by another cause," or by "weariness of life . . . lunacy, or fear of dishonor." Since this covered every rational cause, all that was left was the utterly irrational suicide "without cause," and that was punishable on the grounds that "whoever does not spare himself would much less spare another." In other words, it was punished because irrational, not because it was a crime. *Id.* at 22–23.

The Romans did sometimes punish suicide. Under Roman law, people convicted of crimes forfeited their property to the Emperor, thereby disinheriting their heirs. Roman law imposed a special penalty on people who were caught committing a crime and then committed suicide prior to conviction to avoid forfeiting the property. To protect the Emperor's interests, the property of people who committed suicide under such circumstances was forfeited, just as if they had been convicted of the crime involved. Marzen at 57–58.

The early Christians saw death as an escape from the tribulations of a fallen existence and as the doorway to heaven. "In other words, the more powerfully the

Church instilled in believers the idea that this world was a vale of tears and sin and temptation, where they waited uneasily until death released them into eternal glory, the more irresistible the temptation to suicide became." *Id.* at 25. The Christian impulse to martyrdom reached its height with the Donatists, who were so eager to enter into martyrdom that they were eventually declared heretics. Gibbon, in the Decline and Fall of the Roman Empire, described them this way:

> They sometimes forced their way into courts of justice and compelled the affrighted judge to give orders for their execution. They frequently stopped travellers on the public highways and obliged them to inflict the stroke of martyrdom by promise of a reward, if they consented—and by the threat of instant death, if they refused to grant so singular a favour.

St. Augustine said of the Donatists, "to kill themselves out of respect for martyrdom is their daily sport." *Id.* at 27. Prompted in large part by the utilitarian concern that the rage for suicide would deplete the ranks of Christians, St. Augustine argued that committing suicide was a "detestable and damnable wickedness" and was able to help turn the tide of public opinion. *Id.* Even staunch opponents of a constitutional right to suicide acknowledge that "there were many examples of Christian martyrs whose deaths bordered on suicide, and confusion regarding the distinction between suicide and martyrdom existed up until the time of St. Augustine (354–430 A.D.)."

In 562 A.D., the Council of Braga denied funeral rites to anyone who killed himself. A little more than a century later, in 693 A.D., the Council of Toledo declared that anyone who attempted suicide should be excommunicated. *Id.* at 27–28. Once established, the Christian view that suicide was in all cases a sin and crime held sway for 1,000 years until philosophers, poets, and even some clergymen— Montesquieu, Voltaire, Diderot, Francis Bacon, David Hume, John Donne, Sir Thomas More, among others—began to challenge the all-encompassing nature of the dominant ideology. In his book Utopia, Sir Thomas More, who was later canonized by the Roman Catholic Church, strongly supported the right of the terminally ill to commit suicide and also expressed approval of the practice of assisting those who wished to hasten their deaths. Hume argued that a decision by a terminally ill patient to end his life was often laudable. France even enacted a statute legalizing suicide in 1790, primarily as a result of the influence of the nation's leading philosophers.

Suicide was a crime under the English common law, at least in limited circumstances, probably as early as the thirteenth century. Bracton, incorporating Roman Law as set forth in Justinian's *Digest,* declared that if someone commits suicide to avoid conviction of a felony, his property escheats to his lords. Bracton said "[i]t ought to be otherwise if he kills himself through madness or unwillingness to endure suffering." Despite his general fidelity to Roman law, Bracton did introduce a key innovation: "[I]f a man slays himself in weariness of life or because he is unwilling to endure further bodily pain . . . he may have a successor, but his movable goods [personal property] are confiscated. He does not lose his inheritance [real property], only his movable goods." Bracton's innovation was incorporated into English common law, which has thus treated suicides resulting from the inability to "endure further bodily pain" with compassion and understanding ever since a common law scheme was firmly established.

Sir Edward Coke, in his *Third Institute* published in 1644, held that killing oneself was an offense and that someone who committed suicide should forfeit his movable property. But Coke listed an exception for someone who "by the rage of sickness or infirmity or otherwise," kills himself "while he is not of compos mentia," or sound mind. In eighteenth century England, many and perhaps most juries compensated for the perceived unfairness of the law by concluding that anyone who killed himself was necessarily *not* of sound mind. Thus, although, formally, suicide was long considered a crime under English common law, in practice it was a crime that was punished leniently, if at all, because juries frequently used their power to nullify the law.

The traditional English experience was also shaped by the taboos that have long colored our views of suicide and perhaps still do today. English common law reflected the ancient fear that the spirit of someone who ended his own life would return to haunt the living. Accordingly, the traditional practice was to bury the body at a crossroads—either so the suicide could not find his way home or so that the frequency of travelers would keep his spirit from rising. As added insurance, a stake was driven through the body.

English attitudes toward suicide, including the tradition of ignominious burial, carried over to America where they subsequently underwent a transformation. By 1798, six of the 13 original colonies had abolished all penalties for suicide either by statute or state constitution. There is no evidence that any court ever imposed a punishment for suicide or attempted suicide under common law in post-revolutionary America. By the time the Fourteenth Amendment was adopted in 1868, suicide was generally not punishable, and in only nine of the 37 states is it clear that there were statutes prohibiting assisting suicide.

The majority of states have not criminalized suicide or attempted suicide since the turn of the century. The New Jersey Supreme Court declared in 1901 that since suicide was not punishable it should not be considered a crime. "[A]ll will admit that in some cases it is ethically defensible," the court said, as when a woman kills herself to escape being raped or "when a man curtails weeks or months of agony of an incurable disease." *Campbell v. Supreme Conclave Improved Order Heptasophs,* 66 N.J.L. 274, 49 A. 550, 553 (1901). Today, no state has a statute prohibiting suicide or attempted suicide; nor has any state had such a statute for at least 10 years. A majority of states do, however, still have laws on the books against assisting suicide.

D. Current Societal Attitudes

Clearly the absence of a criminal sanction alone does not show societal approbation of a practice. Nor is there any evidence that Americans approve of suicide in general. In recent years, however, there has been increasingly widespread support for allowing the terminally ill to hasten their deaths and avoid painful, undignified, and inhumane endings to their lives. Most Americans simply do not appear to view such acts as constituting suicide, and there is much support in reason for that conclusion. *See infra* at p. 824.

Polls have repeatedly shown that a large majority of Americans—sometimes nearing 90%—fully endorse recent legal changes granting terminally ill patients, and sometimes their families, the prerogative to accelerate their death by refusing or terminating treatment. Other polls indicate that a majority of Americans favor doctor-assisted suicide for the terminally ill. In April, 1990, the Roper Report found that 64% of Americans believed that the terminally ill should have the right to request and receive physician aid-in-dying. Another national poll, conducted in October 1991, shows that "nearly two out of three Americans favor doctor-assisted suicide and euthanasia for terminally ill patients who request it." A 1994 Harris poll found 73% of Americans favor legalizing physician-assisted suicide. Three states have held referenda on proposals to allow physicians to help terminally ill, competent adults commit suicide with somewhat mixed results. In Oregon, voters approved the carefully-crafted referendum by a margin of 51 to 49 percent in November of 1994. In Washington and California where the measures contained far fewer practical safeguards, they narrowly failed to pass, each drawing 46 percent of the vote. As such referenda indicate, there is unquestionably growing popular support for permitting doctors to provide assistance to terminally ill patients who wish to hasten their deaths.

Just as the mere absence of criminal statutes prohibiting suicide or attempted suicide does not indicate societal approval so the mere presence of statutes criminalizing assisting in a suicide does not necessarily indicate societal disapproval. That is especially true when such laws are seldom, if ever, enforced. There is no reported American case of criminal punishment being meted out to a doctor for helping a patient hasten his own death. The lack of enforcement of statutes prohibiting assisting a mentally competent, terminally ill adult to end his own life would appear to reflect widespread societal disaffection with such laws.

Our attitudes toward suicide of the type at issue in this case are better understood in light of our unwritten history and of technological developments. Running beneath the official history of legal condemnation of physician-assisted suicide is a strong undercurrent of a time-honored but hidden practice of physicians helping terminally ill patients to hasten their deaths. According to a survey by the American Society of Internal Medicine, one doctor in five said he had assisted in a patient's suicide. Accounts of doctors who have helped their patients end their lives have appeared both in professional journals and in the daily press.

The debate over whether terminally ill patients should have a right to reject medical treatment or to receive aid from their physicians in hastening their deaths has taken on a new prominence as a result of a number of developments. Two hundred years ago when America was founded and more than one hundred years ago when the Fourteenth Amendment was adopted, Americans died from a slew of illness and infirmities that killed their victims quickly but today are almost never fatal in this nation—scarlet fever, cholera, measles, diarrhea, influenza, pneumonia, gastritis, to name a few. Other diseases that have not been conquered can now often be controlled for years, if not decades—diseases such as diabetes, muscular dystrophy, Parkinson's disease, cardiovascular disease, and certain types of cancer. As a result, Americans are living longer, and when they finally succumb to illness, lingering longer, either in great pain or in a stuporous, semi-comatose condition that results from the infusion of vast amounts of pain killing medications. Despite the marvels of technology, Americans frequently die with less dignity than they did in the days when ravaging diseases typically ended their lives quickly. AIDS, which often subjects its victims to a horrifying and drawn-out demise, has also contributed to the growing number of terminally ill patients who die protracted and painful deaths.

One result has been a growing movement to restore humanity and dignity to the process by which Americans die. The now recognized right to refuse or terminate treatment and the emergent right to receive medical assistance in hastening one's death are inevitable consequences of changes in the causes of death, advances in medical science, and the development of new technologies. Both the need and the capability to assist individuals end their lives in peace and dignity have increased exponentially.

E. Prior Court Decisions

Next we examine previous Court decisions that delineate the boundaries of substantive due process. We believe that a careful examination of these decisions demonstrates that there is a strong liberty interest in determining how and when one's life shall end, and that an explicit recognition of that interest follows naturally, indeed inevitably, from their reasoning.

The essence of the substantive component of the Due Process Clause is to limit the ability of the state to intrude into the most important matters of our lives, at least without substantial justification. In a long line of cases, the Court has carved out certain key moments and decisions in individuals' lives and placed them beyond the general prohibitory authority of the state. The Court has recognized that the Fourteenth Amendment affords constitutional protection to personal decisions relating to marriage, *Loving v. Virginia,* 388 U.S. 1, 87 S.Ct. 1817, 18 L.Ed.2d 1010 (1967), procreation, *Skinner v. Oklahoma,* 316 U.S. 535, 62 S.Ct. 1110, 86 L.Ed. 1655 (1942), family relationships, *Prince v. Massachusetts,* 321 U.S. 158, 64 S.Ct. 438, 88 L.Ed. 645 (1944), child rearing and education, *Pierce v. Society of Sisters,* 268 U.S. 510, 534–535, 45 S.Ct. 571, 573–574, 69 L.Ed. 1070 (1925), and intercourse for purposes other than procreation, *Griswold v. Connecticut,* 381 U.S. 479, 85 S.Ct. 1678, 14 L.Ed.2d 510 (1965). The Court has recognized the right of individuals to be free from government interference in deciding matters as personal as whether to bear or beget a child, *Eisenstadt v. Baird,* 405 U.S. 438, 92 S.Ct. 1029, 31 L.Ed.2d 349 (1972), and whether to continue an unwanted pregnancy to term, *Roe v. Wade,* 410 U.S. 113, 93 S.Ct. 705, 35 L.Ed.2d 147 (1973).

A common thread running through these cases is that they involve decisions that are highly personal and intimate, as well as of great importance to the individual. Certainly, few decisions are more personal, intimate or important than the decision to end one's life, especially when the reason for doing so is to avoid excessive and protracted pain. Accordingly, we believe the cases from *Pierce* through *Roe* provide strong general support for our conclusion that a liberty interest in controlling the time and manner of one's death is protected by the Due Process Clause of the Fourteenth Amendment.

While the cases we have adverted to lend general support to our conclusion, we believe that two relatively recent decisions of the Court, *Planned Parenthood v. Casey,* 505 U.S. 833, 112 S.Ct. 2791, 120 L.Ed.2d 674 (1992) and *Cruzan v. Director, Missouri Dept. of Health,* 497 U.S. 261, 110 S.Ct. 2841, 111 L.Ed.2d 224 (1990), are fully persuasive, and leave little doubt as to the proper result.

F. Liberty Interest under *Casey*

In *Casey,* the Court surveyed its prior decisions affording "constitutional protection to personal decisions relating to marriage, procreation, contraception, family relationships, child rearing, and education," *id.* at 851, 112 S.Ct. at 2807 and then said:

> These matters, involving the most intimate and personal choices a person may make in a lifetime, choices central to personal dignity and autonomy, are central to the liberty protected by the Fourteenth Amendment. At the heart of liberty is the right to define one's own concept of existence, of meaning, of the universe, and of the mystery of human life. Beliefs about these matters could not define the attributes of personhood were they formed under compulsion of the State.

Id. at 851, 112 S.Ct. at 2807. The district judge in this case found the Court's reasoning in *Casey* "highly instructive" and "almost prescriptive" for determining "what liberty interest may inhere in a terminally ill person's choice to commit suicide." *Compassion in Dying,* 850 F.Supp. at 1459. We agree.

Like the decision of whether or not to have an abortion, the decision how and when to die is one of "the most intimate and personal choices a person may make in a lifetime," a choice "central to personal dignity and autonomy." A competent terminally ill adult, having lived nearly the full measure of his life, has a strong liberty interest in choosing a dignified and humane death rather than being reduced at the end of his existence to a childlike state of helplessness, diapered, sedated, incontinent. How a person dies not only determines the nature of the final period of his existence, but in many cases, the enduring memories held by those who love him.

Prohibiting a terminally ill patient from hastening his death may have an even more profound impact on that person's life than forcing a woman to carry a pregnancy to term. The case of an AIDS patient treated by Dr. Peter Shalit, one of the physician-plaintiffs in this case, provides a compelling illustration. In his declaration, Dr. Shalit described his patient's death this way:

> One patient of mine, whom I will call Smith, a fictitious name, lingered in the hospital for weeks, his lower body so swollen from oozing Kaposi's lesions that he could not walk, his genitals so swollen that he required a

catheter to drain his bladder, his fingers gangrenous from clotted arteries. Patient Smith's friends stopped visiting him because it gave them nightmares. Patient Smith's agonies could not be relieved by medication or by the excellent nursing care he received. Patient Smith begged for assistance in hastening his death. As his treating doctor, it was my professional opinion that patient Smith was mentally competent to make a choice with respect to shortening his period of suffering before inevitable death. I felt that I should accommodate his request. However, because of the statute, I was unable to assist him and he died after having been tortured for weeks by the end-phase of his disease.

For such patients, wracked by pain and deprived of all pleasure, a state-enforced prohibition on hastening their deaths condemns them to unrelieved misery or torture. Surely, a person's decision whether to endure or avoid such an existence constitutes one of the most, if not the most, "intimate and personal choices a person may make in a life-time," a choice that is "central to personal dignity and autonomy." *Casey,* 505 U.S. at 851, 112 S.Ct. at 2807. Surely such a decision implicates a most vital liberty interest.

G. Liberty Interest under *Cruzan*

In *Cruzan,* the Court considered whether or not there is a constitutionally-protected, due process liberty interest in terminating unwanted medical treatment. The Court said that an affirmative answer followed almost inevitably from its prior decisions holding that patients have a liberty interest in refusing to submit to specific medical procedures. Those cases include *Jacobson v. Massachusetts,* 197 U.S. 11, 24–30, 25 S.Ct. 358, 360–363, 49 L.Ed. 643 (1905), in which the Court balanced an individual's liberty interest in declining an unwanted small pox vaccine against the State's interest in preventing disease; *Washington v. Harper,* 494 U.S. 210, 229, 110 S.Ct. 1028, 1041, 108 L.Ed.2d 178 (1990), in which the Court said: "The forcible injection of medication into a nonconsenting person's body represents a substantial interference with that person's liberty"; and *Parham v. J.R.,* 442 U.S. 584, 600, 99 S.Ct. 2493, 2503, 61 L.Ed.2d 101 (1979), in which it said: "[A] child, in common with adults, has a substantial liberty interest in not being confined unnecessarily for medical treatment." Writing for a majority that included Justices O'Connor and Scalia, Chief Justice Rehnquist said that those cases helped answer the first critical question at issue in *Cruzan,* stating: "The principle that a competent person has a constitutionally protected liberty interest in refusing unwanted medical treatment may be inferred from our prior decisions." *Cruzan,* 497 U.S. at 278, 110 S.Ct. at 2851 (emphasis added).

In her concurrence, Justice O'Connor explained that the majority opinion held (implicitly or otherwise) that a liberty interest in refusing medical treatment extends to all types of medical treatment from dialysis or artificial respirators to the provision of food and water by tube or other artificial means. As Justice O'Connor said: "I *agree* that a protected liberty interest in refusing unwanted medical treatment may be inferred from our prior decisions, and that the refusal of artificial delivery of food and water is encompassed in that liberty interest." *Cruzan,* 497 U.S. 261, 287, 287, 110 S.Ct. 2841, 2856 (O'Connor, J., concurring) (emphasis added).

Justice O'Connor further concluded that under the majority's opinion, "[r]equiring a competent adult to endure such procedures against her will burdens the patient's liberty, dignity, and freedom to determine the course of her own treatment." *Id.* at 289, 110 S.Ct. at 2857 (O'Connor, J., concurring). In the majority opinion itself, Chief Justice Rehnquist made a similar assertion, writing:

> *The choice between life and death is a deeply personal decision of obvious and overwhelming finality.* We believe Missouri may legitimately seek to safeguard the personal element of this choice through the imposition of heightened evidentiary requirements. *It cannot be disputed that the Due Process Clause protects* an interest in life as well as *an interest in refusing life-sustaining medical treatment.*

Cruzan, 497 U.S. at 281, 110 S.Ct. at 2852–53 (emphasis added).

These passages make it clear that *Cruzan* stands for the proposition that there is a due process liberty interest in rejecting unwanted medical treatment, including the provision of food and water by artificial means. Moreover, the Court majority clearly recognized that granting the request to remove the tubes through which *Cruzan* received artificial nutrition and hydration would lead inexorably to her death. *Cruzan,* 497 U.S. at 267–68, 283, 110 S.Ct. at 2846, 2853. Accordingly, we conclude that Cruzan, by recognizing a liberty interest that includes the refusal of artificial provision of life-sustaining food and water, necessarily recognizes a liberty interest in hastening one's own death.

H. Summary

Casey and *Cruzan* provide persuasive evidence that the Constitution encompasses a due process liberty interest in controlling the time and manner of one's death—that there is, in short, a constitutionally recognized "right to die." Our conclusion is strongly influenced by, but not limited to, the plight of mentally competent, terminally ill adults. We are influenced as well by the plight of others, such as those whose existence is reduced to a vegetative state or a permanent and irreversible state of unconsciousness. *See* note 68 *supra*.

Our conclusion that there is a liberty interest in determining the time and manner of one's death does not mean that there is a concomitant right to exercise that interest in all circumstances or to do so free from state regulation. To the contrary, we explicitly recognize that some prohibitory and regulatory state action is fully consistent with constitutional principles.

In short, finding a liberty interest constitutes a critical first step toward answering the question before us. The determination that must now be made is whether the state's attempt to curtail the exercise of that interest is constitutionally justified.

V. Relevant Factors and Interests

To determine whether a state action that impairs a liberty interest violates an individual's substantive due process rights we must identify the factors relevant to the case at hand, assess the state's interests and the individual's liberty interest in light of those factors, and then weigh and balance the competing interests. The relevant factors generally include: 1) the importance of the various state interests, both in general and in the factual context of the case; 2) the manner in which those interests are furthered by the state law or regulation; 3) the importance of the liberty interest, both in itself and in the context in which it is being exercised; 4) the extent to which that interest is burdened by the challenged state action; and, 5) the consequences of upholding or overturning the statute or regulation.

A. The State's Interests

We analyze the factors in turn, and begin by considering the first: the importance of the state's interests. We identify six related state interests involved in the controversy before us: 1) the state's general interest in preserving life; 2) the state's more specific interest in preventing suicide; 3) the state's interest in avoiding the involvement of third parties and in precluding the use of arbitrary, unfair, or undue influence; 4) the state's interest in protecting family members and loved ones; 5) the state's interest in protecting the integrity of the medical profession; and, 6) the state's interest in avoiding adverse consequences that might ensue if the statutory provision at issue is declared unconstitutional.

1. Preserving Life

The state may assert an unqualified interest in preserving life in general. As the Court said in *Cruzan,* "we think a State may properly decline to make judgments about the 'quality' of life that a particular individual may enjoy, and simply assert an unqualified interest in the preservation of human life . . ." *Cruzan,* 497 U.S. at 282, 110 S.Ct. at 2853. Thus, the state may assert its interest in preserving life in all cases, including those of terminally ill, competent adults who wish to hasten their deaths.

Although the state's interest in preserving life may be unqualified, and may be asserted regardless of the quality of the life or lives at issue, that interest is not always controlling. Nor is it of the same strength in each case. To the contrary, its *strength* is dependent on relevant circumstances, including the medical condition and the wishes of the person whose life is at stake.

Most tellingly, the state of Washington has already decided that its interest in preserving life should ordinarily give way—at least in the case of competent, terminally ill adults who are dependent on medical treatment—to the wishes of the patients. In its Natural Death Act, RCW 70.122.020 *et seq.*, Washington permits adults to have "life-sustaining treatment withheld or withdrawn in instances of a terminal condition or permanent unconsciousness." RCW 70.122.010. In adopting the statute, the Washington legislature necessarily determined that the state's interest in preserving life is not so weighty that it ought to thwart the informed desire of a terminally ill, competent adult to refuse medical treatment.

Not only does Washington law acknowledge that terminally ill and permanently unconscious adults have a right to refuse life-sustaining treatment, the statute includes specific legislative findings that appear to recognize that a due process liberty interest underlies that right. The statute states:

> The legislature finds that adult persons have the fundamental right to control the decisions relating to the rendering of their own medical care, including the decision to have life-sustaining procedures withheld or withdrawn in instances of terminal condition.
>
> The legislature further finds that modern medical technology has made possible the artificial prolongation of human life beyond natural limits.
>
> The legislature further finds that, in the interest of protecting individual autonomy, such prolongation of life for persons with a terminal condition may cause loss of patient dignity, and unnecessary pain and suffering, while providing nothing medically necessary or beneficial to the patient.

RCW 70.122.010.

The Washington statute permits competent adults to reject life-sustaining medical treatment in advance by means of living wills and durable powers of attorney. RCW 70.122.010–030. Even in cases in which the Washington Natural Death Act does not authorize surrogate decision-making, the Washington Supreme Court has found that legal guardians may sometimes have life-sustaining treatment discontinued. *In re Guardianship of Grant,* 109 Wash.2d 545, 747 P.2d 445 (Wash.1987); *In re Colyer,* 99 Wash.2d 114, 660 P.2d 738 (Wash.1983).

There is nothing unusual about Washington's recognition that the state's interest in preserving life is not always of the same force and that in some cases at least other considerations may outweigh the state's. More than 40 other states have adopted living will statutes that permit competent adults to declare by advance directive that they do not wish to be kept alive by medical treatment in the latter stages of a terminal illness. Like Washington, many states also permit competent adults to determine in advance that they do not wish any medical treatment should they become permanently and irreversibly unconscious. Also, like Washington, many states allow patients to delegate decision-making power to a surrogate through a durable power of attorney, health care proxy, or similar device, or permit courts to appoint surrogate decision-makers. Finally, Congress favors permitting adult patients to refuse life-sustaining treatment by advance directive and requires hospitals receiving federal financial support to notify adult patients of their rights to execute such instruments upon admission.

As the laws in state after state demonstrate, even though the protection of life is one of the state's most important functions, the state's interest is dramatically diminished if the person it seeks to protect is terminally ill or permanently comatose and has expressed a wish that he be permitted to die without further medical treatment (or if a duly appointed representative has done so on his behalf). When patients are no longer able to pursue liberty or happiness and do not wish to pursue life, the state's interest in forcing them to remain alive is clearly less compelling. Thus, while the state may still seek to prolong the lives of terminally ill or comatose patients or, more likely, to enact regulations that will safeguard the manner in which decisions to hasten death are made, the strength of the state's interest is substantially reduced in such circumstances.

2. Preventing Suicide

a. While the state's general commitment to the preservation of life clearly encompasses the prevention of suicide, the state has an even more particular interest in deterring the taking of one's own life. The fact that neither Washington nor any other state currently bans suicide, or attempted suicide, does not mean that the state does not have a valid and important interest in preventing or discouraging that act.

During the course of this litigation, the state has relied on its interest in the prevention of suicide as its primary justification for its statute. The state points to statistics concerning the rate of suicide among various age groups, particularly the young. *Compassion in Dying,* 850 F.Supp. at 1464. As the state notes, in 1991, suicide was the second leading cause of death after accidents for the age groups 15–19, 20–24, and 25–34 and one of the top five causes of death for age groups 35–44 and 45–54. These figures are indeed distressing.

Although suicide by teenagers and young adults is especially tragic, the state has a clear interest in preventing anyone, no matter what age, from taking his own life in a fit of desperation, depression, or loneliness or as a result of any other problem, physical or psychological, which can be significantly ameliorated. Studies show that many suicides are committed by people who are suffering from treatable mental disorders. Most if not all states provide for the involuntary commitment of such persons if they are likely to physically harm themselves. For similar reasons, at least a dozen states allow the use of nondeadly force to prevent suicide attempts.

While the state has a legitimate interest in preventing suicides in general, that interest, like the state's interest in preserving life, is substantially diminished in the case of terminally ill, competent adults who wish to die. One of the heartaches of suicide is the senseless loss of a life ended prematurely. In the case of a terminally ill adult who ends his life in the final stages of an incurable and painful degenerative disease, in order to avoid debilitating pain and a humiliating death, the decision to commit suicide is not senseless, and death does not come too early. Unlike "the depressed twenty-one year old, the romantically devastated twenty-eight year old, the alcoholic forty-year old," *Compassion in Dying,* 49 F.3d at 590–91, or many others who may be inclined to commit suicide, a terminally ill competent adult cannot be cured. While some people who contemplate suicide can be restored to a state of physical and mental well-being, terminally ill adults who wish to die can only be maintained in a debilitated and deteriorating state, unable to enjoy the presence of family or friends. Not only is the state's interest in preventing such individuals from hastening their deaths of comparatively little weight, but its insistence on frustrating their wishes seems cruel indeed. As Kent said in *King Lear,* when signs of life were seen in the dying monarch:

> Vex not his ghost: O! let him pass; he hate him That would upon the rack of this tough world Stretch him out longer.

b. The state has explicitly recognized that its interests are frequently insufficient to override the wishes of competent, terminally ill adult patients who desire to bring their lives to an end with the assistance of a physician. Step by step, the state has acknowledged that terminally ill persons are entitled in a whole variety of circumstances to hasten their deaths, and that in such cases their physicians may assist in the process. Until relatively recently, while physicians routinely helped patients to hasten their deaths, they did so discreetly because almost all such assistance was illegal. However, beginning about twenty years ago a series of dramatic changes took place. Each provoked the type of division and debate that surrounds the issue before us today. Each time the state's interests were ultimately subordinated to the liberty interests of the individual, in part as a result of legal actions and in part as a result of a growing recognition by the medical community and society at large that a more enlightened approach was essential.

The first major breakthrough occurred when the terminally ill were permitted to reject medical treatment. The line was drawn initially at extraordinary medical treatment because the distinction between ordinary and extraordinary treatment appeared to some to offer the courts an objective, scientific standard that would enable them to recognize the right to refuse certain medical treatment without also recognizing a right to suicide or euthanasia. That distinction, however, quickly proved unworkable, and after a while, terminally ill patients were allowed to reject *both* extraordinary and ordinary treatment. For a while, *rejection* of treatment, often through "do not resuscitate" orders, was permitted, but *termination* was not. This dividing line, which rested on the illusory distinction between commission and omission (or active and passive), also appeared for a short time to offer a natural point of repose for doctors, patients and the law. However, it, too, quickly proved untenable, and ultimately patients were allowed both to *refuse* and to *terminate* medical treatment, ordinary as well as extraordinary. Today, many states also allow the terminally ill to order their physicians to discontinue not just traditional medical treatment but the artificial provision of life-sustaining food and water, thus permitting the patients to die by self-starvation. Equally important, today, doctors are generally permitted to administer death-inducing medication, as long as they can point to a concomitant pain-relieving purpose.

In light of these drastic changes regarding acceptable medical practices, opponents of physician-assisted suicide must now explain precisely what it is about the physician's conduct in assisted suicide cases that distinguishes it from the conduct that the state has explicitly authorized. The state responds by urging that physician-assisted suicide is different in kind, not degree, from the type of physician-life-ending conduct that is now authorized, for three separate reasons. It argues that "assisted suicide": 1) requires doctors to play an active role; 2) causes deaths that would not result from the patient's underlying disease; and 3) requires doctors to provide the causal agent of patients' deaths.

The distinctions suggested by the state do not individually or collectively serve to distinguish the medical practices society currently accepts. The first distinction—the line between commission and omission—is a distinction without a difference now that patients are permitted not only to decline all medical treatment, but to instruct their doctors to *terminate* whatever treatment, artificial or otherwise, they are receiving. In disconnecting a respirator, or authorizing its disconnection, a doctor is unquestionably *committing* an act; he is taking an *active* role in bringing about the patient's death. In fact, there can be no doubt that in such instances the doctor intends that, as the result of his action, the patient will die an earlier death than he otherwise would.

Similarly, drawing a distinction on the basis of whether the patient's death results from an underlying disease no longer has any legitimacy. While the distinction may once have seemed tenable, at least from a metaphysical standpoint, it was not based on a valid or practical legal foundation and was therefore quickly abandoned. When Nancy Cruzan's feeding and hydration tube was removed, she did not die of an underlying disease. Rather, she was allowed to starve to death. In fact, Ms. Cruzan was not even terminally ill at the time, but had a life expectancy of 30 years. Similarly, when a doctor provides a conscious patient with medication to ease his discomfort while he starves himself to death—a practice that is not only legal but has been urged as an alternative to assisted suicide—the patient does not die of any underlying ailment. To the contrary, the doctor is helping the patient end his life by providing medication that makes it possible for the patient to achieve suicide by starvation.

Nor is the state's third and final distinction valid. Contrary to the state's assertion, given current medical practices and current medical ethics, it is not possible to distinguish prohibited from permissible medical conduct on the basis of whether the medication provided by the doctor will cause the patient's death. As part of the tradition of administering comfort care, doctors have been supplying the causal agent of patients' deaths for decades. Physicians routinely and openly provide medication to terminally ill patients with the knowledge that it will have a "double effect"—reduce the patient's pain and hasten his death. Such medical treatment is accepted by the medical profession as meeting its highest ethical standards. It commonly takes the form of putting a patient on an intravenous morphine drip, with full knowledge that, while such treatment will alleviate his pain, it will also indubitably hasten his death. There can be no doubt, therefore, that the actual cause of the patient's death is the drug administered by the physician or by a person acting under his supervision or direction. Thus, the causation argument is simply "another bridge crossed" in the journey to vindicate the liberty interests of the terminally ill, and the state's third distinction has no more force than the other two.

c. We acknowledge that in some respects a recognition of the legitimacy of physician-assisted suicide would constitute an additional step beyond what the courts have previously approved. We also acknowledge that judicial acceptance of physician-assisted suicide would cause many sincere persons with strong moral or religious convictions great distress. Nevertheless, we do not believe that the state's interest in preventing that additional step is significantly greater than its interest in preventing the other forms of life-ending medical conduct that doctors now engage in regularly. More specifically, we see little, if any, difference for constitutional or ethical purposes between providing medication with a double effect and providing medication with a single effect, as long as one of the known effects in each case is to hasten the end of the patient's life. Similarly, we see no ethical or constitutionally cognizable difference between a doctor's pulling the plug on a respirator and his prescribing drugs which will permit a terminally ill patient to end his own life. In fact, some might argue that pulling the plug is a more culpable and aggressive act on the doctor's part and provides more reason for criminal prosecution. To us, what matters most is that the death of the patient is the intended result as surely in one case as in the other. In sum, we find the state's interests in preventing suicide do not make its interests substantially stronger here than in cases involving other forms of death-hastening medical intervention. To the extent that a difference exists, we conclude that it is one of degree and not of kind.

d. Moreover, we are doubtful that deaths resulting from terminally ill patients taking medication prescribed by their doctors should be classified as "suicide." Certainly, we see little basis for such a classification when deaths that result from patients' decisions to terminate life support systems or to refuse life-sustaining food and water, for example, are not. We believe that there is a strong argument that a decision by a terminally ill patient to hasten by medical means a death that is already in process, should not be classified as suicide. Thus, notwithstanding the generally accepted use of the term "physician-assisted suicide," we have serious doubt that the state's interest in preventing suicide is even implicated in this case.

e. In addition to the state's purported interest in preventing suicide, it has an additional interest in preventing deaths that occur as a result of errors in medical or legal judgment. We acknowledge that it is sometimes impossible to predict with certainty the duration of a terminally ill patient's remaining existence, just as it is sometimes impossible to say for certain whether a borderline individual is or is not mentally competent. However, we believe that sufficient safeguards can and will be developed by the state and medical profession, *see infra* p. 833, to ensure that the possibility of error will ordinarily be remote. Finally, although life and death decisions are of the gravest order, should an error actually occur it is likely to benefit the individual by permitting a victim of unmanageable pain and suffering to end his life peacefully and with dignity at the time he deems most desirable.

3. Avoiding the Involvement of Third Parties, and Precluding the Use of Arbitrary, Unfair, or Undue Influence

a. A state may properly assert an interest in prohibiting even altruistic assistance to a person contemplating suicide on the grounds that allowing others to help may increase the incidence of suicide, undercut society's commitment to the sanctity of life, and, adversely affect the person providing the assistance. In addition, joint action is generally considered more serious than action by a single person. While we recognize that these concerns are legitimate, the most important—the first two—diminish in importance to the same extent that the state's interest in preventing the act itself diminishes. All are at their minimums when the assistance is provided by or under the supervision or direction of a doctor and the recipient is a terminally ill patient.

In upholding Washington's statute, the majority of the three-judge panel relied heavily on the state's interest in preventing the exercise of undue, arbitrary
or unfair influences over the individual's decision to end his life. *Compassion in
Dying,* 49 F.3d at 592–93. We agree that this is an important interest, but for entirely different reasons than the majority suggests. One of the majority's prime
arguments is that the statute is necessary to protect "the poor and minorities
from exploitation," 49 F.3d at 592—in other words, to protect the disadvantaged
from becoming the victims of assisted suicide. This rationale simply recycles one
of the more disingenuous and fallacious arguments raised in opposition to the legalization of abortion. It is equally meretricious here. In fact, as with abortion,
there is far more reason to raise the opposite concern: the concern that the poor
and the minorities, who have historically received the least adequate health care,
will not be afforded a fair opportunity to obtain the medical assistance to which
they are entitled—the assistance that would allow them to end their lives with a
measure of dignity. The argument that disadvantaged persons will receive *more*
medical services than the remainder of the population in one, and only one,
area—assisted suicide—is ludicrous on its face. So, too, is the argument that the
poor and the minorities will rush to volunteer for physician-assisted suicide because of their inability to secure adequate medical treatment.

Our analysis is similar regarding the argument relating to the handicapped.
Again, the opponents of physician-assisted suicide urge a variation of the dis-
credited anti-abortion argument. Despite the dire predictions, the disabled were
not pressured into seeking abortions. Nor is it likely that the disabled will be pressured into committing physician-assisted suicide. Organizations representing the
physically impaired are sufficiently active politically and sufficiently vigilant that
they would soon put a halt to any effort to employ assisted suicide in a manner
that affected their clients unfairly. There are other more subtle concerns, however, advanced by some representatives of the physically impaired, including the
fear that certain physical disabilities will erroneously be deemed to make life "val-
ueless." While we recognize the legitimacy of these concerns, we also recognize
that seriously impaired individuals will, along with non-impaired individuals, be
the beneficiaries of the liberty interest asserted here—and that if they are not afforded the option to control their own fate, they like many others will be compelled, against their will, to endure unusual and protracted suffering. The resolution that would be best for all, of course, would be to ensure that the practice
of assisted suicide is conducted fairly and well, and that adequate safeguards sufficient to avoid the feared abuses are adopted and enforced.

b. There is a far more serious concern regarding third parties that we must
consider—one not even mentioned by the majority in the panel opinion. That
concern is the fear that infirm, elderly persons will come under undue pressure
to end their lives from callous, financially burdened, or self-interested relatives,
or others who have influence over them. The risk of undue influence is real—and
it exists today. Persons with a stake in the outcome may now pressure the terminally ill to reject or decline life-saving treatment or take other steps likely to hasten their demise. Surrogates may make unfeeling life and death decisions for
their incompetent relatives. This concern deserves serious consideration, as it

did when the decision was made some time ago to permit the termination of life-support systems and the withdrawal or withholding of other forms of medical treatment, and when it was decided to recognize living wills, durable powers of attorney, and the right of courts to appoint substitute decision-makers. While we do not minimize the concern, the temptation to exert undue pressure is ordinarily tempered to a substantial degree in the case of the terminally ill by the knowledge that the person will die shortly in any event. Given the possibility of undue influence that already exists, the recognition of the right to physician-assisted suicide would not increase that risk unduly. In fact, the direct involvement of an impartial and professional third party in the decision-making process would more likely provide an important safeguard against such abuse.

We also realize that terminally ill patients may well feel pressured to hasten their deaths, not because of improper conduct by their loved ones, but rather for an opposite reason—out of concern for the economic welfare of their loved ones. Faced with the prospect of astronomical medical bills, terminally ill patients might decide that it is better for them to die before their health care expenses consume the life savings they planned to leave for their families, or, worse yet, burden their families with debts they may never be able to satisfy. While state regulations can help ensure that patients do not make rash, uninformed, or ill considered decisions, we are reluctant to say that, in a society in which the costs of protracted health care can be so exorbitant, it is improper for competent, terminally ill adults to take the economic welfare of their families and loved ones into consideration.

Throughout its analysis, the dissent relies heavily on Professor Kamisar, a long-time, outspoken, and nationally-recognized opponent of assisted suicide. Following Professor Kamisar's lead, our dissenting colleagues suggest that the nation's priorities are misplaced because some of the problems we address result from the "lack of universal access to medical care." Dissent at 852. We would be inclined to agree that the country's refusal to provide universal health care, and the concomitant suffering so many Americans are forced to undergo, demonstrates a serious flaw in our national values. One answer, of course, is that concerns over the absence of decent medical coverage in this country should be addressed to Congress, which, if it recognizes the values the dissenters and others espouse, will surely enact the sorely-needed, health-care legislation it has up to now rejected. As members of the judicial branch, however, we are compelled to stand aside from that battle. On the other hand, we are certainly not obligated to pile injury upon injury by holding that all of our citizens may be subjected to the prospect of needless pain, suffering, and degradation at the end of their lives, either because of our concern over Congress' failure to provide government-insured health care or alternatively in order to satisfy the moral or religious precepts of a portion of the population.

    c. We are also aware of the concern that doctors become hardened to the inevitability of death and to the plight of terminally ill patients, and that they will treat requests to die in a routine and impersonal manner, rather than affording the careful, thorough, individualized attention that each request deserves. The day of the family doctor who made house calls and knew the frailties and strengths of each family member is long gone. So, too, in the main, is the intense personal interest that doctors used to take in their patients' welfare and activities. Doctors like the rest of society face constantly increasing pressures, and may not always have the patience to deal with the elderly, some of whom can be both difficult and troublesome. Nevertheless, there are many doctors who specialize in geriatric care and there are many more who are not specialists but who treat elderly patients with great compassion and sensitivity. We believe that most, if not all, doctors would not assist a terminally ill patient to hasten his death as long as there were any reasonable chance of alleviating the patient's suffering or enabling him to live under tolerable conditions. We also believe that physicians would not assist a patient to end his life if there were any significant doubt about the patient's true wishes. To do so would be contrary to the physicians' fundamental training, their conservative nature, and the ethics of their profession. In any case, since doctors are highly-regulated professionals, it should not be difficult for the state or the profession itself to establish rules and procedures that will ensure that the occasional negligent or careless recommendation by a licensed physician will not result in an uninformed or erroneous decision by the patient or his family.

Having said all this, we do not dismiss the legitimate concerns that exist regarding undue influence. While steps can be taken to minimize the danger substantially, the concerns cannot be wholly eliminated. Accordingly, they are of more than minimal weight and, in balancing the competing interests, we treat them seriously.

4. Effect on Children, Other Family Members, and Loved Ones

The state clearly has a legitimate interest in safeguarding the interests of innocent third parties such as minor children and other family members dependent on persons who wish to commit suicide. That state interest, however, is of almost negligible weight when the patient is terminally ill and his death is imminent and inevitable. The state cannot help a minor child or any other innocent third party by forcing a terminally ill patient to die a more protracted and painful death. In fact, witnessing a loved one suffer a slow and agonizing death as a result of state compulsion is more likely to harm than further the interests of innocent third parties.

5. Protecting the Integrity of the Medical Profession

The state has a legitimate interest in assuring the integrity of the medical profession, an interest that includes prohibiting physicians from engaging in conduct that is at odds with their role as healers. We do not believe that the integrity of the medical profession would be threatened in any way by the vindication of the liberty interest at issue here. Rather, it is the existence of a statute that criminalizes the provision of medical assistance to patients in need that could create conflicts with the doctors' professional obligations and make covert criminals out of honorable, dedicated, and compassionate individuals.

The assertion that the legalization of physician-assisted suicide will erode the commitment of doctors to help their patients rests both on an ignorance of what numbers of doctors have been doing for a considerable time and on a misunderstanding of the proper function of a physician. As we have previously noted, doctors have been discreetly helping terminally ill patients hasten their deaths for decades and probably centuries, while acknowledging privately that there was no other medical purpose to their actions. They have done so with the tacit approval of a substantial percentage of both the public and the medical profession, and without in any way diluting their commitment to their patients.

In addition, as we also noted earlier, doctors may now openly take actions that will result in the deaths of their patients. They may terminate life-support systems, withdraw life-sustaining gastronomy tubes, otherwise terminate or withhold all other forms of medical treatment, and, may even administer lethal doses of drugs with full knowledge of their "double effect." Given the similarity between what doctors are now permitted to do and what the plaintiffs assert they should be permitted to do, we see no risk at all to the integrity of the profession. This is a conclusion that is shared by a growing number of doctors who openly support physician-assisted suicide and proclaim it to be fully compatible with the physicians' calling and with their commitment and obligation to help the sick. Many more doctors support physician-assisted suicide but without openly advocating a change in the legal treatment of the practice. A recent study of Oregon physicians found that 60% of those who responded believed that physician-assisted suicide should be legal. A recent study of attitudes among physicians in Michigan, where the state legislature adopted a law banning assisted suicide as a result of Dr. Jack Kevorkian's activities, found that only 17.2% of the physicians who responded favored a law prohibiting assisted suicide. Almost all the rest supported one of three options: legalizing physician-assisted suicide (38.9%); permitting the medical profession to regulate the practice (16.1%); or leaving decisions about physician-assisted suicide to the doctor-patient relationship (16.6%). Thus over 70% of the Michigan doctors answering the poll appear to believe that professional ethics do not preclude doctors from engaging in acts that today are classified as "assisted suicide." Even among those doctors who oppose assisted suicide medical ethics do not lie at the heart of the objections. The "most important personal characteristic" separating those doctors from their colleagues is a strong religious identification.

Whether or not a patient can be cured, the doctor has an obligation to attempt to alleviate his pain and suffering. If it is impossible to cure the patient or retard the advance of his disease, then the doctor's primary duty is to make the patient as comfortable as possible. When performing that task, the doctor is performing a proper medical function, even though he knows that his patient's death is a necessary and inevitable consequence of his actions.

As noted earlier, the American Medical Association filed an amicus brief urging that we uphold the practice of administering medicine with a dual effect. At the same time, it takes the position that physician-assisted suicide should not be legalized, at least as of this time. Twenty years ago, the AMA contended that performing abortions violated the Hippocratic Oath; today, it claims that assisting terminally ill patients to hasten their death does likewise. Clearly, the Hippocratic Oath can have no greater import in deciding the constitutionality of physician-assisted suicide than it did in determining whether women had a constitutional right to have an abortion. In *Roe,* the Court cited a scholar's conclusion that the

Hippocratic Oath "originated in a group representing only a small segment of Greek opinion and that it certainly was not accepted by all ancient physicians." The Court stressed the Oath's "rigidity" and was not deterred by its prohibitory language regarding abortion. As *Roe* shows, a literalist reading of the Hippocratic Oath does not represent the best or final word on medical or legal controversies today. Were we to adhere to the rigid language of the oath, not only would doctors be barred from performing abortions or helping terminally ill patients hasten their deaths, but according to a once-accepted interpretation, they would also be prohibited from performing any type of surgery at all, a position that would now be recognized as preposterous by even the most tradition-bound AMA members. More important, regardless of the AMA or its position, experience shows that most doctors can readily adapt to a changing legal climate. Once the Court held that a woman has a constitutional right to have an abortion, doctors began performing abortions routinely and the ethical integrity of the medical profession remained undiminished. Similarly, following the recognition of a constitutional right to assisted suicide, we believe that doctors would engage in the permitted practice when appropriate, and that the integrity of the medical profession would survive without blemish.

Recognizing the right to "assisted suicide" would not require doctors to do anything contrary to their individual principles. A physician whose moral or religious beliefs would prevent him from assisting a patient to hasten his death would be free to follow the dictates of his conscience. Those doctors who believe that terminally ill, competent, adult patients should be permitted to choose the time and manner of their death would be able to help them do so. We believe that extending a choice to doctors as well as to patients would help protect the integrity of the medical profession without compromising the rights or principles of individual doctors and without sacrificing the welfare of their patients.

6. Fear of Adverse Consequences

We now consider the state's final concern. Those opposed to permitting physician-assisted suicide often point to a concern that could be subsumed under the state's general interest in preserving life, but which for clarity's sake we treat separately. The argument is a purely pragmatic one that causes many people deep concern: permitting physician-assisted suicide would "open Pandora's Box."

Once we recognize a liberty interest in hastening one's death, the argument goes, that interest will sweep away all restrictions in its wake. It will only be a matter of time, the argument continues, before courts will sanction putting people to death, not because they are desperately ill and want to die, but because they are deemed to pose an unjustifiable burden on society. Known as a slippery slope argument or what one commentator has called the "thin edge of the wedge" argument, the opponents of assisted suicide conjure up a parade of horribles and insist that the only way to halt the downward spiral is to stop it before it starts. *See Compassion in Dying*, 49 F.3d at 590–91 (providing list of horribles).

This same nihilistic argument can be offered against any constitutionally-protected right or interest. Both before and after women were found to have a right to have an abortion, critics contended that legalizing that medical procedure would lead to its widespread use as a substitute for other forms of birth control or as a means of racial genocide. Inflammatory contentions regarding ways in which the recognition of the right would lead to the ruination of the country did not, however, deter the Supreme Court from first recognizing and then two decades later reaffirming a constitutionally-protected liberty interest in terminating an unwanted pregnancy. In fact, the Court has *never* refused to recognize a substantive due process liberty right or interest merely because there were difficulties in determining when and how to limit its exercise or because others might someday attempt to use it improperly.

Recognition of any right creates the possibility of abuse. The slippery slope fears of *Roe*'s opponents have, of course, not materialized. The legalization of abortion has not undermined our commitment to life generally; nor, as some predicted, has it led to widespread infanticide. Similarly, there is no reason to believe that legalizing assisted suicide will lead to the horrific consequences its opponents suggest.

The slippery slope argument also comes in a second and closely related form. This version of the argument states that a due process interest in hastening one's death, even if the exercise of that interest is initially limited to the terminally ill, will prove infinitely expansive because it will be impossible to define the term "terminally ill." *See Compassion in Dying,* 49 F.3d at 593. (After all, all of us are terminal in some sense of the word, are we not?). *See id.* The argument rests on two false premises. First it presupposes a need for greater precision than is required in constitutional law. Second, it assumes that the terms "terminal illness" or "terminal condition" cannot be defined, even though those terms have in fact been defined repeatedly. They have, for example, been defined in a model statute, The Uniform Rights of the Terminally Ill Act, and in more than 40 state natural death statutes, including Washington's. The model statute and some of the state statutes have defined the term without reference to a fixed time period; others have taken the opposite approach, defining terminal to mean that death is likely to ensue within six months. As we have noted earlier, the Washington Act, like some others, includes persons who are permanently unconscious, that is in an irreversible coma or a persistent vegetative state. RCW 70.122.020(6). While defining the term "terminally ill" is not free from difficulty, the experience of the states has proved that the class of the terminally ill is neither indefinable nor undefined. Indeed, all of the persons described in the various statutes would appear to fall within an appropriate definition of the term. In any event, it is apparent that purported definitional difficulties that have repeatedly been surmounted provide no legitimate reason for refusing to recognize a liberty interest in hastening one's death.

We do not dispute the dissent's contention that the prescription of lethal medication by physicians for use by terminally ill patients who wish to die does not constitute a clear point of demarcation between permissible and impermissible medical conduct. We agree that it may be difficult to make a principled distinction between physician-assisted suicide and the provision to terminally ill patients of other forms of life-ending medical assistance, such as the administration of drugs by a physician. We recognize that in some instances, the patient may be unable to self-administer the drugs and that administration by the physician, or a person acting under his direction or control, may be the only way the patient may be able to receive them. The question whether that type of physician conduct may be constitutionally prohibited must be answered directly in future cases, and not in this one. We would be less than candid, however, if we did not acknowledge that for present purposes we view the critical line in right-to-die cases as the one between the voluntary and involuntary termination of an individual's life. In the first case—volitional death—the physician is aiding or assisting a patient who wishes to exercise a liberty interest, and in the other—involuntary death—another person acting on his own behalf, or, in some instances society's, is determining that an individual's life should no longer continue. We consider it less important who administers the medication than who determines whether the terminally ill person's life shall end. In any event, here we decide only the issue before us—the constitutionality of prohibiting doctors from prescribing medication for use by terminally ill patients who wish to hasten their death.

B. The Means by Which the State Furthers Its Interests

In applying the balancing test, we must take into account not only the strength of the state's interests but also the means by which the state has chosen to further those interests.

1. Prohibition—A Total Ban for the Terminally Ill

Washington's statute prohibiting assisted suicide has a drastic impact on the terminally ill. By prohibiting physician assistance, it bars what for many terminally ill patients is the only palatable, and only practical, way to end their lives. Physically frail, confined to wheelchairs or beds, many terminally ill patients do not have the means or ability to kill themselves in the multitude of ways that healthy individuals can. Often, for example, they cannot even secure the medication or devices they would need to carry out their wishes.

Some terminally ill patients stockpile prescription medicine, which they can use to end their lives when they decide the time is right. The successful use of the stockpile technique generally depends, however, on the assistance of a physician, whether tacit or unknowing (although it is *possible* to end one's life with over-the-counter medication). Even if the terminally ill patients are able to accumulate sufficient drugs, given the pain killers and other medication they are taking, most of them would lack the knowledge to determine what dose of any given drug or drugs they must take, or in what combination. Miscalculation can be tragic. It can lead to an even more painful and lingering death. Alternatively, if the medication reduces respiration enough to restrict the flow of oxygen to the brain but not enough to cause death, it can result in the patient's falling into a comatose or vegetative state.

Thus for many terminally ill patients, the Washington statute is effectively a prohibition. While technically it only prohibits one means of exercising a liberty interest, practically it prohibits the exercise of that interest as effectively as prohibiting doctors from performing abortions prevented women from having abortions in the days before *Roe*.

2. Regulation—a Permissible Means of Promoting State Interests

State laws or regulations governing physician-assisted suicide are both necessary and desirable to ensure against errors and abuse, and to protect legitimate state interests. Any of several model statutes might serve as an example of how these legitimate and important concerns can be addressed effectively.

By adopting appropriate, reasonable, and properly drawn safeguards Washington could ensure that people who choose to have their doctors prescribe lethal doses of medication are truly competent and meet all of the requisite standards. Without endorsing the constitutionality of any particular procedural safeguards, we note that the state might, for example, require: witnesses to ensure voluntariness; reasonable, though short, waiting periods to prevent rash decisions; second medical opinions to confirm a patient's terminal status and also to confirm that the patient has been receiving proper treatment, including adequate comfort care; psychological examinations to ensure that the patient is not suffering from momentary or treatable depression; reporting procedures that will aid in the avoidance of abuse. Alternatively, such safeguards could be adopted by interested medical associations and other organizations involved in the provision of health care, so long as they meet the state's needs and concerns.

While there is always room for error in any human endeavor, we believe that sufficient protections can and will be developed by the various states, with the assistance of the medical profession and health care industry, to ensure that the possibility of error will be remote. We do not expect that, in this nation, the development of appropriate statutes and regulations will be taken lightly by any of the interested parties, or that those charged with their enforcement will fail to perform their duties properly.

In treating a prohibition differently from a regulation, we are following the approach that the Court took in the only right-to-die case to come before it. In *Cruzan,* the Court recognized that the states had a legitimate role to play in regulating the process of refusing or terminating life-sustaining medical treatment even if they could not prohibit the making of decisions that met applicable state standards. The Court explicitly recognized that states did not have to refrain from acting, but rather could adopt appropriate regulations to further their legitimate interests. Missouri's requirement for clear and convincing evidence of a patient's wishes was a regulation designed to reduce the risk of erroneous decisions. The Court upheld that regulation, a requirement that, of course, had far less impact on the exercise of the due process liberty interest than the de facto prohibition at issue here.

To those who argue that courts should refrain from declaring that the terminally ill have a constitutional right to physician-assisted suicide and that we should leave such matters to the individual states, we reply that where important liberty interests are at stake it is not the proper role of the state to adopt statutes totally prohibiting their exercise. Rather, the state should enact regulatory measures that ensure that the exercise of those interests is properly circumscribed and that all necessary safeguards have been provided. In the case of abortions and in the case of the withdrawal of life-sustaining medical treatment, the Court permitted states to enact appropriate regulations that would further its legitimate interests. In this case, like the others, the guiding principle is found in the words of Justice O'Connor. "[T]he more challenging task of crafting appropriate procedures for safeguarding . . . [terminally ill patients'] liberty interests is entrusted to the 'laboratory' of the states in the first instance." *Cruzan* 497 U.S. at 287, 292, 110 S.Ct. at 2856, 2859 (O'Connor, J., concurring) (internal citation omitted).

C. The Strength of the Liberty Interest

Earlier in the opinion we described the liberty interest at issue here and explained its importance. We also explained that the strength of that interest is dependent on a number of factors, especially the individual's physical condition. We noted that an individual's liberty interest in hastening his death is at its low point when that person is young and healthy, because forcing a robust individual to continue living does not, at least absent extraordinary circumstances, subject him to "pain . . . [and] suffering that is too intimate and personal for the State to insist on. . . ." *Casey,* 505 U.S. at 852, 112 S.Ct. at 2807. As we also made clear, when a mentally competent adult is terminally ill, and wishes, free of any coercion, to hasten his death because his remaining days are an unmitigated torture, that person's liberty interest is at its height. For such a person, being forced to live is indeed being subjected to "pain . . . [and] suffering that is too intimate and personal for the State to insist on. . . ." *Id.*

D. The Burden on the Liberty Interest

We have also previously discussed at some length the nature and extent of the burden that the Washington statute imposes on the liberty interest. Here, we need only mention some of the specific evidence introduced by the plaintiffs and refer to some of our earlier analysis. The plaintiffs offered considerable specific testimony involving individual patients that strongly supports their claims that the Washington statute frequently presents an insuperable obstacle to terminally ill persons who wish to hasten their deaths by peaceful means. The testimony produced by the plaintiffs shows that many terminally ill patients who wish to die with dignity are forced to resort to gruesome alternatives because of the unavailability of physician assistance. One such patient, a 34-year-old man dying from AIDS and lymphoma, asked his physician for drugs to hasten his inevitable death after enduring four excruciatingly painful months because he did not wish to die in a hospital in a drug-induced stupor. His doctor, Dr. Harold Glucksberg, one of the physician plaintiffs in this case, refused because he feared prosecution under Washington Statute RCW 9A.36.060. Denied medical assistance, the patient ended his life by jumping from the West Seattle bridge and plummeting to his death. Fortunately, he did not survive the plunge and require permanent hospitalization in an even more exacerbated state of pain.

Deprived of physician assistance, another terminally ill patient took his own life by withholding his insulin and letting himself die of insulin shock. Like many terminally ill patients, one individual killed himself in a secretive and lonely fashion, in order to spare his family from possible criminal charges; as a result he was deprived of a chance to die in a dignified manner with his loved ones at his side. The man's daughter described her father's death this way:

> When he realized that my family was going to be away for a day, he wrote us a beautiful letter, went down to his basement, and shot himself with his 12 gauge shot gun. He was 84 . . . My son-in-law then had the unfortunate and unpleasant task of cleaning my father's splattered brains off the basement walls.

The plaintiffs also produced testimony showing that some terminally ill patients who try to kill themselves are unsuccessful, maiming instead of killing themselves, or that they succeed only after subjecting themselves to needless, excruciating pain. One such terminally ill patient, a mentally competent woman in her 80s suffering from metastatic breast cancer, sought medication to hasten her death from her primary care physician, Dr. Abigail Halperin, one of the physician plaintiffs in this case. Although Dr. Halperin believed, in her professional judgment, that she should accommodate her patient's wishes, she did not do so because she feared prosecution under Washington statute RCW 9A.36.060. The patient acted on her own to hasten her death by placing a plastic bag over her head, securing it so no more air could enter. She suffocated to death, an end that was certainly more painful and inhumane than the death she would have experienced had she been given the prescriptions she sought.

Next, the plaintiffs produced testimony showing that many terminally ill patients are physically or psychologically unable to take their lives by the violent means that are almost always their only alternatives in the absence of assistance from a physician. One man declared that his terminally ill wife "wanted to die but we did not know how to do it. We could not ask her doctors . . . She feared over-the-counter pills, hearing of all the cases where the person woke up a vegetable. Carbon monoxide was out since she wanted the dignity of dying in her own bed, surrounded by the things she loved." Another woman told how her father, "to whom dignity was very important, lay dying, diapered, moaning in pain, begging to die."

Following the approach of the Court in *Casey*, 505 U.S. at 891, 112 S.Ct. at 2828, we note that there is also an extensive body of legal, medical, and sociological literature, lending support to the conclusion that a prohibition on physician assistance imposes an onerous burden on terminally ill, competent adults who wish to hasten their deaths. That conclusion is further buttressed by extensive anecdotal evidence compiled in newspapers and magazines. Although the statute at issue does not totally prohibit the exercise of the liberty interest by all who possess it, it does effectively prohibit its exercise by almost all of the terminally ill. In fact, as applied, the ban on the liberty interest is close to complete; for, there are few terminally ill persons who do not obtain illicit help from someone in the course of their efforts to hasten their deaths.

There is an additional burden on loved ones and family members that is often overlooked. Some terminally ill persons enlist their children, parents, or others who care for them deeply, in an agonizing, brutal and damaging endeavor, criminalized by the state, to end their pain and suffering. The loving and dedicated persons who agree to help—even if they are fortunate enough to avoid prosecution, and almost all are—will likely suffer pain and guilt for the rest of their lives. Those who decline to assist may always wonder whether they should have tried to save their parent or mate from enduring, unnecessary and protracted agony. This burden would be substantially alleviated if doctors were authorized to assist terminally ill persons to end their lives and to supervise and direct others in the implementation of that process.

E. The Consequences of Upholding or Overturning the Statutory Provision

In various earlier sections of this opinion, we have discussed most of the consequences of upholding or overturning the Washington statutory provision at issue, because in this case those consequences are best considered as part of the discussion of the specific factors or interests. The one remaining consequence of significance is easy to identify: Whatever the outcome here, a host of painful and agonizing issues involving the right to die will continue to confront the courts. More important, these problems will continue to plague growing numbers of Americans of advanced age as well as their families, dependents, and loved ones. The issue is truly one which deserves the most thorough, careful, and objective attention from all segments of society.

VI. Application of the Balancing Test and Holding

Weighing and then balancing a constitutionally-protected interest against the state's countervailing interests, while bearing in mind the various consequences of the decision, is quintessentially a judicial role. Despite all of the efforts of generations of courts to categorize and objectify, to create multi-part tests and identify weights to be attached to the various factors, in the end balancing entails the exercise of judicial judgment rather than the application of scientific or mathematical formulae. No legislative body can perform the task for us. Nor can any computer. In the end, mindful of our constitutional obligations, including the limitations imposed on us by that document, we must rely on our judgment, guided by the facts and the law as we perceive them.

As we have explained, in this case neither the liberty interest in choosing the time and manner of death nor the state's countervailing interests are static. The magnitude of each depends on objective circumstances and generally varies inversely with the other. The liberty interest in hastening death is at its strongest when the state's interest in protecting life and preventing suicide is at its weakest, and vice-versa.

The liberty interest at issue here is an important one and in, the case of the terminally ill, is at its peak. Conversely, the state interests, while equally important in the abstract, are for the most part at a low point here. We recognize that in the case of life and death decisions the state has a particularly strong interest in avoiding undue influence and other forms of abuse. Here, that concern is ameliorated in large measure because of the mandatory involvement in the decision-making process of physicians, who have a strong bias in favor of preserving life, and because the process itself can be carefully regulated and rigorous safeguards adopted. Under these circumstances, we believe that the possibility of abuse, even when considered along with the other state interests, does not outweigh the liberty interest at issue.

The state has chosen to pursue its interests by means of what for terminally ill patients is effectively a total prohibition, even though its most important interests could be adequately served by a far less burdensome measure. The consequences of rejecting the as-applied challenge would be disastrous for the terminally ill, while the adverse consequences for the state would be of a far lesser order. This, too, weighs in favor of upholding the liberty interest.

We consider the state's interests in preventing assisted suicide as being different only in degree and not in kind from its interests in prohibiting a number of other medical practices that lead directly to a terminally ill patient's death. Moreover, we do not consider those interests to be significantly greater in the case of assisted suicide than they are in the case of those other medical practices, if indeed they are greater at all. However, even if the difference were one of kind and not degree, our result would be no different. For no matter now much weight we could legitimately afford the state's interest in preventing suicide, that weight, when combined with the weight we give all the other state's interests, is insufficient to outweigh the terminally ill individual's interest in deciding whether to end his agony and suffering by hastening the time of his death with medication prescribed by his physician. The individual's interest in making that vital decision is compelling indeed, for no decision is more painful, delicate, personal, important, or final than the decision how and when one's life shall end. If broad general state policies can be used to deprive a terminally ill individual of the right to make that choice, it is hard to envision where the exercise of arbitrary and intrusive power by the state can be halted. In this case, the state has wide power to regulate, but it may not ban the exercise of the liberty interest, and that is the practical effect of the program before us. Accordingly, after examining one final legal authority, we hold that the "or aids" provision of Washington statute RCW 9A.36.06 is unconstitutional as applied to terminally ill competent adults who wish to hasten their deaths with medication prescribed by their physicians.

A. One Possible Obstacle

The final legal obstacle we examine is an opinion of the District Court of Oregon issued after the panel decision in this case. In *Lee v. State of Oregon,* 891 F.Supp. 1429, 1438 (D.Or.1995), Chief Judge Hogan held that the Oregon Death With Dignity Act, a voter initiative that permits doctors to prescribe medications for terminally ill patients for use in ending their lives, violates the Equal Protection Clause of the Fourteenth Amendment because it deprives terminally ill persons of a *benefit* that is afforded to the non-terminally ill. The *benefit* that the Oregon District Court thought the terminally ill were being deprived of is an Oregon statutory *prohibition* making it a crime for anyone, including doctors, to assist any person, including terminally ill patients, to end their lives, by providing medical assistance or otherwise. The Oregon District Court's reasoning conflicts squarely with the reasoning of this opinion and with the legal conclusions we have reached. Here, we determine that a statute that prohibits doctors from aiding terminally ill persons to hasten their deaths by providing them with prescription medications unconstitutionally *burdens* the liberty interests of the terminally ill. The *benefit* we conclude the terminally ill are entitled to receive in this case—the right to physician-assisted suicide—is precisely what Judge Hogan determined to be a burden and thus unlawful. In short, *Lee* treats a *burden* as a *benefit* and a *benefit* as a *burden*. In doing so, Judge Hogan clearly erred. *Lee* not only does not aid us in reaching our decision, it's reasoning is directly contrary to our holding.

B. Is There an Equal Protection Violation?

In the case before us, Chief Judge Rothstein struck down the "or aids" provision of the Washington statute as it applies to the terminally ill, not only on due process grounds but also on the ground that it violates the Equal Protection Clause. Because we are convinced that her first reason is correct, we need not consider the second. One constitutional violation is enough to support the judgment that we reach here.

VII. Conclusion

We hold that a liberty interest exists in the choice of how and when one dies, and that the provision of the Washington statute banning assisted suicide, as applied to competent, terminally ill adults who wish to hasten their deaths by obtaining medication prescribed by their doctors, violates the Due Process Clause. We recognize that this decision is a most difficult and controversial one, and that it leaves unresolved a large number of equally troublesome issues that will require resolution in the years ahead. We also recognize that other able and dedicated jurists, construing the Constitution as they believe it must be construed, may disagree not only with the result we reach but with our method of constitutional analysis. Given the nature of the judicial process and the complexity of the task of determining the rights and interests comprehended by the Constitution, good faith disagreements within the judiciary should not surprise or disturb anyone who follows the development of the law. For these reasons, we express our hope that whatever debate may accompany the future exploration of the issues we have touched on today will be conducted in an objective, rational, and constructive manner that will increase, not diminish, respect for the Constitution.

There is one final point we must emphasize. Some argue strongly that decisions regarding matters affecting life or death should not be made by the courts. Essentially, we agree with that proposition. In this case, by permitting the *individual* to exercise the right to *choose* we are following the constitutional mandate to take such decisions out of the hands of the government, both state and federal, and to put them where they rightly belong, in the hands of the people. We are allowing individuals to make the decisions that so profoundly affect their very existence—and precluding the state from intruding excessively into that critical realm. The Constitution and the courts stand as a bulwark between individual freedom and arbitrary and intrusive governmental power. Under our constitutional system, neither the state nor the majority of the people in a state can impose its will upon the individual in a matter so highly "central to personal dignity and autonomy," *Casey,* 505 U.S. at 851, 112 S.Ct. at 2807. Those who believe strongly that death must come without physician assistance are free to follow that creed, be they doctors or patients. They are not free, however, to force their views, their religious convictions, or their philosophies on all the other members of a democratic society, and to compel those whose values differ with theirs to die painful, protracted, and agonizing deaths.

AFFIRMED.

Court Opinion in:
Washington
v.
Glucksberg

117 S.Ct. 2258
United States Supreme Court

Chief Justice Rehnquist delivered the opinion of the Court.

The question presented in this case is whether Washington's prohibition against "caus[ing]" or "aid[ing]" a suicide offends the Fourteenth Amendment to the United States Constitution. We hold that it does not.

It has always been a crime to assist a suicide in the State of Washington. In 1854, Washington's first Territorial Legislature outlawed "assisting another in the commission of self-murder." Today, Washington law provides: "A person is guilty of promoting a suicide attempt when he knowingly causes or aids another person to attempt suicide." Wash. Rev.Code 9A.36.060(1) (1994). "Promoting a suicide attempt" is a felony, punishable by up to five years' imprisonment and up to a $10,000 fine. §§ 9A.36.060(2) and 9A.20.021(1)(c). At the same time, Washington's Natural Death Act, enacted in 1979, states that the "withholding or withdrawal of life-sustaining treatment" at a patient's direction "shall not, for any purpose, constitute a suicide." Wash. Rev.Code § 70.122.070(1).

Petitioners in this case are the State of Washington and its Attorney General. Respondents Harold Glucksberg, M. D., Abigail Halperin, M. D., Thomas A. Preston, M. D., and Peter Shalit, M. D., are physicians who practice in Washington. These doctors occasionally treat terminally ill, suffering patients, and declare that they would assist these patients in ending their lives if not for Washington's assisted-suicide ban. In January 1994, respondents, along with three gravely ill, pseudonymous plaintiffs who have since died and Compassion in Dying, a non-profit organization that counsels people considering physician-assisted suicide, sued in the United States District Court, seeking a declaration that Wash RevCode 9A.36.060(1) (1994) is, on its face, unconstitutional. *Compassion in Dying v. Washington,* 850 F.Supp. 1454, 1459 (W.D.Wash. 1994).

The plaintiffs asserted "the existence of a liberty interest protected by the Fourteenth Amendment which extends to a personal choice by a mentally competent, terminally ill adult to commit physician-assisted suicide." *Id.,* at 1459. Relying primarily on *Planned Parenthood v. Casey,* 505 U.S. 833, 112 S.Ct. 2791, 120 L.Ed.2d 674 (1992), and *Cruzan v. Director, Missouri Dept. of Health,* 497 U.S. 261, 110 S.Ct. 2841, 111 L.Ed.2d 224 (1990), the District Court agreed, 850 F.Supp., at 1459–1462, and concluded that Washington's assisted-suicide ban is unconstitutional because it "places an undue burden on the exercise of [that] constitutionally protected liberty interest." *Id.,* at 1465. The District Court also decided that the Washington statute violated the Equal Protection Clause's requirement that "'all persons similarly situated . . . be treated alike.'" *Id.,* at

1466 (quoting *Cleburne v. Cleburne Living Center, Inc.*, 473 U.S. 432, 439, 105 S.Ct. 3249, 3253–3254, 87 L.Ed.2d 313 (1985)).

A panel of the Court of Appeals for the Ninth Circuit reversed, emphasizing that "[i]n the two hundred and five years of our existence no constitutional right to aid in killing oneself has ever been asserted and upheld by a court of final jurisdiction." *Compassion in Dying v. Washington,* 49 F.3d 586, 591 (1995). The Ninth Circuit reheard the case en banc, reversed the panel's decision, and affirmed the District Court. *Compassion in Dying v. Washington,* 79 F.3d 790, 798 (1996). Like the District Court, the en banc Court of Appeals emphasized our *Casey* and *Cruzan* decisions. 79 F.3d, at 813–816. The court also discussed what it described as "historical" and "current societal attitudes" toward suicide and assisted suicide, *id.,* at 806–812, and concluded that "the Constitution encompasses a due process liberty interest in controlling the time and manner of one's death—that there is, in short, a constitutionally-recognized 'right to die.'" *Id.,* at 816. After "[w]eighing and then balancing" this interest against Washington's various interests, the court held that the State's assisted-suicide ban was unconstitutional "as applied to terminally ill competent adults who wish to hasten their deaths with medication prescribed by their physicians." *Id.,* at 836, 837. The court did not reach the District Court's equal-protection holding. *Id.,* at 838. We granted certiorari, 519 U.S. —, 117 S.Ct. 37, 135 L.Ed.2d 1128 (1996), and now reverse.

I.

We begin, as we do in all due-process cases, by examining our Nation's history, legal traditions, and practices. See, *e.g., Casey,* 505 U.S., at 849–850, 112 S.Ct., at 2805–2806; *Cruzan,* 497 U.S., at 269–279, 110 S.Ct., at 2846–2842; *Moore v. East Cleveland,* 431 U.S. 494, 503, 97 S.Ct. 1932, 1937–1938, 52 L.Ed.2d 531 (1977) (plurality opinion) (noting importance of "careful 'respect for the teachings of history'"). In almost every State—indeed, in almost every western democracy—it is a crime to assist a suicide. The States' assisted-suicide bans are not innovations. Rather, they are longstanding expressions of the States' commitment to the protection and preservation of all human life. *Cruzan,* 497 U.S., at 280, 110 S.Ct., at 2852 ("[T]he States—indeed, all civilized nations—demonstrate their commitment to life by treating homicide as a serious crime. Moreover, the majority of States in this country have laws imposing criminal penalties on one who assists another to commit suicide"); see *Stanford v. Kentucky,* 492 U.S. 361, 373, 109 S.Ct. 2969, 2977, 106 L.Ed.2d 306 (1989) ("[T]he primary and most reliable indication of [a national] consensus is . . . the pattern of enacted laws"). Indeed, opposition to and condemnation of suicide—and, therefore, of assisting suicide—are consistent and enduring themes of our philosophical, legal, and cultural heritages. See generally, Marzen, O'Dowd, Crone & Balch, Suicide: A Constitutional Right?, 24 Duquesne L.Rev 1, 17–56 (1985) (hereinafter Marzen); New York State Task Force on Life and the Law, When Death is Sought: Assisted Suicide and Euthanasia in the Medical Context 77–82 (May 1994) (hereinafter New York Task Force).

More specifically, for over 700 years, the Anglo-American common-law tradition has punished or otherwise disapproved of both suicide and assisting suicide. *Cruzan,* 497 U.S., at 294–295, 110 S.Ct., at 2859–2860 (Scalia, J., concurring). In the 13th century, Henry de Bracton, one of the first legal-treatise writers, observed that "[j]ust as a man may commit felony by slaying another so may he do so by slaying himself." 2 Bracton on Laws and Customs of England 423 (f.150) (G. Woodbine ed., S. Thorne transl., 1968). The real and personal property of one who killed himself to avoid conviction and punishment for a crime were forfeit to the king; however, thought Bracton, "if a man slays himself in weariness of life or because he is unwilling to endure further bodily pain . . . [only] his movable goods [were] confiscated." *Id.,* at 423–424 (f.150). Thus, "[t]he principle that suicide of a sane person, for whatever reason, was a punishable felony was . . . introduced into English common law." Centuries later, Sir William Blackstone, whose Commentaries on the Laws of England not only provided a definitive summary of the common law but was also a primary legal authority for 18th and 19th century American lawyers, referred to suicide as "self-murder" and "the pretended heroism, but real cowardice, of the Stoic philosophers, who destroyed themselves to avoid those ills which they had not the fortitude to endure. . . ." 4 W. Blackstone, Commentaries *189. Blackstone emphasized that "the law has . . . ranked [suicide] among the highest crimes," *ibid,* although, anticipating later developments, he conceded that the harsh and shameful punishments imposed for suicide "borde[r] a little upon severity." *Id.,* at *190.

For the most part, the early American colonies adopted the common-law approach. For example, the legislators of the Providence Plantations, which would later become Rhode Island, declared, in 1647, that "[s]elf-murder is by all agreed to be the most unnatural, and it is by this present Assembly declared, to be that, wherein he that doth it, kills himself out of a premeditated hatred against his own life or other humor: . . . his goods and chattels are the king's custom, but not his debts nor lands; but in case he be an infant, a lunatic, mad or distracted man, he forfeits nothing." The Earliest Acts and Laws of the Colony of Rhode Island and Providence Plantations 1647–1719, p. 19 (J. Cushing ed.1977). Virginia also required ignominious burial for suicides, and their estates were forfeit to the crown. A. Scott, Criminal Law in Colonial Virginia 108, and n. 93, 198, and n. 15 (1930).

Over time, however, the American colonies abolished these harsh common-law penalties. William Penn abandoned the criminal-forfeiture sanction in Pennsylvania in 1701, and the other colonies (and later, the other States) eventually followed this example. *Cruzan,* 497 U.S., at 294, 110 S.Ct., at 2859–2860 (Scalia, J., concurring). Zephaniah Swift, who would later become Chief Justice of Connecticut, wrote in 1796 that

> "[t]here can be no act more contemptible, than to attempt to punish an offender for a crime, by exercising a mean act of revenge upon lifeless clay, that is insensible of the punishment. There can be no greater cruelty, than the inflicting [of] a punishment, as the forfeiture of goods, which must fall solely on the innocent offspring of the offender. . . . [Suicide] is so abhor-

rent to the feelings of mankind, and that strong love of life which is implanted in the human heart, that it cannot be so frequently committed, as to become dangerous to society. There can of course be no necessity of any punishment." 2 Z. Swift, A System of the Laws of the State of Connecticut 304 (1796).

This statement makes it clear, however, that the movement away from the common law's harsh sanctions did not represent an acceptance of suicide; rather, as Chief Justice Swift observed, this change reflected the growing consensus that it was unfair to punish the suicide's family for his wrongdoing. *Cruzan, supra,* at 294, 110 S.Ct., at 2859 (SCALIA, J., concurring). Nonetheless, although States moved away from Blackstone's treatment of suicide, courts continued to condemn it as a grave public wrong. See, *e.g., Bigelow v. Berkshire Life Ins. Co.,* 93 U.S. 284, 286, 23 L.Ed. 918 (1876) (suicide is "an act of criminal self-destruction"); *Von Holden v. Chapman,* 87 A.D.2d 66, 70–71, 450 N.Y.S.2d 623, 626–627 (1982); *Blackwood v. Jones,* 111 Fla. 528, 532, 149 So. 600, 601 (1933) ("No sophistry is tolerated . . . which seek[s] to justify self-destruction as commendable or even a matter of personal right").

That suicide remained a grievous, though nonfelonious, wrong is confirmed by the fact that colonial and early state legislatures and courts did not retreat from prohibiting assisting suicide. Swift, in his early 19th century treatise on the laws of Connecticut, stated that "[i]f one counsels another to commit suicide, and the other by reason of the advice kills himself, the advisor is guilty of murder as principal." 2 Z. Swift, A Digest of the Laws of the State of Connecticut 270 (1823). This was the well established common-law view, see *In re Joseph G.,* 34 Cal.3d 429, 434–435, 194 Cal.Rptr. 163, 166, 667 P.2d 1176, 1179 (1983); *Commonwealth v. Mink,* 123 Mass. 422, 428 (1877) ("'Now if the murder of one's self is felony, the accessory is equally guilty as if he had aided and abetted in the murder'") (quoting Chief Justice Parker's charge to the jury in *Commonwealth v. Bowen,* 13 Mass. 356 (1816)), as was the similar principle that the consent of a homicide victim is "wholly immaterial to the guilt of the person who cause[d] [his death]," 3 J. Stephen, A History of the Criminal Law of England 16 (1883); see 1 F. Wharton, Criminal Law §§ 451–452 (9th ed. 1885); *Martin v. Commonwealth,* 184 Va. 1009, 1018–1019, 37 S.E.2d 43, 47 (1946) ("'The right to life and to personal security is not only sacred in the estimation of the common law, but it is inalienable'"). And the prohibitions against assisting suicide never contained exceptions for those who were near death. Rather, "[t]he life of those to whom life ha[d] become a burden—of those who [were] hopelessly diseased or fatally wounded—nay, even the lives of criminals condemned to death, [were] under the protection of law, equally as the lives of those who [were] in the full tide of life's enjoyment, and anxious to continue to live." *Blackburn v. State,* 23 Ohio St. 146, 163 (1872); see *Bowen, supra,* at 360 (prisoner who persuaded another to commit suicide could be tried for murder, even though victim was scheduled shortly to be executed).

The earliest American statute explicitly to outlaw assisting suicide was enacted in New York in 1828, Act of Dec. 10, 1828, ch. 20, § 4, 1828 N.Y. Laws 19 (codified at 2 N.Y.Rev.Stat. pt. 4, ch. 1, tit. 2, art. 1, § 7, p. 661 (1829)), and many of the new States and Territories followed New York's example. Marzen 73–74. Between 1857 and 1865, a New York commission led by Dudley Field drafted a criminal code that prohibited "aiding" a suicide and, specifically, "furnish[ing] another person with any deadly weapon or poisonous drug, knowing that such person intends to use such weapon or drug in taking his own life." *Id.,* at 76–77. By the time the Fourteenth Amendment was ratified, it was a crime in most States to assist a suicide. See *Cruzan, supra,* at 294–295, 110 S.Ct., at 2859–2860 (SCALIA, J., concurring). The Field Penal Code was adopted in the Dakota Territory in 1877, in New York in 1881, and its language served as a model for several other western States' statutes in the late 19th and early 20th centuries. Marzen 76–77, 205–206, 212–213. California, for example, codified its assisted-suicide prohibition in 1874, using language similar to the Field Code's. In this century, the Model Penal Code also prohibited "aiding" suicide, prompting many States to enact or revise their assisted-suicide bans. The Code's drafters observed that "the interests in the sanctity of life that are represented by the criminal homicide laws are threatened by one who expresses a willingness to participate in taking the life of another, even though the act may be accomplished with the consent, or at the request, of the suicide victim." American Law Institute, Model Penal Code § 210.5, Comment 5, p. 100 (Official Draft and Revised Comments 1980).

Though deeply rooted, the States' assisted-suicide bans have in recent years been reexamined and, generally, reaffirmed. Because of advances in medicine and technology, Americans today are increasingly likely to die in institutions, from chronic illnesses. President's Comm'n for the Study of Ethical Problems in Medicine and Biomedical and Behavioral Research, Deciding to Forego Life-Sustaining Treatment 16–18 (1983). Public concern and democratic action are therefore sharply focused on how best to protect dignity and independence at the end of life, with the result that there have been many significant changes in state laws and in the attitudes these laws reflect. Many States, for example, now permit "living wills," surrogate health-care decisionmaking, and the withdrawal or refusal of life-sustaining medical treatment. See *Vacco v. Quill,* — U.S. —, — – —, 117 S.Ct. 2293, — – —, 138 L.Ed.2d 834; 79 F.3d, at 818–820; *People v. Kevorkian,* 447 Mich. 436, 478–480, and nn. 53–56, 527 N.W.2d 714, 731–732, and nn. 53–56 (1994). At the same time, however, voters and legislators continue for the most part to reaffirm their States' prohibitions on assisting suicide.

The Washington statute at issue in this case, Wash. RevCode § 9A.36.060 (1994), was enacted in 1975 as part of a revision of that State's criminal code. Four years later, Washington passed its Natural Death Act, which specifically stated that the "withholding or withdrawal of life-sustaining treatment . . . shall not, for any purpose, constitute a suicide" and that "[n]othing in this chapter shall be construed to condone, authorize, or approve mercy killing. . . ." Natural Death Act, 1979 Wash. Laws, ch. 112, §§ 8(1), p. 11 (codified at Wash. RevCode §§ 70.122.070(1), 70.122.100 (1994)). In 1991, Washington voters rejected a ballot initiative which, had it passed, would have permitted a form of physician-assisted suicide. Washington then added a provision to the Natural Death Act expressly excluding physician-assisted suicide. 1992 Wash. Laws, ch. 98, § 10; Wash. RevCode § 70.122.100 (1994).

California voters rejected an assisted-suicide initiative similar to Washington's in 1993. On the other hand, in 1994, voters in Oregon enacted, also through ballot initiative, that State's "Death With Dignity Act," which legalized physician-assisted suicide for competent, terminally ill adults. Since the Oregon vote, many proposals to legalize assisted-suicide have been and continue to be introduced in the States' legislatures, but none has been enacted. And just last year, Iowa and Rhode Island joined the overwhelming majority of States explicitly prohibiting assisted suicide. See Iowa Code Ann. §§ 707A.2, 707A.3 (Supp.1997); R.I. Gen. Laws §§ 11–60–1, 11–60–3 (Supp.1996). Also, on April 30, 1997, President Clinton signed the Federal Assisted Suicide Funding Restriction Act of 1997, which prohibits the use of federal funds in support of physician-assisted suicide. Pub.L. 105–12, 111 Stat. 23 (codified at 42 U.S.C. § 14401 *et seq*).

Thus, the States are currently engaged in serious, thoughtful examinations of physician-assisted suicide and other similar issues. For example, New York State's Task Force on Life and the Law—an ongoing, blue-ribbon commission composed of doctors, ethicists, lawyers, religious leaders, and interested laymen—was convened in 1984 and commissioned with "a broad mandate to recommend public policy on issues raised by medical advances." New York Task Force vii. Over the past decade, the Task Force has recommended laws relating to end-of-life decisions, surrogate pregnancy, and organ donation. *Id.,* at 118–119. After studying physician-assisted suicide, however, the Task Force unanimously concluded that "[l]egalizing assisted suicide and euthanasia would pose profound risks to many individuals who are ill and vulnerable. . . . [T]he potential dangers of this dramatic change in public policy would outweigh any benefit that might be achieved." *Id.,* at 120.

Attitudes toward suicide itself have changed since Bracton, but our laws have consistently condemned, and continue to prohibit, assisting suicide. Despite changes in medical technology and notwithstanding an increased emphasis on the importance of end-of-life decisionmaking, we have not retreated from this prohibition. Against this backdrop of history, tradition, and practice, we now turn to respondents' constitutional claim.

II.

The Due Process Clause guarantees more than fair process, and the "liberty" it protects includes more than the absence of physical restraint. *Collins v. Harker Heights,* 503 U.S. 115, 125, 112 S.Ct. 1061, 1068–1069, 117 L.Ed.2d 261 (1992) (Due Process Clause "protects individual liberty against 'certain government actions regardless of the fairness of the procedures used to implement them'") (quoting *Daniels v. Williams,* 474 U.S. 327, 331, 106 S.Ct. 662, 665, 88 L.Ed.2d 662 (1986)). The Clause also provides heightened protection against government interference with certain fundamental rights and liberty interests. *Reno v. Flores,* 507 U.S. 292, 301–302, 113 S.Ct. 1439, 1446–1447, 123 L.Ed.2d 1 (1993); *Casey,* 505 U.S., at 851, 112 S.Ct., at 2806–2807. In a long line of cases, we have held that, in addition to the specific freedoms protected by the Bill of Rights, the "liberty" specially protected by the Due Process Clause includes the rights to marry, *Loving v. Virginia,* 388 U.S. 1, 87 S.Ct. 1817, 18 L.Ed.2d 1010 (1967); to have children, *Skinner v. Oklahoma ex rel. Williamson,* 316 U.S. 535, 62 S.Ct. 1110, 86 L.Ed. 1655 (1942); to direct the education and up-bringing of one's children, *Meyer v. Nebraska,* 262 U.S. 390, 43 S.Ct. 625, 67 L.Ed. 1042 (1923); *Pierce v. Society of Sisters,* 268 U.S. 510, 45 S.Ct. 571, 69 L.Ed. 1070 (1925); to marital privacy, *Griswold v. Connecticut,* 381 U.S. 479, 85 S.Ct. 1678, 14 L.Ed.2d 510 (1965); to use contraception, *ibid; Eisenstadt v. Baird,* 405 U.S. 438, 92 S.Ct. 1029, 31 L.Ed.2d 349 (1972); to bodily integrity, *Rochin v. California,* 342 U.S. 165, 72 S.Ct. 205, 96 L.Ed. 183 (1952), and to abortion, *Casey, supra.* We have also assumed, and strongly suggested, that the Due Process Clause protects the traditional right to refuse unwanted lifesaving medical treatment. *Cruzan,* 497 U.S., at 278–279, 110 S.Ct., at 2851–2852.

But we "ha[ve] always been reluctant to expand the concept of substantive due process because guideposts for responsible decisionmaking in this unchar-tered area are scarce and open-ended." *Collins,* 503 U.S., at 125, 112 S.Ct., at 1068. By extending constitutional protection to an asserted right or liberty inter-est, we, to a great extent, place the matter outside the arena of public debate and legislative action. We must therefore "exercise the utmost care whenever we are asked to break new ground in this field," *ibid,* lest the liberty protected by the Due Process Clause be subtly transformed into the policy preferences of the members of this Court, *Moore,* 431 U.S., at 502, 97 S.Ct., at 1937 (plurality opinion).

Our established method of substantive-due-process analysis has two primary features: First, we have regularly observed that the Due Process Clause specially protects those fundamental rights and liberties which are, objectively, "deeply rooted in this Nation's history and tradition," *id.,* at 503, 97 S.Ct., at 1938 (plu-rality opinion); *Snyder v. Massachusetts,* 291 U.S. 97, 105, 54 S.Ct. 330, 332, 78 L.Ed. 674 (1934) ("so rooted in the traditions and conscience of our people as to be ranked as fundamental"), and "implicit in the concept of ordered liberty," such that "neither liberty nor justice would exist if they were sacrificed," *Palko v. Connecticut,* 302 U.S. 319, 325, 326, 58 S.Ct. 149, 152, 82 L.Ed. 288 (1937). Second, we have required in substantive-due-process cases a "careful descrip-tion" of the asserted fundamental liberty interest. *Flores, supra,* at 302, 113 S.Ct., at 1447; *Collins, supra,* at 125, 112 S.Ct., at 1068; *Cruzan, supra,* at 277–278, 110 S.Ct., at 2850–2851. Our Nation's history, legal traditions, and practices thus provide the crucial "guideposts for responsible decisionmaking," *Collins, supra,* at 125, 112 S.Ct., at 1068, that direct and restrain our exposition of the Due Process Clause. As we stated recently in *Flores,* the Fourteenth Amendment "forbids the government to infringe . . . 'fundamental' liberty inter-ests *at all,* no matter what process is provided, unless the infringement is nar-rowly tailored to serve a compelling state interest." 507 U.S., at 302, 113 S.Ct., at 1447.

Justice SOUTER, relying on Justice Harlan's dissenting opinion in *Poe v. Ull-man,* would largely abandon this restrained methodology, and instead ask "whether [Washington's] statute sets up one of those 'arbitrary impositions' or 'purposeless restraints' at odds with the Due Process Clause of the Fourteenth Amendment," *post,* at 2275 (quoting *Poe,* 367 U.S. 497, 543, 81 S.Ct. 1752,

1776–1777, 6 L.Ed.2d 989 (1961) (Harlan, J., dissenting)). In our view, however, the development of this Court's substantive-due-process jurisprudence, described briefly above, *supra*, at 2267, has been a process whereby the outlines of the "liberty" specially protected by the Fourteenth Amendment—never fully clarified, to be sure, and perhaps not capable of being fully clarified—have at least been carefully refined by concrete examples involving fundamental rights found to be deeply rooted in our legal tradition. This approach tends to rein in the subjective elements that are necessarily present in due-process judicial review. In addition, by establishing a threshold requirement—that a challenged state action implicate a fundamental right—before requiring more than a reasonable relation to a legitimate state interest to justify the action, it avoids the need for complex balancing of competing interests in every case.

Turning to the claim at issue here, the Court of Appeals stated that "[p]roperly analyzed, the first issue to be resolved is whether there is a liberty interest in determining the time and manner of one's death," 79 F.3d, at 801, or, in other words, "[i]s there a right to die?," *id.*, at 799. Similarly, respondents assert a "liberty to choose how to die" and a right to "control of one's final days," Brief for Respondents 7, and describe the asserted liberty as "the right to choose a humane, dignified death," *id.*, at 15, and "the liberty to shape death," *id.*, at 18. As noted above, we have a tradition of carefully formulating the interest at stake in substantive-due-process cases. For example, although *Cruzan* is often described as a "right to die" case, see 79 F.3d, at 799; — U.S., at —, 117 S.Ct., at 2307 (STEVENS, J., concurring in judgment) (*Cruzan* recognized "the more specific interest in making decisions about how to confront an imminent death"), we were, in fact, more precise: we assumed that the Constitution granted competent persons a "constitutionally protected right to refuse lifesaving hydration and nutrition." *Cruzan*, 497 U.S., at 279, 110 S.Ct., at 2843; *id.*, at 287, 110 S.Ct., at 2856 (O'CONNOR, J., concurring) ("[A] liberty interest in refusing unwanted medical treatment may be inferred from our prior decisions"). The Washington statute at issue in this case prohibits "aid[ing] another person to attempt suicide," Wash. RevCode § 9A.36.060(1) (1994), and, thus, the question before us is whether the "liberty" specially protected by the Due Process Clause includes a right to commit suicide which itself includes a right to assistance in doing so.

We now inquire whether this asserted right has any place in our Nation's traditions. Here, as discussed above, *supra*, at 2262–2267, we are confronted with a consistent and almost universal tradition that has long rejected the asserted right, and continues explicitly to reject it today, even for terminally ill, mentally competent adults. To hold for respondents, we would have to reverse centuries of legal doctrine and practice, and strike down the considered policy choice of almost every State. See *Jackman v. Rosenbaum Co.*, 260 U.S. 22, 31, 43 S.Ct. 9, 9–10, 67 L.Ed. 107 (1922) ("If a thing has been practiced for two hundred years by common consent, it will need a strong case for the Fourteenth Amendment to affect it"); *Flores*, 507 U.S., at 303, 113 S.Ct., at 1447 ("The mere novelty of such a claim is reason enough to doubt that 'substantive due process' sustains it").

Respondents contend, however, that the liberty interest they assert is consistent with this Court's substantive-due-process line of cases, if not with this Nation's history and practice. Pointing to *Casey* and *Cruzan*, respondents read our jurisprudence in this area as reflecting a general tradition of "self-sovereignty," Brief of Respondents 12, and as teaching that the "liberty" protected by the Due Process Clause includes "basic and intimate exercises of personal autonomy," *id.*, at 10; see *Casey*, 505 U.S., at 847, 112 S.Ct., at 2804–2805 ("It is a promise of the Constitution that there is a realm of personal liberty which the government may not enter"). According to respondents, our liberty jurisprudence, and the broad, individualistic principles it reflects, protects the "liberty of competent, terminally ill adults to make end-of-life decisions free of undue government interference." Brief for Respondents 10. The question presented in this case, however, is whether the protections of the Due Process Clause include a right to commit suicide with another's assistance. With this "careful description" of respondents' claim in mind, we turn to *Casey* and *Cruzan*.

In *Cruzan*, we considered whether Nancy Beth Cruzan, who had been severely injured in an automobile accident and was in a persistive vegetative state, "ha[d] a right under the United States Constitution which would require the hospital to withdraw life-sustaining treatment" at her parents' request. *Cruzan*, 497 U.S., at 269, 110 S.Ct., at 2846–2847. We began with the observation that "[a]t common law, even the touching of one person by another without consent and without legal justification was a battery." *Ibid.* We then discussed the related rule that "informed consent is generally required for medical treatment." *Ibid.* After reviewing a long line of relevant state cases, we concluded that "the common-law doctrine of informed consent is viewed as generally encompassing the right of a competent individual to refuse medical treatment." *Id.*, at 277, 110 S.Ct., at 2851. Next, we reviewed our own cases on the subject, and stated that "[t]he principle that a competent person has a constitutionally protected liberty interest in refusing unwanted medical treatment may be inferred from our prior decisions." *Id.*, at 278, 110 S.Ct., at 2851. Therefore, "for purposes of [that] case, we assume[d] that the United States Constitution would grant a competent person a constitutionally protected right to refuse lifesaving hydration and nutrition." *Id.*, at 279, 110 S.Ct., at 2852; see *id.*, at 287, 110 S.Ct., at 2856 (O'Connor, J., concurring). We concluded that, notwithstanding this right, the Constitution permitted Missouri to require clear and convincing evidence of an incompetent patient's wishes concerning the withdrawal of life-sustaining treatment. *Id.*, at 280–281, 110 S.Ct., at 2852–2853.

Respondents contend that in *Cruzan* we "acknowledged that competent, dying persons have the right to direct the removal of life-sustaining medical treatment and thus hasten death," Brief for Respondents 23, and that "the constitutional principle behind recognizing the patient's liberty to direct the withdrawal of artificial life support applies at least as strongly to the choice to hasten impending death by consuming lethal medication," *id.*, at 26. Similarly, the Court of Appeals concluded that "*Cruzan*, by recognizing a liberty interest that includes the refusal of artificial provision of life-sustaining food and water, necessarily recognize[d] a liberty interest in hastening one's own death." 79 F.3d, at 816.

The right assumed in *Cruzan*, however, was not simply deduced from abstract concepts of personal autonomy. Given the common-law rule that forced medication was a battery, and the long legal tradition protecting the decision to refuse unwanted medical treatment, our assumption was entirely consistent with this Nation's history and constitutional traditions. The decision to commit suicide with the assistance of another may be just as personal and profound as the decision to refuse unwanted medical treatment, but it has never enjoyed similar legal protection. Indeed, the two acts are widely and reasonably regarded as quite distinct. See *Vacco v. Quill,* — U.S., at — – —, 117 S.Ct., at 2298–2302. In *Cruzan* itself, we recognized that most States outlawed assisted suicide—and even more do today—and we certainly gave no intimation that the right to refuse unwanted medical treatment could be somehow transmuted into a right to assistance in committing suicide. 497 U.S., at 280, 110 S.Ct., at 2852.

Respondents also rely on *Casey*. There, the Court's opinion concluded that "the essential holding of *Roe v. Wade* should be retained and once again reaffirmed." *Casey,* 505 U.S., at 846, 112 S.Ct., at 2804. We held, first, that a woman has a right, before her fetus is viable, to an abortion "without undue interference from the State"; second, that States may restrict post-viability abortions, so long as exceptions are made to protect a woman's life and health; and third, that the State has legitimate interests throughout a pregnancy in protecting the health of the woman and the life of the unborn child. *Ibid.* In reaching this conclusion, the opinion discussed in some detail this Court's substantive-due-process tradition of interpreting the Due Process Clause to protect certain fundamental rights and "personal decisions relating to marriage, procreation, contraception, family relationships, child rearing, and education," and noted that many of those rights and liberties "involv[e] the most intimate and personal choices a person may make in a lifetime." *Id.,* at 851, 112 S.Ct., at 2807.

The Court of Appeals, like the District Court, found *Casey* "'highly instructive'" and "'almost prescriptive'" for determining "'what liberty interest may inhere in a terminally ill person's choice to commit suicide'":

> "Like the decision of whether or not to have an abortion, the decision how and when to die is one of 'the most intimate and personal choices a person may make in a lifetime,' a choice 'central to personal dignity and autonomy.'" 79 F.3d, at 813–814.

Similarly, respondents emphasize the statement in *Casey* that:

> "At the heart of liberty is the right to define one's own concept of existence, of meaning, of the universe, and of the mystery of human life. Beliefs about these matters could not define the attributes of personhood were they formed under compulsion of the State." *Casey,* 505 U.S., at 851, 112 S.Ct., at 2807.

Brief for Respondents 12. By choosing this language, the Court's opinion in *Casey* described, in a general way and in light of our prior cases, those personal activities and decisions that this Court has identified as so deeply rooted in our history and traditions, or so fundamental to our concept of constitutionally ordered liberty, that they are protected by the Fourteenth Amendment. The opinion moved from the recognition that liberty necessarily includes freedom of conscience and belief about ultimate considerations to the observation that "though the abortion decision may originate within the zone of conscience and belief, it is *more than a philosophic exercise.*" *Casey,* 505 U.S., at 852, 112 S.Ct., at 2807 (emphasis added). That many of the rights and liberties protected by the Due Process Clause sound in personal autonomy does not warrant the sweeping conclusion that any and all important, intimate, and personal decisions are so protected, *San Antonio Independent School Dist. v. Rodriguez,* 411 U.S. 1, 33–35, 93 S.Ct. 1278, 1296–1298, 36 L.Ed.2d 16 (1973), and *Casey* did not suggest otherwise.

The history of the law's treatment of assisted suicide in this country has been and continues to be one of the rejection of nearly all efforts to permit it. That being the case, our decisions lead us to conclude that the asserted "right" to assistance in committing suicide is not a fundamental liberty interest protected by the Due Process Clause. The Constitution also requires, however, that Washington's assisted-suicide ban be rationally related to legitimate government interests. See *Heller v. Doe,* 509 U.S. 312, 319–320, 113 S.Ct. 2637, 2642–2643, 125 L.Ed.2d 257 (1993); *Flores,* 507 U.S., at 305, 113 S.Ct., at 1448–1449. This requirement is unquestionably met here. As the court below recognized, 79 F.3d, at 816–817, Washington's assisted-suicide ban implicates a number of state interests. See 49 F.3d, at 592–593; Brief for State of California et al. as *Amici Curiae* 26–29; Brief for United States as *Amicus Curiae* 16–27.

First, Washington has an "unqualified interest in the preservation of human life." *Cruzan,* 497 U.S., at 282, 110 S.Ct., at 2853. The State's prohibition on assisted suicide, like all homicide laws, both reflects and advances its commitment to this interest. See *id.,* at 280, 110 S.Ct., at 2852; Model Penal Code § 210.5, Comment 5, at 100 ("[T]he interests in the sanctity of life that are represented by the criminal homicide laws are threatened by one who expresses a willingness to participate in taking the life of an other"). This interest is symbolic and aspirational as well as practical:

> "While suicide is no longer prohibited or penalized, the ban against assisted suicide and euthanasia shores up the notion of limits in human relationships. It reflects the gravity with which we view the decision to take one's own life or the life of another, and our reluctance to encourage or promote these decisions." New York Task Force 131–132.

Respondents admit that "[t]he State has a real interest in preserving the lives of those who can still contribute to society and enjoy life." Brief for Respondents 35, n. 23. The Court of Appeals also recognized Washington's interest in protecting life, but held that the "weight" of this interest depends on the "medical condition and the wishes of the person whose life is at stake." 79 F.3d, at 817. Washington, however, has rejected this sliding-scale approach and, through its assisted-suicide ban, insists that all persons' lives, from beginning to end, regardless of physical or mental condition, are under the full protection of the law. See *United States v. Rutherford,* 442 U.S. 544, 558, 99 S.Ct. 2470, 2478–2479, 61 L.Ed.2d 68 (1979) ("... Congress could reasonably have determined to protect the terminally ill, no less than other patients, from the vast range of self-styled panaceas that inventive minds can devise"). As we have previously affirmed, the States "may properly decline to make judgments about the 'quality' of life that a particular individual may enjoy," *Cruzan,* 497 U.S., at 282, 110 S.Ct., at 2853. This remains true, as *Cruzan* makes clear, even for those who are near death.

Relatedly, all admit that suicide is a serious public-health problem, especially among persons in otherwise vulnerable groups. See Washington State Dept. of Health, Annual Summary of Vital Statistics 1991, pp. 29–30 (Oct. 1992) (suicide is a leading cause of death in Washington of those between the ages of 14 and 54); New York Task Force 10, 23–33 (suicide rate in the general population is about one percent, and suicide is especially prevalent among the young and the elderly). The State has an interest in preventing suicide, and in studying, identifying, and treating its causes. See 79 F.3d, at 820; *id.,* at 854 (Beezer, J., dissenting) ("The state recognizes suicide as a manifestation of medical and psychological anguish"); Marzen 107–146.

Those who attempt suicide—terminally ill or not—often suffer from depression or other mental disorders. See New York Task Force 13–22, 126–128 (more than 95% of those who commit suicide had a major psychiatric illness at the time of death; among the terminally ill, uncontrolled pain is a "risk factor" because it contributes to depression); Physician-Assisted Suicide and Euthanasia in the Netherlands: A Report of Chairman Charles T. Canady to the Subcommittee on the Constitution of the House Committee on the Judiciary, 104th Cong., 2d Sess., 10–11 (Comm. Print 1996); cf. Back, Wallace, Starks, & Pearlman, Physician-Assisted Suicide and Euthanasia in Washington State, 275 JAMA 919, 924 (1996) ("[I]ntolerable physical symptoms are not the reason most patients request physician-assisted suicide or euthanasia"). Research indicates, however, that many people who request physician-assisted suicide withdraw that request if their depression and pain are treated. H. Hendin, Seduced by Death: Doctors, Patients and the Dutch Cure 24–25 (1997) (suicidal, terminally ill patients "usually respond well to treatment for depressive illness and pain medication and are then grateful to be alive"); New York Task Force 177–178. The New York Task Force, however, expressed its concern that, because depression is difficult to diagnose, physicians and medical professionals often fail to respond adequately to seriously ill patients' needs. *Id.,* at 175. Thus, legal physician-assisted suicide could make it more difficult for the State to protect depressed or mentally ill persons, or those who are suffering from untreated pain, from suicidal impulses.

The State also has an interest in protecting the integrity and ethics of the medical profession. In contrast to the Court of Appeals' conclusion that "the integrity of the medical profession would [not] be threatened in any way by [physician-assisted suicide]," 79 F.3d, at 827, the American Medical Association, like many other medical and physicians' groups, has concluded that "[p]hysician-assisted suicide is fundamentally incompatible with the physician's role as healer." American Medical Association, Code of Ethics § 2.211 (1994); see Council on Ethical and Judicial Affairs, Decisions Near the End of Life, 267 JAMA 2229, 2233 (1992) ("[T]he societal risks of involving physicians in medical interventions to cause patients' deaths is too great"); New York Task Force 103–109 (discussing physicians' views). And physician-assisted suicide could, it is argued, undermine the trust that is essential to the doctor-patient relationship by blurring the time-honored line between healing and harming. Assisted Suicide in the United States, Hearing before the Subcommittee on the Constitution of the House Committee on the Judiciary, 104th Cong., 2d Sess., 355–356 (1996) (testimony of Dr. Leon R. Kass) ("The patient's trust in the doctor's whole-hearted devotion to his best interests will be hard to sustain").

Next, the State has an interest in protecting vulnerable groups—including the poor, the elderly, and disabled persons—from abuse, neglect, and mistakes. The Court of Appeals dismissed the State's concern that disadvantaged persons might be pressured into physician-assisted suicide as "ludicrous on its face." 79 F.3d, at 825. We have recognized, however, the real risk of subtle coercion and undue influence in end-of-life situations. *Cruzan*, 497 U.S., at 281, 110 S.Ct., at 2852. Similarly, the New York Task Force warned that "[l]egalizing physician-assisted suicide would pose profound risks to many individuals who are ill and vulnerable. . . . The risk of harm is greatest for the many individuals in our society whose autonomy and well-being are already compromised by poverty, lack of access to good medical care, advanced age, or membership in a stigmatized social group." New York Task Force 120; see *Compassion in Dying*, 49 F.3d, at 593 ("[A]n insidious bias against the handicapped—again coupled with a cost-saving mentality—makes them especially in need of Washington's statutory protection"). If physician-assisted suicide were permitted, many might resort to it to spare their families the substantial financial burden of end-of-life health-care costs.

The State's interest here goes beyond protecting the vulnerable from coercion; it extends to protecting disabled and terminally ill people from prejudice, negative and inaccurate stereotypes, and "societal indifference." 49 F.3d, at 592. The State's assisted-suicide ban reflects and reinforces its policy that the lives of terminally ill, disabled, and elderly people must be no less valued than the lives of the young and healthy, and that a seriously disabled person's suicidal impulses should be interpreted and treated the same way as anyone else's. See New York Task Force 101–102; Physician-Assisted Suicide and Euthanasia in the Netherlands: A Report of Chairman Charles T. Canady, at 9, 20 (discussing prejudice toward the disabled and the negative messages euthanasia and assisted suicide send to handicapped patients).

Finally, the State may fear that permitting assisted suicide will start it down the path to voluntary and perhaps even involuntary euthanasia. The Court of Appeals struck down Washington's assisted-suicide ban only "as applied to competent, terminally ill adults who wish to hasten their deaths by obtaining medication prescribed by their doctors." 79 F.3d, at 838. Washington insists, however, that the impact of the court's decision will not and cannot be so limited. Brief for Petitioners 44–47. If suicide is protected as a matter of constitutional right, it is argued, "every man and woman in the United States must enjoy it." *Compassion in Dying*, 49 F.3d, at 591; see *Kevorkian*, 447 Mich., at 470, n. 41, 527 N.W.2d, at 727–728, n. 41. The Court of Appeals' decision, and its expansive reasoning, provide ample support for the State's concerns. The court noted, for example, that the "decision of a duly appointed surrogate decision maker is for all legal purposes the decision of the patient himself," 79 F.3d, at 832, n. 120; that "in some instances, the patient may be unable to self-administer the drugs and . . . administration by the physician . . . may be the only way the patient may be able to receive them," *id.*, at 831; and that not only physicians, but also family members and loved ones, will inevitably participate in assisting suicide. *Id.*, at 838, n. 140.

Thus, it turns out that what is couched as a limited right to "physician-assisted suicide" is likely, in effect, a much broader license, which could prove extremely difficult to police and contain. Washington's ban on assisting suicide prevents such erosion.

This concern is further supported by evidence about the practice of euthanasia in the Netherlands. The Dutch government's own study revealed that in 1990, there were 2,300 cases of voluntary euthanasia (defined as "the deliberate termination of another's life at his request"), 400 cases of assisted suicide, and more than 1,000 cases of euthanasia without an explicit request. In addition to these latter 1,000 cases, the study found an additional 4,941 cases where physicians administered lethal morphine overdoses without the patients' explicit consent. Physician-Assisted Suicide and Euthanasia in the Netherlands: A Report of Chairman Charles T. Canady, at 12–13 (citing Dutch study). This study suggests that, despite the existence of various reporting procedures, euthanasia in the Netherlands has not been limited to competent, terminally ill adults who are enduring physical suffering, and that regulation of the practice may not have prevented abuses in cases involving vulnerable persons, including severely disabled neonates and elderly persons suffering from dementia. *Id.*, at 16–21; see generally C. Gomez, Regulating Death: Euthanasia and the Case of the Netherlands (1991); H. Hendin, Seduced By Death: Doctors, Patients, and the Dutch Cure (1997). The New York Task Force, citing the Dutch experience, observed that "assisted suicide and euthanasia are closely linked," New York Task Force 145, and concluded that the "risk of . . . abuse is neither speculative nor distant," *id.*, at 134. Washington, like most other States, reasonably ensures against this risk by banning, rather than regulating, assisting suicide. See *United States v. 12 200-ft Reels of Super 8MM Film,* 413 U.S. 123, 127, 93 S.Ct. 2665, 2668, 37 L.Ed.2d 500 (1973) ("Each step, when taken, appear[s] a reasonable step in relation to that which preceded it, although the aggregate or end result is one that would never have been seriously considered in the first instance").

We need not weigh exactingly the relative strengths of these various interests. They are unquestionably important and legitimate, and Washington's ban on assisted suicide is at least reasonably related to their promotion and protection. We therefore hold that Wash. RevCode § 9A.36.060(1) (1994) does not violate the Fourteenth Amendment, either on its face or "as applied to competent, terminally ill adults who wish to hasten their deaths by obtaining medication prescribed by their doctors." 79 F.3d, at 838.

* * *

Throughout the Nation, Americans are engaged in an earnest and profound debate about the morality, legality, and practicality of physician-assisted suicide. Our holding permits this debate to continue, as it should in a democratic society. The decision of the en banc Court of Appeals is reversed, and the case is remanded for further proceedings consistent with this opinion.

It is so ordered.

Contributors

Howard Brody teaches family practice and medical ethics and humanities at Michigan State University. He has written numerous articles and several books on medical ethics and philosophy, including *The Healer's Power* (1992). He is coauthor of a recent book for a general audience, *The Placebo Response*.

Rebecca Dresser is a professor of law and ethics in medicine at Washington University–St. Louis, and she has written prolifically on many parts of those subjects. Her book *When Science Offers Salvation: Patient Advocacy and Research Ethics* will be published by Oxford University Press in 2001.

Arthur W. Frank is a professor of sociology and an adjunct professor of nursing at the University of Calgary in Alberta, Canada. Author of *At the Will of the Body: Reflections on Illness* (1991) and *The Wounded Storyteller: Body, Illness, and Ethics* (1995), he also has written extensively in a wide variety of journals.

Peter J. Hammer is an assistant professor of law at the University of Michigan. After receiving his J.D. and his Ph.D. in economics from that institution, he served as an associate at the Los Angeles office of O'Melveny & Myers, where he maintained an active practice in antitrust and health law and the presentation of expert economic testimony. He now specializes in federal antitrust law and legal issues surrounding changes in the health-care industry.

Yale Kamisar, Clarence Darrow Distinguished University Professor at the University of Michigan, has written about euthanasia and assisted suicide since 1958, when he published an article, "Some Non-Religious Views Against Proposed 'Mercy-Killing' Legislation," which is widely regarded as stating the classic case against legalizing euthanasia. He is also a prominent authority on constitutional law and criminal procedure.

Christopher McCrudden is a professor of human rights law at Oxford University, a Fellow of Lincoln College, Oxford, and a visiting professor at the University of Michigan Law School. He specializes in human rights (international, European, and comparative) and has recently concentrated on the relationship between international economic law and human rights.

Martin S. Pernick, Richard Hudson Research Professor of History at the University of Michigan, studies the history of value issues in medicine and the relation between medicine and mass culture. He is the author of two books: *A Calculus of Suffering* (1985) and *The Black Stork* (1996). He is currently completing a book tentatively titled *When Are You Dead?,* which investigates the history of uncertainty about the definition of death from the eighteenth-century's fear of premature burial to today's debates over brain death.

Carl E. Schneider, Chauncey Stillman Professor of Law and Professor of Internal Medicine at the University of Michigan, has written in several fields, including bioethics, constitutional law, and family law. His recent book, *The Practice of Autonomy: Patients, Doctors, and Medical Decisions,* examines how power to make medical decisions is and should be divided between doctors and patients and, more largely, explores the role of autonomy in American culture.

Sonia M. Suter became an associate professor of law at George Washington University in 1999 after completing a Greenwall Fellowship in bioethics and health policy at Georgetown and Johns Hopkins Universities and after serving as a visiting professor at the University of Michigan. Professor Suter has a master's degree in human genetics and worked for two years as a genetics counselor; her scholarship focuses on legal issues in medicine and genetics as well as bioethics.

Index